COLLECTED PLAYS
Volume Three

Collected Plays

Brian Friel

COLLECTED PLAYS

Volume Three

Edited by Peter Fallon

FABER & FABER

Gallery Books

Collected Plays: Volume Three
is first published in paperback and in a clothbound edition
by The Gallery Press and in paperback by Faber and Faber Limited
in 2016. Originated at The Gallery Press.

The Gallery Press   Faber and Faber Limited
Loughcrew   Bloomsbury House,
Oldcastle   74–77 Great Russell Street,
County Meath   London WCIB 3DA
Ireland   England

This collection © the Estate of Brian Friel 2016
For Acknowledgements see page 515

The right of Brian Friel to be identified as Author of this Work
has been asserted in accordance with Section 77 of the Copyright,
Designs and Patents Act 1988

ISBN 978–0–571–33178 –9

A CIP catalogue record for this book is available from
the British Library

Contents

THREE
SISTERS

after Chekhov

Characters

ANDREY PROZOROV
NATASHA, his fiancée, later his wife
OLGA ⎫
MASHA ⎬ his sisters
IRINA ⎭
FYODOR KULYGIN, a schoolmaster, Masha's husband
ALEXANDER VERSHININ, a lieutenant-colonel
BARON TUSENBACH, a lieutenant
CAPTAIN VASSILY SOLYONY
DOCTOR IVAN CHEBUTYKIN, an army lieutenant
ALEKSEY FEDOTIK, a second lieutenant
VLADIMIR RODDEY, a second lieutenant
FERAPONT, a porter from the county council
ANFISA, an old nurse

Time and Place

The action takes place in the Prozorov home in a provincial town in Russia.

ACT ONE	Spring
ACT TWO	Winter, a year and a half later
ACT THREE	Summer, a year and a half later
ACT FOUR	Autumn, two years later

Three Sisters was first produced by Field Day Theatre Company at the Guildhall, Derry, on 8 September 1981, with the following cast:

ANDREY PROZOROV	John Quinn
NATASHA	Nuala Hayes
OLGA	Sorcha Cusack
MASHA	Eileen Pollock
IRINA	Olwen Fouéré
FYODOR KULYGIN	Patrick Waldron
ALEXANDER VERSHININ	James Ellis
BARON TUSENBACH	Niall Buggy
CAPTAIN SOLYONY	Colm Meaney
DOCTOR CHEBUTYKIN	Eamon Kelly
FEDOTIK	Gary Lilburn
RODDEY	Michael Burlington
FERAPONT	Michael Duffy
ANFISA	Máirín D O'Sullivan

Directed by	Stephen Rea
Designed by	Eileen Diss
Lighting by	Rory Dempster
Costumes by	Dany Everett
Music by	Mícheál Ó Súilleabháin
Artist	Basil Blackshaw

for Sally and David

ACT ONE

The Prozorov house is situated outside a large provincial Russian town (population 100,000) and close to a river. It is the month of May, a bright and sunny morning just before noon.

A drawing room with columns beyond which is a large dining room. In the drawing room there is a draught-screen, a large iron stove, a full-size mirror, a piano.

In both the drawing room and the dining room there are flowers everywhere — flowers on the tables, flowers on the piano, flowers on the mantelpiece, flowers in vases on the floor.

ANFISA *is helping two young maids who are laying the dining-room table for buffet lunch.*

OLGA *is wearing the regulation dark blue dress of a secondary schoolteacher. She is correcting exercise books.*

MASHA *is dressed in black; her hat on her lap; reading.*

IRINA *is in a white dress. She has a basket filled with flowers and is arranging them in vases around the room.*

Silence except for the sound of ANDREY *playing the violin in his room off right.*

OLGA *stops working.*

> OLGA Hard to believe it's only a year since Father's death, isn't it? Twelve months to the day. The 5th of May. Your name day, Irina. Do you remember how cold it was? And there was snow falling. I thought then I'd never get over it. And you collapsed — d'you remember? — just passed out. But a year *has* gone by and we can talk about it calmly now, can't we? And you're wearing white again and you look . . . radiant! (*Clock strikes*) The clock struck twelve then, too. Remember the band playing when they were carrying the coffin out of the room here? And firing the salute in the cemetery? General Prozorov,

Brigade Commander! All the same very few local people turned up. But it was a terrible day, wasn't it? All that rain and sleet and —

IRINA (*Closing her eyes*) Olga, please!

> BARON TUSENBACH, DOCTOR CHEBUTYKIN *and* CAPTAIN SOLYONY *enter the dining room and talk in undertones among themselves.* CHEBUTYKIN *is engrossed in his paper.* OLGA *opens all the windows. As she does:*

OLGA There's real warmth in the air today, isn't there? It's such a relief to be able to fling the windows wide open. And we won't feel until the birch trees are in leaf. I'm sure they're already in leaf in Moscow . . . D'you remember the day we left there? Eleven years ago. I remember it as if it were yesterday. Father had finally got his brigade and we were posted here. Early in May. Just like now. And it seemed as if everything was just about to . . . to blossom. And Moscow, beautiful, beautiful Moscow was bathed in sunshine and warmth. Eleven whole years. What happened to them? But when I woke this morning and saw the heat haze I knew that finally, finally spring had come. And I felt elated. No, exalted! And suddenly and with all my soul I yearned to go back home again.

CHEBUTYKIN (*Tapping his paper*) Rubbish-rubbish-rubbish.

BARON You're right, Doctor. Only words — all rubbish.

> MASHA, *absorbed in her book, whistles softly through her teeth.*

OLGA Masha, would you mind . . . please . . . my migraine's back. All day at school and all evening at this (*corrections*) — it's turning me into a crabbed old maid, isn't it? Four years in that secondary school and every day, every single hour of every day, I feel my youth and my energy draining away.

All I'm left with is a resolution, a determination, a passion —

IRINA To go back to Moscow.

OLGA Yes!

IRINA To sell this house, to pack up here and to go home to Moscow.

OLGA Yes! Yes! Home to Moscow! But it must be soon, Irina! It has got to be soon!

CHEBUTYKIN *and the* BARON *both laugh.*

IRINA Once Andrey becomes a professor he won't stay on here. So there'll be nothing to stop us — (*remembering*) except poor Masha.

OLGA Masha'll come and spend the summer in Moscow — the whole summer, every summer!

MASHA *whistles softly.*

IRINA I hope to God it all works out. (*Runs to the window and looks out*) Isn't it a wonderful day! I don't know why it is but I feel so — so joyous! (*Turning round again*) I'd forgotten all about my name day until I woke this morning and suddenly I felt so happy, so happy! I just lay there thinking about when I was young and Mama was alive and life was so simple and there was so much happiness; and just to think about them made me so excited again.

OLGA You really are radiant today. I've never seen you look so beautiful. Masha's beautiful too. And Andrey would be quite handsome if he lost some of that weight. I'm the only one of the four of us that — that's standing the times badly. Oh yes; I know I've become lean and hard — I suppose because those girls at school make me so irritable. But today I'm free. And at home. The migraine's suddenly vanished and I feel younger than I felt yesterday. I'm only twenty-eight, amn't I? So. All's well. Everything's in God's good hands. All the same I'd prefer to be married and be at home every day. If I had a husband I would really love him.

BARON TUSENBACH *breaks away from the others and comes down to the drawing room. As he descends:*

BARON   Talk-talk-talk. Endless silly talk. That's all they do is talk. I meant to tell you: you're having a visitor today — our new battery commander — Lieutenant Colonel Vershinin.

He sits at the piano and begins playing 'Won't You Buy My Pretty Flowers?' His playing is heavy and enthusiastic. MASHA *turns away as if to avoid the sound.*

(*Sings*) 'There are many sad and weary, / In this pleasant world of ours . . . '

IRINA   Oh my God. What's his name?

BARON   Vershinin. (*Sings*) 'Crying every night so dreary, / Won't you buy my pretty flowers?'

IRINA   I'm sure he's ancient.

BARON   (*Stops playing*) Sorry?

IRINA   I said I'm sure he's ancient.

BARON   Somewhere between forty and forty-five. Is that ancient? I think you'll like him. Talks too much but he's a decent man.

IRINA   I'm sure he's a bore.

BARON   No, he's not! Let's see: married — this is his second wife and he has a mother-in-law and two young daughters. You'll hear all about them. He's going round the town making courtesy calls and every-one's being told about 'my wife and my two little girls'. The wife has nervous trouble: wears her hair in a pigtail like a schoolgirl and every so often makes a stab at killing herself — just to keep him on his toes, I suspect. If she were my wife I'd have left her years ago. But he endures it. It gives him a valid reason for feeling sorry for himself.

SOLYONY *and* CHEBUTYKIN *come down.* CHEBUTYKIN *is engrossed in his paper and pays no attention to* SOLYONY. *As they descend:*

SOLYONY With one hand I can lift only half-a-hundredweight. Right? But with two hands I can lift a hundredweight and a half. So what does that suggest? That two men aren't just twice as strong as one man but three times as strong, maybe four or five times as strong. Isn't that a reasonable deduction?

CHEBUTYKIN (*Reads*) 'A cure for alopecia.' (*He produces a notebook and pencil*) Must make a note of this. (*Reads*) 'Mix two ounces of naphthalene with one half-pint of surgical spirits. Apply daily and dissolve.' Apply daily and diss- — Shouldn't that be 'Dissolve and apply daily'? Why would I write that nonsense! Rubbish-rubbish-rubbish.

IRINA *runs to him and catches both his hands.*

IRINA Darling Doctor, dozy Doctor.

CHEBUTYKIN What is it, little sweetheart?

IRINA You'll know the answer.

CHEBUTYKIN Of course. What's the question?

IRINA Why am I so happy today? I feel as if I had become ethereal — as if I were gliding along with the great blue sky above me and huge white birds all around me!

He kisses her hands tenderly.

CHEBUTYKIN You're my beautiful white fledgling —

IRINA D'you know what happened to me this morning just after I'd washed and dressed?

CHEBUTYKIN Tell me.

IRINA I had a revelation!

CHEBUTYKIN Good.

IRINA A genuine epiphany. Everything made immediate sense. Suddenly I knew how life would be

17

lived. Suddenly I possessed profound wisdom. Are you listening to me, dozy Doctor?

CHEBUTYKIN Avidly.

IRINA Man must work. He must toil by the sweat of his brow. That's the only thing that gives life purpose and meaning. That's the only thing that guarantees contentment and happiness. My God, what I'd give to be a labourer with the council, up at the crack of dawn and out smashing stones! Or a sheep farmer. Or a bus driver. Or a teacher slogging away, expanding young minds. Because if I'm just a slut having my breakfast in bed and then spending a couple of hours dithering over what I'll wear, then wouldn't I be far better off being a carthorse or an ox — anything at all just as long as I can work, work, work. You know how you'd give anything for a cool drink in the middle of a hot summer day? Well, that's exactly what I feel about work — I thirst for it! So from this moment, dozy Doctor, if I'm not up at dawn and out there toiling, never ever break breath with me again.

CHEBUTYKIN Never ever.

OLGA We were all up at seven when Father was alive. Irina still wakes at seven but somehow she never manages to rise for at least two more hours. But then she's having revelations.

Everybody laughs.

IRINA You think it's funny when I'm serious because you consider me a child. But I'm twenty, Olga.

The BARON gets up from the piano.

BARON Irina's right. My God, how well I know that thirst for work. And why do I know it? Because in all my life I've never done a hand's turn! I'd come home from cadet school. A footman to pull off my riding boots. Me making it difficult for him. And Mother

18

gazing at me in admiration and actually offended when others didn't find me quite as engaging as she did. The point is: I was *shielded* from work. *But:* we can't be shielded finally because we are on the threshold of a revolution. An avalanche is about to descend on us. A tremendous hurricane is about to rise up. And all the laziness, complacency, rottenness, boredom, shirking of work — all are going to be purged out of society as we know it now. So not only am I myself absolutely determined to work, but in another twenty-five or thirty years, everyone everywhere . . . will work.

CHEBUTYKIN Except me.

BARON You don't count.

SOLYONY (*Smiling at the* BARON *with icy sweetness*) In twenty-five years' time you won't be around, thank God. Some happy day soon you'll have a coronary. Or maybe I'll get really angry with you and — (*he mimes putting a revolver to his head and pulling the trigger*) — phwt! (*Looking around*) When he stands there like that doesn't he remind you of a duck? (*To the* BARON, *softly and with accompanying gesture of his left hand*) Quack-quack, quack-quack, quack-quack.

He takes a bottle of eau de cologne from his pocket and sprinkles some on his hands.

CHEBUTYKIN Now that I think about it — I've never worked either! Never lifted a finger since the day I graduated! Never even opened a book! The only thing I read now is newspapers. See? But of course I extract lots of very profound information from these same newspapers. For example I see here that there is a critic called — (*Knocking from below*) Ah! Wanted downstairs. Somebody wants to consult me! (*Calls*) Coming! Coming!

He leaves.

IRINA He's up to something.

BARON (*Knowingly*) It wouldn't surprise me if he were away to get your name-day present.

IRINA Oh no. Stop him, Olga.

OLGA How do you stop a stupid man being stupid?

MASHA 'A green oak grows by a curving shore
And on that oak a gold chain hangs;
And on that oak a gold chain hangs.'

OLGA You're very quiet today, Masha.

MASHA, *humming, puts on her hat.*

Where are you going?

MASHA Home.

BARON Aren't you going to wait for your sister's party?

MASHA Party? (*Suddenly remembering; to* IRINA) Of course. Of course. I'll be back this evening. 'Bye, love. (*Kisses her*) And once more — all the happiness in the world. (*To everybody*) In the old days when Father was alive we always had thirty or forty young officers here at our name-day parties. Remember the mad fun there used to be? Now we're reduced to one man (BARON) and one boy (SOLYONY) and a house as quiet as a library . . . Sorry. I'd better go. Pay no attention to me. I'm so depressed today I almost — I — I'm — (*She laughs through her tears and hugs* IRINA) We'll have a chat later. See you all then. I've got to get out, out, away —

IRINA Masha, are you sick?

OLGA (*Crying and embracing* MASHA) I know exactly how you feel.

SOLYONY (*Smiling his icy smile*) When a man attempts to philosophize the chances are you'll hear something approaching philosophy — or at least a kind of sophistry. But when a woman attempts to philosophize — or better still a pair of women — d'you know what you get? *You* know, Baron. (*The hand gesture and his face close to* TUSENBACH's *face*) Quack-quack, quack-quack, quack-quack.

MASHA You really are a twisted little pup!

SOLYONY Me? 'Tweedle-de-dum and tweedle-de-dee / Is there a bird as happy as we?'

MASHA (*Angrily, to* OLGA) Stop snivelling, Olga!

> SOLYONY *crosses the stage silently miming his duck sounds with his mouth and his left hand. Enter* ANFISA *and* FERAPONT *with a large cake.*

ANFISA Come on, slowcoach — hurry up — move, move, move! Your boots are clean enough. (*To* IRINA) A name-day cake from Mr Protopopov!

IRINA (*Puzzled*) Is it for me?

ANFISA Well it's not my name day. From the county council — from Mr Protopopov, the chairman.

> IRINA *takes the cake.*

IRINA (*To* FERAPONT) Thank you. And thank Mr Protopopov for me —

FERAPONT Wha's tha', Miss?

IRINA (*Loudly*) Please thank Mr Protopopov for me.

> FERAPONT *is bewildered and looks from* ANFISA *to* IRINA *and back.*

OLGA Give him a cup of tea, Nanny. (*Loudly*) Anfisa will get you something to eat in the kitchen, Ferapont.

FERAPONT Wha's tha', Miss?

ANFISA Come on! Come on with me! (*As she leads him off she looks back*) Old people!

> *They exit.*

MASHA I don't like that Protopopov. He shouldn't be invited here.

IRINA Who's invited him?

MASHA Haven't you?

IRINA Never.

MASHA Good.

> CHEBUTYKIN *enters followed by an orderly carrying a silver samovar. A buzz of surprise and dismay at the inappropriateness of the gift.*

OLGA Look at what he's got her! A samovar! Oh my God!

IRINA That's what you give to old maids!

> OLGA *goes up to the dining room and busies herself.*

BARON (*Laughs*) Didn't I tell you!

IRINA Darling, dozy Doctor, why did you do that?

MASHA Because he's beyond talking to — that's why.

CHEBUTYKIN Because, my darling girls, you're all I have. Because you're more precious to me than anything in the world. I'm nearly sixty, a lonely old man, a useless old man. But if there's anything good about me it's my love for you three. If it wasn't for you, I — I'd — I'd have packed it in long ago. (*Quietly, to* IRINA) And because I loved your mother — loved her with a great, great . . . may God have mercy on her soul. And I have loved you since the day you were born. When you were a baby — (*to* ALL) I used to rock her to sleep in my arms. Yes.

IRINA You have got to stop buying me these expensive presents. There's to be no more!

CHEBUTYKIN (*Wiping his eyes and angrily*) Who gives a damn about expense! (*To orderly*) Take that damned thing in there! (*Imitating her*) 'Expensive presents'!

> *The orderly takes the samovar into the dining room.* ANFISA *enters — carrying a tray.*

ANFISA Colonel Somebody-or-Other has arrived. He's taken off his coat if you don't mind and he's on his way upstairs. Irina, you behave yourself now, madam.

Pause as she goes up to the dining room.

And I suppose you're complaining that your lunch is late. Well, I've only one pair of hands, you know!

BARON Must be Vershinin.

VERSHININ *enters.*

It is. (*He bows*) Colonel Vershinin, sir.

VERSHININ (*To* MASHA) May I introduce myself? My name's Vershinin. It's a great pleasure to be here at last, a very great pleasure. God, how you've changed! My God, I would never —

Suddenly realizing what he is saying he breaks off. An awkward silence.

IRINA You're very welcome, Colonel. Here — sit down.

VERSHININ (*With great animation*) It really is a great, great pleasure to see you again. But there were three of you, weren't there? Three sisters? I distinctly remember three little girls, Colonel Prozorov's three little daughters. The faces — they're gone. But that there were three of you — oh, yes, I'm sure of that. (*Indicating three small children*) Where have the years gone to?

BARON Colonel Vershinin's from Moscow.

IRINA You're from Moscow?!

VERSHININ I served in the same brigade as your father when he was battery commander there. (*To* MASHA) There is something about your face that I seem to remember.

MASHA I've no memory of you.

IRINA Olga! Olga! Come here, Olga!

OLGA *comes down to the drawing room.*

This is Colonel Vershinin — my sister, Olga. And she's Masha. And I'm Irina. And guess what, Olga — he's from Moscow!

VERSHININ That's where I joined up. I've been stationed there ever since. Then this posting came up and I escaped. Actually I don't really remember you. I just remember that there were three sisters. Your father — oh, I remember your father all right. (*He mimes a large, straight man*) Oh, yes, the General I remember vividly. I was a regular visitor in your house in Moscow.

OLGA And I thought I remembered everybody and every tiny detail. But now — suddenly —

VERSHININ Vershinin? Alexander Vershinin? Lieutenant Vershinin in those days?

IRINA And now Colonel Vershinin. And from Moscow. Olga, it's an omen!

VERSHININ It's a — ?

OLGA What she means is — we're moving to Moscow. We'll be there by autumn. That's our home — Moscow. That's where we were born. In Old Basmanny Street.

OLGA *and* IRINA *both laugh.*

MASHA Out of nowhere — someone from home walks in. It's so — (*suddenly and eagerly*) — Yes, I do remember! Olga, d'you remember the man they used to call the Lovesick Major? (*To* VERSHININ) That's you! You were a lieutenant then. And you must have been in love. And everyone took a hand at you and called you Major for some reason!

VERSHININ (*Laughs*) Unmasked! The Lovesick Major — that's me!

MASHA You had a moustache in those days. Lord, how you've aged! (*Through her tears*) Good Lord, how you've aged!

She suddenly realizes what she has said. A momentary awkward silence.

VERSHININ Yes . . . well . . . the Lovesick Major was a young

man then, wasn't he? . . . And in love . . . That's all
finished now, isn't it?

OLGA There's not a grey hair in your head. And of course
you're older — aren't we all? Nowadays we call
that 'a mature look'.

VERSHININ It would need to be: I'll soon be forty-three. Is it
long since you left Moscow?

OLGA ⎫
IRINA ⎰ Eleven years!

They laugh with embarrassment.

IRINA Masha, what are you crying for? (*Beginning to cry*)
Now look what you've done: you have me crying,
too!

MASHA Who's crying? Tell me, where did you live in
Moscow?

VERSHININ Old Basmanny Street.

OLGA That's where we lived!

IRINA I've told him that, Olga.

VERSHININ I used to live in Nyemetsky Street. I could walk to
the Red Barracks from there. And on the way you
had to cross this black bridge and underneath
you could just hear the water — a kind of throaty,
strangled sound. It wasn't the liveliest place to
pass on your way to work every morning by yourself. (*Sudden interest in the view from the window*)
Well, look at that! And the river! Isn't that a really
beautiful view!

OLGA It's cold. It's always cold here. And the midges
would devour you.

VERSHININ You have the ideal Russian climate here. And you
have the forest and the river and — those are silver
birches over there, aren't they? Gentle, modest birch
trees; they're my favourite. You don't know how
lucky you are to be living here. But would someone
please explain something to me? Why is the railway
station fifteen miles from the town! Nobody seems
to know!

SOLYONY I do. (*Everybody looks at him*) Because if the station were here, it wouldn't be fifteen miles away. However, if it were fifteen miles away, as it is — (*pause*) — then it can't be here, as it isn't.

SOLYONY's *explanation is received in total silence.*

BARON (*To* VERSHININ) Solyony's sense of humour is . . . his own.

OLGA I'm sure I remember you now. I must remember you. Yes. I do.

VERSHININ I knew your mother well.

CHEBUTYKIN Ah! Their mother . . . May God have mercy on her soul.

IRINA Mother's buried in Moscow.

OLGA In the old cemetery.

MASHA I can hardly remember what she looked like. Isn't that strange? Not that we'll be remembered either. We'll be forgotten, too.

VERSHININ Nothing you can do about that. Even the issues we consider so 'serious' today, in time they'll be completely forgotten. (*Pause*) The trouble is, we've no way of knowing now what will be thought serious or significant and what will seem frivolous and trivial. Look at Columbus. Look at Copernicus. People dismissed them as cranks. And yet the rubbish spouted by some fool who was a contemporary of theirs — that was hailed as a revelation! God alone knows how the way we live will be assessed. To us it's — it's how we live. But maybe in retrospect it will look foolish. Maybe even . . . morally wrong. Well . . .

He spreads his hands in dismissal of his solemnity.

BARON You have a point. On the other hand perhaps our age will be called a great age and looked back on with admiration. We've no torture chambers, no public executions, no invasions. On the other hand there is still an unacceptable level of human suffering and —

SOLYONY Quack-quack, quack-quack, quack-quack. Our Baron's a philosopher, a real ideas man.

BARON Leave me alone, Solyony. (*Moves away*) I'm asking you. Please.

SOLYONY (*Smiling, softly*) Quack-quack. (*Then two more quacks in mime*)

BARON My point is simply this: that the suffering we see around us — and God knows I deplore it as much as anybody — but the fact that it is *only* suffering and not actual — (*Out of the corner of his eye he sees* SOLYONY *miming a quack-quack at him and his line of thought is gone*) — What I'm suggesting is that it is no worse than suffering — that our society has in fact developed to a higher plane of moral awareness and sensitivity than obtained . . . a higher level of morality than that same society, in other words *this* society, had reached — has reached — is now — is . . . (*He is lost*)

CHEBUTYKIN I know what your point is, Tusenbach. This is a great era. It's just people who are small. (*He rises and stands to his full height*) Not the height of tuppence. But all you have to do is *tell* me I live in a great age and I'll believe I'm a giant.

Sound of a violin being played offstage.

VERSHININ You have a musician in the house?

MASHA Andrey, our brother.

IRINA Andrey's going to be an academic.

MASHA That was Father's wish.

IRINA We think he's destined for a brilliant career as a university professor.

OLGA In the meantime he's in love. We've been teasing him all morning.

IRINA A local girl. You'll probably meet her later.

MASHA With her poor-but-honest provincial face. And be dazzled by her yellows and greens and purples.

OLGA She dresses . . . distinctively.

MASHA I know nobody who risks so many startling com-
binations of colours. Miss Natasha's taste is . . .
peccable.

OLGA She's —

MASHA Vulgar, for God's sake! Downright vulgar! Andrey
in love with her! Come on, Olga; he's got some
taste. *He's* teasing *us*. I know he is: somebody told
me yesterday she's going with that Protopopov
creature, the chairman of the county council. Sounds
a perfect match. (*She crosses to a door right*) Andrey,
have you a moment? Could you come out for a
moment, Andrey?

> ANDREY *emerges awkwardly, his face half averted.*
> MASHA *hugs him warmly. He is in his twenties;*
> *plump; thick glasses; very shy. He is both cosseted*
> *and overwhelmed by his three sisters.*

MASHA Our Tchaikovsky!

VERSHININ My name's Vershinin.

ANDREY Prozorov.

> *Pause.* ANDREY *mops his face with his handker-*
> *chief. Nobody speaks. Then simultaneously:*

VERSHININ ⎱ I was —
ANDREY ⎰ You're just —

> *Again a silence.*

VERSHININ Sorry?

ANDREY You're the new battery commander here, aren't you?

OLGA Colonel Vershinin's from Moscow, Andrey! Isn't
that wonderful?

ANDREY Yes? Ah. Well. In that case, God help you. You won't
get a moment's peace from my darling sisters.

VERSHININ I'm afraid your darling sisters are already bored
with me.

IRINA   Look what Andrey gave me today — this little picture frame. (*She hands it to* VERSHININ) He made it
himself.

       VERSHININ *looks at the frame. He does not know
what to say.*

VERSHININ   Well. That — that's very — that would certainly —
frame a picture, wouldn't it?

IRINA   And the one on top of the piano — he made that
too.

       ANDREY *makes an impatient gesture and moves
away.*

OLGA   Andrey's a scholar and a musician and an artist.
He has all the talents. No slipping away, Andrey.
Come back here, Andrey!

       MASHA *and* IRINA *run after him and arrest him.
Laughing, they lead him back to the centre of the
room.*

MASHA   No, no, no you don't.

ANDREY   Please . . . please . . . please . . .

IRINA   (*Child's chant*) 'Andrey is huffing! Andrey is huffing.'

ANDREY   Please . . .

MASHA   They used to call Alexander the Lovesick Major
and he didn't huff — did you?

VERSHININ   Never!

MASHA   So I'm going to christen you the Lovesick Fiddler.

IRINA   The Lovesick Professor.

OLGA   Poor little Andrey's in love. Are you madly in love,
Andrey?

       *By now the three girls have encircled him and
dance aound him, repeating: 'Andrey is huffing!
Andrey is huffing' and 'The Lovesick Fiddler' and*

29

> '*Poor little Andrey. What does it feel like, little Andrey?*' *And now* CHEBUTYKIN *comes up from behind and puts his arm round* ANDREY'*s waist.*

CHEBUTYKIN 'For love alone did nature make us / That it might bend and try to break us.'

> CHEBUTYKIN *returns to his chair and his paper.* ANDREY *breaks away from his sisters.*

ANDREY All right — all right. Come on. That's enough. Please . . . please . . . (*He wipes the perspiration off his face*) I'm not feeling too well today. Didn't close an eye all night. I sat up studying till four and then when I went to bed my mind was too active —

IRINA (*Coyly*) Ah-ha!

ANDREY Then when I was about to drop off, suddenly it's daylight and the sun's pouring in the damned window.

VERSHININ What are you studying?

ANDREY An English text I'm hoping to translate over the summer.

VERSHININ Do you know English?

ANDREY And French. And German. We all do — don't we? Irina's fluent in Italian too. Father had a mania about 'learning'. 'The lightest load you'll ever carry,' he used to say.

MASHA You can imagine how useful it is to be able to speak three languages in a town like this! Like having a sixth finger. Everything we know is . . . useless.

VERSHININ Oh, come on! (*Laughs*) That's just not true. Educated, intelligent people are valuable in every community, even more valuable in a place like this. What's the population of this town? One hundred thousand? And there are three of you. Three Prozorovs encircled by one hundred thousand ignorant uneducated people. Of course you'll be eroded bit by bit, day by day, until finally the one hundred thousand will overwhelm you. But the fact that you're swallowed up doesn't mean you'll have made no impact. Because you will. You'll have influenced perhaps — let's say six other people. And in turn those six will influence twelve more. And that twelve another twenty-four. Until finally, finally people like you will be in the majority. Until finally in two or three hundred years' time the quality of life on this earth will be transformed and beautiful and marvellous beyond our imagining. Because *that's* the life man longs for and aspires to. And even though he hasn't achieved it yet, he must look forward to it, dream about it, prepare for it. But he can prepare for it only if he has more vision and more knowledge than his father or his grandfather. (*Again he spreads his hands in embarrassment and apology*) Well . . . (*Laughs. To* MASHA) Just because you said that nearly everything you know is . . . what was it? — 'useless'?

Pause. MASHA *looks at him. Then, still looking at him, she resolutely takes off her hat.*

MASHA I'm staying for lunch.
IRINA (*To* VERSHININ; *in awe*) Do you know something? Every word you've said should be written down.

ANDREY *has slipped away unnoticed.*

BARON Your point is that in some future time life on this earth will be beautiful and marvellous. That is possible. *But*: if we are to have a part in it now, even at this distance, we must prepare for it, we must work for it, we must —
VERSHININ (*Cutting him off*) Indeed. My God, I've never seen so many flowers. The whole place — it's so elegant; it has the whiff of women about it. I spend my life flitting from one shabby flat to another. A couple of chairs, a camp bed, a stove that always seems to

31

smoke. Flowers! That's what's been missing from my life! Flowers like these!

BARON No doubt about it — work is the answer. And if you think that's just Baron Tusenbach indulging in German sentimentality you're wrong. Despite the name I'm one hundred per cent Russian. Don't even speak a word of German. In fact my father was a practising Orthodox long before —

VERSHININ (*Walking around the room*) Did you ever wonder what it would be like if you could begin your life over again — with the knowledge that you have now? Supposing you could just put aside the life you've already lived, as if it were just a try-out, and then start the other one, the real life. D'you know the first thing you'd do? You'd make absolutely sure you wouldn't repeat yourself. You'd try to create a different environment for yourself: a house like this, spacious, lots of light, flowers, the whiff of women . . . I should have told you: I'm married. I've two little girls. My wife is . . . delicate. But the first rule must be: never repeat yourself. Oh, no. Never. Never.

Enter KULYGIN *wearing a schoolteacher's uniform.*

KULYGIN Ah! The name-day girl herself! May I wish you, dear Irina, from the bottom of my heart a most happy occasion and whatever it is a young woman of your age wishes for herself — and I suspect that may well be robust good health. Am I right? And may I present to you this little volume. (*Hands her a book*) A history of our secondary school, covering the past fifty years. Written by yours truly. A modest little enterprise executed in moments of leisure but still worth a casual perusal. Good afternoon, everybody! (*To* VERSHININ) Kulygin's the name. By profession a teacher in the local secondary school. And for my sins a humble member of the county council. (*To* IRINA) Consists of lists of all the pupils

who have passed through our hands in the last
fifty years. *Feci quod potui; faciant meliora potentes.* I
have done what I can; let those with more talent
do better. (*He kisses* MASHA)

IRINA You gave me a copy of this last Easter, Fyodor.

KULYGIN (*Laughs*) I didn't — did I? In that case give it back to
me or, better still, give it to the colonel. (*He presents
it to* VERSHININ) There you are, Colonel. Dip into it
when you've nothing better to do.

VERSHININ Thank you. (*Preparing to leave*) I'm very glad to have
met you all.

OLGA You're not leaving already, are you?

IRINA Stay and have lunch with us. Please.

OLGA Yes; everything's ready.

VERSHININ I feel I've intruded on a family —

OLGA Please.

VERSHININ Well . . .

He looks directly at MASHA. *She holds his look for
a second; then turns away.*

Why not! I'd love to. And a very happy name day,
Irina.

He and OLGA *go into the dining room.*

KULYGIN Sunday, gentlemen! The day of rest! So we must all
relax and enjoy ourselves with as much brio as each
of us is capable. Those carpets will have to be lifted
for the summer and put away until next winter.
Must remember to get mothballs or naphthalene;
they're equally effective. Why were the Romans a
healthy people? The Romans were a healthy people
because they knew how to work *and* how to rest.
In consequence *mens sana in corpore sano*. Their life
had pattern, form. As our headmaster says, the most
important thing in life is its form; that which loses
its pattern cannot survive. Isn't he right? (*He puts
his arm around* MASHA'S *waist and laughs*) Masha

loves me. Yes. My wife loves me. Yes. And we must put those winter curtains away with the carpets. I'm really happy today; joyous in fact. Masha, we're invited to the headmaster's house at four this afternoon. An outing has been arranged for the teachers and their families.

MASHA I'm not going.

KULYGIN (*Dismayed*) My darling — why not?

MASHA We'll talk about it later.

KULYGIN But arrangements have all been —

MASHA (*Angrily*) All right — I'll go — I'll go! But for God's sake leave me alone now, will you . . . please . . .

She moves away from him.

KULYGIN And after the outing we'll spend the rest of the evening with the headmaster. Despite his indifferent health he is a man of enormous integrity, of enviable perspicacity. Do you know what he said to me after the staff meeting yesterday? 'Kulygin,' he said, 'Kulygin, I am tired.' (*He looks at the clock and then at his watch*) Your clock is seven minutes fast. Yes; his precise words — 'I am tired.'

Sounds of the violin being played offstage.

OLGA Come and eat, everybody! The food's going cold.

KULYGIN Coming, Olga! Yesterday I worked from early morning until almost midnight and I can tell you I was just spent. But today? Exuberant! The most astonishing thing about the human spirit is its resilience.

He goes up to the dining room.

CHEBUTYKIN Did someone say food? Excellent.

He puts away his paper and combs his beard.

MASHA Remember — just because it's a name day doesn't mean you can take a drink.

CHEBUTYKIN Me?

MASHA You can't handle it.

CHEBUTYKIN I never think of it. I've been dry for five hundred and ninety seven and a half days now.

MASHA For your own good.

CHEBUTYKIN 'My own good'! Who gives a damn about that, my love?

MASHA I do. And well you know it.

She takes his arm. She speaks quietly and angrily.

Another boring evening at the headmaster's!

BARON If I were you I just wouldn't go.

CHEBUTYKIN He's right, my love. Don't go.

MASHA 'Don't go'! Hah! Damn this — this — this bloody, dreary, grinding life.

She goes up to the dining room. CHEBUTYKIN *follows her.*

CHEBUTYKIN Easy, my love, easy . . .

As SOLYONY *passes the* BARON:

SOLYONY (*Barely audible*) Quack-quack, quack-quack.

BARON Leave me alone, Solyony. I'm asking you. Formally.

SOLYONY *responds with his left-hand mime and his icy smile. Only* IRINA *and the* BARON *are left in the drawing room.*

KULYGIN Your very good health, Colonel. I'm Masha's husband. A schoolteacher by profession and happily by inclination and, if I may say so myself, very much an integral part of the household here. As for Masha, my wife, Masha is the very personification of kindness and consideration and —

VERSHININ I'll try some of this dark vodka, I think. (*Toast*) To the Prozorov family. (*To* OLGA) I'm very happy to be here with you all.

Welcoming sounds. General talk. OLGA *serves the meal.*

IRINA (*To* TUSENBACH) Masha's in bad form today. She was only eighteen when they got married; and at that age he probably seemed the cleverest man in the world. Things have changed. He's a very kind man but hardly the cleverest.

OLGA Andrey! Are you coming or are you not!

ANDREY (*Off*) Coming.

He enters and goes straight to the table.

BARON What are you thinking about?

IRINA Just that I don't like your friend, Solyony. There's something sinister about him. I think I'm frightened of him.

BARON He's an odd fish. I'm equally sorry for him and irritated by him. No, that's not accurate. I'm more sorry than irritated. I think he's shy. When we're alone together he's quite normal — very relaxed, even warm. But when there are others around he becomes aggressive and — (IRINA *moves towards the dining room*) Don't go in yet. Wait till they've all sat down. Let me just stand beside you for a while. (*Pause*) What are you thinking about? (*Pause*) You're only twenty and I'm not thirty yet and stretching out before us, waiting for us, are all those years — days and days to be filled with my love for you and —

IRINA Please — please don't talk like that. I —

BARON I have two great passions: my thirst for life, for work, for challenges; the other is my love for you. And somehow these two passions have fused and become one: life is beautiful because *you* are so beautiful. What are you thinking about?

IRINA 'Life is beautiful' — you say it so easily. Life for us three sisters hasn't been very 'beautiful' so far, has it? (*She is fingering flowers in a vase and now picks out a withered one*) Life can stifle, too, you know. Look — it never got a chance to blossom. And now I'm crying. Stupid, amn't I? (*She hurriedly wipes away her tears and tries to smile*) What we must do is work, and work, and work. If we're unhappy it's because we don't know what work means; and we don't know what it means because we're descended from people who despised it.

NATASHA enters wearing a pink dress and a green sash.

NATASHA Sweet Mother of God, I'm late — they're at the dinner already! (*Quick look in the mirror. She adjusts her hair*) It'll have to do now. (*She sees* IRINA *and goes to her. Her accent becomes slightly posh*) Irina darling, many, many happy returns. (*She gives* IRINA *a vigorous and prolonged kiss*) And look at the crowd of guests! Goodness gracious, I could never face in there! Baron, how d'you do.

OLGA comes down from the dining room.

OLGA Ah, Natasha. How are you, Natasha?

NATASHA All right, I suppose. (*They kiss*) God but that's a terrible big crowd, Olga. I could never face that crowd.

OLGA Of course you can. They're our friends. (*Quietly*) And you're wearing a green sash. That's . . . unusual.

NATASHA You mean it's unlucky? Is it a bad omen, Olga?

OLGA It's just that against the pink — it's quite distinctive.

NATASHA (*Tearfully*) You're right. It's wrong. But it's not really a greeny green, is it? Like I mean it's more a sort of kind of neutral green, isn't it?

She follows OLGA *into the dining room. The drawing room is now empty.*

KULYGIN And now, Irina, what you have got to do is seek out an eligible young man for yourself. Isn't it about time you were contemplating matrimony?

CHEBUTYKIN Isn't it about time Natasha found herself an eligible young man, too?

KULYGIN My spies tell me that Natasha has already found her man. Am I correct, Natasha?

MASHA *deliberately drops her plate on the table.*

MASHA I want some wine! Why are you keeping the damned wine hidden up there?

KULYGIN Language, Masha, language! Black mark, my darling.

VERSHININ Try this. This is very good. What is it made of?

SOLYONY Crushed cockroaches.

IRINA My God, you're disgusting.

OLGA Tonight we're having roast turkey and apple pie for dinner. I'm free as the wind today and I'm going to do all the cooking myself. So I want you all to join us again tonight.

VERSHININ (*To* MASHA) Does that include me?

IRINA Of course it includes you.

VERSHININ Good.

NATASHA (*Coyly*) We don't stand on ceremony in this house, do we?

CHEBUTYKIN (*Into* ANDREY's *ear*) 'For love alone did nature make us / That it might bend and try to break us.' (*Laughs*)

ANDREY (*Angrily*) For God's sake! Do you never get sick of your own jokes?

Enter FEDOTIK *and* RODDEY, *two young lieutenants. Between them they are carrying an enormous wicker basket full of flowers.* FEDOTIK *also carries a camera*

mounted on a tripod and RODDEY *a guitar.* RODDEY
speaks with an affected lisp.

FEDOTIK We're late. They've already begun.
RODDEY You're right, my petal. We *are* late.

FEDOTIK *mounts his camera.*

FEDOTIK Look this way everybody, please!

*A response from the group — a mixture of sur-
prise and delight and embarrassment.* FEDOTIK
disappears behind his black cloth.

RODDEY I think they're all just lovely!
FEDOTIK Only take a second. Big smile. Come on — you can
do better than that! Smile, Andrey! Smile! Yes!
Lovely! Terrific!

*He takes his picture — a puff of smoke from his
camera. A response to this.*

Don't move — one more — just one more. That's
it. Hold it there. That's perfect.
RODDEY They all look just divine, don't they?
FEDOTIK What are the sad faces for? Come on, Irina! That's
more like it. Terrific! Terrific!

*Another puff of smoke. Laughter. Clapping. The
group begins to break up.* RODDEY *and* FEDOTIK
*go up to the dining room where they are greeted
noisily.*

RODDEY Irina, my petal, many, many happy returns and
may all your sweet little dreams come true. And
what a day for celebration! Magnificent, isn't it?
You'd never guess where I've been all morning
— out with the boys from the secondary school!
Jogging — as we call it!

IRINA Roddey, you're — !

RODDEY I'm their instructor in physical education — didn't you know?

Another puff of smoke — FEDOTIK *has taken a picture of* IRINA *alone.*

FEDOTIK Thank you, Irina. That's all. Relax now. My God you're looking terrific today.

RODDEY (*Drily*) We all know that. Now go away and snap somebody else.

FEDOTIK *is fumbling in his bag.*

FEDOTIK Wait — wait — wait — wait. (*Produces a tiny top*) Here we are. Happy name day.

IRINA What is it?

FEDOTIK A top. A spinning top. A top that . . . spins.

IRINA Thank you, Fedotik.

FEDOTIK This is how you work it.

He demonstrates.

MASHA 'A green oak grows by a curving shore
And on that oak a gold chain hangs;
And on that oak a gold chain . . . '
Those lines of Pushkin have been haunting me all day. Why is that?

KULYGIN Ah-hah! Thirteen at table!

RODDEY Good heavens, the man's superstitious! You're surely not superstitious, are you?

Laughter.

KULYGIN If there are thirteen at table it means that somebody's in love. It wouldn't be yourself, Doctor, would it?

Laughter.

CHEBUTYKIN That's all in the past for me. But Natasha's a fine healthy colour. Why's that, Natasha?

Loud laughter. NATASHA *rushes down to the drawing room.* ANDREY *follows her. As he does:*

ANDREY Nastasha — please — don't listen to them — (*They are now both in the drawing room*) Wait — please — wait — don't go away —

NATASHA (*Crying*) What did I do that for — making an eejit of myself before everybody. (*To* ANDREY) Because they make fun of me all the time — that's the why! I know it was shocking bad manners — I know that! — but I couldn't help myself, Andrey. Honest to God I just couldn't — I couldn't —

She covers her face with her hands.

ANDREY Shhhhh, my darling, shhh — shhh — shhh. Please don't cry. They were only teasing; they meant no harm. They're good, generous people. They're fond of us both; I know they are. Come over here to the window. They can't see us there.

NATASHA I'm just not used to mixing with posh people like —

ANDREY Posh! Oh my God, you're so innocent, so beautiful, so magnificently innocent. Please don't cry. If you only knew — if I could only tell you — how I feel about you. I'm wildly in love with you. I'm besotted by you. (*He takes her in his arms*) We can't be seen now. (*As he kisses her face and hair and neck*) Where did we meet? How did I come to fall in love with you? When did it happen? I don't know. I know nothing anymore. All I know is that I love you, love you more than I've ever loved anyone in my life. Will you marry me, my beautiful innocent? Please, will you marry me?

They kiss. As they kiss FEDOTIK *and* RODDEY *come*

down to the drawing room and stare at them.

RODDEY Oh my goodness me! Just look at those two happy
petals!

Quick black. End of Act One.

ACT TWO

It is now late January, over a year and a half later; a Thursday night. The same scene as in Act One. The stage is in darkness. In the far distance a girl hums 'Won't You Buy My Pretty Flowers?' and is accompanied by a piano accordion. The music is slow and haunting and sad. A quick brief gust of howling wind and NATASHA *enters. Her hair in curlers, wearing a housecoat, carrying a candle. She crosses the stage and stops at the door of Andrey's room.*

NATASHA What are you doing, Andrey? (*She opens his door and puts her head in*) Are you reading? It's all right — don't stir — don't stir — just checking.

She closes the door, goes to an adjoining door, opens it, peers in, closes it again. ANDREY *emerges with a book in his hand.*

ANDREY What *are* you at, Natasha?

NATASHA Looking around in case the servants might have left a light burning. Staff! You couldn't watch them these days. And this carnival week has them astray in the head altogether. D'you hear? Singing in the streets! Have people no homes to go to? D'you know what I found last night in there? A candle! Burning! At midnight! But who left it there? Oh, nobody, nobody! What time is it?

ANDREY (*Checks watch*) A quarter past eight.

NATASHA Sweet Mother of God, it's not — is it? (*She fingers her curlers briefly, anxiously*) And poor Olga and Irina aren't back from work yet, the creatures. Olga has a staff meeting, I think, and this is one of Irina's late nights at the post office. I was just saying to Irina

43

this very morning, 'You really must take better care of yourself, darling.' Not that your sister heeds the like of me. A quarter past eight? It's little Bobik — that's what has me all throughother. He's not well at all. One minute he's cold and the next he's sweating like a pig. I just keep throwing up with worry.

ANDREY There's nothing wrong with Bobik, Natasha. The child's perfectly healthy.

NATASHA He is — isn't he? All the same I must pack more food into him. God, I worry so much about him. And I'm told we're having a group of mummers calling in about nine on their way to the carnival. It would be better if they didn't come, Andrey.

ANDREY Why would it? They've been invited and —

NATASHA When the wee darling woke up this morning he looked straight up at me — and he *smiled*! Honest to God! He knew me! 'Morning, Bobik,' I said. 'Morning, my darling little gosling.' And he *laughed*! They understand, you know. They understand everything. That's what I'll do then, Andrey; I'll just tell the maid not to let the mummers in.

ANDREY But my sisters invited them — and after all this is their house —

NATASHA Yes, it's their house, too. I'll have a word with them; they're *very* understanding.

She moves off, forgetting the candle burning on the table. ANDREY *lifts it as if to offer it to her, but with typical irresolution leaves it down again on the table.*

You're having yogurt for supper. The doctor says you must eat nothing but yogurt or you'll never lose weight. I know why Bobik's always cold — that damp room he's in! We've got to shift him, at least until the weather's warmer. Irina's room — that would be perfect for him! She can go in with Olga for the time being. Anyhow she's out all day long. She only sleeps there. (*Pause*) Andrey, love, why don't you say something?

ANDREY What about? There's nothing to say, is there?

NATASHA Something else in my head . . . Yes, Ferapont's here from the county council offices. He wants to see you.

ANDREY (*Wearily*) Tell him to come up.

> *She leaves.* ANDREY *sits at the table and reads by the light of the candle.* FERAPONT *enters encased in heavy, woollen, shabby clothes. A scarf around his ears.*

Over here, Ferapont. What do you want?

FERAPONT The chairman sent you these, the minute book and some papers.

> *He hands over the book and papers.*

ANDREY Thank you. You're working late, aren't you? It's after eight.

FERAPONT It's late, sir, isn't it? But I've been here since before dark only she wouldn't let me in. She said you were busy.

ANDREY Who said —

FERAPONT I know myself you're a busy man. And I'm not rushing off to the festival dance in the marquee, hee-hee-hee — (*He stops suddenly, thinking* ANDREY *has said something*) Wha's tha', sir?

ANDREY (*Leafing through the minute book*) Nothing . . . nothing . . . This is Thursday, isn't it? There won't be a meeting until next week. But I might as well go in tomorrow and write these up, I suppose. It will be at least as exciting as moping about here. (*Directly to* FERAPONT *but very quietly*) I'll tell you something, Ferapont: life bamboozles us all. I was messing about in my room today and look what I came across — (*holds up a book*) — my old university lectures! Go ahead and laugh, man, hee-hee-hee. I did. Andrey Prozorov, part-time clerk in the county council, temporary secretary to Mr Protopopov, the chairman, but with reasonable expectations of being made permanent — oh, yes, Andrey Prozorov still has ambitions. And every night, Ferapont, that part-time Andrey Prozorov dreams the same dream: that he is Professor Andrey Prozorov of Moscow University, the distinguished academician, one of Russia's leading intellectuals.

Pause. FERAPONT *sees he has stopped talking.*

FERAPONT No point in asking me, sir. I don't hear hardly nothing anymore.

ANDREY (*Softly*) If you could hear me, Ferapont, I wouldn't be talking to you. But I must talk to somebody. To coin a phrase, 'My wife doesn't understand me.' And for some reason I'm afraid of the girls. Ridiculous, isn't it? Afraid they'll laugh at me . . . (*Loudly*) D'you know where I'd love to be at this very moment? In the restaurant of the Great Moscow Hotel! Or better still in Tyestov's Grill Room! Not eating, not drinking, just sitting there.

FERAPONT There was a building contractor in the office the other day and he told me this story. Two Moscow businessmen went into this eating house. First fella orders forty pancakes. Devours the lot. Second fella orders fifty pancakes. Devours his pile. (*Pause*) Second fella — *poof* — drops dead, hee-hee-hee . . .

ANDREY You can sit in any of the bigger Moscow restaurants and, even though you know nobody and nobody knows you, you still don't feel you're alone. But here, where you know everyone and everybody knows you, you don't belong at all.

FERAPONT That same contractor told me another thing.

ANDREY Yes?

FERAPONT He says there's a huge rope stretched right across the width of Moscow.

ANDREY A rope.

FERAPONT In the front of Moscow, through the middle and straight out the back.

ANDREY Why?

FERAPONT Must be a very long rope.

ANDREY Why in the name of God would —

FERAPONT How long would that rope be, sir?

ANDREY I have no idea, Ferapont.

FERAPONT Do you think he was taking a hand at me?

ANDREY Have you ever been to Moscow?

FERAPONT Oh, God, no. Moscow? Oh, never, never. If it had been the will of God I would have been, though.

ANDREY All right. Off you go.

FERAPONT Wha's tha'?

ANDREY Thank you. Goodnight. (ANDREY *rises*) Come back tomorrow morning. I'll have some of these done by then.

FERAPONT Wha's tha', sir?

ANDREY Goodnight. Goodnight. Goodnight.

FERAPONT *goes.*

Oh my God . . .

ANDREY *goes into his room. Offstage a nurse is singing a lullaby to Bobik.* MASHA *and* VERSHININ *enter, shaking the snow off their coats. A maid lights candles and a lamp in the dining room.*

MASHA Maybe you *are* right — maybe there is no difference between army people and civilians. Maybe it's a question of what you're used to. I remember after Father's death we couldn't get used to the idea that we hadn't a houseful of orderlies to wait on us!

VERSHININ I'm very thirsty.

MASHA No, there *is* a difference. Maybe other provincial towns aren't as dreary as this one. But in this town the only courteous, the only civilized people are the military.

VERSHININ I'd love a glass of tea.

MASHA Look at me for example.

VERSHININ Happily.

He reaches out to hold her. She moves away.

MASHA I got married when I was eighteen and at that age
I was in awe of Fyodor because he had taught me
and I'd only just left school myself. I thought he
was clever, sophisticated; a man of significance.
Wasn't I mature?

VERSHININ You are —

Again he tries to hold her. Again she eludes him.

MASHA What were we talking about? Civilians! Anyhow,
what I'm saying is that most of them are coarse,
ill-mannered . . . louts! I can't stand their rudeness,
their boorishness; their ignorance! You've never
been in a group of Fyodor's colleagues? That's something you must experience!

VERSHININ All I tried to say was —

MASHA (*Laughs*) That you want a glass of tea!

VERSHININ I just suggested that people everywhere — this
town, any other town, civilian, military — they all
have one thing in common: they are all equally
dreary. Talk to any soldier, any civilian who's
capable of looking objectively at his life, and what
will he tell you? That he's sick and tired of it all.
Sick and tired of his wife, his family, his home, his
job — the whole thing. We Russians are a people
whose aspirations are magnificent; it's just living
we can't handle. (*His usual embarrassment. He spreads
his hands*)

MASHA And why can't we?

VERSHININ Am I the one to ask? Sick and tired of his wife. Sick
and tired of his children. And his wife and children are just as sick and tired of him.

MASHA *catches his hand.*

48

MASHA You're in bad form today.

VERSHININ I've had nothing to eat since breakfast! (*He kisses her hand and holds it against his cheek*) One of the girls is sick. When anything's wrong with them I get so . . . I feel guilty about them and responsible to them because of their mother's condition, as if it were *all* my fault. You should have seen her this morning; she really is a vixen. The fighting began at seven, earlier than usual. Finally about nine I walked out and slammed the door. (*Again he kisses her hands. Pause*) Funny thing is, you're the only one I've ever talked to about it. Do you realize how privileged you are? (*Kisses her again*) I've no one, Masha, no one in the world but you.

Pause.

MASHA The wind's howling in the stove. It made a noise like that too just before Father died.

VERSHININ Are you superstitious?

MASHA Very.

VERSHININ (*Suddenly he kisses her hands rapidly and repeatedly*) You're the most wonderful woman I've ever known. Wonderful and marvellous! Even though it's dark, your eyes are luminous.

She moves away from him.

MASHA There's more light here.

He goes to her and holds her in his arms.

VERSHININ I love you, Masha, love you, love you, love you. I love your eyes. I love the way you move. Everything you do is wonderful, marvellous, marvellous, wonderful!

MASHA (*Laughing softly*) When you talk to me like that, somehow I can't help laughing even though I'm frightened at the same time. So please don't . . .

(*Very softly*) Yes, do; do. (*She covers her face with her hands*) Please do. I want you to. Yes, do . . . (*A long kiss. Then suddenly she breaks away*) Somebody's coming!

IRINA *and* TUSENBACH *enter the dining room.*

BARON Yes I *have* a triple-barrelled name: Baron Tusenbach-Krone-Altschauer. *But*: I was baptized in the Greek Orthodox Church and I'm every bit as Russian as you are. Not a trace of German ancestry in me except the way I persist in leaving you home every evening, boringly, predictably, so 'Teutonically'.

IRINA God, I'm exhausted.

BARON And I will persist in calling for you at the post office every evening. I'll keep it up for ten years, for twenty years until you *order* me out of your life. (*Seeing* MASHA *and* VERSHININ) Ah. And how are you two?

IRINA Home at last. (*She flops exhausted into a seat*) We're just about to close up when in comes this peasant woman. Wants to send a telegram to her brother to tell him that her son died today. Where does this brother live? In Saratov. Where in Saratov? No idea. Saratov town or Saratov county? Didn't know. Just Saratov. So off it went without an address — just to Saratov! And she was crying all the time. And I was so bitchy with her. 'You're wasting my time, dear.' My time! My God. (*She leaps to her feet, suddenly brisk*) Well, at least we're having the mummers tonight, aren't we?

MASHA Yes.

IRINA (*Weary again*) I must lie down for a while. I'm falling apart. (*She sits*)

BARON (*To* MASHA) When she comes home from work she always looks very, very young and very, very vulnerable. Doesn't she?

IRINA (*Eyes closed*) Weary . . . weary . . . weary . . . I hate working in that place. Really hate it.

MASHA You do look younger, Irina; sort of boyish-looking.
BARON It's the way she does her hair.
IRINA (*Eyes closed*) Must find another job. I'm wilting in
that place. (*Eyes open*) Remember what I used to
dream of? — Work that was stimulating, fulfilling,
'creative'. Look what I've ended up with — sheer
damn drudgery. (*Knocking on the floor from below*)
That's the doctor. Signal back to him, Nikolai. I'm
too tried. (*The* BARON *stamps on the floor in response*)
Now he'll be up like a light. Did you know that
Andrey and himself were at the card school in the
club last night and lost again? I'm told Andrey lost
two hundred roubles on one hand alone. Something must be done about it.
MASHA (*Indifferently*) A bit late in the day.
IRINA He lost a lot of money two weeks' ago, too, and
even more in December. If he'd just go and gamble
away everything we've got the sooner we might
escape from this place. D'you know — every night,
every single night in life, I dream about Moscow.
Sometimes I think I'm going off my head. (*Laughs*)
Yes, yes, I *know* we're moving there in June. But
it's — what? — February, March, April, May — it's
almost six months till June!
MASHA Natasha mustn't find out about his gambling.
IRINA Of course she knows. Does she care anymore?

CHEBUTYKIN *enters the dining room. He has been
sleeping. He combs his beard, sits at the table, and
begins reading a paper.*

MASHA Quite a dandy, isn't he? Has he paid any rent since?
IRINA (*Laughs*) Since what? Not for eight months! It just
never occurs to him.

MASHA *laughs with her.*

MASHA And would you look at him — like a little bantam
rooster.

All three laugh except VERSHININ.

IRINA You're very quiet.

VERSHININ Am I? I've had nothing to eat since breakfast.

MASHA He's dying for a glass of tea.

CHEBUTYKIN Irina!

IRINA Hello.

CHEBUTYKIN Have you a moment? *Venez ici.*

IRINA *Vengo subito* — correct?

She goes and sits at the table with him.

CHEBUTYKIN What would I do without you?

She lays out the cards for patience. Silence.

VERSHININ Well, since nobody's going to bring us tea, can't we at least talk?

BARON (*With excessive enthusiasm*) Excellent idea! What will our topic be, Colonel?

VERSHININ Topic? Oh . . . let's . . . just . . . chatter.

BARON Splendid! What will we chatter about?

VERSHININ What life will be like long after we're dead and gone — say in two or three hundred years' time.

BARON We're dead and buried? Excellent! Firstly, people will glide across the great blue sky in enormous balloons. (*Response from* IRINA) Secondly, there will be totally new styles in men's jackets. (MASHA *and* VERSHININ *exchange suppressed smiles*) Thirdly, it is conceivable that a sixth sense may be discovered and developed. But life will be essentially the same. It will still be as difficult and as mysterious and as joyous as it is now. I promise you. And in a thousand years from now you'll still have people whining about how 'dreary' their life is. But those self-same whiners will still be as scared of dying as we are. Right, Colonel?

VERSHININ Yes, of course there'll be change — that's inevitable. But in two or three hundred years' time, in a thousand years' time — I think, yes, I'm convinced a new kind of life, a truly happy life, will evolve. We won't experience it, of course. But our lives here, now — our work, our anxieties, our sufferings — that's all a kind of preparation for what is to come. That's the purpose of our existence. And because it is our purpose, it is the only possibility of happiness we have.

MASHA *laughs quietly.*

BARON What are you laughing at, Masha?

MASHA I don't know. Sorry. I've been laughing all day.

VERSHININ I went to the same cadet school as you did but I never made it to staff college. Even though I read a lot I was never a discriminating reader. But the longer I live the more I want to know. I'm going grey; I'm getting old; and I know so little. But one thing I do know: we're never going to know happiness in our time. We mustn't expect it. We have no right to it. Our fate is to work and work and work. I'll never experience happiness. Neither will you. But there is a possibility that my children's children may. (*His dismissive gesture*) Well . . .

FEDOTIK *and* RODDEY *enter the dining room and sit at the end of the table.* RODDEY *plays the guitar* — 'Won't You Buy My Pretty Flowers?' — *and hums softly.*

BARON So that even to dream of happiness is futile? *But*: supposing I say to you, as indeed I do, 'I am happy now.'

VERSHININ (*Casually, dismissively*) You're not.

TUSENBACH *claps his hands and laughs loudly.*

BARON But I am! I am! How do you talk to a man like that!

> MASHA *laughs quietly, privately.*

Masha, I wish you'd either share your joke with us or else —

MASHA Sorry — sorry.

BARON No, no, life does not change. It follows its own strange laws that are beyond our understanding. Two hundred years, three hundred years, a million years, everything will be the same. Look at the cranes that head south every winter. Do they understand why they migrate? Not at all! They just fly south instinctively. And if there is a single thought in their heads when they're flying, does that matter? Let them philosophize as much as they like as long as they keep on flying. And I promise you, they will.

MASHA So the whole thing has no meaning?

BARON It's snowing out there. What's the 'meaning' of that?

MASHA I think we must have a faith, or look for one. Because if we don't life is empty and senseless. There must be some explanation why cranes fly south, why children are born, why there are stars in the sky. Either you know what you are living for or else nothing matters — the whole thing is absurd.

> VERSHININ *has been gazing at her throughout her speech.*

VERSHININ I know just one thing.

MASHA What's that?

VERSHININ I'm not a young man anymore.

> *She laughs, goes to him, and catches his arm reassuringly.*

MASHA What's that line from Gogol? 'Life on earth is a complete bore, my friends.'

BARON And arguing with you two is impossible, my friends. 'Faith'! For God's sake!

CHEBUTYKIN (*Reads*) 'Balzac was married in Berdichev town.' Must make a note of that.

> *As before he produces his pencil and notebook but puts them away almost immediately.*

Why would I write that nonsense? Rubbish.

> IRINA *picks up the line and dreamily sings a polka-style melody.*

IRINA (*Sings*) 'Balzac was married in Berdichev town.'

> RODDEY *picks up the melody and plays the line once on his guitar.* IRINA *leaves down the cards and sings the line again.*

'Balzac was married in Berdichev town.'

> IRINA *and* FEDOTIK *now sing together to* RODDEY'S *accompaniment.*

'Balzac was married in Berdichev town.'
FEDOTIK (*Without breaking the rhythm*) Who to?
IRINA (*Sings*) 'To a Polish girl called Hanska.'

> *Pause. There is a sense that this moment could blossom, that suddenly everybody might join in the chorus — and dance — and that the room might be quickened with music and laughter. Everyone is alert to this expectation; it is almost palpable, if some means of realizing it could be found.* VERSHININ *moves close to* MASHA. FEDOTIK *moves close to* IRINA *(to* RODDEY'S *acute annoyance).* TUSENBACH *sits at the piano. As soon as he begins picking out the melody:*

FEDOTIK Good man, Baron!

And to encourage him IRINA *and* FEDOTIK *sing the first two lines again to* RODDEY's *accompaniment. The* BARON *is all thumbs — the melody is drowned.*

BARON Can't play without music. Useless. Sorry.

He shrugs his shoulders and rises from the piano. The moment is lost. IRINA *picks up the cards.* MASHA *drifts away from* VERSHININ, FEDOTIK *moves away from* IRINA *and goes back to* RODDEY. *There is an atmosphere of vague embarrassment. And* RODDEY *now picks out the melody at an ironic, funereal pace.*

I forgot to tell you; I've taken the plunge; I've resigned my commission!

This evokes no response whatever. TUSENBACH *waits. Silence.*

What d'you make of that, Masha?
MASHA Sorry?
BARON I'm leaving the army!
MASHA (*Vaguely*) Oh! . . . yes, yes; good . . .
BARON So I'm practically a civilian!
MASHA I prefer military men.
BARON Do you? Ah . . .

RODDEY *strikes one deep quivering note on his guitar.*

The only people who get promotion in the army these days are the pretty boys. That rules me out.

He strikes one high, mocking note.

I'm going to get a real job, and I'm going to work so hard that when I come home in the evening I'll collapse exhausted into bed and fall asleep instantly. The people who sleep really soundly are labourers — unskilled labourers.

> *And as he goes up to the dining room* RODDEY *plays a final cadence — an amen cadence — on his guitar.*

FEDOTIK (*To* IRINA) I got you these colouring crayons in that new toy shop in Moscow Street.

IRINA Why do you treat me like a child?

FEDOTIK And this penknife.

IRINA I'm a young woman and you must — (*She breaks off, her face lighting up with childish pleasure at the crayons*) Oh they're lovely, they're really lovely!

FEDOTIK And I got this knife for myself. What about that! (*Their heads together like two children as they examine the toys. Demonstrating*) One blade. Two blades. Three blades. Four blades!

IRINA And a nail file!

FEDOTIK And a pair of tiny scissors!

IRINA And a thing for taking stones out of horses' hooves! A miniature miracle, isn't it?

FEDOTIK 'Miniature miracle'!

> *They laugh together.*

RODDEY (*Irritable with jealousy*) Doctor!

CHEBUTYKIN Yes?

RODDEY Do *you* still play children's games? What age are you?

CHEBUTYKIN Thirty-two.

> *Laughter at this.* FEDOTIK *and* RODDEY *stare angrily at one another. Then* FEDOTIK *turns to* IRINA.

FEDOTIK I've learned another kind of patience. Let me show it to you.

He sits beside IRINA *at the table, and immediately* RODDEY *sings raucously and in parody.*

RODDEY 'Balzac was married in Berdichev town . . . ' (*To the end*)

As he sings ANFISA *carries in the samovar and* NATASHA *brings two plates of food.* SOLYONY *enters.*

SOLYONY Evening. Evening. Evening.

As he passes the BARON *he mimes his quack-quack and goes to the table.*

VERSHININ There's a wind getting up.

MASHA I'm sick of winter. I can't remember what summer feels like.

IRINA It's working out! Look! It's an omen! That means we *will* go to Moscow.

FEDOTIK It's not working out. That eight shouldn't be on top of the two of spades. So you won't go to Moscow.

CHEBUTYKIN (*Reads*) 'An outbreak of smallpox in Manchuria is of epidemic proportions.' (*Mock horror*) We're all doomed!

ANFISA (*Coming down to* MASHA) Masha, the tea's poured, love. (*To* VERSHININ) If you'd come up here, sir, your honour — I beg your pardon — what's this your name is again?

VERSHININ It's —

MASHA Bring it down here, Nanny. I'm not going in there.

IRINA Nanny!

ANFISA 'Nanny! Nanny!' Coming-coming!

NATASHA *hands tea to* SOLYONY *who is sprinkling his hands with perfume.*

NATASHA They understand everything, you know.

SOLYONY Of course they do. Who?

NATASHA 'Morning, Bobik,' I said. 'Morning, my darling little

gosling.'
SOLYONY 'Gosling'?

And he looks quickly across at the BARON *and gives his quack-quack mime.*

NATASHA And d'you know what he did?
SOLYONY (*With exaggerated interest*) What did he do?
NATASHA He gave me this cold, penetrating look. It was uncanny! And now you're thinking that's just a silly, doting mammy talking. But you're wrong. I'm telling you, Captain: the child is extraordinary.
SOLYONY Extraordinary.
NATASHA You're so right, Captain. Mammies know these things.
SOLYONY If he were my child, d'you know what I'd do?
NATASHA What?
SOLYONY Fillet him, roast him and eat him. Bobik stroganoff!

And immediately he lifts his glass and comes down to the drawing room.

NATASHA The army has put no manners on you, you pup you!
MASHA If you're happy you wouldn't notice whether it's summer or winter. If I were in Moscow I don't think I'd give a damn what the weather was like.
VERSHININ I've just been reading the diary of a French cabinet minister that he wrote in jail — he was sentenced over the Panama Canal swindle. He writes with such enthusiasm about the birds he sees from his cell window — birds he'd never even noticed when he was outside. And now he's out of jail he pays no more attention to the birds than he did before. Like you and Moscow: once you're living there, it'll mean nothing to you. Happiness? I don't believe it exists. Happiness is just an aspiration.

ANFISA *hands him a cup of tea and a letter.*

ANFISA A letter for you, sir.
VERSHININ For me?

> TUSENBACH *picks up the chocolate box from the* *table.*

BARON What happened the chocolates?
IRINA Solyony ate them.
BARON The whole box?

> *He looks at* SOLYONY. SOLYONY *mimes his quack-* *quack at him.*

VERSHININ (*To* MASHA) From my daughter. One line on an exercise book.
MASHA Is something wrong?
VERSHININ I've got to go, Masha. I'm sorry. I won't have tea.
MASHA What is it?
VERSHININ Another crisis.
MASHA Can't you tell me?
VERSHININ My wife — she's taken an overdose again. I'll just slip out quietly. It's all so . . . grotesque . . . (*He kisses her hand*) My darling — my wonderful, marvellous darling. I'll leave by the back stairs.

> *He leaves.*

ANFISA Where's *he* away to? Haven't I just poured him his tea! What sort of an odd fish is he?
MASHA (*Angrily*) Shut up, will you! You keep nagging, nagging, nagging! I'm sick of your damned nagging, you old bag.

> *She goes up to the dining room with her cup.*

ANFISA Did I do something wrong, darling?
ANDREY (*Off*) Anfisa! Anfisa!
ANFISA 'Anfisa! Anfisa!' He sits in there all day and expects . . .

> *She is too exasperated to finish. She goes off.* MASHA
> *is now at the dining-room table.*

MASHA Where am I supposed to sit? (*She sweeps the cards
aside*) Must the whole table be covered with cards?

IRINA Oh my, aren't we cranky.

MASHA If I'm cranky don't talk to me then. Just leave me
alone.

CHEBUTYKIN (*Laughing*) Don't touch her! Careful! Do not touch!

MASHA Look at him, would you — sixty if he's a day —
and mouthing rubbish like a bloody child.

NATASHA Masha, please! Must you use coarse language like
that? You who could have entré into the very best
society. But when you use vernacular vulgarities
— oh my goodness! *Je vous prie. Pardonnez-moi,
mais vous avez des manières peu-grossières.*

> *The situation is defused.* TUSENBACH *can scarcely
> suppress his laughter.*

BARON Isn't there brandy somewhere? Where's the brandy
gone?

NATASHA *Il paraît que mon Bobik déjà ne dort pas* — the little
darling's awake. He's out of sorts today. If you'll
excuse me . . .

> *She leaves.*

IRINA (*To* MASHA) Where's the colonel?

MASHA Gone.

IRINA Gone where?

MASHA 'Home'. His wife's done something . . . theatrical
again.

> TUSENBACH, *already slightly intoxicated, goes with
> the bottle of brandy to* SOLYONY *who is sitting
> apart as usual.*

BARON You're always sitting by yourself, brooding about

something or other, God alone knows what. Come on, Solyony, let's have a brandy together. (*They drink*) A little refreshment before the mummers arrive 'cause then I'll be stuck at the piano all bloody night — to use a vernacular vulgarity.

SOLYONY I've never quarrelled with you. What have we to make up?

BARON Just that I have the feeling that there's some tension between us. I'll tell you what you are, Solyony.

SOLYONY Here we go.

BARON You are what Kulygin would call a *rara avis*, a rare bird.

SOLYONY 'I may be odd, but who is not; Aleko, be not angry.'

> *While they are talking* ANDREY *enters with his book and sits at the table.*

BARON Is that Pushkin?

SOLYONY When I'm alone with somebody I'm perfectly relaxed and normal. It's only when I'm in company that I become difficult, aggressive.

> FEDOTIK *comes down beside them, picks up the brandy bottle, looks at it, leaves it down again.*

FEDOTIK Sorry. Looking for vodka.

> *He moves away.*

SOLYONY At the same time I'm a lot more honest, a lot less difficult, than some people I could name.

BARON And I'll be honest with you, Solyony. I do get angry with you — when you deliberately set out to bait me. *But*: I like you — yes, I like Solyony. Oh, what the hell — I'm going to get loaded tonight. Let's get loaded together.

SOLYONY Why not. (*They drink*) No, I've nothing against you, Baron. Just that I'm a Lermontov type.

BARON A what type?

SOLYONY You know the writer, Lermontov? I've his temp-
erament — disenchanted, bored, caustic. (*Quietly,
confidentially*) I've even been told I resemble him
physically, too.

He perfumes his hands.

BARON I've resigned my commission, Solyony. Thought
about it for five years and now it's done. Now I'm
going to get a real job, a man's job.

SOLYONY 'Aleko, be not angry.'

BARON From now on it's going to be all work, work, work.

SOLYONY 'Forget, forget your dreams.'

CHEBUTYKIN *comes down to the drawing room
with* IRINA.

CHEBUTYKIN I was there for only one night but the food they
gave us was genuine Caucasian: vegetable soup
followed by chemartma — a kind of meat dish.

SOLYONY Onion.

CHEBUTYKIN Sorry?

SOLYONY Cheremsha's a kind of onion. Bit like a shallot.

CHEBUTYKIN I'm talking about a mutton dish called chemartma.

SOLYONY Cheremsha's made from onions.

CHEBUTYKIN We're talking about two different dishes, Solyony.
Anyhow you've never been to the Caucasus. Or
eaten chemartma.

SOLYONY Because I can't stand the smell of it. Stinks, like
garlic.

ANDREY For God's sake will you two please stop!

BARON I want the mummers! Bring on the dancing mummers!

IRINA They promised they'd be here about nine. Should
be here any time now.

TUSENBACH *goes unsteadily to* ANDREY *and embraces him.*

BARON (*Sings*) 'There are many sad and weary — '
ANDREY (*Sings*) '— in this pleasant world of ours.'
TOGETHER 'Crying every night so dreary, / Won't you buy my pretty flowers?'

They laugh raucously and TUSENBACH *kisses* ANDREY.

BARON Dammit, let's have one more modest drink. (*Toast*) To my eternal friendship with Andrey Prozorov. And when Andrey Prozorov goes back to Moscow University, his eternal friend goes, too.
SOLYONY Goes where?
BARON To Moscow University.
SOLYONY Which one?
BARON There is only one Moscow University.
SOLYONY Two universities in Moscow.
BARON One.
SOLYONY Two.
BARON One.
ANDREY Who cares if there's a hundred. The more the merrier.
SOLYONY Two.

Good-humoured booing and hissing and cries of 'Shut up, Solyony!'

In Moscow there are two universities. (*Louder protests.* SOLYONY *now has to shout to be heard*) But if you find me too unpleasant I can always go somewhere else, can't I?

He leaves.

BARON And good riddance, too. (*Laughs*) Everybody on the floor, my friends. A *rara avis*, Solyony. Ignore him — ignore him.

He sits at the piano and thumps out the 'Blue

> Danube' *waltz.* MASHA *dances by herself. As before there is the possibility that the occasion might blossom. But there is less possibility this time.*

MASHA (*Sings*) 'The baron is drunk, is drunk, is drunk;
The baron is drunk is drunk as a skunk . . . '

> *While she sings* NATASHA *enters.*

NATASHA Where's the doctor?
CHEBUTYKIN Hello!

> NATASHA *passes* MASHA *to go to* CHEBUTYKIN *and, as she passes,* MASHA *sings directly to her.*

MASHA 'The baron is pissed, is pissed, is pissed;
I wished I were pissed, full pissed, mad pissed.
Was she ever pissed, full pissed, half-pissed? . . . '

> NATASHA *has whispered into* CHEBUTYKIN's *ear and now leaves.* CHEBUTYKIN *goes to the piano and whispers to the* BARON. *The* BARON *stops playing. Silence — apart from* MASHA's *singing, and she persists.*

MASHA Ta-ra-ra-ra-ra, ta-ra, ta-ra;
Ta-ra-ra-ra-ra . . .

> *Now she fades out.*

IRINA (*To* CHEBUTYKIN) What's the matter?
CHEBUTYKIN Time we were going. Goodnight.
BARON Goodnight, everybody. Time to pack up.
IRINA Wait a minute! What about the mummers?
ANDREY The mummers aren't coming! (*Now very embarrassed*)
Bobik's not well according to his mother . . . and
. . . and . . . that's that. That's all I know. Just what
I'm told.

He exits quickly. CHEBUTYKIN *follows him.*

IRINA (*Shrugs*) If Bobik's not well . . .

MASHA What the hell. If we're being evicted (*shouts*) then we ought to leave quietly, mustn't we? (*To* IRINA) Nothing the matter with Bobik. Just another theatrical mammy. (*Loudly*) Bitch!

FEDOTIK And I was looking forward to a good night. But of course if the baby's sick . . . I'll get him some toys tomorrow. 'Bye.

RODDEY Such a disappointment, my petals. And you'd never guess what I did this afternoon — went to bed for an hour so that I'd be in positively dazzling form this evening! I thought we'd be dancing all night, didn't I? We can't let the night end like this, my petals — can we? It's only nine o'clock!

MASHA We'll go outside. We'll decide then what to do.

They all leave. Voices off calling 'Goodnight — goodnight'. The BARON *sings 'The baron is drunk, is drunk, is drunk' and laughs drunkenly. Gradually the sounds fade.* ANFISA *and a maid enter, clear the table, put out the lights. Offstage a nurse sings to the baby.* ANDREY *and* CHEBUTYKIN *enter, preparing to go out.*

CHEBUTYKIN No, I never got round to marrying. Somehow life went past too quickly. Anyhow, the only woman I ever loved was your mother; and she was already married.

ANDREY (*Not listening*) Nobody should get married. Ever. Marriage is a suffocation.

CHEBUTYKIN Perhaps. But the alternative is loneliness. And loneliness can crush you, too. What matter. Who gives a damn!

ANDREY Come on. Let's get out of here.

CHEBUTYKIN Take your time. We're too early.

ANDREY Will you move before Natasha comes in and stops me?

CHEBUTYKIN Right, right.

ANDREY I'm not going to gamble tonight. I'm just going to sit and watch. I don't feel so well.

CHEBUTYKIN Yes?

ANDREY I get this shortness of breath. What should I take for it?

CHEBUTYKIN You're asking *me*? I wouldn't know. I don't remember.

ANDREY We'll go out through the kitchen.

> *They go out. The doorbell rings.* ANFISA *goes to the window and looks down. The bell rings again. Voices and laughter off — the mummers have arrived.* IRINA *enters.*

IRINA Who is it, Nanny?

ANFISA (*Whispers*) The mummers! All dressed up!

IRINA Tell them there's no one at home. Say you're very sorry but there's nobody here but you.

> ANFISA *goes off.* SOLYONY *enters.*

SOLYONY (*Astonished*) Where's everybody gone?

IRINA Home.

SOLYONY So you're on your own?

IRINA Yes. Goodnight, Solyony.

SOLYONY I'm sorry. I behaved badly just now. That shouldn't have happened. But you're not like the others, Irina: I think you understand me. I know you do. (*Pause*) I'm in love with you, Irina. I love you deeply. I love you passionately.

IRINA You'd better go. Goodnight, Solyony.

SOLYONY I can't live without you.

> *She moves away. He follows.*

Just to be with you. Just to gaze at you. Just to see those magical, amazing eyes of yours —

IRINA Please, Captain.

SOLYONY The first time I've ever told you how much I love you and, just to be able to say it to you, it makes me feel . . . transformed.

IRINA Stop it! At once!

Pause.

SOLYONY Of course I can't force you to love me . . . naturally . . . But understand this: I won't let anybody else have you. Because if there is somebody else — (*pause*) — I will kill him. (*Again he moves towards her*) Irina, my beautiful, beautiful Irina, please listen for a second to —

He breaks off because NATASHA *enters wearing her housecoat and carrying a candle. As before she opens doors, peers in, closes them again. As she passes Andrey's room she taps on the door but does not open it.*

NATASHA Just checking, Andrey. Don't stir. (*Now she sees* SOLYONY. *Coldly*) You'll have to excuse me, Captain. I know I'm not dressed for guests.

SOLYONY Who cares?

He leaves.

NATASHA Irina, darling — (*kisses her*) — you're exhausted: you should try to get to bed a bit earlier.

IRINA Is Bobik asleep?

NATASHA Restless, tossing about. By the way, darling, I keep meaning to ask you but either you're out or else I'm too busy. Bobik's nursery — it's cold and gloomy. Now your room — it'd be just perfect for a baby. Darling, would you ever think of moving in with Olga for a while?

IRINA (*Not understanding*) Move in where?

A troika with bells is heard drawing up outside.

NATASHA *responds briefly but pursues her present task.*

NATASHA Into Olga's room. For the time being. Then Bobik can have your room. (*Doorbell rings*) That'll be Olga. Isn't she late? (*Back to her task*) That's a weight off my mind. He's such a darling. This morning I said to him, 'Morning, Bobik. Morning, my darling little gosling.' And d'you know what he did? He —

She breaks off because a maid has entered and whispers in her ear.

(*Sharply*) What is it? What is it? (*More whispering. Coyly*) Protopopov? Lord, isn't he a caution! (*To* IRINA) Protopopov — inviting me out for a drive in his new troika. The naughty boy. (*Laughs*) Men! You couldn't be up to them. Maybe I'll go for a quarter-of-an-hour or so — what d'you think? Sure what harm's in it? (*To maid*) Tell him I'll be down in a minute. (*Doorbell again*) That'll be Olga now.

She goes off. Pause. Then VERSHININ, OLGA *and* KULYGIN *enter.*

KULYGIN I thought you said we were going to have a party?
VERSHININ I thought so. I left only half-an-hour ago and they were expecting the mummers then.
IRINA Everybody's gone. Everybody's left.
KULYGIN Masha, too? Where did she go? And what's Protopopov doing out there in his troika? Who's he waiting for? And where's the baron and —
IRINA Fyodor, please. Please. I'm tired.
KULYGIN Now-now — don't be a Little-Miss-Cross-Patch-Draw-The-Latch!
OLGA The staff meeting has only just finished and I'm just spent. And the headmistress is sick and I've got to take on her work. This migraine's becoming

unbearable. (*She drops into a seat*) And the whole town's talking about Andrey: he lost two hundred roubles at cards last night.

KULYGIN That meeting was a bit testing, wasn't it?

He sits. Pause.

VERSHININ What happened was . . . my wife decided to give me a fright . . . tried to poison herself . . . Another false alarm. Everything's in hand now, I think . . . So there's no party? I suppose we should go, then? (*Suddenly eager*) Kulygin, what about you and I going somewhere ourselves? Come on, man! I can't face going home just yet. What d'you say?

KULYGIN Some other time. (*He stands up*) I'm really very tired. Do you think Masha has gone home?

IRINA I suppose so.

KULYGIN Well — goodnight. (*Kisses* IRINA's *hand*) At least we have the weekend to recuperate. (*He moves off*) I would have liked a refreshing cup of tea and an evening of relaxed sociability. But there you are. *O fallacem hominum spem*; the false hopes that men entertain.

VERSHININ I'll go somewhere by myself then. Goodnight.

VERSHININ *and* KULYGIN *leave.*

OLGA This migraine's getting unbearable . . . Did I tell you? — Andrey lost two hundred roubles; it's the talk of the town. Yes, I did tell you . . . I'm off to bed. No work tomorrow or the next day; thanks be to God for that . . . Oh my poor head . . .

She leaves. As at the opening of this Act in the far distance a girl hums 'Won't You Buy My Pretty Flowers?' and is accompanied by a piano accordion. The music is slow and haunting. NATASHA *enters and crosses the stage briskly. She is wearing an expensive fur coat and matching fur hat. A maid trots behind her carrying a matching fur muff.*

NATASHA Back in half-an-hour! Just going for a little drive!
Au revoir!

IRINA *is alone on stage. Long silence.*

IRINA Oh, Moscow! Moscow! Moscow!

Quick black. End of Act Two.

ACT THREE

It is almost 3.00 a.m., a midsummer night. A year and a half has passed. The bedroom shared by OLGA *and* IRINA. *Two beds, one stage left and one stage right, each with a screen around it. A large sofa stage left. Also a wardrobe. A wash-handbasin and jug stage right. Above it a large mirror. Offstage a bell is ringing: fire has broken out in the town some time previously. Nobody in the house has gone to bed.* MASHA, *dressed in black as usual, is lying on the sofa, her eyes closed.* OLGA *enters. She is very agitated.* ANFISA *trots exhaustedly behind her.*

ANFISA They're sitting down there now, the poor wee souls, crying their eyes out. I've told them a dozen times to come upstairs. But I can't get a budge out of them. 'Where's Daddy?' they're crying. 'Maybe Daddy's burned to death.' There's a crowd outside in the yard, too, with hardly a stitch on them. According to them Kirsanovsky Street's burned to the ground.

> OLGA *rapidly pulls dresses out of the wardrobe, choosing certain garments only. She flings them into* ANFISA's *open arms.*

OLGA Take this grey one, Nanny. And this blouse. And this skirt. God, what a disaster! Here — take this — and this — and this. (ANFISA *almost staggers under the weight*) The Vershinins got a terrible fright — their house is badly damaged. They must stay the night here. And poor Fedotik lost everything — not a single thing saved.

ANFISA You'd better call Ferapont, love. (OLGA *rings a hand bell*) I'm not fit to carry all —

OLGA Why doesn't he come when I ring? (*She flings open the door and calls*) Come on, come on, Ferapont! (*Through the open door can be seen a window red with the fire*) Oh my God, this is terrible, terrible!

> FERAPONT *enters.* OLGA *returns to the wardrobe and now strips it indiscriminately.*

Here, man, take these downstairs. Give them to the Kolotilin girls to distribute. Here, give them this too.

FERAPONT In the year one thousand, eight hundred and twelve Moscow was burned down too — just like this. And when the French saw it they were so shocked they —

OLGA Will you move, man!

FERAPONT Wha's tha', Miss?

OLGA Go! Go! Go!

FERAPONT Yes, Miss. Certainly.

> *He leaves.*

OLGA Give them everything we have, Nanny.

> *She empties what is left in the wardrobe onto the bed.*

Give it all away — everything — everything.

> OLGA *is suddenly exhausted. She sits on the bed, then rises immediately.*

No, we must keep going. Now. The Vershinins will stay the night. The two little girls can sleep in the drawing room and their father can go in with Baron Tusenbach in the back bedroom. Fedotik can sleep there too. We can put no one in with the doctor. I'm so angry with him. What sort of a man goes and gets drunk on a night like this! Who else is there? Vershinin's wife. She'd better go into the drawing room too, with her two little girls.

ANFISA (*Exhausted, speaking softly*) Don't send me away, Miss Olga. Please don't send me away.

OLGA What are you talking about, Nanny? (*She goes to her*) Who's sending you away? What sort of silly talk is that?

She sits beside ANFISA *who puts her head on* OLGA*'s shoulder.*

ANFISA I work as hard as I can, love. Honest to God I do. But the moment I'm not fit to carry on I'll be told to go. And sure I've nowhere to go to, Olga, you know that. I'm eighty, love, amn't I? No. I must be over eighty, I must be eighty-one or eighty-two or —

OLGA Shhhhh, Nanny darling. You're worn out tonight, that's all. So just sit here and rest for a while. Shhhhh . . .

And she rocks ANFISA *in her arms for a few seconds.* NATASHA *enters. She moves around the room as she talks, mentally noting the clothes on the floor, the empty wardrobe, etc.*

NATASHA They're talking about setting up a relief committee for the families that have lost their homes. I'm all for that. (*She studies herself in the mirror*) If the privileged classes don't undertake their civic responsibilities, I mean to say, who will? They're fast asleep — Bobik and wee Sophie — dead to the world. Have you seen the mob downstairs? God bless us and save us! — like the harvest fair day! There's a bad 'flu going about. I hope the wee ones don't get it.

OLGA It's so peaceful in this room. You wouldn't know there was a fire at all.

NATASHA   Sweet Mother of God, would you look at that hair! D'you think I've put on weight? People tell me I'm not near as *soigné* as I was before Sophie was born. What d'you think? (*She turns round*) Ah! Poor Masha's asleep, the creature. Exhausted, the soul. Sure aren't we all?

> *Now for the first time she sees* ANFISA. *Her fury is instant, almost hysterical.*

You! How dare you sit in my presence! (ANFISA *rises quickly. So does* OLGA) Get up and get out! Out! Out! Out! Immediately!

> ANFISA *leaves.*

I'll never understand why you keep that old woman about the place!

OLGA   And, if you'll forgive me, Natasha, I don't understand how —

NATASHA   She's no use anymore! She's a peasant and that's where she belongs — out in the bogs! You have her spoiled! If this house is ever to be run properly we cannot hang on to old bags like that.

> OLGA *sits.* NATASHA *is suddenly calm again. She strokes* OLGA's *cheek.*

Ah, poor Olga's tired. Our headmistress is exhausted. Do you realize that when wee Sophie grows up and goes to grammar school I'll be scared of you?

OLGA   I won't be made headmistress.

NATASHA   Oh but you will, darling. That's all been arranged.

OLGA   I'll turn it down. I couldn't do it. I could never handle it. (*She takes a drink of water*) You were very rude to Nanny just now, Natasha. I'm sorry but I just cannot endure that sort of behaviour; it makes me feel . . . weak.

NATASHA I'm sorry, Olga. Sure I wouldn't upset you for all the tea in China.

MASHA *stands up, takes her pillow, and exits angrily.*

OLGA Maybe the way we were brought up seems peculiar to you. But to hear a servant talked to like that upsets me terribly. I just can't — it just makes me feel . . . physically sick.

NATASHA (*Kissing her*) I'm sorry — I'm sorry — I'm sorry — I'm sorry —

OLGA Even a rude word — I know it's stupid — even a tactless word —

NATASHA And sure nobody's more tactless than I am. I know. I know. All the same, darling, at her time of day she'd be happier in her own village — now wouldn't she?

OLGA She's been with our family for thirty years, Natasha.

NATASHA (*Softly, reasonably*) But she can't work anymore, can she? Either I don't understand you or you don't want to understand me. *She is not able to work.* Is that not right? All she does is sleep or sit about.

OLGA Then let her sit about!

NATASHA Let her sit about! Sweet Mother of God! She's a servant, isn't she? (*Crying*) I don't understand you, Olga. I have a nanny for Bobik and a wet nurse for the baby and we share a maid and a cook. So what do we keep that old bag for? Just tell me — what in God's name *for*?

The fire bell rings in the distance.

OLGA I feel I have aged ten years this night.

NATASHA We must come to an understanding, Olga . . . Your place is in the school. Mine is in the home. You teach your classes. I run this house. And when I make a decision about the servants that decision will be respected. Is that understood? Right. So: that old hag, that thieving old bitch clears out of this house tomorrow. (*Suddenly almost hysterical again*) And don't you ever cross me again! D'you hear me? Ever-ever-ever! (*As suddenly in control again*) God bless us and save us, if you don't go downstairs we'll end up having a little tiff; and that would be awful, wouldn't it? Lord, we could never have that!

KULYGIN *enters.*

KULYGIN Is Masha not here? It's time we went home. I'm told the fire's under control now. (*He stretches himself*) Only one street of houses was burned down despite that wind. At one point it looked as if the whole town was going to go up. (*Sits*) I *am* tired. I'll tell you something, Olga: if I hadn't married Masha, I'd have married you. You are such a *femina benevola* — such a considerate woman. Oh, I really am tired. Shhhhh. (*Listens*) The doctor has to pick a night like this to go on the tear. (*Rises*) I think he's coming up here. Yes, that's him. (*Laughs*) What a man! I'm getting out of the way.

He goes behind one of the screens.

OLGA He doesn't touch a drop for two years, and then on the one night — the only night — when he could be of some use —

She moves up to the back of the bedroom where NATASHA *is doing her hair before a small mirror.* CHEBUTYKIN, *walking very erect, enters. He looks round the room, sees nobody. He goes to the wash-handbasin and begins washing his hands.*

CHEBUTYKIN To hell with the whole lot of them. Just because

I'm called 'Doctor' they think I can make them all
. . . whole! Me! Who knows sweet damn all! Even
the sweet damn all I used to know, that's forgotten
too. Gone — gone — gone.

OLGA *and* NATASHA *slip out unnoticed.*

So to hell with them all. (*To his reflection*) And to
hell with you specifically, my friend. You know
why you're drunk, don't you? Last Wednesday —
correct? That woman that came to see you and
you diagnosed appendicitis — correct? (*Shakes his
head very slowly*) But your diagnosis was incorrect
and the lady died, my friend. (*He splashes water on
his face*) Twenty-five years ago I knew one or two
things; but they're vanished too — all gone, gone,
gone . . . (*He touches his reflection with his fingertip*)
Maybe you're the reality. Maybe this (*body*) is the
image. Maybe this hasn't arms and legs and a head
at all. Maybe this just pretends to exist . . . pretends
to walk about and eat and sleep . . . I wish that were
true. Oh God, how I wish this (*body*) didn't exist
. . . (*He cries. Then suddenly*) What the hell do I care?
That conversation in the club the other day — (*to
mirror*) remember? About Shakespeare and Voltaire.
You've never read Shakespeare or Voltaire — not a
line. But you all pretended you were experts, didn't
you? Shysters! Shabby, grubby shysters! And then
suddenly you remembered the woman you had
killed, expert doctor. And then you realized how
bogus and empty you are. So you went out and got
sloshed. What a magnificent creature you are.

IRINA, VERSHININ *and* TUSENBACH *enter.* VERSHININ
is dishevelled and dirty with the fire. The BARON
is immaculate in a stylish new civilian suit.

IRINA Come in here and sit down. It's quieter here.
VERSHININ Only for the soldiers the whole town would have

been burned down. They were superb. I was so
proud of them.

> KULYGIN *emerges from behind the screen. He is
> winding his watch.*

KULYGIN Anybody got the correct time?

BARON Ten past three. It'll soon be dawn.

IRINA Everybody's just sitting down there in the draw-
ing room. Nobody seems to want to move. (*To*
TUSENBACH) Your friend, Solyony, is down there too.
Don't you think you should go to bed, Doctor?

CHEBUTYKIN I'm perfectly all right, thank you very much
indeed.

KULYGIN You naughty boy, you're inebriated, Doctor! —
'Correct'? (*He slaps him on the back*) *In vino veritas*
— 'Correct'?

BARON Everybody's on to me to get up a benefit concert
for the fire victims.

IRINA Who would you get to perform in a town like this?

BARON I suppose it's possible. Masha could play the piano.
She's a beautiful pianist.

KULYGIN Indeed she is. Splendid.

IRINA She's forgotten it all now. She hasn't touched a
piano for three or four years.

BARON Trouble is, nobody in this town appreciates good
music — apart from myself. And I can assure you,
Masha plays magnificently, almost with genius.

KULYGIN Absolutely right, Baron. I'm very fond of Masha.
Masha is a wonderful human being.

BARON Can you imagine what it's like to play so magnificently and to know that nobody appreciates you?

KULYGIN (*Sighs*) Difficult, indeed. But would it be — you
know — perhaps *infra dignitatem* for the wife of a
schoolmaster to play in a concert? Maybe not. I'm
sure it would be perfectly proper. Our headmaster
is an understanding man, a highly intelligent man.
But, he does have certain inflexible attitudes. Not
that this would have anything to do with him. All

the same perhaps I should have a word with him
. . . if you like.

CHEBUTYKIN *picks up a china clock and examines it.*

VERSHININ That fire has ruined my clothes. Must go and change.
(*Pause*) There was a rumour going about yesterday that our brigade may be transferred. Poland
was mentioned. And Siberia. You may be sure —
somewhere in the back of beyond.

BARON Thank God I'm finished with all that. Well, when
you people leave this will be a real ghost town!

IRINA We're going away, too.

CHEBUTYKIN *drops the clock which smashes into
pieces.*

CHEBUTYKIN Smashed to smithereens!

There is a very brief, shocked silence. KULYGIN
*moves first. He gets down on his hands and knees
and begins to pick up the pieces.*

KULYGIN Oh, Doctor, Doctor, Doctor — a valuable piece like
that! Oh, black mark, Doctor! Definitely a black
mark for that!

IRINA That was Mother's clock.

CHEBUTYKIN (*Quickly, angrily*) I know that, don't I? (*Controlled*)
Maybe it's not smashed. Maybe it only seems to be
smashed. Maybe we don't exist. Maybe we're not
here at all. (*Leaving*) Sweet damn all I know. Sweet
damn all anybody knows. (*Stops at door*) What are
you all staring at me for? Natasha's having an affair
with Protopopov — stare at that for a change! But
you'd rather not, wouldn't you? You'd rather sit with
your eyes closed while Natasha and Protopopov
are carrying on under your very noses! Hah! (*Sings*)
'There was I, waiting at the church, waiting at the
church, waiting at the church — '

He breaks off, stares briefly at them and leaves.

VERSHININ (*Speaks*) 'Waiting at the church!' (*Shakes his head slowly*) It has been such a strange day . . . As soon as the fire started I ran home as fast as I could. As I got near I could see it wasn't in danger. My two little girls were standing at the front door in their pyjamas. No sign of their mother. People charging about, shouting, screaming — horses terrified, dogs going mad. If you'd seen the look on the children's faces: a mixture of terror and entreaty. That was more terrifying than all the horrors around me. And I thought: my God, I thought, how much more have these children to go through in the years ahead. I grabbed them and ran back here with them and all the time I was running I could think only one thing: how much more they will have to go through in this world. (*Fire alarm, off*) When I got here my wife was here already, ranting and screaming and acting out some tantrum of her own.

MASHA *enters with her pillow and sits on the sofa.*

Telling them about seeing my two little girls standing at the front door in their pyjamas and the street in flames and everybody panicking. Like a scene from years and years ago when armies would make sudden raids on towns and burn and plunder them. And it struck me how different those days were to our time now. And things will get better still. Before very long — in two or three hundred years' time — people will look back on our way of life the way we look back on those old days, with genuine horror; because they'll regard our way of life as really 'nasty, brutish and short'. Oh yes, life is going to get better and better and better and better! (*He laughs and spreads his hands*) Vershinin, your instant philosopher — (*Looking at the BARON and KULYGIN who are both asleep*) — guaranteed to electrify. (*Laughs*) Actually

81

I'm in deadly earnest — not that that makes any difference. (*Softly to* MASHA *who is hugging her pillow, her eyes closed*) You're not asleep, are you? (*She shakes her head*) Yes — great, great times ahead. (*To* IRINA) Today there are only three people like you in the whole of this town. But in the generations to come there will be more and more; and a time will arrive when things will have changed so radically that your lifestyle will be the norm. And when that happens, then even your enlightened attitudes will become outmoded and an even more enlightened generation will emerge. Hurrah! (*Laughs*) The gospel according to Vershinin! (*Laughs*) I want so desperately, so passionately to live . . .
(*Sings*) 'We yield to love at every age
And fruitful are its pains.' (*Laughs*)

MASHA   (*Eyes still closed*) Ta-ra-ra-ra.
VERSHININ   (*Delighted*) Ta-ra.
MASHA   Ta-ra-ra-ra.
VERSHININ   Ta-ra. (*And again he laughs*)

FEDOTIK *enters.*

FEDOTIK   Everything gone! Burned to ashes! Not a single thing left. (*Laughs*)
IRINA   What's funny about that? Was nothing saved?
FEDOTIK   (*Laughs*) Camera, guitar, clothes, letters, dress uniform — all up in smoke! Even a little notebook I had for you — gone!

Enter SOLYONY.

IRINA   No, no, Captain. Please go away. You can't come in here.
SOLYONY   Why not?
IRINA   Please.
SOLYONY   The baron's allowed in. Why amn't I?
VERSHININ   It's time we were all going. What's the news of the fire?

SOLYONY Dying down. (*To* IRINA) Well? Why do you allow the baron in and not me?

He sprinkles his hands with perfume.

VERSHININ (*Softly to* MASHA) Ta-ra-ra-ra.
MASHA (*Softly to* VERSHININ) Ta-ra.
VERSHININ (*Laughing, to* SOLYONY) Come on, man. We'll go down to the dining room.
SOLYONY (*To* IRINA) That's all right. That's fine with me. I'll not forget this. (*His icy smile*) 'This issue will be made more clear; / But not before the duck, my dear.'

As he passes the sleeping BARON *he does his quack-quack mime into the* BARON's *face. Then he and* VERSHININ *and* FEDOTIK *all leave.*

IRINA (*Opening a window*) Everywhere that man goes reeks with his damned lotions. (*She shakes* TUSENBACH) Wake up, Baron. Wake up.

TUSENBACH *sits up.*

BARON What? What's the matter?
IRINA Time to go home.
BARON (*Rising and stretching*) I was dead out there. The brickworks — that's the solution. I've spoken to the manager. I'm to start work there first thing in the morning — one of these days. No, I'm not talking in my sleep. It's all been arranged. (*He catches her hands*) You look so pale and so beautiful and so radiant. Even your paleness has a luminosity. Yes, yes, yes, I know you're depressed; I know how unhappy you are with the way things have turned out. So we'll go away together, just the two of us; we'll go away and work together, somewhere far, far away.
MASHA Nikolai, go home please, will you?
BARON All right — all right — I'm going. (*He doesn't move.*

He gazes at IRINA) D'you remember a party you had on your name day? — oh, it must be four years ago — d'you remember that party? — and you told us you had a revelation, an epiphany — and you spoke about the excitement, the joy of work — d'you remember that? I remember so clearly how happy, how vibrant you were that day. And you were so confident you made everything sound so possible for all of us ... What happened to all that? ... All those possibilities? (*He kisses her hand again*) Don't cry, Irina. (*Kiss*) You should be in bed. (*Kiss*) It's beginning to get light. (*Kiss*) It's almost morning. (*Kiss*) I would like to — I'd be happy to — to —

IRINA   What?

BARON   (*Very simply*) I wish I could give my life for you ...

MASHA   Nikolai, have you no home to go to?

BARON   I'm away.

Again he kisses IRINA's *hand and leaves.* MASHA *stretches out on the sofa and closes her eyes.*

MASHA   Are you asleep, Fyodor?

KULYGIN   What's that?

MASHA   Why don't you go home?

KULYGIN   My good Masha, my precious Masha, I —

IRINA   She's very tired. Let her rest, Fyodor.

KULYGIN   You're right. I'll go. Masha, my love, I love you, I love only you, I love nobody but —

MASHA   (*Softly, bitterly*) Amo, amas, amat, amamus, amatis, amant.

KULYGIN   (*Laughs*) Perfectly conjugated. And what does 'amamus' mean? First person plural? 'We love' — correct? (*To* IRINA) Isn't she marvellous? Seven whole years since she and I were conjugated — ha-ha — but it seems to me as if that happy occasion took place only yesterday. (*To* MASHA) You are a wonderful, wonderful human being. (*To* IRINA) I'm so happy, happy, happy.

MASHA   And I'm so bored, bored, bored. (*She sits up*) There's

something I've got to tell you. I can't keep it to
myself any longer. I —

KULYGIN (*Momentary panic*) Masha, if it's something to do
with you and —

MASHA Andrey has mortgaged this house to the bank and
that wife of his has taken the money. And the
point is, this house belongs to the four of us. And
damn-well he knows that — if there's any decency
left in him!

KULYGIN (*Relieved*) Oh, come on, Masha. Why bring that up
now? You know he owes money all over the town.
Poor old Andrey, he has his own bothers.

MASHA It's a rotten thing for him to have done! Just rotten!

She lies down again.

KULYGIN You and I are comfortably off, aren't we? I have my
job in the secondary school, and there's the odd
private pupil, and — and — and everything's in
hand, isn't it? But then I'm just your plain, average
Omnia mea mecum porto — whatever I am, there it
is before you.

MASHA It's the injustice of the thing that sickens me. Why
don't you go home, Fyodor?

KULYGIN (*Kisses her*) You're tired. Rest for half-an-hour. I'll
go downstairs and wait for you. Right? Oh, I'm so
happy, happy, happy.

He leaves.

IRINA 'Poor old Andrey'. That's accurate enough. Living
with that woman has put years on him. I've never
known anyone disintegrate as quickly. Professor
Andrey Prozorov! Remember that ambition? And
only yesterday he was boasting to me that they've
made him permanent on the county council staff,
thanks, no doubt, to Mr Protopopov, the chairman.
He's the talk of the town. Everybody's laughing at
him. Doesn't he see what's happening? And to-

night when every other man was out fighting the
fire, where's Andrey? Sitting in his room, fiddling!
(*Cries*) I really don't think I can stand much more.

OLGA *enters.*

I don't think I can carry on much longer. I'm beginning to disintegrate, too.

OLGA (*Alarmed*) What's the matter, my darling?

IRINA (*Sobbing*) What's become of everything? Where has
it all gone to? Oh my God, I've forgotten everything. Everything's chaotic in my head. What's the
Italian word for window — or ceiling? I don't know.
Gone. And every day I forget something more . . .
My life, too — haemorrhaging away on me — never
to be recovered. And we'll never go to Moscow —
never, never — I know that now.

OLGA *holds her in her arms and rocks her as she
did* ANFISA.

OLGA Shhhhh, my darling, shush-shush-shush.

IRINA I'm so unhappy, Olga. I'm sick working in the county
council office. I can't go on working there. I won't
go on working there. It's far, far worse than the post
office. I dread and detest every second I spend in it.
I'm twenty-three, Olga. And it has all been work,
work, work. I've become desiccated in mind and in
body. Look at me — I've got thin and ugly and old.
I'll soon be twenty-four and what have I to show for
it? Nothing. And time is slipping away. Every day
that races past I *know* I'm losing touch with everything that has even the whiff of hope about it —
no, no, worse than losing touch — sinking, being
sucked down into a kind of abyss. I am despairing,
Olga. Do you understand what I'm saying? I am
desperate. I see no reason to go on living. I see no
reason why I shouldn't end it now.

OLGA Don't cry, my darling. Please don't cry. I get so upset when I see you crying.

IRINA I'm not crying. Look — I've stopped. There. No more crying. No more scenes.

OLGA Darling, may I say something to you? The advice of an older sister, a friend? (*Pause*) Marry the baron. (IRINA *begins crying again quietly*) Shhhhh. Listen to me. You admire him and you respect him. He may not be the most handsome man in the world, but he is a kind man and he is a decent-minded man, and what you must understand, my darling, is that one doesn't marry for love; one marries out of duty. I would marry a man I didn't love. I would marry any man who would ask me as long as he was a kind man, a decent man. I would even marry an old man.

IRINA D'you know what I used to imagine? That when we'd go home to Moscow I'd meet the great love of my life, the man I'd dreamed of, genuinely loved in anticipation. Wasn't I the stupid fool?

OLGA (*Embracing her*) I know, my darling, I know, I do know. I actually cried myself the first time I saw the baron in civilian clothes just after he resigned his commission. He looked so . . . ordinary. He asked me why I was crying. What could I say? But if he did marry you, if that was the will of God, I'd be happy for you. Because that's really as much as you can hope for now.

>   NATASHA *enters left, a lit candle in her hand. Without looking left or right she crosses the stage at a brisk pace and exits right.*

MASHA (*Sitting up*) Would you look at that! Our very own Lady Macbeth!

OLGA (*Laughs*) Masha, you're awful.

MASHA I wouldn't be surprised if she started the fire.

OLGA Honest to God, you're the silliest of the three of us.

>   *Pause.* MASHA *rises.*

MASHA   There's something I've got to tell you both. I want
        to tell only you two and then I'll never breathe a
        word of it again to anyone. (*Pause*) I'm in love with
        Vershinin.

OLGA   You're — !

MASHA   (*Slightly louder*) I'm in love with Vershinin.

OLGA   Masha, stop that!

MASHA   (*Proclamation*) I am in love with Lieutenant Colonel
        Alexander Vershinin!

OLGA dashes behind a screen.

OLGA   Can't hear a word you're saying. Not a single word.

MASHA   At first I thought he was strange. Then I felt sorry
        for him. Then I began to love him — love every-
        thing about him — the way he walks, the way he
        talks, his unhappy life, his two little girls —

OLGA   I'm not listening. Talk all the rubbish you want —

MASHA   I am in love with Vershinin. There's nothing more
        to say. Fate, destiny — call it whatever you like.
        And he loves me. Terrifying, isn't it? (*She catches
        IRINA's hands*) The question is: how are we to live
        the rest of our lives? What's to become of us? Like
        a situation in a novel, isn't it? Except that in a novel
        it always seems jaded and obvious. But when you
        fall in love yourself you *know* this is unique. There
        are no precedents, no guidelines. You are the first
        ever explorer . . . That's all. Now I'll keep quiet.
        Like that madman in Gogol's short story: silence
        . . . silence . . . shhhhh.

Enter ANDREY followed by FERAPONT.

ANDREY   (*Angrily*) Stop mumbling! What is it? What is it?

FERAPONT (*Standing at the door*) I've asked you a dozen times
          already, Mister Andrey, if you'd —

ANDREY   And don't call me Mister Andrey. Call me Sir.

FERAPONT It's the firemen, Mister. They want to know can
          they bring their hoses through your garden to the

river. They've been lugging them round the long
way all night and you know yourself it takes —

ANDREY All right! All right!

FERAPONT Wha's tha', Mister?

ANDREY (*Shouts*) All right! Tell them — all right!

FERAPONT *leaves.*

Damned hoses! (*To* IRINA) Where's Olga?

OLGA *comes from behind the screen.*

I'm looking for the duplicate key of the sideboard.
I've lost mine. You know the one. About this size
and has a brass —

OLGA *silently holds out a key to him.* IRINA *goes
behind a screen.*

Terrible fire, wasn't it? . . . It's dying down now . . .
Poor old Ferapont, I lost the head with him, told
him to address me Sir, for God's sake . . . Why don't
you speak, Olga? (*Pause*) Isn't it about time you
stopped this bloody sulking? If I even knew what
you were sulking about! (*Pause*) All right. All right.
The three of you are here now — fine — fine — let's
clear the air for once and for all. What have you all
got against me?

OLGA (*Wearily*) Not now, Andrey. Tomorrow maybe. We've
all had a bad night.

ANDREY (*His voice rising*) No need to shout at me. I'm asking a calm, reasonable question — what have you
all got against me? I would like a calm, reasonable
answer.

VERSHININ (*Off*) Ta-ra-ra-ra.

MASHA *gets instantly to her feet and responds
delightedly.*

MASHA   Ta-ra. Ta-ra. Goodnight, Olga. Take care of yourself.

Runs behind the screen and kisses IRINA.

Sleep well, my darling. (*To* ANDREY *as she rushes past
him*) Not tonight, Andrey — they're exhausted.
Leave it till tomorrow.

She runs off.

OLGA   Please, Andrey. Leave it till tomorrow. It's time we
were all in bed.

She goes behind a screen. Now only ANDREY *is
visible.*

ANDREY   I want to say just one thing; then I'll go. First of all
you've got something against Natasha. I've been
aware of this ever since the day we got married.
Natasha is a fine, honest, high-principled woman.
That is my opinion of her: I love my wife and I
respect my wife and I expect others to respect her,
too. As I have said, she is a decent woman and a
high-principled woman. And your objections to her
— whatever those objections are — have no basis
whatever in — in — in — in reality. (*He pauses and
mops his face with his handkerchief*) Secondly, you're
disappointed in me and annoyed with me because
I'm not a professor engaged in academic pursuits.
But I happen to work for the county council. I am
engaged in public service. And I consider that profession every bit as noble and as honourable as a life
in the academy. In fact I derive more pride and self-
fulfilment from my work in the public interest than
I could have had I — have I — had I not been in the
public service. (*Again he pauses and mops his face
with his handkerchief*) Right. Thirdly, I know that I
mortgaged this house without your permission. I

shouldn't have done that. I apologize. I had to do it because of my debts — I owe thirty-five thousand roubles. I've stopped gambling. I gave it up long ago. And the only excuse I have to offer is that you girls get the annuity Father left you whereas I have no income, no inherited income.

KULYGIN *(Off)* Masha? Masha? *(His head around the door)* Isn't she here? I left her sleeping there. Good heavens, that's strange!

He exits. Pause.

ANDREY *(Softly, wearily)* They won't listen to me. I'm telling you: Natasha is a good wife and a good mother; she is a fine woman, a decent woman, a high-principled . . .

He begins to cry. He tries to stop but cannot. He sinks down onto the edge of the couch, slides off it and is now on his knees, facing upstage.

When we got married I thought we would be happy . . . all of us . . . together . . . happy . . . Oh my God . . . My dear sisters, my darling sisters, everything I've said is lies . . . everything . . . Don't believe a word of it . . . not a single word . . .

Pause. Then he gets quickly to his feet and stumbles off.

KULYGIN *(Head around the door and now very agitated)* Where *is* Masha? She's not downstairs. Where *is* she? Extraordinary.

He exits. Fire alarm off. The stage is empty. Silence. Then IRINA *and* OLGA *talk behind their screens.*

IRINA Olga.

OLGA Yes?

IRINA Who's that knocking on the floor?

OLGA The doctor. He's drunk.

IRINA God. What a night. (*Pause*) Olga.

OLGA What?

> IRINA *now appears from behind her screen. She is in her nightdress.*

IRINA Did you hear the news? They're moving our brigade. They're being sent to some place far away.

OLGA That's only a rumour.

IRINA We'll be all on our own then, Olga.

OLGA So.

> Pause.

IRINA I do respect the baron, Olga. I have a very high opinion of him. I think he is a very . . . worthy man. And I *will* marry him, Olga. I will, if we can go to Moscow then. I'm asking you, Olga — I'm begging you — please. Let us go to Moscow. There's nowhere in the world like Moscow. Let us go, Olga. Please, let us go.

> *Bring down lights slowly. End of Act Three.*

ACT FOUR

Almost two years have passed. Autumn. Noon. Diluted sunshine —
the first snow of winter is imminent.

The old garden of the Prozorov house. Stage left a garden swing.
Stage right the verandah of the house. On the verandah a table with
glasses and empty champagne bottles. In the distance a long avenue
of fir trees beyond which one can see the river. Beyond the river is a
wood.

CHEBUTYKIN *sits at the table, drinks champagne, and reads his*
paper. He is in a benevolent mood which lasts throughout the entire
Act. He is waiting to be summoned for the duel, his army cap and
stick on the table beside him.

IRINA, KULYGIN *(wearing a decoration round his neck and with*
his moustache shaved off) and TUSENBACH *emerge from the house.*
FEDOTIK *and* RODDEY *are with them. They all stand on the steps of the*
verandah to say goodbye. FEDOTIK *and* RODDEY *are in field uniform.*

BARON (*Embracing* FEDOTIK) We had a lot of fun together,
        Fedotik. I'm going to miss you. (*He embraces* RODDEY)
        You, too, Roddey. Goodbye, friends. Goodbye, old
        comrades.
IRINA Correction. *Au revoir.*
FEDOTIK It's goodbye and well you know it.
RODDEY (*About to cry*) Please, my petals . . . please . . .
FEDOTIK We'll never see each other again.
KULYGIN You don't know that. (*Wiping his eyes; to* RODDEY)
        Now you have me crying, too.
IRINA Yes, we all *will* meet again. I know we will.
FEDOTIK (*Lining up camera shot*) Maybe in ten or fifteen years'
        time. And by then we'd be strangers. We wouldn't
        even recognize one another. Hold it like that!
RODDEY Oh my goodness me!
FEDOTIK (*Flash*) Lovely.

RODDEY   Lovely! My eyes are all blotchy!

FEDOTIK   And another, please — just one more. You all look so distinguished.

RODDEY   Who wants to look distinguished! We just want to look pretty! (*Another camera flash. Embracing* TUSENBACH) We'll never meet again, Baron. Goodbye, my friend, and great good luck — (*kisses* IRINA) to both of you. May you have every happiness together, Irina, and may you both be —

He is overcome and rushes upstage.

FEDOTIK   Hold on, Roddey! I'm coming!

BARON   Irina's right: we *will* meet again. And in the meantime you'll write to us both, won't you?

RODDEY   (*Going round garden*) Goodbye, trees. (*Shouts*) Goodbye!

ECHO   'Bye-bye-bye . . .

RODDEY   (*Shouts*) Goodbye, echo.

ECHO   Echo-echo-echo . . .

KULYGIN   (*To* FEDOTIK) You'll not be three months in Poland till you find yourself a splendid Polish wife. And every night she'll throw her arms around you and whisper. (*He whispers in* FEDOTIK's *ear*)

FEDOTIK   (*Pretended shock*) Kulygin!

KULYGIN   (*Confused*) It means — it simply means — sleep well.

FEDOTIK   (*Looks at his watch*) Less than an hour to go. Solyony's the only man from our battery going on the barge. We're with the men. Three battery divisions move out today; three more tomorrow. Then the town will return to peace and quiet again.

BARON   Boredom's more like it. Sheer damned boredom.

RODDEY   (*Upstage*) Where's Masha?

KULYGIN   In the garden somewhere.

FEDOTIK   Must say goodbye to her.

RODDEY   'Bye, everyone.

He looks back at them. Then on impulse he returns to them, embracing TUSENBACH *and* KULYGIN *and kissing* IRINA*'s hand — all exactly as before.*

My petals, can you believe it's been almost five
years? — five wonderful, sensational, fantastic years.
I'll remember every detail for — for — for as long
as —

FEDOTIK (*To* KULYGIN; *a pen*) A little souvenir for you,
Kulygin, to —

RODDEY (*Irritably, in tears*) Toys! Toys! When are you going
to grow up!

And again he rushes upstage.

FEDOTIK A miniature pen and notebook.

KULYGIN I'm really most —

FEDOTIK (*Now embarrassed*) This is the quickest way back,
isn't it?

He joins RODDEY. *They both begin to leave together.*

RODDEY (*Shouts*) 'Bye!

ECHO 'Bye-bye-bye . . .

KULYGIN (*Shouts*) Goodbye!

As they exit they meet MASHA. *All three leave
together. Brief pause.*

IRINA That's the end of that.

She sits on the verandah steps.

CHEBUTYKIN They forgot to say goodbye to me.

IRINA Did you say goodbye to them?

CHEBUTYKIN Good point. Anyhow, I'll be seeing them before
long. I'm off tomorrow. One more day left here. But
when I get my pension in twelve months' time I'll
come back and spend the remainder of my days
here with you. And I'll be so changed you won't
know me. I'll be a quiet, benign (*lifting his glass*)

95

and totally abstemious old gentleman.

IRINA We certainly won't know you.

CHEBUTYKIN Well, the aspiration is noble, isn't it? (*Sings softly*) 'There was I, waiting at the church, waiting at the church, waiting at the — '

KULYGIN You're incorrigible, Doctor.

CHEBUTYKIN Maybe you should take me in hand. Would that have any effect?

IRINA (*To* CHEBUTYKIN) Fyodor's shaved off his moustache. (*To* KULYGIN) I liked you the way you were.

KULYGIN Did you? What's wrong with it now?

IRINA I preferred you the way you were.

KULYGIN Well, this is the new style. Moustaches are out. Our headmaster got rid of his, and the day I was appointed assistant-head, off went mine. Oddly enough nobody seems to like it. Not that that matters. I'm perfectly happy. With a moustache — without a moustache — I'm perfectly . . .

He fades out, stands irresolutely for a second, and sits. ANDREY *enters, his nose deep in a book, pushing a pram. He crosses the back of the stage and exits. Pause. Then* IRINA *goes to* CHEBUTYKIN.

IRINA Darling, dopey Doctor —

CHEBUTYKIN You haven't called me that in ages.

IRINA I'm worried sick.

CHEBUTYKIN Little sweetheart, what is it?

IRINA You were in town last night. What happened?

CHEBUTYKIN Happened?

IRINA Outside the theatre — there was a row of some sort.

CHEBUTYKIN Was there?

IRINA You know there was. Between the baron and Solyony.

CHEBUTYKIN Oh, that.

IRINA What happened?

CHEBUTYKIN Nothing. (*Opens his paper*) Nothing. Hot air. Big words. Nothing. Nothing.

KULYGIN The story I heard was that just as the baron came

out of the theatre he met Solyony and for no apparent reason Solyony squared up to him and —

BARON Stop it, will you! Stop it! Stop it! (*Now controlled*)
It's nobody's business but mine and —

He rushes into the house.

KULYGIN Solyony began picking on him. The baron got angry,
insulted Solyony.

CHEBUTYKIN All you know is what you've picked up from gossip. Anyhow, the whole thing — it's ridiculous, just
ridiculous. Two supposedly adult people behaving
like children. Ridiculous!

KULYGIN Interesting word that — 'ridiculus'. From the Latin
verb *rideo-ridere-risi-risum*, meaning to laugh. Hence
ridicule, ridiculous, risible etc. etc. Actually the
gossip is — if you'll pardon me, Doctor — the
gossip is that Solyony's in love with Irina! Yes!
And *that's* why he detests the baron. And that's
perfectly understandable. Because Irina is a wonderful human being. Oh yes, you are. In many
respects very like my Masha. Not as — as — as
introspective as Masha. You're more outgoing.
Though Masha on occasion and in a certain humour,
my Masha can indeed be very outgoing herself.
Oh, I do love Masha.

From offstage the sound of FEDOTIK *calling
'Goodbye' and the echoing answers of 'Bye-bye-
bye . . . ' They listen until the last sound dies
away.*

IRINA (*Shivering*) Something eerie about that sound.
Everything seems to frighten me today. (*Rapidly
and with sudden desperate resolution*) Well, at least
things are all organized. My stuff's all packed
and goes off on the evening train; and tomorrow
morning, immediately after we're married, the
baron and I go straight to the brickworks — just

like your migrating bird, except of course that we're heading north, away from the sun. And the morning after that I begin my first teaching job. One-two-three — just like that — wife, teacher, and a whole new life all in the space of three hectic days. But Olga assures me everything's in God's hands. And Olga's right, isn't she? . . . The day I got my teaching diploma I was so happy I — I cried . . .

CHEBUTYKIN goes to her and puts his arms around her.

CHEBUTYKIN Little sweetheart, my tiny white bird, of course you're going to fly away to the sun, up and away with the great blue sky above you and hundreds of other beautiful white birds all around you. Fly away, little sweetheart. For God's sake, fly away while you're still young. This place is only fit for old moulting things that can't keep up with the flock anymore. (*Into her ear*) He didn't shave off that moustache. He's moulting, too.

KULYGIN The Order of Saint Stanislaus, second class. You've seen my decoration, Doctor, haven't you?

CHEBUTYKIN Once or twice, I believe.

The sound of somebody playing 'The Maiden's Prayer' on the piano, off.

KULYGIN 'For dutiful service to the cause of education.' I'm wearing it today to celebrate the army pulling out and our return to the way things used to be. There's a lot to be said for routine. All things considered. I'm a very fortunate man. I enjoy my work, exhausting though it may be. And I have my Masha, my loyal and faithful Masha. Yes, people would consider me a very fortunate man. I'm sure they would. I mean to say, why wouldn't they?

98

As before he tails off into a private misery. Pause.

IRINA   This time tomorrow night I won't be listening to 'The Maiden's Prayer'.

CHEBUTYKIN   Or seeing Mr Protopopov ensconced in the drawing room with Natasha.

IRINA   Shhh. He's in there now.

CHEBUTYKIN   Isn't he always?

KULYGIN   Where's Olga? Has the new headmistress not arrived yet?

IRINA   She'll be here soon. Lucky Olga. I envy her living in that schoolhouse. And I envy her her full, busy life. I hate this house without her. I've been relegated to the back bedroom — did you know that? Hate it and bored by it. But I am becoming . . . 'reconciled' — isn't that the word, Doctor?

ANDREY *enters with his book and pram.*

CHEBUTYKIN   No, no, no. Fly, white bird. Fly.

IRINA   Because if I can't go to Moscow I must accept that Moscow's out. That is God's will and I accept that. (*Pause*) So, when the baron asked me to marry him, I said yes, yes I would marry him. Because he is a kind man, a genuinely good man, a decent-minded man. And the moment I said yes to him I felt a great sense of relief and the old passion for work, work, work suddenly possessed me again. I think I was almost happy again. And then when I heard about the incident outside the theatre last night I had a sense that something sinister is going to happen.

CHEBUTYKIN   For God's sake —

NATASHA   (*At the window*) The headmistress is here!

KULYGIN   Ah! Let's go outside. She'll have all the gossip about her staff.

He leads IRINA *into the house.* CHEBUTYKIN *pours himself a drink, checks the time, and opens his paper, all the time singing 'There was I, waiting at the church, waiting at the church, waiting at the church . . . '* MASHA *enters.*

MASHA You look very comfortable sitting there.

CHEBUTYKIN And why not? What's happening?

MASHA What in God's name could be happening? (*Pause*) Were you in love with my mother? (*Pause*) Doctor.

CHEBUTYKIN (*Simply*) Desperately.

MASHA Was she in love with you?

CHEBUTYKIN I don't remember — where's Vershinin?

MASHA He's on his way. (*Pause*) When you've had to snatch at whatever happiness you can in furtive little grabs and then lose it all, as I've lost it all, you become hard and bitter. (*Calmly and softly*) I am seething inside, Doctor.

ANDREY, *who has been standing and reading, moves slowly across the back of the stage.*

Look at him — Andrey Prozorov — academician, musician, gentleman about town. There's defeat for you, Doctor.

A sudden loud sound of dishes falling and smashing, off, and of maids shouting at one another.

ANDREY Is this racket never going to stop, for God's sake! When are we going to get some peace in this house!

MASHA There go all our hopes.

CHEBUTYKIN I wonder what's keeping them?

MASHA What's keeping who?

CHEBUTYKIN (*Looking at his watch*) Nice old-fashioned watch, isn't it? Listen.

He presses a button on it and the watch chimes.

MASHA You're up to something. What is it?

ANDREY *moves down beside him.*

CHEBUTYKIN The First, Second and Fifth batteries are pulling out at one o'clock sharp. I leave tomorrow.

ANDREY For good?

CHEBUTYKIN Most likely. I don't know. Maybe I'll come back in a year's time. God alone knows. Does it matter?

A harp and a violin in the far distance play 'Won't You Buy My Pretty Flowers?'

ANDREY The town'll seem deserted now. Now we'll really go to seed. (*He puts down his book and removes his glasses*) What happened outside the theatre last night?

CHEBUTYKIN Sheer stupidity. Solyony said something that angered the baron. The baron flared up and insulted Solyony. One word led to another and the outcome was that Solyony had to challenge him to a duel. (*Looks at watch*) It's about to begin; twelve-thirty in the forest, just across the river there. Bang-bang. (*Laughs*) Did you know that Solyony imagines he's like Lermontov, the writer? He even writes poetry! Joking apart though, this is his third duel.

MASHA They ought to be stopped.

CHEBUTYKIN D'you think so?

MASHA He might wound the baron. He might still even kill him. He might. And the baron's not a bad sort. But one baron more or less in the world — does that matter? Let them tear away. Who cares?

Shouts from a distance: 'Hello there! Hello! Hello!'

CHEBUTYKIN (*Quietly*) Oh, shut up! That's Skvorstov calling the boat. He's one of Solyony's seconds.

ANDREY *steels himself to make a pronouncement.*

ANDREY I'm no expert in ethics. But it is absolutely crystal clear to me that — that — that —

CHEBUTYKIN That what?

> MASHA *drifts into a reverie and hums her* MASHA/
> VERSHININ *theme.* ANDREY *falters, partly because
> he is distracted by* MASHA*'s humming.*

ANDREY That to attend a duel, even as a doctor, especially
as a doctor, is — is — is immoral. That's what.

CHEBUTYKIN Do you think so?

ANDREY That's what I think. Yes. That's how it seems to me.

CHEBUTYKIN Ah! That's how it 'seems' to you. But we don't exist.

ANDREY We — ?

CHEBUTYKIN We're not real at all. Nothing in the world is real.
It only seems to us that we exist. And even if we
did exist, finally, finally does it all matter one —
little — whit?

MASHA Talk-talk-talk. Nothing but talk the whole damn
day long. (*She moves towards the house*) As if this
bloody awful climate with snow about to fall any
minute weren't enough, we have to listen to all
this blathering!

> *She is about to go into the house when she is
> arrested by* NATASHA*'s stilted laughter and her line:*

NATASHA Where's your manners, Bobik! Say 'Goodday, Mr
Protopopov'.

MASHA Christ! Is there nowhere to go!

> *She moves up the garden, stops, calls back:*

Let me know when Vershinin comes, will you?
(*She looks up at the sky*) Look. The swans are escap-
ing south already. Lucky, happy swans; happy,
lucky swans.

> *She goes off.* ANDREY *moves beside* CHEBUTYKIN
> *and sits down.*

ANDREY With the officers gone and you gone and Irina getting married I'll be alone here.

CHEBUTYKIN What about your wife?

ANDREY What about my wife? *(He shrugs)* What is there to
say? My wife is a fine woman. My wife is an honest,
straightforward, high-principled woman. Oh dear
God . . . May I talk to you in confidence, Doctor? My
wife is an animal — a mean, gross, grubbing animal.
There's not a trace of humanity left in her. And
yet — and yet I still love her, Doctor. *Love* her, for
God's sake, despite her vulgarity, despite everything that she is, everything she does. I'm so be-
wildered I don't know what I think anymore. God
alone knows why I still love her, if I still love her
. . . *(Natasha's loud laughter off)* What I'm trying to
say to you is that I don't think I can stand any
more. I — I — I'm desperate, Doctor.

CHEBUTYKIN *(Rising)* I'm going away tomorrow, Andrey. The
chances are we'll never meet again. So I *will* give
you my advice. Put on your hat, take up your
walking-stick, and leave.

ANDREY But —

CHEBUTYKIN And the further you go, the better.

> SOLYONY *enters resolutely, crossing stage with his
> second. He sees* CHEBUTYKIN *and comes down to
> him. The second goes off.* SOLYONY *is icy and elated.*

SOLYONY Twelve-thirty, Doctor. Time to go.

CHEBUTYKIN Coming — coming. God, I'm sick of you all. *(To
ANDREY)* If anybody asks where I am just say I'll be
back soon.

> *He goes to* ANDREY, *embraces him very warmly.*

As far away as possible.

> FERAPONT *enters and waits his chance to address*
> ANDREY.

SOLYONY   What are you lamenting about, old man? 'Tweedle-
de-dum and tweedle-de-dee / Is there a bird as
happy as we?'
CHEBUTYKIN (*Leaving*) Come on.
SOLYONY   Aren't you looking forward to it?
CHEBUTYKIN I can hardly wait!
SOLYONY   All right. Keep calm. I'm not going to do the big job
on him. Just wing him — the way I'd bring down
a woodcock. (*Sprinkling his hands with perfume*) I've
used up a whole bottle already today and they still
smell of . . . decay. 'But he rebellious, seeks the storm
/ As if in storms lay peace.' Lermontov. D'you
know that poem?
CHEBUTYKIN How's this it goes? 'There was I waiting at the
church, waiting at the church, waiting at the
church . . . '

CHEBUTYKIN *and* SOLYONY *leave together.*

SOLYONY   (*Off, shouting*) Hello, Skvorstov! Hello, there!
VOICE   (*Off, shouting*) Hello! Hello!

FERAPONT *moves down beside* ANDREY.

FERAPONT   Excuse me, sir. I've some papers here for you to
sign, if you —
ANDREY   Leave me alone, will you? Will you for the love of
God leave me alone!

ANDREY *goes off rapidly with the pram.*

FERAPONT   What am I to do with these papers? I mean, like, if
official papers aren't signed, what becomes of them?

He follows ANDREY *off.* IRINA *and* TUSENBACH *enter
from the house. The* BARON *is wearing a straw hat.
Just as they enter* KULYGIN *crosses the back of the
stage, calling softly and anxiously.*

KULYGIN Masha? Ma-sha! Where are you, love?

BARON He'll be the only person in the town who'll be glad to see the army leaving.

IRINA Would you blame him? The town'll die now.

BARON I'll be back in a minute, my darling.

IRINA Where are you going?

BARON Just down to the camp — to say goodbye to the men.

IRINA You're not telling me the truth, Nikolai. What happened outside the theatre last night?

BARON Give me half-an-hour and I'll be straight back to you. (*He takes her hand and kisses it*) My beautiful Irina. (*Holds her in his arms*) Five years since I first fell in love with you and I'm still surprised, amazed, staggered by it all. Every day, every hour of every day you become more and more beautiful, more and more exquisite. And tomorrow I'll take you away from here and we'll marry and we'll work and we'll be rich and everything I ever dreamed of will be realized. And you'll be happy, too, because I'll —

IRINA Nikolai, I —

He puts his hand across her mouth.

BARON I know — I know — only just don't say it — please. But you do *like* me, don't you? I mean you don't dislike me — I know you don't. And in time, my darling, in time, what you do like about me may grow and blossom and you'll get to like me more and more. And in time, in time — give it time — you may even begin to — to love me just a little bit . . .

IRINA I *do* like you, Nikolai. I like you very much. And I will marry you and honour you and obey you; and that won't be difficult because I am very fond of you. But I don't love you, Nikolai. (*She begins to cry*) I've never been in love. I've dreamed about it all my life. But it has never happened to me.

Sometimes I think that all that's needed is a magic key, a code, a password — and suddenly all that pent-up, waiting love will spill out . . . Something's wrong. Tell me what it is.

BARON I didn't sleep last night. Thinking about that elusive key. Say something encouraging to me — please — anything.

IRINA What can I say?

BARON A phrase — a word — a look —

IRINA I can't — I can't — you know I can't —

Suddenly SOLYONY *shouts, now further away.*

SOLYONY Hello, there!

VOICE Hello! Hello!

Pause.

BARON Strange that it's never the great passions, the great ambitions, that determine the course our lives take, but some trivial, piddling little thing that we dismiss and refuse to take seriously; until it's too late. And then we recognize that the piddling little thing has manoeuvred us into a situation that is irrevocable and . . . final.

IRINA It's to do with Solyony! What happened outside the theatre — and you and Solyony are —

BARON (*Delighted*) There! You're concerned for me! And suddenly I feel elated — exalted! I love you! I love life! I love everybody and everything! Look at those fir trees, those maples, those birches — I've never seen them before! Aren't they beautiful? And look, Irina — they're looking back at me — they're alert — they're watchful — they're waiting for something to happen. Aren't they beautiful? Aren't they wise? With beautiful, wise trees like that around you life should be beautiful too!

SOLYONY (*Far off*) Hello!

VOICE (*Far off*) Hello! Hello!

Again the BARON's *mood changes.*

BARON I have to go now. Look — there's a tree that's dead. But it's still swaying in the breeze with the others. I have that sense about myself, too: even if I die, somehow or other I'll still be part of life. Goodbye, my darling.

IRINA Nikolai, I —

BARON Shhhhh. (*He kisses her hand*) The postcards you sent me each summer, they're in the top drawer of my desk.

IRINA I'm going with you.

BARON (*Quietly, firmly*) You're staying here.

He moves briskly away and stops before exiting.

Irina.

IRINA Yes? (*Pause. He stares strangely at her*) What is it, Nikolai?

BARON I — I — I didn't get a cup of coffee this morning. Would you ask them to get some for me?

He leaves. She stares after him; then goes to the swing and sits there. ANDREY *with his book and pram enters, followed by* FERAPONT.

FERAPONT Mister Andrey, sir, these papers aren't mine, you know; they're official papers. I didn't invent them.

ANDREY *now addresses* FERAPONT *as he did in Act Two, speaking very softly, almost in quiet soliloquy.*

ANDREY D'you know what I find difficult to believe, Ferapont? That there *was* a time in my life when I was young and happy and eager, when I had noble dreams and huge ambitions, when the future was almost breathless with hope. Because there was such a time, wasn't there? But if there was, why can't I remember it? How could it just vanish so completely? And why is it, Ferapont, that at a certain point in our lives — there we are, young, bright, eager, about to inherit the earth — why is it that instead of taking possession of that waiting world, we suddenly become weary and dull and apathetic? I wonder why that is. Look at this town. One hundred thousand people — all indistinguishable. In the two hundred years this town has been in existence it hasn't produced one person of any distinction — not one saint, not one scholar, not one artist. Just one hundred thousand identical, drab people, eating, sleeping, working, eating, sleeping, dying. Isn't it puzzling? And in order to invest their drab lives with some little excitement, they gossip and drink and gamble and take each other to court for broken fences and for slander actions — because if they didn't they'd die of overwhelming boredom. That's why wives deceive their husbands — not for pleasure but just to reassure themselves they are still alive. And that's why husbands pretend they hear nothing and see nothing. Their pretence is a faint whisper that they're alive too. Isn't it ridiculous? And into this charade children are born with their own hopes and their own dreams and then in time become spectres like the rest of us. It's all absurd. Can I help you?

FERAPONT These papers still have to be signed.

ANDREY (*Without impatience*) You're a pest, Ferapont.

FERAPONT *hands over the papers.*

FERAPONT Do you know what the porter in the tax office told me this morning?

ANDREY (*Leafing through the papers*) Yes?

FERAPONT In Petersburg last winter they had two hundred degrees of frost!

ANDREY But we have got to keep believing that all this squalor, all this degradation — this endless round of vodka and cabbage-and-bacon and gossip and pretence — it will end soon and we must keep believing in a future for our children that is open and honest and free. Anyhow, that's what I believe. I'm absolutely convinced of that, Ferapont — absolutely . . .

FERAPONT Two hundred people froze to death that winter. That's what the porter said, hee-hee-hee.

ANDREY I know it's no excuse at all, Ferapont, but I haven't got a hat and I haven't got a walking stick . . .

He begins to cry. FERAPONT *watches him blankly.*

My dear sisters . . . my wonderful sisters . . . Masha, my darling sister . . .

NATASHA's *head appears at the window.*

NATASHA Who's making that racket out there? Sweet Mother of God, how can wee Sophie sleep with a racket like that? (*Controlled again*) *Il ne faut pas faire du bruit, la Sophie est dormée déjà. Vous êtes un ours.* (*Furious again*) If you can't keep your big mouth shut let someone else mind the child. You there, Ferapont, take that pram away from Mr Prozorov!

FERAPONT Yes, Ma'am. Certainly, Ma'am.

She withdraws. FERAPONT *takes the pram.*

ANDREY I didn't think I was making any . . .

He tails off, then picks up the papers.

NATASHA (*Off*) Bobik! Don't you dare spit into Mr Protopopov's good hat. Don't you dare, you bad, bad boy!

ANDREY I'll go through these tonight and sign the ones that need signing.

FERAPONT Wha's tha', sir?

ANDREY (*Quietly*) I'll have them ready for you tomorrow . . .

(*As he leaves*) . . . or the day after . . .

FERAPONT *wheels the pram off.*

NATASHA (*Off*) Now, Bobik, who's this? Bobik, stop that! That's dirty, dirty! Now, darling, who's this? You know who it is. It's Auntie Olga. Say 'Good afternoon, Auntie Olga'.

> *While* NATASHA *is talking two itinerant musicians enter, an old man and his daughter. He is the violinist and she the harpist. They look around.* VERSHININ, OLGA *and* ANFISA *enter from the house.*

OLGA Our garden's become like a public road — everybody seems to walk through it. Nanny, give those musicians something.

> IRINA *leaves her swing and joins the others.* ANFISA *gives money to the musicians.*

ANFISA There you are. Thank you. Off you go.

> *The musicians leave.*

God help them, the creatures; sure if they had a full stomach they wouldn't be traipsing about the countryside like that. (*Now seeing* IRINA *for the first time*) Irina! My wee pet! How are you?

> *They kiss and embrace.*

IRINA You're looking great, Nanny.
ANFISA And why wouldn't I? Amn't I living the life of a queen? The flat's as big as a palace and it's right beside the school. And you'll never guess, love: I've a lovely big room of my own. Looking out over the playground. All paid for by the Department of Education. Thanks be to God, but He's made me a

IRINA very contented aul' woman in my old age. Sometimes I wake up in the middle of the night and I think to myself: thanks be to God and His holy Mother, I'm the happiest aul' woman in the world.

IRINA I'm delighted for you, Nanny.

VERSHININ We're about to leave, Olga. I've got to run. (*Shakes her hand*) I hope *you* get even some of the happiness you deserve . . . Have you any idea where Masha is?

IRINA She's about somewhere. I'll get her.

VERSHININ Thanks. I'm late already.

ANFISA Sure you couldn't find your right hand. I'll get her. Masha! Masha!

ANFISA goes off. IRINA smiles at the others and follows.

VERSHININ (*Looking at his watch*) We've just been at the town hall . . . farewell lunch . . . champagne, the usual . . . the mayor made a long speech . . . I'm not too sure what happened. My mind was here all the time. I never seem to be away from here.

He looks around anxiously for MASHA.

OLGA Will we ever see each other again?

VERSHININ Unlikely, isn't it? (*Pause*) My wife and my two little girls are staying on until I can send for them. Maybe if they need anything, or if anything were to happen, would it be too much trouble to —

OLGA Of course, of course. I'll take care of them.

VERSHININ Thank you.

OLGA It'll be strange not to see military uniforms on the streets from tomorrow on. All we'll have is our memories of you. We'll have to begin putting a new life together . . . Nothing ever turns out the way we want it to, does it? I never wanted to be a headmistress; now I'm a headmistress. I did want to go home to Moscow; now I never will go home to Moscow.

She is about to cry and to hide her embarrassment she imitates Vershinin's gesture of spreading her hands.

Well . . .

He mimes the gesture back.

VERSHININ I know. Anyway, thank you for everything. And sorry for boring you with my endless talk. Thank you, too, Olga, for being so . . . tolerant. I know you were uneasy — unhappy — that Masha and I were —

OLGA (*Drying her eyes, very briskly*) What *is* keeping her?

VERSHININ I must have some final wisdom to impart. Surely to God I'm not tongue-tied! (*Laughs uneasily*) Let's see. 'Life is not a bed of roses. Indeed it may appear to many to be totally bleak and hopeless. But there is evidence that it is improving. And perhaps the time is not too far away when it may be described as almost hopeful.' What about that? (*Looks at his watch*) I really can't stay much longer. Yes, there *has* been a great improvement. Seriously. There was a time when man's entire life was taken up with the search for food and shelter, with cultivating a patch of land and defending it against intruders, with feeding and clothing himself and his family. And now that those basic concerns have been taken care of, there is a great emptiness in man's life, and he's searching for something to fill it. He doesn't know yet what it is he wants. But he's seeking and he will find it. But until he does my solution for his sense of emptiness is education and work, hard work and education. (*He laughs, then mocks himself with his gesture*) Well . . . (*Looks at watch*) I've really got to go.

OLGA Here she is.

MASHA *enters.*

VERSHININ I came to say goodbye.

>OLGA *moves upstage.*

MASHA Goodbye.

>*Pause as they look at each other. Then suddenly they embrace. A long kiss.* OLGA *looks away.*

OLGA Please! Please! For God's sake — please!

>MASHA *sobs loudly.*

VERSHININ Write to me, my darling. And when you think about me —

>MASHA *flings her arms around him.*

I have got to leave now, Masha. Olga, please. I must go. I'm late already.

>OLGA *takes* MASHA, *still sobbing, in her arms.* VERSHININ *takes* OLGA's *free hand and kisses it. Then he leaves.* MASHA *emits a long, anguished howl.*

OLGA Shhhhh, my darling, please . . . please, my darling, shhh . . .

>KULYGIN *enters. He is very embarrassed.*

KULYGIN Let her cry . . . doesn't matter . . . let her cry . . . doesn't matter at all . . . My Masha, my good kind Masha, you are my wife and I am happy no matter what . . . Oh Jesus Christ . . . I'm not complaining — not blaming you at all. Isn't that right, Olga? Have I ever complained, Olga? Ever? What we'll do is — what we'll have to do is go back to the way we used to be before — before — And I promise you, my darling, I'll never ever make any reference to — to — ever say a single word about — about . . .

He breaks down.

MASHA 'A green oak grows by a curving shore
And on that oak a gold chain hangs;
And on that oak a gold chain hangs . . . '
I'm going mad, Olga. 'A green oak grows by a curving shore . . . '

OLGA Shhhhh, my love, shhhhh — easy, easy — don't talk — (*To* KULYGIN) — a glass of water.

MASHA No more crying.

KULYGIN No more crying. All over and done with. All finished.

Distant sound of a gunshot.

MASHA 'A green oak hangs by a golden shore — a hanging shore — And on that chain a green oak curves — a green chain curves — a gold oak hangs — '
I've got it all mixed up. (*Drinks water*) It's all a mess, all a confusion. I'll be all right in a minute. No more crying. What's that line again? 'A green oak hangs by a golden shore' — what's that supposed to mean? If I can't get those lines out of my head, Olga, I know I'll go mad.

IRINA *enters.*

OLGA No, you won't. You're better already.

MASHA No more crying.

OLGA Good. Now, give me your hand. We'll go inside together.

MASHA I am not going into that house! (*Sobbing again, softly*) I'm not going into that house ever again.

IRINA That's all right. We'll all just sit here for a while and not speak at all.

KULYGIN I took this beard and moustache from a boy in the

third form yesterday. (*He puts it on*) Look, Masha. Who's this? Who am I?

OLGA Who?

KULYGIN Our German master! (*Laughs*) Exactly like him, Masha, isn't it?

OLGA Very like him.

KULYGIN It's him! (*In heavy German accent*) 'Who is beautiful three sisters that sits in those garden — *ja*?'

> IRINA *laughs. Then* OLGA. *Finally* MASHA. *The laughter lives for a few seconds. Now* MASHA *cries again.* NATASHA *enters, talking to the maid who trots behind her.*

NATASHA Two things I want done: bring Master Bobik up-stairs and wash his hands and face — (*The maid is about to leave:* NATASHA *shouts at her*) — I said two things, didn't I? Are you thick? (*Controlled again*) And tell Mr Prozorov to take Miss Sophie for a walk along the bank of the river.

> *The maid exits. To the sisters:*

Children! Never a moment to call your own. You girls don't know how lucky you are. (*To* IRINA) And you're leaving us tomorrow, Irina. That's a shame. Could you not stay on for another week? (*Now seeing* KULYGIN *for the first time*) Jesus, Mary and Joseph! You put the heart across me!

KULYGIN (*German accent*) 'What means I put the heart across you?'

> *He removes the mask.*

NATASHA You're a bold, bold boy, Fyodor. Isn't he? (*To* IRINA) I've got so used to having you in the house that I'm going to miss you terribly. Yes, that's just what I'll do — Andrey can move into your room and he can saw away on his fiddle to his heart's content back there and he'll bother nobody. And wee Sophie can move into his room. That's that all sorted. She's a real darling, isn't she? If you'd seen her this morning when she woke up. She smiled up at me — this is as true as God — and she said, 'Mama'.

KULYGIN There's no doubt about it — she's a very pretty child.

NATASHA So from tomorrow I'm to be all alone here then? Well — *c'est la vie*. The first thing I'll do is get that avenue of fir trees cut down and then get rid of that maple — it's such a depressing aul' thing in the dark evenings. (*To* IRINA) And you're wearing a green sash, darling. I wouldn't have thought green was your colour. And I'm going to plant flowers everywhere — all kinds of flowers — all over the place. I want the whole garden to be saturated with aromic . . . aromas.

The maid has entered again — just as NATASHA *discovers a fork lying on the ground.*

What's that fork doing here? (*In a fury*) What in God's name is a valuable, stamped-silver fork lying out here for? And don't you dare answer me back, madam, don't you dare!

She pursues the maid off.

KULYGIN There she goes again.

A military band plays in the distance.

OLGA Listen. They're leaving.

They all listen. CHEBUTYKIN *enters.*

MASHA God be with him. God be with them all . . . (*Suddenly brisk, to* KULYGIN) We'd better go home.

Where's my hat and coat?
KULYGIN I left them inside. I'll get them.

He exits.

OLGA Yes; it's time we all went home.
CHEBUTYKIN (*Softly*) Olga.

She goes to him.

OLGA What is it?
CHEBUTYKIN Nothing . . . I don't know how to say it . . .

He whispers in her ear.

OLGA Oh my God!
CHEBUTYKIN I know . . . shocking . . . what's there to say . . . I
feel ancient.
IRINA What's wrong, Olga?

OLGA *goes to* IRINA *and puts her arms around her.*

OLGA My darling — my darling — there's been a terrible
accident. I don't know how to —
IRINA What is it? Tell me quickly — what is it? (*Momentary
pause*) For God's sake *tell* me, Olga.
OLGA The baron has been killed in a duel.

IRINA *begins to cry.*

IRINA I knew it . . . I knew it . . .

CHEBUTYKIN *goes to the back of the stage and sits.*

CHEBUTYKIN Ancient and exhausted.

*He takes out a paper, looks at it, lets it fall to the
ground.*

117

Crying's no harm . . . they say that a good cry can even be salutary, if being salutary matters . . . (*Speaks*) 'When I found she'd left me in the lurch, Oh how it did upset me . . . '

The three sisters are standing close together.

MASHA Listen to that music. They're going away forever. They'll never be back. And we must begin to put our lives together again because we have got to go on living. That's what we must do.

IRINA (*Resting her head on* OLGA's *shoulder*) All this unhappiness, all this suffering — what is it all for? Some day we'll know the answer. But in the meantime life goes on and we must work and work and think of nothing but work. I'll go off by myself tomorrow and teach in a school somewhere and spend the rest of my life serving people who need me. It's autumn now. It will be winter soon, and the snow will come and cover everything everywhere, and I will keep on working and working.

OLGA *puts her arms around* MASHA *and* IRINA.

OLGA Just listen to that music. It's so assured, so courageous. It makes you want to go on, doesn't it? Yes, of course we will die and be forgotten — everything about us, how we looked, how we spoke, that there were three of us. But our unhappiness, our suffering, won't be wasted. They're a preliminary to better times, and because of them the people who come after us will inherit a better life — a life of peace and content and happiness. And they will look on us with gratitude, and with love. But our life isn't over yet. By no means! We are going to go on living! And that music is so confident, so courageous, it almost seems as if it is about to be revealed very soon why we are alive and what our suffering is for. If only we knew that. If only we knew that.

The music fades slowly. KULYGIN *enters with Masha's hat and coat and stands waiting with infinite patience.* ANDREY *enters at the back of the stage with his book and his pram and pauses.*

CHEBUTYKIN (*Sings softly*) 'There was I, waiting at the church, waiting at the church, waiting at the church; When I found she'd left me in the lurch, Oh how it did upset — '

He stops abruptly, sits upright and stares in front of him.

Matters sweet damn all . . . sweet damn all it matters . . .

OLGA If we only knew. Oh, if we only knew.

Bring lights down slowly.

THE
COMMUNICATION
CORD

Characters

TIM GALLAGHER
JACK McNEILIS
NORA DAN
CLAIRE HARKIN
SENATOR DOCTOR DONOVAN
SUSAN DONOVAN
BARNEY THE BANKS
EVETTE GIROUX

Time and Place

The present, early in October; a sunny, gusty afternoon (Act One) and that evening (Act Two).

A restored thatched cottage close to the sea in the remote townland of Ballybeg, County Donegal.

The Communication Cord was first produced by Field Day Theatre Company at the Guildhall, Derry, on 21 September 1982, with the following cast:

TIM GALLAGHER	Stephen Rea
JACK McNEILIS	Gerard McSorley
NORA DAN	Pat Leavy
CLAIRE HARKIN	Fidelma Cullen
SENATOR DOCTOR DONOVAN	Kevin Flood
SUSAN DONOVAN	Ann Hasson
BARNEY THE BANKS	Ian McElhinney
EVETTE GIROUX	Ruth Hegarty

Directed by	Joe Dowling
Designed by	Margo Harkin
Lighting by	Rory Dempster
Music by	Keith Donald

for Tom Paulin

ACT ONE

The action takes place in a 'traditional' Irish cottage. The open-hearth
fireplace, with the crook and the black hanging pot, occupies most of
the wall right. (Left and right from the point of view of the audience.)
A string is stretched across the breast of the fireplace as a clothes line.
Hanging on it is a pink nightdress. Downstage on the same wall is a
door leading to a bedroom. The back wall contains most of the furnishings. Stage right, in the corner close to the fireplace, is a settle bed which
is concealed behind curtains. Next to the bed is a kitchen table posi-
tioned in front of a small square window. The window is curtained
with lace. Beside the table is a dresser, fully stocked with plates, cups,
bowls, etc. Next to the dresser is the double door. When the big door
is open we can see the half-door beyond it. Left of the door is a large
churn; a creel for holding turf; a wooden flail. On the wall left there
are three wooden posts complete with chains where cows were chained
during milking. (A hundred years ago this was the area of the house
where animals were bedded at night.)

A wooden stairway, beginning downstage left, leads up to the loft.
This loft (unseen) is immediately above the kitchen. A substantial beam
of wood at right angles to the kitchen floor supports the floor of this
loft. This beam should be placed wherever it causes least masking —
perhaps downstage right (below the fireplace) or downstage left (below
the stairs).

Apart from a few chairs and stools (all 'traditional') the entire centre
of the stage is free of furnishings.

Every detail of the kitchen and its furnishings is accurate of its
time (from 1900 to 1930). But one quickly senses something false about
the place. It is too pat, too 'authentic'. It is in fact a restored house,
a reproduction, an artefact of today making obeisance to a home of
yesterday.

TIM GALLAGHER is in his late twenties/early thirties, a junior lecturer without tenure in a university. A serious, studious young man
with a pale face and large glasses. The business of coping with every-

*day life makes him nervous and seems to demand more than ordinary
concentration. He is relaxed and assured only when he is talking
about his work: he is doing his Ph.D in an aspect of linguistics. The
enterprise he is now reluctantly embarked on has made him very
agitated.*

JACK McNEILIS, *his friend, is the same age. He is a barrister.* JACK
has all the characteristics that TIM *lacks. He is quick-talking, self-
confident, able to handle everybody and every situation. He considers
himself to be a man of vast and worthwhile experience.*

*We hear a motorbike approach the house. It stops. Voices off. Then
the latch is lifted and the big door is pushed open.* TIM *looks into the
room across the half-door.*

TIM It was open, Jack.
JACK What?
TIM The door — it wasn't locked.

       Cut the sound of the engine.

JACK Can't hear you.
TIM The door was open.
JACK You're turning the key the wrong way.

      TIM *looks at the key in his hand.*

TIM Am I?
JACK Turn it clockwise — OK?
TIM Yes.
JACK Now just lift the latch and give it a good push.
TIM Yes.
JACK Got it now?
TIM Yes.
JACK Good.

      TIM *draws the bolt on the half-door and enters. He takes
off his crash helmet, searches his pockets, finds a handkerchief and wipes his watering eyes. He searches his
pockets again, finds his glasses, blows on them, cleans
them and puts them on. Now he can see properly. He*

surveys the kitchen. He is wearing a dark, well-worn, three-piece suit, black shoes, white shirt and dark tie. He shudders occasionally from cold after the motorbike trip.

JACK *enters. He is carrying his helmet, an overnight bag and a plastic bag full of groceries. He is casually but carefully dressed: a suede jacket, open-neck lemon shirt, tan trousers, stylish shoes. Unlike* TIM's *his appearance bears no signs of the journey and the ravages of the wind.*

TIM *wanders around uneasily, looking vaguely and without much interest at the furnishings, touching them abstractedly.*

JACK *closes both doors behind him as he enters and immediately begins unpacking — putting groceries on the dresser, his bag in the bedroom, etc.*

(*Entering*) Two and a half hours exactly from the city centre to the bottom of the lane. That's not bad going. And now you know why I haven't a Ferrari: at least with the old Honda I can drive up that bloody lane, right up to the door.

TIM (*Scarcely hearing*) Yes.

JACK When the parents or the sisters come for a weekend they have to leave the car down at the main road and walk up. It's hell in winter — water, muck, slush, bloody cow manure. You arrive soaked and spent. But Father believes that the penance of that introduction is somehow part of the soul and authenticity of the place.

The big door blows open. JACK *closes it.*

That south wind hits the front of the house. Are you cold?

TIM Just a bit.

JACK I'll light the fire.

TIM No, no. I'll be fine in a minute. Do you use it much?

JACK Depends. When my services as the country's leading

barrister aren't in demand — which is nearly always; and as often as I can ensure the company and the consolations of a female companion. Make yourself at home.

TIM Thanks.

JACK Did you get a glimpse of the beach? It's just at the bottom of that field.

TIM Yes.

JACK Dramatic, isn't it?

TIM Yes.

JACK *goes into the bedroom.*

JACK You might have time for a swim. But you'd need to be careful near the rocks at the far side — there's a heavy undertow. (*In his abstracted way* TIM *is touching the pink nightdress on the line. He is vaguely aware of its incongruity here*) That's where Claire Harkin was nearly drowned — just below the sandbanks.

TIM (*Alarmed*) When? Recently?

JACK *enters. Almost guiltily* TIM *takes his hand quickly off the nightdress.*

JACK No; years ago. Here for Easter with the sisters and was almost dragged away. Artificial respiration; all that stuff. I'll take that (*crash helmet*).

TIM You used to go with Claire, didn't you?

JACK Lasted a week.

TIM I always thought —

JACK I'm exaggerating — two days. A golden rule, professor: never take out a friend of your sisters; from the word go the moral standard is pitched too high. Absolutely.

He produces a bottle of whiskey from his grocery bag and surveys it.

Too early for a charge, is it? Yes. Later — if there's time.

He takes the bottle off to the bedroom.

You took her out a few times yourself, didn't you?

TIM Claire?

JACK We all thought that was terminal at the time. What happened between you?

TIM Between Claire and me?

JACK That's who we're talking about, isn't it?

> TIM *in some embarrassment is abstractedly and gently punching the beam with his fist.*

TIM Yes . . . oh that was years ago . . . a student thing . . . she — she — she — there was nothing much to —

JACK (*Entering*) Don't touch that! Christ, man, do you want to bring the bloody loft down on us!

TIM Sorry.

JACK It's OK, professor. But that beam's only a temporary job we stuck up one day when the ceiling began to sag.

TIM Sorry.

JACK No harm done. We're getting a proper job done on it this winter. (*Looking around*) Well, what do you think of it?

TIM I think my grandmother was probably reared in a house like this.

JACK Everybody's grandmother was reared in a house like this. Do you like it?

TIM It — it — it's very . . .

JACK What?

TIM Nice.

JACK 'Nice'! The ancestral seat of the McNeilis dynasty, restored and refurbished with love and dedication, absolutely authentic in every last detail, and all you can say is 'nice'. For one who professes the English language, your vocabulary is damned limp. Listen, professor. (*In parody*) This is where we all come from. This is our first cathedral. This shaped all our souls. This determined our first pieties. Yes. Have reverence for this place. (*Laughs heartily*) Come on; since it's going to be your property for the next few hours you'd better know something about it. Hold on — let's get the timetable right first. Absolutely. (*Looks at his watch*) What time do you make it? (TIM *looks at his watch*)

TIM I forgot to wind it.

JACK Wind it now, Tim. It's three o'clock exactly. When are Susan and Daddy Senator passing through?

TIM She wasn't sure. She just said sometime after lunch. I think she said maybe sometime in the early afternoon.

JACK You'd be a great witness.

TIM I remember now. What she said was that her father had to be in Sligo at six for this political dinner he's speaking at.

JACK That means he'll have to leave here at four thirty at the latest. Fine. Let's say they arrive at three thirty. So you'll have from three thirty until four thirty — one full hour. That should be adequate. I'll disappear for that hour — go for a swim, maybe — and the moment I see them leave I'll return and drive you down to the bus. Great.

JACK *begins working again.*

TIM But you're going to be here, aren't you? I mean to meet them?

JACK Like hell I am.

TIM Jack, the understanding was that both of us were to —

JACK You have misunderstood the understanding, professor. What I said was that I'd be happy to see Susan, with whom I once had a little fling, as you know, and for whom I still have a huge affection, despite the fact that she is a sly, devious and calculating little puss, if you don't mind my saying so. But I made it clear to you that I would not meet Senator Doctor Donovan who went for me like a savage one night just because

I was ten minutes late for a date with little Susan. 'My only child — my innocent little daughter' — I got all that stuff. No, sir. Oh don't be disarmed by the suave tongue of Dr Bollocks.

TIM So that when they arrive I'm to be here alone?!

JACK Absolutely. And not trembling, I hope. So that's the schedule. This is your house until four thirty. If for any reason they haven't left by then you've got to get rid of them. Right?

TIM Yes. But —

JACK And the moment they leave I'll return, drive you into the town on Brother Honda, put you on the evening bus, pick up Evette and bring her here. Excellent. Couldn't be simpler.

TIM Evette? Evette who?

JACK *does not know her surname.*

JACK Evette — Evette — Evette the French girl — from the Consulate — she's been around for years. What do you mean, 'Evette who'? The same Evette we bumped into at the party last Saturday. I promised I'd show her some of Donegal over the weekend. Right. That's the timetable. Mess it up and we're all in trouble.

The big door blows open. He closes it.

Must be something wrong with that latch. Now — the tour. (*Very rapidly*) A bedroom there, known as the 'room down'; one double bed. Fireplace. Usual accoutrements. Tongs. Crook. Pot — iron. Kettle — black. Hob. Recess for clay pipes. Stool. Settle bed. Curtains for same. Table. Chairs —

TIM Slower — slower, Jack, please.

JACK Have I lost you somewhere, professor? Where did I lose you?

TIM The settle bed.

JACK Ah. This is the settle bed. Right?

TIM Yes.

JACK Absolutely. (*Rapidly again*) Table. Lamp. Window. Curtains — lace. Clock — stopped. Dresser. Again the usual accoutrements. Cups. Bowls. Plates — functional. Plates — ornamental. Egg cups. (*Lifts bottle*) Paraffin? (*Sniffs*) Vodka. Good. Give Susan a charge — not that she needs it.

TIM I need it. Is there a glass?

JACK A glass! The gaff's blown already. Bowls, professor, bowls! Never glasses! Have you no sense of the authentic? You *are* going to mess it. Door. Half-door beyond — even though you can't see it, I assure you it's there. Churn. Flail. Creel. Stairs to —

TIM What's that again?

JACK That is a creel.

TIM No, that thing there.

JACK That is a flail for — (*in exasperation*) — for special orgies on midsummer night — an old and honoured Donegal ritual. Two single beds up there. One beam or upright to support the loft — and you're perfectly safe up there as long as some fool doesn't shift this thing. Posts and chains for tethering cows at night — a relict from the days when your granny and the animals shared the same roof. And that's about it. What else do you need to know?

TIM It's not going to work, Jack.

JACK Professor, you're —

TIM I want to call it all off. It seemed a good idea in the comfort of my flat —

JACK Comfort?

TIM — but I can see now that it's stupid and dangerous. It was very kind of you to offer me your house —

JACK My father's house.

TIM Thank you very much. But I want to scrap the whole thing. It's crazy. For God's sake, I'm not even sure that I *like* Susan!

JACK Who mentioned liking her, professor? You're going with her — that's all. And it's a perfect match: you're ugly and penniless, she's pretty and rich.

TIM That's not why I'm going with her as you know

damned well. And please stop calling me professor. I'm a bloody junior lecturer in linguistics. Without tenure.

JACK But your thesis is nearly finished, isn't it?

TIM I don't know. Maybe.

JACK What's it on again?

TIM Talk.

JACK What about?

TIM That's what the thesis is about — talk, conversation, chat.

JACK Ah.

TIM Discourse Analysis with Particular Reference to Response Cries.

JACK You're writing your thesis on what we're doing now?

TIM It's fascinating, you know. Are you aware of what we're doing now?

JACK We're chatting, aren't we?

TIM (*Warming up*) Exactly. But look at the process involved. You wish to know what my thesis is about and I wish to tell you. Information has to be imparted. A message has to be sent from me to you and you have to receive that message. How do we achieve that communication?

JACK You just tell me.

TIM Exactly. Words. Language. An agreed code. I encode my message; I transmit it to you; you receive the message and decode it. If the message sent is clear and distinct, if the code is fully shared and subscribed to, if the message is comprehensively received, then there is a reasonable chance — one, that you will understand what I'm trying to tell you — and two, that we will have established the beginnings of a dialogue. All social behaviour, the entire social order, depends on our communicational structures, on words mutually agreed on and mutually understood. Without that agreement, without that shared code, you have chaos.

JACK Chaos. Absolutely. Why?

TIM Because communication collapses. An extreme example: I speak only English; you speak only German;

no common communicational structure. The result? Chaos. Or when I was opening that big door, you were broadcasting on one wavelength, I was receiving on another. No shared context in which the common code can function. But let's stick with the situation where there is a shared context and an agreed code, and even here we run into complications.

JACK So soon?

TIM The complication that perhaps we are both playing roles here, not only for one another but for ourselves. But let's stick to basics. You ask me what my thesis is about. You ask me that question every so often and I tell you every time. Information requested; information transmitted; information received. But by the very fact of asking me as often as you do, you do something more than look for information, something more than try to set up a basic discourse; you desire to share my experience.

JACK I don't — do I?

TIM And because of that desire our exchange is immediately lifted out of the realm of mere exchange of basic messages and aspires to something higher, something much more important — conversation.

JACK God!

TIM A response cry! And that's really the kernel of my thesis. A response cry blurted out as an involuntary reaction to what you've just heard. And what does it tell me? Does your 'God!' say: I never knew that before? Does it say: This is fascinating — please continue? Does it say: Yes, I do desire to share your experience? Does it say: Tim, you're boring me? Or is your expletive really involuntary? Maybe — because we're both playing roles, if we're both playing roles — maybe your 'God!' is a *pretence* at surprise, at interest, at boredom. And if it is a pretence, why is it a pretence? Do you see the net we're weaving about ourselves now?

JACK I do, professor. Absolutely. One — we're wasting time. And two — our plan goes ahead.

TIM   Plan? What plan?

JACK This is your house for an hour.

TIM   Oh my God!

JACK A response cry that goes straight past my heart. Or maybe it's a prayer: Please, God, receive my message.

TIM   Jack, I'm not going through with it! I'm not! I'm not!

JACK Right. Right. Calm down. We've been over all this before. Will you trust me in this? Just trust me, Timothy, will you?

TIM   When someone says that to you, you know you're being betrayed. I'm sorry, Jack. I didn't mean that. I'm sorry. It's just that there's something shabby, something damned perfidious about the whole thing.

JACK Wasn't it Susan's idea?

TIM   Hers — mine — yours — I've forgotten now how it originated. I think it began almost as a joke, didn't it? And suddenly here we are!

JACK But she sees nothing unprincipled in it.

TIM   That worries me, too. Look at what I'm doing: for two furtive hours on a sunny October afternoon I'm to pretend I'm the owner of a-a-a-a miniature museum just because Susan thinks that would impress her pompous father who fancies himself as an amateur antiquarian.

JACK One furtive hour.

TIM   All right. All right. One hour then.

JACK And Dr Bollocks also happens to be a senator who can help you secure your tenure.

TIM   If that's how I were to get it I'd refuse it.

JACK Of course. The worthy and penniless Timothy Gallagher — all nobility and no nous. Look at it from Susan's point of view. Just because she's crazy about you —

TIM   Ah, come on, Jack!

JACK — is it unnatural that she should want her poor widowed father who dotes on his only child — and why wouldn't he? — what father wouldn't dote on such an estimable offspring? — is it unnatural, I ask you, that she should want him to share with her her regard, her respect, her admiration, yes, yes, even her love for you? — Is that unnatural?

TIM Jack, I'm not a jury.

JACK So they drop in here on their way to their political dinner and have a quick look around and Daddy Senator suddenly realizes that there's more to you than the stooped, whingeing, trembling, penniless, myopic, part-time junior lecturer without tenure. 'Good heavens, the lad has a noble soul like myself. Good gracious, this is a kindred spirit. My blessing on you both.' And her wealth that I once lusted after is safe in your pocket — or as near as bedamned. And they head off to address the party faithful and everybody's happy — Susan, Dr Bollocks, yourself.

TIM It's still —

JACK Shabby, furtive, perfidious, unprincipled. Dear God, surround me with people of no morals — (*sudden delight*) — Giroux! — That's her name! — Evette Giroux! How could that have slipped my mind? I'm away to the well for a bucket of the purest of pure spring water.

> *He picks up a wooden bucket and is about to exit when he sees* NORA DAN *passing the window.*

Goddammit, Nora Dan! The quintessential noble peasant — obsessed with curiosity and greed and envy.

> NORA DAN *knocks.*

Come in, Nora! (*Softly*) Distant relative of the family. Convinced this house is legally hers.

> NORA DAN *enters. She is in her sixties and single. A country woman who likes to present herself as a peasant.*

NORA Ah, Jack.

JACK How are you doing, Nora?

NORA Ah sure I'm only half-middling, Jack. You're welcome — you're welcome. And who's this young gentleman?

JACK Tim Gallagher, a friend of mine. Nora Dan.

NORA A friend of yours. Isn't that grand? You're welcome, sir, welcome.

TIM Thank you, Mrs Dan.

NORA (*Laughs*) 'Mrs Dan'! Glory be to God, isn't that a good one! Sure I was never a missus in my life, Tim. I get the Dan from my father — that's the queer way we have of naming people about here. (*To* JACK) I didn't find yous coming. Are yous here long?

JACK We've just arrived.

NORA You have surely. And you'll be staying for the week-end?

JACK I will, Nora. Tim's going home on the evening bus.

NORA The evening bus. He must be a very busy man. And how's Mammy and Daddy and the girls?

JACK They're fine, thanks. They send their love.

NORA They do surely.

JACK (*To* TIM) Nora very kindly looks after the house when we're not here. She's a far-out relation of Mother.

NORA Daddy.

JACK Father. What is it? — A third cousin?

NORA Second and third.

JACK (*To* TIM) That's it.

NORA Twice removed.

JACK Twice removed.

NORA I'm sure this gentleman has a powerful big job, too?

JACK Tim works in the University.

NORA In the University. Oh, he'll be the smart man.

JACK Brilliant, Nora.

NORA He is surely. And it'll be the big wages he'll earn in a place like that?

JACK Absolutely. And what's the news about Ballybeg, Nora?

NORA Ah sure what news would there be in a place like this? Sure we see nobody and hear nothing here. I'm sure you were never in as backward a place as this, Tim?

TIM   No — yes — oh, yes.

NORA   You were surely — you're a travelled man. (*To* JACK) And how's Miss Tiny? I often think of Miss Tiny.

JACK   (*Embarrassed*) Who's that, Nora?

NORA   Miss Tiny — the big lady that was here with you last month.

JACK   Oh, Tiny — Tiny — she's — a — she's fine — she's fine.

NORA   She's fine, thanks be to God. (*To* TIM) I'm sure you know Miss Tiny?

TIM   I don't think I ever —

NORA   Oh, a great big stirk of a girl. Black as your boot and a head of wee tight curls on her like a lamb in March. She used to lie all day in the salt water, rolling about like a big seal — Lord, and not a stab on her! Patsy the Post — (*to* JACK) you know Patsy — wee Patsy was cycling home from Mass that Sunday morning and looked down and there she was, stretched out on her back in the water; and d'you know, didn't the poor man fall off his bike and into the tide! And you know yourself, Jack, there's no more modest man in Ballybeg than Patsy — married with nine children. He said afterwards that he thought it was a porpoise through the salmon nets. Lord, it was the talk of the town!

JACK   Did I notice a caravan at the far end of the sand-banks, Nora?

NORA   (*To* TIM) He misses nothing, the same Jack. (*To* JACK) Indeed and you did. He's a German gentleman. I couldn't tell you his right name; all he gets about here is Barney the Banks but sure that wouldn't be his real name at all, would it?

JACK   Unlikely.

NORA   Unlikely, indeed. He's about the same age and build as yourself. A civiler man you couldn't meet except when he has — (*indicates drinking*) — you know your-self; and he'd be apt to gulder a wee bit then. But no harm in him; no harm at all. And he has me deaved asking about this house — says he never seen any-

thing like it and he'd give a fortune to buy it. (*To* TIM)
You know the way strangers get queer notions about
a place like this; and foreigners is the worst. (*To* JACK)
I gave him Daddy's address but I'm sure he never
wrote, did he?

JACK Not that I know of.

NORA Not that you know of. Ah, sure what would a foreign
gentleman want to be living in a backward place like
this for anyway? Yous have plenty milk and potatoes?

JACK We're fine, Nora, thanks.

NORA Yous are fine, surely. Well, yous'll want peace for
your holidays. I've just made a wee cake of soda
bread — I'll bring yous over some of it later. Enjoy
yourself now, Tim.

TIM Thank you.

NORA Not that yous'll have much chance to spend your
fortune about here. But sure the three of yous'll
make your own fun together.

JACK See you later, Nora.

She leaves. TIM *laughs.*

What's she talking about — 'the three of yous'?

TIM 'He misses nothing, the same Jack.'

JACK That's because the moment I first saw her I recognized her as a nosy, hypocritical, treacherous old
bitch. Now she'll be over every half-hour, smelling
around. Maybe you should light the fire.

TIM How do I light it?

JACK How would he light it? As our forebears lit it for thousands of years — by rubbing flint stones together!

Again he picks up the bucket and exits. TIM *goes to
the fireplace and studies it.* JACK *suddenly reappears
at the half-door.*

What about this, professor? When Susan and Daddy
Senator are here I'll appear disguised as Barney the
Banks and offer you a fortune for the place.

TIM   For God's sake, Jack —

JACK   It's not a bad idea, you know. (*Loudly, in German accent*) 'I hear you sell your house, Herr Gallagher — ja? I give you a fortune to buy it.'

TIM   Jack!

JACK   Of course you'll scorn the notion of flogging your heritage — and in Dr Bollocks's eyes your stock will rise even higher. You'll have tenure before the night's out!

TIM   How is it you never told me about Miss Tiny?

JACK   'A million Deutsche Mark, Herr Gallagher. I hoffer you any monies you hask for.'

TIM   Was she really as black as your boot?

JACK   (*With dignity*) You know, Tim, there are times when you surprise and disappoint me. Tiny was a princess from Mysore; and her skin was the colour of ripe damsons; and it so happens that when she went back to India a part of me died. Bastard!

> *He disappears.*
>
> TIM *looks at his watch, shakes it, holds it against his ear. His anxiety returns. He goes to the dresser, picks up the vodka bottle, chooses a cup, decides against a cup, takes a bowl, pours himself a large drink and drinks some of it quickly. He now returns to the fire-place (and again notices the nightdress) and feels along the top of the mantelpiece where he finds a box of matches. He strikes a match and holds it — at arm's length and with his face averted as if the fire were dangerous — against a piece of turf he holds in his hand. The turf does not ignite. The match burns his fingers and dies. He picks up his bowl and drifts off to explore the bedroom.*
>
> CLAIRE *enters. She is about thirty — competent, open, humorous. She is barefooted and dressed in jeans and a T-shirt. She is carrying a wet, bright yellow, two-piece swimsuit and is drying her hair as she enters. She leaves her towel across the back of a chair and hangs the wet swimsuit on the clothes line. She*

takes matches from the mantelpiece and lights the fire. It ignites instantly. She takes her nightdress from the line and goes upstairs.

TIM reappears. Again he looks at his watch. He drinks again from his bowl. He looks at the fireplace and immediately notices that the nightdress has been replaced by the swimsuit. He fingers the swimsuit and discovers it is wet. His bewilderment increases. He looks around — there is nobody there. He fingers the swimsuit again, could it belong to . . . ?

TIM (*Calling gently*) Nora Dan?

Silence. Now he sees that the fire is lit. He stoops down to have a closer look and is suddenly enveloped in a blow-down.

Oh my God!

He staggers, coughing, into the centre of the kitchen and — as he did on his first entrance — takes off his glasses, dries his eyes, cleans the glasses. CLAIRE has heard the noise downstairs.

CLAIRE (*Off*) Is that you, Nora?

TIM hears the voice which comes from the direction of the door.

TIM I'm here, Jack.
CLAIRE I'll be straight down.
TIM Who's there?

CLAIRE appears at the top of the stairs. She is wearing a dress now and is brushing her hair.

CLAIRE Who's that?
TIM Just a minute. I'm —
CLAIRE Who are you? What do you want?

TIM *now has his glasses on. He looks up and recog-*
nizes her.

TIM (*Undisguised joy*) Oh my God — it's Claire! Oh my
God!

She comes down the remaining steps.

CLAIRE Tim? Is it you?
TIM Yes — yes! It's me — Tim! God, I'm glad to see you,
Claire.
CLAIRE I'm glad to see you, too.
TIM And you were nearly drowned!
CLAIRE Was I?
TIM Yes!
CLAIRE Just now?
TIM No! Years ago! One Easter!
CLAIRE Oh.
TIM God, that was a close thing, Claire!
CLAIRE It was. Yes.

Pause.

TIM Must have been terrifying. There's a heavy under-
tow over there . . .
CLAIRE What are you doing here, Tim?
TIM I came with Jack.
CLAIRE Jack McNeilis?
TIM We've just arrived.
CLAIRE For the whole weekend?
TIM For an hour — three thirty to four thirty.
CLAIRE That's all you can spare.
TIM Jack says that should be adequate. Are you staying
the weekend?
CLAIRE Until next Wednesday.
TIM God, I wish I could stay. I'm going home on the even-
ing bus, but Jack's staying on. Maybe I should sneak
back for a few minutes after half four — I'll ask Jack
if I can. You only just missed him. He's gone to the

well wherever it is — you've been here before — I suppose you know where it is — anyhow that's where he's away to, with a big wooden pail like Little Miss Moffat and pretending he's Barney the Banks, the German visitor that lives in the caravan, and guldering about 'hoffering me a million Deutsche Mark' if I would sell him this house —

As he tells this story he acts it: imitating Jack with his pail and Barney drinking and staggering and guldering, then suddenly, realization — and even greater panic than before.

Oh my God! Get out — get out — get out! Now! Now! They'll be here any minute!

He grabs her towel and thrusts it violently into her hands.

For God's sake, will you move! What else have you got? Have you stuff upstairs? Have you a case? Oh my God!

CLAIRE (*With great concern*) Tim, are you not well? What's the — ?

TIM (*Shouts*) Will you for God's sake go!

JACK *enters.*

JACK I'm off, professor. There's a big car stopped at the foot of the lane and two figures coming up the — (*He sees* CLAIRE) Oh, Christ!

TIM A response cry uttered to convey that the utterer finds the world disappointing.

JACK What are you raving about?

CLAIRE What are you two up to?

JACK The question is: what are you doing here, Claire?

CLAIRE I'm here at your mother's request — to keep an eye on your youngest sister, Elizabeth, who is arriving tomorrow morning —

JACK Elizabeth?

TIM You can't leave now, Jack — neither of you.

CLAIRE And I'm here because I'm free until next Wednesday apart from one lecture on Tuesday morning which a friend is going to take for me.

TIM We'll all stay. We'll all meet them. You two are married — you're on your honeymoon — I'm your best man —

CLAIRE Is he drunk?

TIM *runs to the door and peers furtively out.*

JACK Claire, many, many years ago you and I were fortunate enough to experience and share an affection that is still one of my most sustaining memories. If that memory means anything to you — and I can't believe it doesn't — will you trust me now and please leave immediately?

CLAIRE Trust you?! I never trusted you, Jack! What are you scheming at now?

JACK I won't take offence at that, Claire. But if I give you my solemn word as an old friend and as a lawyer —

CLAIRE Hah!

JACK — that your presence here over this weekend — and Elizabeth's — may jeopardize Tim's entire academic future —

CLAIRE In what way?

JACK — and I am aware that you and he were much, much closer than you and I ever were — but if I give you my solemn word —

TIM *has run back to them.*

TIM Susan's gone back to the car for something. He's at the bend in the lane.

CLAIRE Susan? Who's Susan?

TIM (*Totally wretched*) I can't go through with it alone, Jack. Both of you stay — please!

CLAIRE (*Brightly*) Yes. The whole weekend.

JACK You're a bloody bitch.

TIM We'll all have a party!

JACK (*To* TIM) And you're a bloody fool.

He goes to the door.

Remember — one hour. Then out — both of you!

He exits. TIM *runs after him.*

TIM Jack — Jack —

CLAIRE It's the sweet little Susan Donovan I've heard so much about!

TIM It is not.

CLAIRE So I've walked in on a love nest!

TIM It's nothing of the kind, Claire.

DONOVAN (*Off*) Hello. Hello. Anybody at home?

CLAIRE I'm going to enjoy this.

TIM I'm asking you, Claire — I'm begging you —

DONOVAN (*Off*) Hello? Hello?

TIM Oh my God! — Your swimsuit — !

> *He runs to the fireplace and has just grabbed the top half of the swimsuit when he is enveloped in a blow-down. He responds as before — Oh my God! — coughing, eyes streaming. Glasses removed, etc.* CLAIRE *watches him for a few seconds and then goes calmly and serenely upstairs.*
>
> DONOVAN, *doctor and senator, enters as he knocks. He is about sixty, well preserved, very conscious of his appearance. He exudes energy and confidence, and considers himself to be a man of great charm and persuasiveness, as indeed he is, particularly with women, more particularly with young women.*

DONOVAN Anybody here? May I come in?

TIM Hello. Yes. Of course come in — come in. I'm having some trouble with the fire. Hello. How are you, Doctor?

DONOVAN I'm well, Tim. How are you?

DONOVAN asks this question with some deliberation because TIM *is cleaning his glasses with a yellow bra.*

TIM   Busy — busy. Just — you know — just doing a bit of dusting.

He thrusts the wet bra into his pocket and holds out his hand.

I was afraid you mightn't have been able to find the house.

For the next five minutes TIM'*s first concern is to establish* CLAIRE'*s whereabouts.*

DONOVAN   It wasn't too difficult. One old man we asked for directions said there were no Gallaghers in Ballybeg. Insisted your name must be McNeilis! (*Seeing* TIM *looking around*) Susie'll be with us in a moment. She went back to the car for our things.

TIM   Things?

DONOVAN   Our cases.

TIM   Suitcases?!

DONOVAN   They're not heavy. She can manage. (*Looking around*) Yes — yes — yes — I'm very glad we made the detour — this is certainly worth seeing. How long have you got it?

TIM   For an hour — oh, you mean — ? Oh, years, years. It belonged to a second and third cousin of Daddy's — Father's.

DONOVAN   Really?

TIM   Twice removed.

DONOVAN   Do you use it much?

TIM   Occasionally — frequently.

DONOVAN   The journey is a bit long but then you're free a lot. You're still only part-time, aren't you?

TIM   Yes.

DONOVAN   So Susie told me. Too bad.

TIM   But I'm hoping to get tenure when I finish my thesis.

DONOVAN (*Looking around, not listening*) Yes . . . yes . . .

TIM It's on Discourse Analysis with Particular Reference to Response Cries.

DONOVAN Good Lord.

TIM Exactly. That sort of thing.

DONOVAN What sort of thing?

TIM 'Good Lord'.

DONOVAN Good Lord what?

TIM That response cry — the imprecation — the expletive. We think we say things like 'Good Lord' casually but of course we don't. Yes, it is a conventionalized utterance but what is distinctive and interesting about it are three things: its form — you didn't, for example, say 'Oh shit' even though in different circumstances you might; the occasion of its utterance — during a not-too relaxed, slightly formal exchange between myself and yourself; and most particularly its social function — you used it not as a response to what I was saying but merely as a reassuring sound that would encourage me to continue talking.

DONOVAN Did I?

TIM Yes.

DONOVAN Good L- . Imagine that.

Pause.

TIM It's nice, isn't it?

DONOVAN What?

TIM The place.

DONOVAN Nice? It's magnificent, Tim. Really magnificent. This is what I need — this silence, this peace, the restorative power of that landscape.

TIM Yes.

Another pause. DONOVAN *is standing in the middle of the kitchen, poised, listening, absolutely still, only his eyes moving.*

It's very nice indeed.

DONOVAN   This speaks to me, Tim. This whispers to me. Does that make sense to you?

TIM   Yes.

DONOVAN   And despite the market-place, all the years of trafficking in politics and medicine, a small voice within me still knows the responses. I was born in a place like this. Did you know that? No, how could you! In County Down. A long, long time ago, Tim. Politics has its place — of course it has. And medicine, too, has its place — God knows it has. But this, Tim, this transcends all those . . . hucksterings. This is the touchstone. That landscape, that sea, this house — this is the apotheosis. Do you know what I'm saying?

TIM   Yes.

DONOVAN   I suppose all I'm really saying is that for me this is the absolute verity. Am I talking nonsense?

TIM   No.

DONOVAN   I envy you, Tim. You know that, don't you?

TIM   Yes.

DONOVAN   That's not true. I don't envy you. You know that, don't you?

TIM   Yes.

DONOVAN   I'm happy for you. I rejoice for you because I think you hear that small voice, too, and I think you know the responses. Thank God for this, Tim. (*He shakes himself as if he were freeing himself of a painful/pleasurable memory*) Well! Aren't you going to show me around? What was it Susie told me? — That this was just four walls when you got it? I don't believe it! Is that true?

TIM   That's all. Only four.

DONOVAN   And you re-roofed it yourself?

TIM   Yes.

DONOVAN   And thatched it?

TIM   Yes.

DONOVAN   By yourself?

TIM   Yes.

DONOVAN   Good L- . Good man. What did you thatch with?

TIM   Thatch.

DONOVAN Straw or bent?

TIM Straw.

DONOVAN It's warmer than bent but not as enduring. Do you find that?

TIM It's not as enduring but it's warmer.

DONOVAN Right. What sort of scollops?

TIM Oh, the usual.

DONOVAN Hazel or sally?

TIM Hazel.

DONOVAN Not as resilient but they last longer. Is that your experience.

TIM They last longer but they're not as resilient.

DONOVAN Exactly. What's this the old Irish expression is? 'The windy day isn't the day to scollop your thatch.' Isn't that it? And this is your bedroom?

> TIM *catches his elbow to stop him going into the bedroom.*

TIM We'll look at this room first. That's just a bedroom in there.

DONOVAN The 'room down'.

TIM The 'room down' — that's it. One double bed. (*Then rapidly*) Fireplace. Usual accoutrements. Tongs. Crook. Pot — iron. Kettle — black. Hob. Recess for clay pipes. Stool. Settle bed. Curtains for same. Table. Chairs. Christ!

> *This expletive because he sees* CLAIRE *coming serenely down the stairs.*

DONOVAN (*Delighted*) And you've held on to the old posts and chains!

> TIM *signals frantically to* CLAIRE *to go back up. She sees his gestures but keeps coming down.* DONOVAN *is crouching down at the posts.*

My God, Tim, that's wonderful, that's really wonderful! I haven't seen these for — my God, it must be over fifty years! And you've incorporated them into the kitchen as of course it should be because that is exactly as it was! Oh, you're no amateur at this, Tim! You know your heritage! Oh, you and I are going to have a lot to say to each other! Marvellous! Just marvellous!

> CLAIRE *is now at the bottom of the stairs and is approaching them. As she approaches* TIM's *panic rises. He scarcely knows what he is saying.*

TIM This is where we all come from.
DONOVAN Indeed.
TIM This is our first cathedral.
DONOVAN Amen to that.
TIM This shaped all our souls. This determined our first pieties. This is a friend of mine.

> DONOVAN, *who has begun to look quizzically at* TIM — *'Surely the young man isn't mocking me?'* — *now turns.* CLAIRE, *silent and smiling, is right behind him. He gets quickly to his feet.*

DONOVAN Ah. Forgive me.
TIM This is Dr Donovan. A doctor of medicine. He is also a senator. In the Senate.
DONOVAN For my sins. How are you? Haven't we met somewhere before?
TIM You couldn't have. She's from here.
DONOVAN Ah.
TIM She lives in a caravan at the far end of the banks. She's married to a German.
DONOVAN Lucky German. When I was a younger man I used to have some German.
TIM She doesn't speak German. She's French. Her name is Evette.
DONOVAN Evette — a charming name.

DONOVAN *and* CLAIRE *shake hands.*

TIM   Evette Giroux.

DONOVAN   Good heavens, that's a coincidence. I know another Evette Giroux. Needless to say, a French girl, too. Not nearly as pretty as you, though. (*Bows gallantly*) *Enchanté, madame.* My great pleasure. Do you speak English?

TIM   She —

CLAIRE *holds up her hand to silence* TIM. *Pause.*

CLAIRE   (*With French accent*) I understand perfectly.

DONOVAN   Of course you do; and if I may make so bold as to say so, you speak —

TIM   She doesn't understand you. 'I understand perfectly' — that's the only English she knows — just one phrase — only one phrase — that's all she ever says —

Again CLAIRE *silences him with her hand. Pause.*

CLAIRE   (*With French accent*) That is a lie.

TIM   Excellent, Evette! A second phrase! When did you learn that? Congratulations! Two phrases — *deux phrases* — excellent!

DONOVAN   And two such wonderful phrases — 'I understand perfectly' and 'That is a lie' — a précis of life, aren't they?

TIM   She's a very clever lady, Evette. She learns very rapidly.

DONOVAN   When you're as young and as beautiful as Madame Giroux language doesn't matter, does it? Words are superfluous, aren't they?

CLAIRE   I understand perfectly.

DONOVAN   Of course you do — (*pointing to his heart*) — here.

CLAIRE   Timothy . . . ?

TIM   Yes?

She takes his arm — she has something private to say to him.

CLAIRE Timothy —

TIM It's time to go — is that it? That's fine — go ahead.

CLAIRE No, no. Please, Timothy, *mon . . . mon . . . (She tosses her head in frustration and points towards the clothes line)*

TIM Thank you for all your good work. (*To* DONOVAN) She's a sort of caretaker — cleans the place for me. (*To* CLAIRE) See you next time I'm back, Evette. Tell Barney I was asking for him. (*To* DONOVAN) Man as communicator — doesn't always work, does it? I mean in a situation like this we can hardly explain the individual as being simultaneously creator and creation of his own communicational possibilities, can we? — Ha-ha-ha.

CLAIRE Timothy, please, *mon . . . mon . . .*

She leads him a few steps away. Now she attempts to mime her request — she touches her midriff with her fingertips.

TIM Ah, you're thirsty! Can I get you a bowl of vodka?

DONOVAN Perhaps I could help, Evette?

CLAIRE No, no, Timothy only. Please, Timothy, *mon, mon . . .*

Again the mime.

TIM I'm sorry. I just don't understand what —

CLAIRE Ah!

Suddenly her eyes light up. She sees the bra protruding from his pocket. She retrieves it and holds it up in triumph.

Ah! *Merci! Merci!*

She smiles sweetly, shyly, at both men and runs into the bedroom.

TIM Ha-ha. I would never have got that. Never. I thought she was ravenous.

DONOVAN Have you something to tell me, Tim?

TIM I certainly have.

DONOVAN I will not have my only child hurt, Tim.

TIM Of course not. It's an ugly story.

DONOVAN I'm listening.

TIM (*Lowering his voice*) When her husband gets drunk he beats her. He's an animal in drink. Only today he tried to drown her near the rocks at the far end of the beach. Artificial respiration; all that stuff. That's why my father gave her the key to this house — so that she can escape from him when things become unbearable. And that's why she insists on doing the housework — it makes her feel she's not a charity. It's the only dignity she has left.

DONOVAN Why doesn't she report him?

TIM She has — several times. But he's a very wealthy man — probably a millionaire. He has a lot of influence.

DONOVAN Even with the authorities here?

TIM Everywhere.

DONOVAN You've met him?

TIM Yes. Oh, yes. He torments me every time I come here.

DONOVAN Torments you?

TIM He wants to buy me out.

DONOVAN This house?

TIM House, land, the whole place. Offers me a fortune for it every weekend.

DONOVAN This drunken German?

TIM Hands me a blank cheque. He never gives up.

DONOVAN Typical bloody German. Overrun you if you gave them half a chance. You're not selling to him, of course?

TIM Never.

DONOVAN Good man. I'm going to make some enquiries about our German friend.

SUSAN (*Off*) Yo-ho! Yo-ho!

DONOVAN Not a word of this to Susie. She's very sensitive. Stories like that affect her badly.

> SUSAN *enters carrying two small suitcases. She is in her early twenties, pert, pretty, assured. She is dressed*

in jeans and a blouse.

SUSAN   Shame on you, Timmy, having me carry these big things. They're a ton weight.

DONOVAN   No, they're not.

TIM   I'm sorry. I didn't —

SUSAN   And shame on you, too, Daddy.

DONOVAN   Don't listen to her.

She leaves the cases in the centre of the floor and kisses TIM *lightly on the cheek.*

SUSAN   Hello, you.

TIM   Hello, Susan.

DONOVAN   I was just saying I'm delighted we made the detour. It's a very special place, isn't it?

SUSAN   (*Looking around*) I love it — I love it — I love it. Don't you love it, Daddy? Isn't it just unbelievable? I think it's just unbelievable.

DONOVAN   I'm going to have a look around. How much land do you own?

TIM   All you can see.

DONOVAN   Really? Splendid. I've a speech to mull over. I'll be back soon.

He leaves and closes both doors behind him.

SUSAN   How are you? Are we very evil deceiving poor Daddy like this? No, we're not. We're just naughty. What did he say? Was he impressed? What does he think?

TIM   He thinks it's unbelievable.

SUSAN   Terrific. That's very important to us. And he's very knowledgeable about old ruins. And you look so miserable.

TIM   Do I?

She throws her arms around him and gives him a long kiss. As before his concern is CLAIRE's *whereabouts.*

SUSAN Are you glad to see me?

TIM Indeed.

SUSAN 'Indeed'! Say it then.

TIM I'm glad to see you.

SUSAN How glad? Tell me how glad.

TIM A very, very large quantity of glad indeed.

SUSAN You're quaint — that's what you are. And I've a crow to pick with you, Timmy Sly Boots.

TIM What crow is that?

SUSAN You never told me you'd bought a motorbike.

TIM Me?

SUSAN A big, old Honda. At the side of the house.

TIM Oh, that — that's not mine.

SUSAN Whose is it?

TIM I have the use of it all right but I don't own it. It belongs to a friend of mine. A local. A neighbour.

SUSAN Who is he?

TIM He's a woman. Nora Dan. Nora the Scrambler. She lets me have it to go scrambling on the sand dunes.

SUSAN She scrambles herself, this Nora Dan?

TIM Brilliant at it. Donegal champion.

SUSAN Is she young?

TIM Ex-champion. She's not so young now.

SUSAN Will you take me out? Please, Timmy! I'd love to go scrambling.

TIM Any time at all. Of course.

SUSAN Now?!

TIM After a while — after you've seen around. How long can you stay? (*Indicating the cases*) What are these for?

SUSAN Our dress clothes for the damned dinner in Sligo this evening. But I was thinking, now that Daddy adores this place, I'll try to persuade him to drive back home this way tomorrow morning and maybe even spend the weekend here. Wouldn't that be unbelievable?

TIM Indeed.

SUSAN Whatever about this damned house I would have made him bring me here today just so that I could see you.

TIM Yes.

SUSAN Kiss me, Timmy.

TIM   Yes.

> *Again she flings her arms around him and kisses him.*

SUSAN   (*Dreamily*) If you only had a job we could make real plans, Timmy.
TIM   I have a job.
SUSAN   Not a real job. I mean they could kick you out any second, couldn't they?
TIM   I suppose so.
SUSAN   And where would we be then? And I was thinking that if you were to talk to Daddy —

> *She breaks off suddenly because, looking over* TIM's *shoulder, she sees the yellow pants on the clothes line.*

What's that, Timmy?
TIM   What?
SUSAN   Who else is in the house?
TIM   Nobody. What do you mean?
SUSAN   Whose are those on the clothes line?
TIM   Those? Oh, those are mine.
SUSAN   They're not!
TIM   They are.
SUSAN   That colour?!
TIM   That's my lucky colour.
SUSAN   Oh, you are a devil.
TIM   They must be dry by now.

> *He rushes to the line, grabs the pants and stuffs them into his pocket.*

Now. You'll want to get changed. Which case is yours?
SUSAN   The blue one. What's the rush?
TIM   Just to get things organized a bit. Time's running out. The blue one it is. Fine. Up we go. I'll lead the way.

> *He goes up the stairs.* SUSAN *follows him.*

So it's a dress affair tonight?

As they go upstairs CLAIRE *enters from the bedroom and hangs a waist-slip on the line.*

SUSAN Boring.

TIM And there'll be speeches?

SUSAN Scores of them.

TIM Wonderful. You'll enjoy that. Dress speeches and scores of dinners. Here we are — in there. I'll see you downstairs.

SUSAN Timmy.

She kisses her fingertips and places them on his lips.

TIM See you when you're ready.

She goes into the loft bedroom. He dashes downstairs and straight to the bedroom door. He flings it open and throws the pants inside.

(*Frantic whisper*) I'm warning you, Claire! Get to hell out of here now or I'll break your bloody neck!

CLAIRE Oh, you are a devil. Why don't you get a real job?

The voice from behind him. He wheels around — CLAIRE *is sitting on the settle bed.*

TIM I'm warning you —

CLAIRE Daddy could get you a real job. He's on the governing body.

TIM You know what you're doing, don't you?

SUSAN'*s head appears over the rail.*

SUSAN Timmy, have you an iron?

He pulls the curtains across the settle bed.

TIM   Have I an iron what?

CLAIRE   (*Behind the curtain*) A smoothing iron, you eejit!

TIM   Oh, a smoothing iron? Sorry. Sorry.

SUSAN   Doesn't matter. I'll just hang this dress up for a while.

She withdraws.

CLAIRE   What would she plug it into? — The thatch? But you were going to tell me what I'm doing to you.

He finds his bowl and pours himself another drink.

TIM   You're doing two things to me. Not only are you ensuring I won't get tenure but that I may even lose the bloody miserable job.

SUSAN's *head appears again.*

SUSAN   Are you talking to somebody, Timmy?

TIM   Just to myself. Preparing a lecture.

SUSAN   You're quaint. And unique. And mine.

She blows a kiss and withdraws.

CLAIRE   'And mine.'

TIM   And secondly — secondly — in the space of half-an-hour you've succeeded in changing the — the — the very high regard I've had for you for a long, long time —

CLAIRE   Regard? Hah!

TIM   — into — into — into bloody hatred of you.

CLAIRE *sticks her head out.*

CLAIRE   If you ever had any regard — as you call it — for me, you certainly succeeded in concealing it from me!

The door suddenly blows open. CLAIRE's *head disappears.*

What was that?

TIM That damned door. It does that all the time.

CLAIRE The latch is faulty.

TIM I know.

CLAIRE Last night about midnight — Nora Dan and I had been sitting chatting and she had just left — I was about to go to bed when suddenly the door burst open and blew out the lamp. Then of course I thought I heard footsteps. And there I was in the pitch black, on the point of tears and groping about for matches. I didn't sleep until morning.

TIM Were you frightened?

CLAIRE Terrified.

TIM I'm sure. Did you ever have a sense that a place hates you? — That it actually feels malevolent towards you? I think this house hates me. I'm convinced that the genii of this house detest me.

CLAIRE 'This shaped all our souls.'

TIM Did you hear me? God, I'm ashamed of myself. But I'm serious about this place. Maybe it's because I feel no affinity at all with it and it knows that. In fact I think I hate it and all it represents. And it senses that. And that's why it's out to get me. D'you see that fireplace? Every time I go near that damned hearth it attacks me — spews its filthy smoke all over me. Maybe it's not malign in itself but it's the willing, the conniving instrument of a malign presence.

CLAIRE (*Laughs*) Rubbish!

TIM Right. Right. Just watch. Are you watching?

Her head appears.

CLAIRE Yes.

He looks at the fireplace. Panic — he sees the slip on the line.

TIM Where did that — ?! You're the malign spirit! I'll get you for this, Claire!

He dashes to the fireplace and grabs the slip. The
smoke bellows and envelops him.

Oh my God.

CLAIRE *exits by the front door.* TIM *is spluttering,*
wiping his eyes etc. when NORA DAN *enters. He*
sticks the slip into his pocket.

NORA Don't cut it until it cools down a bit. But maybe you
      don't care for homemade bread, do you?

TIM Thank you very much. I love it.

NORA You love it surely. And you have a bit of reek? Ah
      sure that aul' chimney never pulled right. Sure this
      aul' house is only a byre by right. People with any
      self-respect wouldn't live in it. Give some of this to
      Claire — she likes it, too. Is she about?

TIM She's having a sleep. She was awake all night.

NORA Was she, the creature? She's tired so.

TIM (*Calls*) Claire.

NORA Let her be if she's —

TIM She's awake now. Claire, it's —

He pulls back the curtains. She is not there. The
usual panic — where is she now?

She was there a second ago.

NORA And I see Jack out swimming in the tide. Lord, the
      comings and goings there is about the place! Weeks,
      months, maybe, and sure we don't see a soul; and
      then all of a sudden the place is throng. There's a fine
      big gentleman out walking the fields, the one that
      left his car down at the road. Oh, the man that owns
      that big car, that's the man with the money. Who
      would he be?

TIM *has been looking into the bedroom, up the stairs,*
out of the door — where is she now?

TIM   Dr Donovan.

NORA   He is indeed.

TIM   He's a senator, too.

NORA   A senator, too. Two big jobs. Wouldn't you know it to
        look at him. And the girl that's with him — she'll be
        his daughter?

TIM   That's right. That's Susan.

NORA   Susan surely. There you are. Oh, they'll be the bucks
        with the money. And what do they make of a poor,
        backward place like this?

TIM   They think it's unbelievable.

NORA   They do surely, the poor creatures. Ah, sure for all
        their money people like that have no sense at all.

        DONOVAN *enters energetically.*

DONOVAN That was good. I needed that. I'm restored now. (*To*
        NORA) Hello.

TIM   This is Dr Donovan. Nora Dan — a neighbour of mine.

DONOVAN How are you?

NORA   You're welcome, Doctor, welcome.

DONOVAN Thank you very much. May I tell you something,
        Nora Dan? You are a privileged woman living in a
        place like this.

NORA   I am surely, Doctor.

DONOVAN Privileged and blessed. Treasure it, Nora. Cherish it.
        (*Taking* TIM *aside*) I'll be speaking to the Chief Super-
        intendent tonight. I'll mention that case to him.

TIM   Case?

DONOVAN The battered wife — the French girl, Evette. Is Giroux
        her married name?

TIM   It's her maiden name.

DONOVAN What's the husband's name, the German thug?

TIM   Munich. Herr Munich.

DONOVAN Did you say Barney?

TIM   That's right. Herr Barney Munich.

DONOVAN Fine. Leave it with me. (*Aloud*) Forgive me, Nora. A
        small act of charity to atone for my sins. There's a
        young man having the time of his life swimming

down there.

NORA That's Jack. His people live in —

TIM He's a local. A fisherman. We call him Jack the Cod.

DONOVAN Jack the Cod! I love that. Call a man Jack the Cod and you tell me his name and his profession and that he's not very good at his profession. Concise, accurate and nicely malicious. Beautiful! Tell me, Nora, what would be the chances of picking up a cottage around here? Or even a site?

NORA Ah, sure what would a gentleman like you want with a place here?

DONOVAN Renewal, Nora. Restoration. Fulfilment. Back to the true centre.

NORA The true centre, surely.

DONOVAN Would there be anything on the market?

NORA Sure I can ask around.

DONOVAN Would you?

NORA A place about this size, maybe?

DONOVAN Ideal. There's just my daughter and myself.

NORA And not too dear. Surely, Doctor, I'll ask around.

DONOVAN You're a great woman.

> SUSAN *comes downstairs in a dressing gown. She has a towel in her hand.*

SUSAN The comb must be in your case, Daddy. (*To* NORA) Hello.

DONOVAN My daughter, Susie.

NORA You're very welcome.

> SUSAN *leaves the towel across the back of a chair.*

DONOVAN This splendid lady lives here. Nora Dan.

SUSAN Nora Dan?

NORA Nora Dan surely.

SUSAN You're the scrambler! She scrambles, Daddy!

DONOVAN She what?

SUSAN She goes scrambling on the sand dunes! (*To* NORA) Isn't that true? (*To* DONOVAN) She's Nora the Scrambler!

The Communication Cord

DONOVAN Jack the Cod I got instantly but Nora the Scrambler
         . . . Give me a clue. Has it to do with eggs? You keep
         hens!

NORA I keep hens, surely.

DONOVAN There! Beautiful!

NORA I have three.

SUSAN Daddy, you fool, I'm talking about motorbikes!

DONOVAN What motorbikes?

SUSAN Who's she?

*CLAIRE has entered carrying an armful of turf which
she deposits into the creel.*

TIM Thank you very much. That's fine. Just throw it there.
     Off you go.

SUSAN Who's that?

NORA (*To* DONOVAN) If I have any news for you, Doctor, I'll
      be straight back. (*As she passes* CLAIRE) You're the
      better of that wee sleep. You're looking grand now.

She leaves.

TIM That's all for today. Thank you very much.

CLAIRE That is a lie.

SUSAN Who is that woman, Daddy?

DONOVAN Shhh. Sordid story. Tell you later.

SUSAN Is she a foreigner?

TIM That's everything now, Evette. Nothing more for you
     to do, thank you.

SUSAN (*To* DONOVAN) Evette?

TIM I can manage everything else myself now.

SUSAN I want to know. Who is that woman?

DONOVAN Shhh. (*To* CLAIRE) *Pardonnez moi, Madame,* I — will —
         help — you. I — understand — perfectly.

SUSAN I don't understand at all! Who is this woman, Timmy?

*CLAIRE is now standing in front of TIM and as before
she begins to mime. She points towards the fireplace
and then strokes her legs and thighs.*

163

CLAIRE   Timothy, please, please, *mon . . .*

SUSAN   Why doesn't she speak English?

DONOVAN   She's French, darling; married to a German.

SUSAN   What the hell does she want?

TIM   Go on. Out you get. That's all for today. Off you go.

CLAIRE   *Mon . . .* please, Timothy . . . *mon . . .*

SUSAN   I heard her speaking English!

> TIM's *panic and confusion suddenly endow him with a desperate authority. He grabs* CLAIRE *by the arm and marches her to the door.*

TIM   Didn't you hear what I said? I said that's all for today.

CLAIRE   Please, Timothy, please . . .

TIM   (*To* DONOVAN) Wouldn't be difficult to analyze this discourse, Doctor? — Ha-ha-ha.

SUSAN   Is he drunk?

TIM   Off you go to your caravan, thank you very much. Your husband will be waiting for you. You'll have a meal to make for him. I'll see you the next time I'm here.

> *He has pushed her outside and closes the half-door behind her.*

CLAIRE   Please, Timothy —

TIM   No please Timothy about it. I've been more than patient with you.

CLAIRE   Ah!

> *She has spotted the slip in his pocket. She reaches across the door, retrieves it and, as before, holds it up in triumph.*

Merci, Timothy. Merci.

> *She runs away.* TIM *is momentarily at a loss. All he can do is brazen it out and continue to parade his bogus authority.*

SUSAN That was her slip, Timmy!

TIM Yes, that was her slip and I had it in my pocket.

SUSAN You —

TIM And why was it in my pocket? I will tell you why it was in my pocket. When she comes in to clean the house I allow her to do her own washing here because she lives in a caravan that has no light and no running water —

SUSAN But you have —

TIM — and when she finishes her washing she hangs her things on that line there even though she knows that the damned fire smokes and ruins her wash. And so just because she's a stupid and stubborn bitch and almost certainly animated by some inexplicable spite against me, what I have to do is run around after her and pull the things off the line and hang them on the backs of chairs. Look. (*Points to Susan's towel across a chair*) That's what I have to do.

SUSAN Timmy, that's mine. I left it there.

TIM Of course you left it there because it wouldn't fit into my pocket, would it? Right. You want to change, Doctor, don't you? In there, if you please. (*Hands* DONOVAN *his case and indicates the bedroom*) And you want a comb, Susan? (*Produces one from his pocket*) There you are. One comb. And, even though the company's good, time is running out and you've got to be in Sligo by six which means that you have got to be out of this house in five minutes at the very outside. Right?

DONOVAN (*Looking at his watch*) God, is that the time? You're right, Tim. We ought to get a move on.

TIM It occurred to me, Doctor, when you were asking Nora Dan about buying a site here, it occurred to me and I'm sure the thought crossed your own mind, too: what about one of my sites?

DONOVAN Actually that did cross my mind but I —

TIM Of course it did. Why wouldn't it? I'll tell you what: get yourself dressed up and we'll talk business then. All right?

DONOVAN Indeed. Excellent. You've no idea, Susie, how special, how very special all this is to me. See those posts and chains over there? Haven't seen those since I was a child. I'll explain them to you before we leave. You're right, Tim, absolutely right. This is the true centre.

> DONOVAN *goes into the bedroom,* SUSAN *stares at* TIM *in amazement.*

TIM An interesting discourse phenomenon that. Called statement transference. I never used the phrase 'This is the true centre' but by imputing the phrase to me, as the Doctor has just done, he both seeks confirmation for his own sentiments and suggests to listeners outside the duologue that he and I are unanimous in that sentiment . . . which we're not . . . (*his bogus authority suddenly deserts him*) . . . not at all . . . Oh my God . . . where's my bowl of vodka?

SUSAN Timmy, are you not well?

TIM I left a drink somewhere.

SUSAN This isn't your house, Timmy. You have no sites for sale.

TIM Where did I put it?

SUSAN And there is no running water in this house. And that — that — that French woman, whoever she is, what is she doing here with you?

TIM I thought I left it there.

> DONOVAN *emerges from the bedroom with the yellow pants in his hand.*

DONOVAN Sorry, I think these must be . . . (TIM *takes them from him*)

TIM Thank you very much, Doctor. I was just looking for them.

> DONOVAN *exits. Aware of* SUSAN's *very cold eye on him* TIM *does not know what to do with the pants. He begins to stuff them into one pocket. No, not that. He*

*looks at the line. No, not that. He begins to stuff them
into the other pocket.*

SUSAN They're your own, aren't they? Why don't you just
put them on?

TIM They're damp.

SUSAN You and I are going to have a business chat, too,
Timmy.

TIM Certainly. Any time that suits you.

SUSAN And that bloody fire doesn't smoke either!

TIM It doesn't smoke, does it not? You just watch this. Do
you see that fire? That fire loathes me!

*He goes to the fireplace and stares challengingly at
it. Nothing happens. Still staring at it he takes the
pants from his pocket and drapes them on the line.
Nothing happens.*

SUSAN Liar!

TIM True as God, every other time I did that, Susan, honest
to God —

*The sudden blow-down with the usual consequences.
He snatches the pants off the line.*

Oh my God.

SUSAN I hope it chokes you.

*She runs upstairs.
He goes through the usual routine with his glasses,
etc. When he has recovered he goes to the dresser to
refill his bowl.*

BARNEY THE BANKS, *the German, enters. As Nora
Dan has said, he is about the same age and build as
Jack; and he is apt to gulder.* TIM, *who has not yet
put on his glasses, assumes he is Jack.*

BARNEY Ah — hello! Finally we encounter — *ja*? At long
length.

167

TIM   Oh — hello. (*Softly*) I told you it wouldn't work, you
bastard you. (*Loudly*) Isn't it a beautiful day?
BARNEY   *Ja, ja.* Beautiful. Beautiful.

> *With both arms fully outstretched and using the
> index finger of both hands as pointers* TIM *signals
> to the bedroom and to the loft to indicate where*
> DONOVAN *and* SUSAN *are.*

TIM   (*Softly*) Doctor. Susan. Doctor. Susan.
BARNEY   I know you are here since I see the motorbike park-
ing outside.
TIM   Yes, parking away there. (*Softly*) It's all falling apart.
(*Pointing again*) Doctor. Susan. (*Loudly*) Welcome.

> BARNEY, *at first puzzled but now assuming that the
> outstretched arms and the upturned index fingers
> must be some form of local greeting, laughs and copies
> the gesture.*

BARNEY   Welcome? Ah, *ja, ja, ja!* Welcome! *Danke schön* —
thank you. And to you also. Welcome home to hand-
some Ballybeg. (*Slight bow*) My name is Willie —
TIM   (*Softly*) Munich — Munich — Munich — Willie
Munich. (*Loudly*) Good to see you again, Willie.
(*Remembering; softly*) No, it's not Willie — it's Barney
— Barney — Barney Munich. (*Loudly*) How have you
been keeping, Barney? (*Softly*) God, I think I'm going
off my head.
BARNEY   Going where? Leaving, *ja?*
TIM   (*Softly*) D'you know what I've just done? I've practi-
cally sold one of your father's fields to Dr Bollocks!
BARNEY   Dr Bollocks? He is selling — ?
TIM   (*Softly*) Shhh. And Claire's doing her damnedest to
ruin me. Oh, I'll get her, all right! But Susan smells a
rat. Susan's no fool.
BARNEY   (*Matching* TIM's *soft tone*) You talk too fast for —
TIM   (*Softly*) Gulder, man! You're supposed to gulder!
(*Loudly*) This is our first cathedral, isn't it? The ques-

tion is: are we worthy of it? (*Softly*) D'you know what she wants me to do? Take her scrambling! On Nora Dan's motorbike!

BARNEY Nora Dan?

TIM (*Softly*) Yes, yours! All right! But I can't even ride a pushbike.

BARNEY *Ja, ja,* I understand. Nora Dan good. But you talk quick, too quick for me.

TIM (*Loudly*) I beg your pardon, Barney. I'll slow down. (*Softly and very rapidly*) Listen carefully, Jack. You're a German thug called Barney Munich and you're married to Claire Harkin whose real name is Evette Giroux. You drink like a fish and beat the tar out of her and he's going to have you arrested. (*Loudly*) Yes, yes, this is indeed the true centre. (*Softly and very rapidly*) In real life you're Jack the Cod, a local fisherman, an eejit — he spotted you out swimming. And I let your wife, Evette Giroux — in real life, Claire — I let her do her washing here because you have no running water in the caravan and I have here — even though in fact I haven't — but I think he hasn't noticed, though sly puss Susan has. (*Loudly*) But if not the true centre, perhaps the true off-centre. Most definitely the true off-centre. (*Softly and very rapidly*) And I own all the land you can see around here and if Susan has her way they'll come back here tomorrow and spend the weekend here and even if I can talk her out of taking her scrambling today, she'll make sure I break my bloody neck at it tomorrow. And your wife persists in leaving her wet clothes on the line even though that damned fire smokes although it smokes only on me and nobody else but that's because it hates me and I hate it, hate the whole damned place, and I've got to go round after her, picking them up — (*Produces the pants from his pocket*) Look! Your wife's!

All of this speech has been delivered urgently into BARNEY's *ear.* BARNEY *has retreated before it and* TIM

169

has pursued him. BARNEY *is now quite nervous. He finds himself up against the door-frame and feels around for a defensive implement. His hand finds the flail. Now* TIM *thrusts the pants into his hands — so* BARNEY *now has the pants in one hand and the flail in the other.*

And now, I suppose, we're going to have your special Donegal midsummer orgy! Terrific, my friend! You have a wonderful sense of humour! (*Totally defeated, he slumps into a chair*) Oh my God, it's out of hand, Jack! I can't go on! It's all in pieces.

BARNEY (*Stiffly*) I come here just to talk to you business, Herr McNeilis, and not to —

TIM (*Suddenly impassioned again; shouts*) You're McNeilis! (*Softly*) You're McNeilis. I'm Gallagher — Gallagher — Gallagher! (*And with both index fingers he jabs at his temple each time he says the word 'Gallagher'*)

BARNEY (*Copying the gesture*) Gallagher — *ja*?

TIM Yes. *Ja*. Gallagher. Gallagher. Tim Gallagher — isn't it? I hardly know myself. God, Jack, get me a drink. There's vodka over there.

BARNEY Vodka? Ah — vodka! *Danke schön*. I like little vodka. Thank you. You are kind. Where is vodka?

TIM On the dresser.

BARNEY Sorry?

TIM Gulder.

BARNEY The gulder? — (*Finds the bottle*) Ah, the gulder, yes. It is a handsome gulder, too. I like it.

TIM What are you raving about, Jack?

BARNEY I come here to talk to you business, Herr McNeilis. But some other day. I write you letter three times from the address Nora Dan give me because I wish to sell this house from you. Are you receiving my letter?

TIM (*Wearily*) Yes . . . yes . . .

BARNEY That is good.

BARNEY *hands* TIM *a bowl of vodka and has a bowl himself.*

Vodka is handsome. Ah — I learn a toast from this
English book I read last night. What is it? *Ja*, I know.
(*Bowl in one hand, pants in the other; both raised:*) 'To us
lovers everywhere!'

TIM (*Wearily*) Cut it out, Jack.

DONOVAN *enters. He is now wearing his dress suit.*

BARNEY Good? *Ja*? 'To us lovers everywhere!'

DONOVAN It looks as if this is not the right moment.

TIM Doctor, this is — this is Barney Munich, the German
I mentioned to you.

DONOVAN I guessed as much.

TIM (*Whispers to* DONOVAN) He's on the bottle. Careful.

BARNEY (*Slight bow*) My name is Willie Hausenbach.

DONOVAN It certainly is not.

BARNEY Welcome to handsome Ballybeg, Dr Bollocks.

And as before BARNEY *stretches his arms out, as he
has learned from* TIM; *index fingers pointing upwards,
arms waving up and down in the welcome gesture.*

TIM Christ, Jack — ! (*Suddenly realizing*) Christ, it's not —

DONOVAN My name, sir, happens to be Donovan, Dr Donovan.
Senator Donovan.

TIM (*To* DONOVAN) He's drunk. He's violent. Humour him.

BARNEY I am sorry — my English it is too bad. You are a doctor of medicine?

DONOVAN I am.

BARNEY May I speak private to you, Doctor?

DONOVAN I'd prefer if you didn't.

BARNEY (*Whispering*) May I say to you, Doctor, I think your
friend, Herr McNeilis, is —

DONOVAN Gallagher?

BARNEY Correct, Doctor. Correct. (*Touching his head*) Just a little
bit gallagher. He says himself so to me. He tells me,
'I'm gallagher — gallagher — gallagher'. So we take
care, Doctor — *ja*? We talk to him soft — *ja*? (*Aloud*)
I come to speak to Herr McNeilis to buy his house

to me because I love it so. But perhaps some other day —

susan, in formal dress, is coming down the stairs.

DONOVAN Go back up, Susie, please. (*To* BARNEY) What were you saying?

susan continues down.

BARNEY I say I speak to your friend some other day perhaps when he is not so — not so frisky. Please to give him this.

He hands the pants to DONOVAN.

DONOVAN What's this?
BARNEY Thank you.
DONOVAN These are Mrs Munich's.

He hands them back to BARNEY.

TIM (*To* DONOVAN) Don't anger him.
BARNEY Mrs — ? Ah, your wife.
DONOVAN Susie is my daughter.
BARNEY (*Bows*) Handsome daughter. Fräulein Bollocks.

BARNEY *hands the pants to* SUSAN.

SUSAN They aren't mine. They're his! (*Tim's*)
DONOVAN Tim's?
SUSAN Yes!
DONOVAN How do you know?

SUSAN *hands the pants to* TIM.

SUSAN They're perfectly dry now!
BARNEY (*To* SUSAN) Welcome to handsome Ballybeg.

And again he mimes the welcome gesture.

TIM Careful — he's getting madder.
SUSAN God, he's obscene! (*Barney*)
BARNEY *Ja, Ja,* very, very.
TIM D'you see?
SUSAN Timmy, whose are they?
TIM Evette's.
SUSAN That French tramp?
TIM His wife's.

TIM *hands the pants to* BARNEY.

DONOVAN Tim's right.
SUSAN How do you know?
DONOVAN He told me.
SUSAN (*To* BARNEY) Your wife — is called — Evette?
BARNEY Ah. *Ja-ja-ja-ja.* Evette. (*Bows again*) Welcome, Evette.
DONOVAN Of course she's called Evette.
SUSAN (*To* TIM) And how did you get them?
TIM I had them in my pocket. Your father was there. He saw it all.
SUSAN (*To* DONOVAN) You were there?
TIM No, I'm wrong. He was only there for the . . .

He imitates Claire's bra mime.

DONOVAN That'll do — that'll do — that'll do! I am not going to argue any longer with a drunkard, a wife-beater, and very probably a man of unnatural vice.
BARNEY Thank you, Doctor.
DONOVAN And I will make it my business this very evening to see that an end is put to his vile gallop. Those are the property of your unfortunate wife, sir.
BARNEY Perhaps I —
DONOVAN And please leave this decent Irish home immediately. You are going to learn very soon, my friend, that there are still places in this world, little pockets of decency and decorum, where your wealth means

nothing at all.

BARNEY (*Puzzled*) I leave them on the gulder for when he is not so gallagher.

NORA DAN *enters.*

NORA I just remembered, Doctor: there's a site near the main road that might suit you; but the man that owns it is away in the town today. Oh, Lord, but you're looking swanky, Doctor!

DONOVAN Thank you, Nora.

NORA And Susan! Oh dear, oh dear, you're beau-ti-ful. Isn't that (*dress*) lovely. You paid a big penny for that. Oh, yous'll stand out, the pair of you, with all those big toffs tonight. And Barney! How are you, Barney?

BARNEY Good, Nora, thank you.

NORA Isn't she just beau-ti-ful?

BARNEY Fräulein Evette? *Ja, ja,* beau-ti-ful.

NORA Would you look at the eyes of him, Doctor! He'll be off with her before you know.

DONOVAN (*Taking* NORA *aside*) Nora, a moment, please.

SUSAN I want to talk to you before I leave, Timmy.

TIM Certainly.

DONOVAN The balance is very delicate, Nora. Don't trifle with him.

NORA Is it Barney the Banks?

DONOVAN Is that what you call him? Of course — because of his wealth! Well named indeed. But be careful, Nora. Unsavoury material that.

NORA Unsavoury surely, Doctor.

DONOVAN I'll talk to the Chief Superintendent about him tonight. Now about the business of the site: don't bother pursuing that, thank you all the same.

NORA Sure I knew that a gentleman like yourself wouldn't want to live in a backward place like this.

DONOVAN Tim has made me an offer.

NORA Tim?

DONOVAN Maybe his own place here. Not a word.

NORA He's selling you this house?

DONOVAN Shhh. Or at least a site. I don't want to rush him.

BARNEY Well, please, I think I leave now. Goodbye. (*To* TIM) Again perhaps we will talk at long length. Nora.

NORA I'll see you later, Barney.

BARNEY Please, yes. (*To* SUSAN) *Auf Wiedersehen*, Evette.

He leaves. The big door is left open, the half-door shut.

SUSAN I'm leaving now, Daddy.

DONOVAN Come here till I show you these first, Susie (*the posts and chains*). Brilliant idea to retain them, Tim. Look, Susie. What happened was this. I drive my cow through the door here — or my two cows if I'm a man of substance.

NORA A man of substance indeed.

DONOVAN There was an old Irish expression for that, wasn't there? What was it? — 'As rich as a woman with two cows' — wasn't that it? Now, if our little scenario takes place in, say, the early nineteenth century, then our fireplace will be there (*centre of the floor*) with the smoke going straight up through a hole in the roof; and that is why the modest but aesthetically satisfying furnishings in the traditional Irish kitchen are always placed along the walls, leaving this area completely free for moving around.

All eyes are on DONOVAN *when* JACK *appears at the half-door* — *pretending he is the German. Only* TIM *sees him. Throughout part of* DONOVAN's *monologue* TIM *and* JACK *mime the following exchange:*

JACK: *I'm the German. I'm coming in, OK?*

TIM: *No, no. Go away. Go away.*

JACK: *What's wrong? I love your house. I want to buy it.*

TIM: *For God's sake — go! The German was here.*

JACK: *Look. My cheque book. My pen. What money do you want?*

TIM: *Please, Jack! Go away!*

175

JACK: *And look at the time! Your time is up!*
TIM: *Please!*

NORA   Moving around surely, Doctor.
DONOVAN But let's bring our little scenario forward in time,
        let's say to the turn of the century. Right. The fire-
        place has been moved up to the gable. This is now
        the heart of the home. That's where we warm our-
        selves. That's where we cook. That's where we kneel
        and pray. That's where we gather at night to tell our
        folk tales and our ancient sagas. Correct, Tim?
TIM   Our ancient sagas surely, Doctor.

        At the very end of the mime above SUSAN *happens to
        glance at* TIM. JACK *immediately crouches down behind
        the half-door. But* TIM *is caught making his final
        impassioned 'Please!'. Aware that* SUSAN *is now look-
        ing at him, he converts the gesture into blowing a
        kiss to her.*

DONOVAN So let us imagine it is night-time. Granny is asleep in
        the settle bed. My wife is knitting by the fireside, the
        children in a circle at her feet. I enter with my most
        valuable worldly possession — my cow! She knows
        the routine perfectly. With her slow and assured gait
        she crosses over there and stands waiting for me
        with her head beside the post where I have already
        placed a battle of hay. An interesting word that —
        'battle' — it must be Irish, Tim?
TIM   Scottish. Sixteenth century.
DONOVAN Is it? Anyhow. I pick up my milking pail and my
        milking stool and I join her. I lift up the chain — (*he
        demonstrates*) and bring it gently round her neck and
        secure it with the little clasp here — like this. Then I
        milk her. And when I'm finished she'll stand here
        for another hour, perhaps two hours, just chewing
        her cud and listening to the reassuring sounds of a
        family preparing to go to bed. Then she will lie down
        and go to sleep. A magical scene, isn't it? It's a little

scene that's somehow central to my psyche.

NORA You're as good as a concert, Doctor. Isn't he?

SUSAN Come on, Daddy. You're going to miss that dinner.

NORA Sure they'll keep it warm for you, won't they? (*Going to the door*) Aren't the days getting very short?

SUSAN goes towards the stairs.

TIM Let me get your case.

SUSAN I can manage.

NORA (*Looking out*) Barney the Banks is a very smart man on his feet. The lights are on in his caravan already.

SUSAN (*To* TIM) 'No light and no running water' — hah!

TIM Susan, I've got to explain to you —

SUSAN I don't think you can — even if you were sober.

TIM When I was at the door there, waving, that was to keep Jack McNeilis out.

DONOVAN (*Tentatively*) Tim . . . ?

SUSAN He's here?

TIM Yes.

SUSAN What for?

TIM He's somewhere out there waving his cheque book because time's running out.

DONOVAN Can you come here for a minute, Tim?

TIM Coming, Doctor.

SUSAN His cheque book?

TIM He wants to buy this house.

SUSAN Why would he buy his own house?

TIM Because he's a German. Don't move.

He dashes over to DONOVAN *who is squatting on the ground — as he demonstrated — and chained to a post. Whether he is crouching down or standing up (never to his full height) he is chained in such a way that he is locked into a position facing the wall. Only with great difficulty and pain can he see over his shoulder — and then only a portion of the kitchen.*

DONOVAN Damned stupid of me. Don't seem to be able to get

177

this clasp opened.

TIM crouches down beside him.

TIM   Is this it?
DONOVAN   Press it and it should open.
TIM   No.
DONOVAN   No — what?
TIM   The spring's broken. It's stuck.
DONOVAN   It was working perfectly a second ago.
TIM   It's getting dark in here. Maybe if you stood up . . .

They rise together.

SUSAN   Are you coming, Daddy?
DONOVAN   That is not a very intelligent question, darling, is it?
— Am I coming when I'm demonstrably stationary.
(*To* TIM) Are you attempting to choke me?
TIM   Sorry. I was only —
DONOVAN   Nora Dan!
NORA   What is it, Doctor?

She goes to him.

DONOVAN   (*To* TIM) Stand back, will you, please, and let Nora Dan
open it. (*To* NORA) Would you open that clip, please.
NORA   Open it surely, Doctor.

*SUSAN runs upstairs. Now TIM, NORA DAN and
DONOVAN are in a huddle together.*

Now — let me see. What did you do, Doctor?
DONOVAN   Isn't it apparent that I have secured myself to this post?
NORA   You have surely. And that aul' chain's that dirty and
rusty it has your good suit ruined. Wait till I wipe —

She begins dusting him vigorously.

DONOVAN   Never — never — never mind the clothes! Just open

178

the clasp!

TIM You press that lever.

NORA What lever?

TIM That thing there.

NORA Sure I haven't had a cow this forty years. It's terrible dark here. (*To* TIM) Would you light the lamp?

TIM Yes.

TIM *goes to the table and lights the lamp. As he does:*

NORA You're grand, Doctor. Just grand. We'll have you free in a minute. Sure this is no place for a gentleman like yourself, tethered there like a brute beast.

DONOVAN I'm quite comfortable actually except when I — when I try to see over —

NORA Don't stir yourself. Just stand still. Sure how can we milk you if you start kicking and flicking your tail about — Ha-ha-ha.

DONOVAN Ha-ha-ha.

TIM *has lit the lamp and is about to lift it off the table when* CLAIRE, *serene and smiling, enters, closing both doors behind her.*

TIM Oh my God.

CLAIRE (*Softly, as she passes him*) I understand perfectly.

And without stopping she crosses the floor and goes into the bedroom. Just as she is about to enter the bedroom SUSAN *emerges from the loft with her case. She gets a glimpse of a figure disappearing into the bedroom and she dashes down the stairs.*

NORA Bring it over here, Tim.

TIM Coming — coming.

SUSAN Somebody's just gone into that room!

NORA That's grand. Now we'll see what we're at.

SUSAN It's that French tramp! She's back!

NORA What's that?

TIM (*Sings*) 'When the lights go on again . . . '

DONOVAN It's not exactly a celebration, Tim, is it?

SUSAN She's in there! I saw her! She's in there now!

NORA Now I can see. Hold it steady there, Tim.

TIM All right?

NORA It's that wee clasp surely. God bless us and save us, I can't get a budge out of it.

SUSAN drops her case in the middle of the floor and proclaims:

SUSAN That French tramp is in that bedroom! What is the French tramp doing in that bedroom?

DONOVAN Will you shut up, Susie! I am in some pain!

SUSAN I will not shut up!

DONOVAN Aaagh! You're severing my head, woman!

NORA Stand still, you brute you, or I'll hop the stick off you!

DONOVAN Madam, I am not an animal!

NORA You're not indeed, Doctor. I'm sorry.

SUSAN dashes to TIM.

SUSAN I want to know what the hell's going on between you and that woman in there! And I want to know now, Timmy!

The big door suddenly bursts open — JACK, pretending he is the German, and guldering:

JACK I hear you sell your house, Herr Gallagher — *ja*? I give you a fortune to buy it.

The moment the door opens the lamp, which TIM is holding in his hand, flickers a few times and now dies. SUSAN screams. For three seconds the stage is in total darkness. During this total blackout:

NORA Will you close that big door, Barney! You've blown the lamp out!

DONOVAN Get that foreign brute out of here!

NORA Has anybody got a box of matches?

> *Now sneak the lights up to half. The assumption will
> be that the stage is still in total darkness. The actors
> behave as if it were.* JACK *is now inside and closes
> both doors behind him.* CLAIRE *has entered from the
> bedroom.*

SUSAN Daddy?!

DONOVAN You're quite safe, darling. Just keep away from the German.

NORA Have you got the lamp, Tim?

CLAIRE (*Into* TIM's *ear*) I understand perfectly.

SUSAN (*Pointing in the wrong direction*) I hear her! She's there!

JACK A million Deutsche Mark, Herr Gallagher. I hoffer you any monies you hask for.

TIM Oh my God.

> *Blackout. Music.*

ACT TWO

The action is continuous. Everybody is in the same position as at the end of Act One. And everybody wants to establish his/her own bearings and then the bearings of everybody else.

JACK   (*Loudly*) A million Deutsche Mark, Herr Gallagher. I hoffer you any monies you hask for.

TIM   Oh my God.

SUSAN   Where are you, Daddy?

DONOVAN   Here, darling. (*Trying to turn round*) Oooh.

TIM   (*Whispers*) Jack?

JACK   (*Loudly*) Herr Gallagher? *Ja*?

TIM   (*Whispers*) Stop that German stuff!

DONOVAN   Put that damned light on!

NORA   Have you got the lamp, Tim?

TIM   I think it's on the table. (*Whispers*) Jack?

> CLAIRE *is now beside* TIM. *She nibbles his ear.*

Who's that? Who's that?

CLAIRE   (*Whispers*) It's unbelievable, isn't it?

TIM   Oh, hello, Susan. How are you?

CLAIRE   (*French accent*) 'ello, my big 'andsome Jack.

TIM   (*Whispers*) Claire, damn you — !

> *She slips away from him.* NORA DAN *is groping at the table.*

NORA   It's not here, Tim.

TIM   It must be.

SUSAN   Daddy?

DONOVAN   Over here, Susie.

> JACK *is feeling in front of him, trying to go towards* TIM's *voice.*

JACK Herr Gallagher?
TIM (*Whispers*) Cut it out, Jack!
NORA No, it's not here. Has anybody got a match?

> JACK's *groping hands now find a figure —* CLAIRE's.

JACK Susan?
TIM There are matches on the mantelpiece, Nora.
JACK Susan? It's Jack. How's it all going?
CLAIRE It's not Susan. It's Evette.
JACK You're here? Christ!

> *Again she slips away.*

When did you arrive . . . ?
NORA You get them for me, Tim.
TIM I can't — that fire attacks me.
NORA Attacks you? What are you blathering about?

> JACK's *hands now find another figure —* SUSAN's.

JACK Hold on, Evette. When did you — ?
SUSAN Take your filthy hands off me, you Hun! Daddy!
JACK Susan, it's —
SUSAN Daddy!
DONOVAN Protect my daughter, Tim! Protect my only child! Oooh.

> SUSAN *finds her way to her father.* CLAIRE *slips upstairs.* TIM *and* JACK *find one another.*

TIM Jack?
JACK Herr Gallagher!
TIM Drop that accent.
NORA Have you no matches, Barney?
TIM (*German accent*) Sorry. No. I don't have none matches.

JACK   I'm supposed to be the German, you fool!

TIM   You're not Willie Hausenbach anymore!

JACK   Who?

TIM   Barney Munich — Barney the Banks. You're an eejit.

JACK   *I'm* an eejit?!

TIM   Jack the Cod — a local fisherman — a fool — you can't fish for nuts.

JACK   Tim —

TIM   The German has been here! Get out, man!

JACK   Tim —

TIM   And the Doctor thinks I'm going to sell this house to him, or at least a site —

SUSAN   Please put the lights on!

TIM   — and I'm an expert scrambler and they're both coming back tomorrow for the weekend and Hausenbach's a transvestite and —

JACK   Shut up and listen to me!

NORA   Will none of yous give me a hand?

JACK   Your time is up! Get them all out!

TIM   I can't. The Doctor's anchored to the wall.

JACK   Evette's here, man!

TIM   Don't I know. Chewing my ear all evening —

JACK   Evette?

NORA DAN strikes a match.

NORA   Ah, that's a bit better. (*To* TIM) And you had the lamp after all.

TIM   Where?

NORA   Where, he says. Isn't it in your hand! God bless us, Tim, are you soft in the head? Take the globe off it.

DONOVAN   I have been wronged.

NORA   You have been wronged surely, Doctor. But we'll soon get you sorted. (*The lamp is now lit*) That's grand. Now we know where we're at. (*Seeing* JACK) And it's you's in it, Jack? God forgive you imitating poor Barney the Banks like that.

She places the lamp on the table.

SUSAN (*To* JACK) What are you doing here?

DONOVAN Who is it, Susie?

TIM It's Jack the Cod.

JACK What's that man doing down there?

SUSAN That's Daddy.

NORA He was imitating a cow for us — weren't you? And he did it very well, too.

JACK Doctor Donovan?!

NORA The Doctor surely. He's a wee bit cross, the creature; naturally.

SUSAN For God's sake, Jack, help him. He's chained there.

DONOVAN It's the village blacksmith I need — not the village idiot!

NORA (*To* JACK) A wee bit upset, the soul. But he'll come round.

JACK (*To* TIM) Where's Evette?

TIM Evette?

SUSAN The French woman?

JACK Yes.

SUSAN You've met her?

JACK Yes. Have you?

SUSAN She's here! With him!

JACK With Tim?

SUSAN With Tim indeed — instead of in her husband's caravan. No wonder he (TIM) looks so hangdog!

JACK Evette's husband is here, too?

SUSAN Why wouldn't he be? He lives here!

JACK Good God!

NORA Will yous all keep quiet and listen to me. I've the solution to the whole thing.

DONOVAN Ooooh.

SUSAN Nora Dan, will you please go on your bike and get help somewhere?

NORA That's what I'm going to do. The man with the smartest pair of hands about here is Barney the Banks — he'll have the Doctor free in no time at all. (*To* TIM) Slip you over and get him.

DONOVAN I will not be rescued by that brute!

NORA Indeed and you will, Doctor, and glad to be, too. (*To*

TIM) Away you go on the bike. The caravan's just across the banks.

SUSAN (*To* TIM) Will you please hurry!

TIM I hardly know him. I couldn't ask him.

NORA You couldn't ask him. Well, I'll ask him then. Come on. Give me a lift over.

TIM Me?!

JACK Off you go, expert scrambler.

SUSAN Will you go, Timmy!

NORA He thinks I'm nervous, the creature.

TIM You're terrified!

NORA You don't know Nora Dan, son.

TIM I've no licence.

NORA He has no licence.

She takes his arm and leads him to the door.

Sure nobody about here has either licence or insurance. (*To* JACK) Mind the lamp when I open the door. The draught in this aul' byre would clean corn. Come on, Tim. Barney'll be glad to help.

TIM Jack, please —

SUSAN Will you hurry, Timmy!

NORA We'll be back in five minutes.

TIM If we're not, you'll know —

SUSAN Go on, Timmy! Move!

NORA leads TIM *outside and closes both doors behind her.* SUSAN *sits dejectedly on a stool.* JACK *puts the lamp back on the table. Sound of the motorbike starting up, cutting out, starting up again. Furious revving — the engine stutters — more revving. The bike moves off erratically.*

DONOVAN Oooh.

JACK Nora Dan should be wearing a helmet.

SUSAN And Timmy.

JACK Well . . .

JACK *now moves around the kitchen. His concern is: where is Evette?*

DONOVAN I'm getting very cold. Are there any spirits in the house?

JACK (*To* SUSAN) There's vodka there somewhere.

He peers into the bedroom and whispers:

Evette?

SUSAN *pours a drink and brings it to* DONOVAN.

DONOVAN What's that?

SUSAN Vodka.

DONOVAN I hate vodka.

SUSAN That's all there is.

DONOVAN Have they far to go?

SUSAN I don't know.

DONOVAN Where's this caravan?

SUSAN I don't know.

DONOVAN You're such a consolation, Susie. Could you at least manage to keep the fire going? — Oooh.

She returns to her stool.

SUSAN I think I'm going to cry, Jack.

JACK No, you're not.

SUSAN And everything was going so perfectly. Daddy just loved the place — thought it was unbelievable.

JACK *peers up the well of the stairs.*

JACK (*Whispers*) Evette?

SUSAN I was even planning to come back this way tomorrow and spend the weekend here. Timmy was all for it; thought it was a great idea. Do you think he meant it, Jack?

JACK Of course.

SUSAN   Why would he say it if he didn't mean it? I just don't
        know anymore. He sounded as if he meant it. He even
        promised he'd take me scrambling on Nora Dan's bike.

JACK   My bike, you mean.

SUSAN   No, Nora Dan's.

JACK   Nora Dan has no bike, for God's sake. That's my bike.
        He told you it was his? The fool can't even drive!

SUSAN   But he's away driving on it now . . . (*Concern*) My
        God, he'll have an accident, Jack!

JACK *peers into settle bed and whispers:*

JACK   Evette?

SUSAN   (*Anger*) My God, I hope he does! Oh, the liar! And of
        course, of course she's not Nora the Scrambler! How
        did I believe that?! — Ex-champion of Donegal! Oh
        my God! Is there running water in this house?

JACK   No.

SUSAN   Another lie! And I'm sure you have a smoothing iron,
        haven't you?

JACK   Yes.

SUSAN   More lies! My God, I hate him! And d'you know what
        he told me, too? — He does her washing!

JACK   Nora Dan's?

SUSAN   That woman he has living with him here — that
        French tramp! Lies, lies, lies — that's all he has told
        me since I got here!

DONOVAN Susie?

SUSAN   I'm putting turf on the fire, Daddy. (*To* JACK) Why
        didn't you tell me he was such a skilled liar, Jack?

JACK *now goes to her.*

JACK   She was here in the house when you arrived?

SUSAN   Walking around as if she owned the place; chatting
        and laughing with Daddy; flirting openly with Timmy.
        He wants to humiliate me, Jack!

TIM   Describe her.

SUSAN   She's common looking, vulgar, brazen manner —

JACK About 28, 29?

SUSAN Yes.

JACK Average height?

SUSAN Yes.

JACK Blonde?

SUSAN It's not natural.

JACK Round-faced?

SUSAN Do you know her?

JACK Absolutely.

SUSAN She has hardly any English.

JACK She was born and bred in Omagh.

SUSAN Her name is Evette.

JACK Her name is Claire Harkin.

SUSAN She's married to a German.

JACK She's single. She is in the English Department with Master Timothy.

SUSAN But I met her husband!

JACK In fact she's an old girlfriend of Master Timothy's from years back.

SUSAN So all that stuff about . . . ? And everything he said about . . . ? And that German character isn't her husband at . . . ? Oh, the bastard! The rotten, lying bastard! (*Cries*) There! I told you I was going to cry!

JACK Shhh.

SUSAN I hope he never gets his bloody thesis finished! I hope they kick him out of that miserable bloody job! I hope he comes off that bike and breaks his bloody neck!

JACK (*His arms around her*) Shhh.

SUSAN God, how I loathe him!

JACK I know — I know.

SUSAN I don't really mean that at all, Jack — I mean about his thesis and his miserable job.

JACK Of course you don't.

SUSAN But I mean all the rest.

JACK I know — shhh — I know — I know. (*A quick furtive look at his watch*) This has been a very unfortunate experience, Susan. You have been treated shabbily. But the important thing now is to protect you from

189

further hurt.

DONOVAN Oooh.

JACK (*Offering handkerchief*) Here.

SUSAN Thanks.

JACK May I tell you something?

SUSAN What?

JACK Many, many years ago, Susan, you and I were fortunate enough to experience and share an affection that is still one of my most sustaining memories. And when we broke up — and I can tell you this now; indeed I embrace the opportunity to make this declaration, however unhappy, however unlikely the circumstances for this kind of confession — but when we broke up — and I suspect that you would be the first to admit that I wasn't exclusively to blame for that unfortunate episode — but when it happened — and I say this now very deliberately and with absolute sincerity — when it happened, Susan, a part of me died.

SUSAN Oh, Jack. (*Sobs*) I'm off again.

JACK Does that sound maudlin?

SUSAN No.

JACK Is this the wrong time to say it?

SUSAN I thought it all meant nothing to you.

JACK We could have been quite a pair.

SUSAN Could we?

JACK We're alike in so many ways.

SUSAN Are we?

JACK So alike it's . . . uncanny. Susan, will you trust me?

DONOVAN Oooh.

SUSAN Poor Daddy's in agony.

JACK Will you trust me, Susan?

SUSAN Yes.

JACK You must leave here immediately.

SUSAN But Daddy's — !

JACK I'll release him. But you must both leave the minute he's free. What I'm really talking about, Susan, is your safety. You must be protected from Tim.

SUSAN My safety?

JACK   That's what brought me here today — to warn you.
DONOVAN   What's keeping them, Susie?
SUSAN   They'll be back soon. (*To* JACK) Warn me?
JACK   He's had a breakdown.
SUSAN   Timmy? When?
JACK   Acute hallucinatory trauma. Cracked up suddenly last Saturday night. We were at a party. Went crazy. Tried to demolish the house — literally. It's a combination of several factors: drinking too much; pressure of work; that damned thesis he's never going to finish. Those lies you talk about — they're not lies to him — he believes them. The psychiatrist says he must have six months' total rest.
SUSAN   Oh, poor Timmy.
JACK   Poor Timmy indeed. But the important thing is: you must be gone before he returns. Right?
SUSAN   Yes.
JACK   (*Rising*) They'll soon be back. Bring that lamp over, will you?

He stoops down and puts his hand on her face.

Trust me, Susan, will you?
SUSAN   Absolutely.

He kisses her forehead.

JACK   Thank you, Susan.

He goes to DONOVAN. *She follows with the lamp.*

Well, Doctor. You got yourself tied up somehow, did you?
DONOVAN   Do you really think so?
JACK   Let's see can we help you.
DONOVAN   Are you a blacksmith?
JACK   Not quite. But we'll soon have you freed. Let's have a look. This is the trouble, is it?
SUSAN   It's that clasp. It won't open.

DONOVAN Who is this?

SUSAN It's Jack, Daddy.

DONOVAN Jack the Cod — wonderful! The village idiot — why not!

SUSAN Jack McNeilis, Daddy. You remember Jack, don't you?

JACK How are you, Doctor?

DONOVAN What's he doing here?

SUSAN He's trying to help you.

DONOVAN What's keeping Tim and that female cattle drover.

SUSAN She said they'd be back in five minutes.

DONOVAN They've gone at least an hour. The circulation isn't reaching the feet. I've lost all feeling in the feet and legs.

JACK Yes — it's that hook. If I could prize it open — (*To* SUSAN) There's a pair of pliers in the drawer of the dresser.

DONOVAN Careful!

JACK Sorry — sorry. These chains haven't been used for over sixty years, not since my father was a boy.

DONOVAN What was your father doing here?

JACK He lived here until he was seven. (*To* SUSAN) Thanks.

DONOVAN So Tim bought it from your father?

JACK I'm afraid Tim has been telling you all a lot of fibs, Doctor. I've just been explaining to Susan: Tim's a very sick man.

SUSAN He's had a breakdown.

DONOVAN God.

JACK This is my house. I let Tim have it for the weekend.

DONOVAN Do you hear this, Susie?

SUSAN Jack's just told me. It's terrible. Apparently he can get very violent.

DONOVAN Good God. The bloody German wasn't so slow.

JACK He spotted it?

DONOVAN He certainly did.

JACK I suppose a stranger would see the symptoms more clearly. Anyhow, the important thing now is to get you freed. Could you move your head just slightly . . . ? That's it! That's better! Now if I can prize this open . . . (*As he works*) Wonderful place this, isn't it,

Doctor? You're an antiquarian yourself, aren't you?

DONOVAN Careful . . .

JACK You're all right. Just sit still . . .

> CLAIRE *comes downstairs, goes to the clothes line and hangs up tights. She then goes into the bedroom.*

Yes, this is where we all come from, isn't it? This is our first cathedral. This shaped our souls.

DONOVAN This determined our first priorities! This is our native simplicity! Don't give me that shit!

SUSAN Daddy!

DONOVAN Forgive me, Susie. (*To* JACK) Stop mouthing, you fool. This is the greatest dump in all — Aaagh! My neck! My neck!

JACK Sorry. You —

DONOVAN You've pierced my neck!

JACK I'm sorry, Doctor, but you moved your —

DONOVAN Look at the blood! Get him away from me!

SUSAN (*To* JACK) Maybe we'd better —

DONOVAN Keep that fool away from me, Susie!

SUSAN We'll wait for the others, Jack.

DONOVAN Get me something to bind the wound!

> SUSAN *dashes into the centre of the kitchen, looks around in panic, sees the tights on the line, grabs them and returns to* DONOVAN.

Oh God, dear God, let me survive this night.

JACK (*To* DONOVAN) I'm sorry, Doctor. It was an accident.

DONOVAN Leave me. Leave me.

SUSAN There you are, Daddy. That's all I can find.

DONOVAN (*As he wraps the tights around his neck*) Thank you. Now please leave me.

> SUSAN *takes* JACK's *arm and leads him away.*

JACK He moved his bloody head just as I was —

SUSAN I know — I know. He's better left alone.

DONOVAN   (*Sings*) 'Abide with me; fast falls the eventide;
            The darkness deepens; Lord, with me abide
            When other helpers fail, and comforts flee,
            Help of the helpless, O abide with me!'

After the first line of the hymn:

JACK   God, what a day!
SUSAN   What's keeping the others? Didn't Nora Dan say
         they'd —

         She suddenly breaks off — she hears CLAIRE *singing
         the hymn with* DONOVAN.

SUSAN   Listen!
JACK   What?
SUSAN   There she is! Evette — Claire — she's in there!
JACK   Where?
SUSAN   In that room there!

         JACK *dashes to the bedroom door.*

JACK   Come out at once, Claire. I know you're in there. (*To*
         SUSAN) Give me that lamp. (*To* CLAIRE) This nonsense
         has got to end now.

         SUSAN *is crossing with the lamp when the big door
         bursts open. The lamp flickers and dies.* DONOVAN
         stops singing.

         Dammit — that bloody latch!
SUSAN   Jaaaack . . . ?
JACK   You're perfectly all right, Susan. Just stand where
         you are. Don't move.
DONOVAN Put that light on!
SUSAN   Please, Jack . . .
DONOVAN What are you doing, McNeilis?
SUSAN   Daddy?
DONOVAN Susie, come over here, darling — oooh . . .

JACK Keep calm, Susan. Everything's in hand.

SUSAN I'm frightened, Jack.

DONOVAN I'm warning you, McNeilis — lay one finger on that child and —

JACK I'm looking for the lamp, Doctor. Where are you, Susan?

> EVETTE *enters. She is a sophisticated, stylish woman in her early thirties. She is carrying a small weekend case. She is French but her English is perfect.*

SUSAN Here. I'm here.

JACK Where? Keep talking.

SUSAN Hello.

EVETTE Hello.

JACK Hello — hello.

EVETTE Hello, Jack.

JACK Good. Again — again.

EVETTE Hello — hello — hello — is that enough?

SUSAN Who's that?

JACK Have you any matches?

EVETTE I have a lighter.

JACK Good.

SUSAN It's her! (*Pointing in the wrong direction*) There she is! Catch her!

> JACK *reaches out and grabs the figure beside him* (EVETTE).

JACK Now, Claire.

EVETTE What are you doing in the dark?

JACK We've had enough of your vicious little pranks.

EVETTE There's the lighter. Aren't you glad to see me?

SUSAN Jack, I don't think it's —

JACK It's quite all right, Susan. Just bring the lamp over here.

EVETTE Susan? Who's Susan?

JACK I warned you you were going to ruin Tim's career. But I'm made of sterner stuff, Claire.

> *He lights the lighter. And at that moment* CLAIRE *is*

crossing towards the stairs.

EVETTE Claire? Who's Claire?

SUSAN There she is, Jack! (*Now seeing* EVETTE) But who's she? (JACK *has now lit the lamp*)

JACK Now, Miss Harkin.

SUSAN Where did she come from?

JACK Christ.

EVETTE You said you'd meet me at the bus.

SUSAN Who's she, Jack?

DONOVAN Oooh!

EVETTE What's that?!

CLAIRE (*Ascending the stairs; sings*) 'Abide with me; fast falls the eventide . . . '

DONOVAN Who's that?

CLAIRE (*To* DONOVAN) Evette. (*She continues singing*)

SUSAN That's her! There she is!

EVETTE Who's that?

JACK That's Claire.

SUSAN Who are you?

JACK That's Evette.

EVETTE Who is she?

JACK That's Susan.

EVETTE You didn't tell me you were going to have a party, Jack!

DONOVAN Oooh.

EVETTE Who's that?

JACK That's Susan's father.

EVETTE What's he doing down there?

JACK I think he's imitating a cow.

EVETTE You're playing charades!

JACK No. He's chained himself there.

EVETTE Why?

JACK How would I know! Because — don't ask me — because he thought this was a cathedral.

DONOVAN This is an evil house.

EVETTE That's Teddy's voice!

SUSAN Whose?

EVETTE What's Teddy doing here?

JACK Who's Teddy?

DONOVAN Is that the female cattle drover?

EVETTE Yes! It is Teddy!

She runs to DONOVAN *and crouches down beside him.*

It's me, Teddy. It's Evette.

DONOVAN Oooh.

EVETTE What's the matter with you?

SUSAN (*To* JACK) Do you know her?

JACK Yes.

SUSAN Is she drunk?

JACK Don't think so.

EVETTE Look at me, Teddy.

DONOVAN Who is it?

EVETTE Evette! Evette! Why are you hiding down here?

DONOVAN A third phrase, Evette. Very good. Excellent.

EVETTE A third phrase? What do you mean? (*To the others*) Is he drunk?

DONOVAN Not that language matters when you're as young and as beautiful as you are.

EVETTE What language, Teddy? What are you talking about? And why have you those tights around your neck? (*To* JACK) What's going on here, Jack?

DONOVAN Words are superfluous.

EVETTE (*To* DONOVAN) What words? (*To the others*) Is he delirious? (*Very slowly and distinctly to* DONOVAN) It's Evette, Teddy. Evette Giroux. We went to Brussels together last month for my birthday — remember? Look — this is the watch you bought me there.

DONOVAN (*Realizing*) Oooh.

SUSAN Who is this woman?

JACK Shhh.

SUSAN Did you ask her here?

JACK Me? Never! Shhh.

EVETTE You remember this watch, don't you?

DONOVAN Who is this woman?

EVETTE Look — you had it inscribed at the back.

DONOVAN Take this woman away. She is a little bit gallagher.

EVETTE   Teddy, I'm —

DONOVAN Take her away and talk to her soft.

EVETTE   He *is* delirious. (*She dashes to* JACK *and* SUSAN) He doesn't know me! Look — (*the watch*) — the inscription and the date. We're old friends. We've known each other for ages and ages. He's taking me to Washington with him next Friday!

SUSAN   Daddy?

EVETTE   He's your — ? Then you're his daughter, Susan! He told me all about you. You're going with a wastrel called Timmy.

SUSAN   His name isn't Teddy. It's Patrick Mary Pious.

EVETTE   I know — I know — Teddy's my pet name for him — short for Teddybear. But he told me you and he were going to Sligo this weekend?

SUSAN   It's unbelievable, Jack.

JACK   Have you the audacity, indeed may I say the insolence, to ask Susan and myself to subscribe to the patently absurd proposition that you and Senator Donovan have, over a considerable period of time —

DONOVAN Oooh.

SUSAN   You mean to say that last month you and Daddy were in Brussels together and next Friday you're going to — ?

DONOVAN Oooh.

SUSAN   Jack, I'm going to cry.

JACK   No, you're not.

EVETTE   Why didn't you tell me Teddy was going to be here?

JACK   He wasn't to be here.

EVETTE   And who's that woman up there?

JACK   That's Tim's girlfriend.

EVETTE   She's Tim's girlfriend!

SUSAN   I certainly am not!

EVETTE   How many more women have you got here?

JACK   How dare you speak to me like that!

SUSAN   She's shameless — she followed him here.

EVETTE   I was invited here — by him (*Jack*).

JACK   That's a lie.

SUSAN   Is she your girlfriend?

JACK She certainly is not!

DONOVAN Oooh.

EVETTE How can you stand about talking? Poor Teddy's ill!

CLAIRE *comes downstairs.*

SUSAN There she is, Jack! Look — there she is! Oh dear God
— (*Begins sobbing*) There. I told you I was going to cry.

Both doors suddenly burst open.

CLAIRE Watch the lamp!

JACK Watch the lamp! Claire, come here, Claire!

TIM, BARNEY *and* NORA DAN *enter noisily.* NORA DAN
is between TIM *and* BARNEY, *her arms around their
shoulders. She has one foot raised off the ground.*
TIM, *too, is dishevelled from the tumble off the bike.*
BARNEY *is very excited and because of his excitement
he behaves as if he were at a party: shouting, laughing, etc.*
As they enter everybody talks simultaneously.

BARNEY We have a little accident here — Ha-ha-ha.

CLAIRE Nora!

NORA Slow, now, slow, slow.

CLAIRE What happened, Nora?

TIM I crashed into the caravan.

CLAIRE Is she hurt?

NORA I want to see the Doctor.

EVETTE Who are these people, Jack?

CLAIRE Are you hurt, Nora?

NORA *is brought to the settle bed and laid down there.*

NORA I'm not too bad.

DONOVAN Oooh.

NORA Oooh.

DONOVAN Go ahead! Ridicule me!

NORA Is that you, Doctor?

SUSAN (*Sobbing*) It's unbelievable — unbelievable.

CLAIRE (*To* SUSAN) Stop that at once!

SUSAN (*Louder*) Oooh.

NORA I'll be all right when I lie down.

BARNEY I am sitting very private with my book and suddenly — boom!

JACK Tie those curtains back.

TIM (*To* JACK) I got it started all right but I couldn't stop it.

BARNEY I think my caravan is bombed — Ha-ha-ha!

CLAIRE (*To* JACK) Is there any spirits in the house?

JACK I've some whiskey in my bag.

He goes off to the bedroom. CLAIRE *takes control.*

NORA I'm afraid we damaged poor Barney's caravan.

BARNEY No, no; it does not matter.

CLAIRE Just ease yourself back there, Nora. You're fine.

NORA I'm fine surely, thanks be to God.

CLAIRE Where are you hurt?

NORA It's the leg. It must be broken.

DONOVAN What's happening back there?

SUSAN (*To* DONOVAN) They came off the motorbike. Nora Dan has broken her leg.

DONOVAN Damn her leg. Did they bring a blacksmith?

BARNEY (*To* EVETTE) Hello. My name is Willie. In English that is Barney.

EVETTE Evette.

BARNEY Evette? Good, ha-ha-ha. (*Pointing to* CLAIRE) Evette also. (*Pointing to* SUSAN) Also Evette. Perhaps is every Irish girl named Evette?

CLAIRE (*To* TIM) Are you all right?

TIM I think so.

CLAIRE There's a hot-water bottle upstairs.

TIM Where?

CLAIRE At the foot of the bed.

He goes upstairs.

BARNEY (*To* EVETTE) Welcome to handsome Ballybeg. (*The gesture*)
CLAIRE We'll have the Doctor with you in a second, Nora. (*To* BARNEY) See can you release the Doctor, Barney.
BARNEY Release the Doctor?
CLAIRE There he is.

BARNEY *now sees* DONOVAN *for the first time.*

BARNEY Ah! I see him!
EVETTE He's chained.
BARNEY Good. He was naughty, *ja*? Ha-ha-ha.

JACK *returns to* CLAIRE *with the whiskey.*

JACK Here you are.
CLAIRE Thanks. Get me a cup.

TIM *returns with the hot-water bottle.*

TIM (*To* JACK, *with great enthusiasm*) That's a terrific bike. I'm going to save up for one.
CLAIRE Now, Nora.
JACK Is it damaged?
TIM I don't think so — (*Sees* EVETTE) Who's that?
JACK Evette. Tim Gallagher.
TIM Ah. You're the real French tramp.
EVETTE And you're Tim the wastrel.
TIM You're welcome.
CLAIRE (*To* TIM) Did you get it?
TIM Coming. Here it is.
CLAIRE For God's sake, it's no good empty. Fill it.

He goes to the fireplace. The usual consequences: Oh my God, *etc. while this is happening:*

BARNEY So we encounter again, Doctor?
DONOVAN Who is this?
SUSAN It's Barney the Banks. He's going to —

DONOVAN Get him away from me! Don't touch me, you —

SUSAN Daddy, stop it! Stop it at once!

DONOVAN I will not be —

SUSAN (*To* BARNEY) Don't listen to him. It's that clasp. It won't open.

BARNEY You punish him because he is bold? Ha-ha-ha. (*To* DONOVAN) Bold doctor — *ja*?

DONOVAN Oooh.

CLAIRE How do you feel now, Nora?

NORA I'm coming round slowly. Is the room very cold?

CLAIRE It's the shock. Hurry up, Tim.

NORA It's the shock surely. Do you think the ankle's broken?

CLAIRE You probably just twisted it. We'll get the Doctor to look at it.

TIM (*Coughing*) There.

CLAIRE Are you sure you're all right?

TIM Yes.

CLAIRE Now, Nora. That'll warm you up.

NORA Thank you, Tim.

CLAIRE That's better, isn't it?

NORA I don't think I'll ever rise from this bed again.

CLAIRE Indeed you will. Here — a spoonful of whiskey.

NORA A spoonful of whiskey, surely. Yous have me spoiled. Oh dear, Oh dear, Oh dear, I doubt if I'll ever be fit to leave this house again.

BARNEY (*To* DONOVAN) I have it now nearly. One more minute.

JACK What did she say there? Did that old bitch just say she'd never —

CLAIRE For God's sake, can't you lower your voice?

JACK (*Whispering*) I will not lower my voice in my own house! I know what she's up to. She thinks she's going to squat here. Well it's not going to work!

CLAIRE Jack, she's hurt.

JACK I don't give a damn if she's paralyzed! She gets out of here in five minutes!

CLAIRE (*To* EVETTE) I'm Claire. You're Evette.

EVETTE How do you know that?

CLAIRE I understand perfectly.

EVETTE You're Tim's girlfriend, aren't you?

CLAIRE Am I?

JACK You all get out of here in five minutes!

EVETTE Me, too?

JACK Especially you.

EVETTE Happily.

JACK You and everybody.

BARNEY There we are! Dr Bollocks is liberated!

SUSAN (*To* BARNEY) Thank you very much.

BARNEY My pleasure, Evette — Ha-ha-ha.

SUSAN (*To* DONOVAN) Can you stand? Give me your arm.

EVETTE Lean on me, Teddy.

DONOVAN Oooh.

> *He gets slowly to his feet. From now on he holds his head to the side. The legs of the tights dangle down his back.*

SUSAN You're all right, aren't you?

DONOVAN I think so.

SUSAN It was Barney that got you free.

DONOVAN I'll survive. (*To* BARNEY) Thank you.

BARNEY Do not be bold again, Doctor — *ja*? Ha-ha-ha.

DONOVAN (*To* SUSAN) Get the cases.

CLAIRE Would you take a look at Nora, Doctor?

DONOVAN I'm in a hurry.

CLAIRE She has hurt her leg.

DONOVAN Where is she?

CLAIRE Over here.

DONOVAN What happened to her?

SUSAN She came off her bike — Timmy's bike — Jack's bike.

DONOVAN Wouldn't one tumble have sufficed?

> TIM *takes the tights from* DONOVAN's *neck.*

TIM I don't think you need these any- . . .

> *He holds them in his hands. Everybody looks at him. Pause. Then he stuffs them into his pocket.*

	They dried. On your neck.
DONOVAN	Not only are you deranged. You are despicable.
BARNEY	May I have a little vodka to celebrate that Nora Dan fall?
JACK	Why not. Help yourself. Make yourself at home.
BARNEY	Thank you. Thank you.
JACK	Anybody else for a drink? Whiskey? Vodka? It's open house!
NORA	It's my ankle, Doctor. It's throbbing and it's hot.
DONOVAN	Are you in pain?
NORA	Pain surely, Doctor. I must have come down heavy on it.
DONOVAN	Can you move it?
NORA	Not a budge, Doctor.
DONOVAN	(*Moving it vigorously*) Indeed you can.
NORA	Lord, Doctor, that's terrible sore. Is it broken?
DONOVAN	Not at all. A slight sprain. Rest it over the weekend. (*Moving away from the bed*) My case is somewhere . . .
CLAIRE	Are you sure she's all right?
DONOVAN	Your English is suddenly very fluent.
CLAIRE	Are you certain nothing's broken?
DONOVAN	My neck is.

He exits to the bedroom.

| EVETTE | Let me help you, Teddy? |

Exits.

JACK	Open house. Wander around. Come and go as you wish.
SUSAN	When are you going home?
JACK	Tonight — now — if my bike's working.
SUSAN	Will you take me with you?
JACK	Absolutely. But what about —
SUSAN	I'm not going with him if she's going with him!
BARNEY	(*To* TIM) You are feeling not so frisky now, Herr McNeilis?
TIM	Yes — no — I'm fine, thanks.

BARNEY So perhaps maybe tomorrow I come and talk to you
about selling this house from you?

JACK Why not! Just give it to him, for Christ's sake!

BARNEY No, no, I buy it — I buy it correct. *Ja?* (*Catching the legs
of the tights*) 'To us lovers everywhere' — Ha-ha-ha.

DONOVAN *and* EVETTE *enter.*

DONOVAN Are you ready, Susie?

SUSAN Is she going with you?

EVETTE I'm not staying here!

SUSAN Then I'll go home with Jack.

DONOVAN You'll come with me.

JACK I'll be happy to drive her home, Doctor — that is, of
course, with your permission.

DONOVAN *surveys them all slowly. Pause.*

DONOVAN Never in all my life . . . in my long career as a politi-
cian and a doctor I have never —

NORA Doctor!

DONOVAN (*To* BARNEY) I am grateful to you for rescuing me, sir.
But I must also say that this island has no need at all
for land-grabbing transvestites of your calibre.

BARNEY Thank you, Doctor. Ha-ha-ha.

DONOVAN I have no idea what your wife's (CLAIRE) game is —

BARNEY Evette? *Ja-ja.*

DONOVAN Whatever alias she uses. She is clearly a liar and a
schemer and I think you are well matched.

TIM (*Whispers to* JACK) What's he talking about? Is he cracking up?

NORA Doctor!

DONOVAN (*To* TIM) As for you; I accept that you are a very ill
man. But I must say this to you: if you ever darken
my door again I will have you arrested.

NORA Doctor!

EVETTE The lady in the bed wants you.

DONOVAN Well?

NORA Could I have a word with you, Doctor?

DONOVAN I've told you: you're perfectly well but much too old for scrambling.

NORA Could the rest of yous move away . . . ?

DONOVAN *and* NORA *are now alone together.*

DONOVAN What is it? What is it?

NORA I was just thinking, Doctor, now that I'm going to be an invalid here, I'll not be needing my own house.

DONOVAN Well?

NORA It's just across the fields there. Two rooms and an acre of land overlooking the strand. The very place you're looking for, Doctor!

DONOVAN Oh Jesus Christ — let me out of . . . !

He grabs his case and almost runs out of the house.

EVETTE Hold on, Teddy! I'm coming! I'm coming!

She follows him.

CLAIRE Watch the lamp!

JACK Watch the lamp!

JACK *closes both doors after them.*

TIM (*Worried*) What does he mean — I'm a very ill man. I only got a scratch on my head.

CLAIRE You've missed the last bus.

TIM (*Looking at his watch*) My watch has stopped. What time is it?

CLAIRE It's gone.

TIM I'll just have to stay then.

CLAIRE Yes.

TIM The whole weekend. After all.

CLAIRE Yes.

TIM Is there room?

CLAIRE When they leave, there is.

TIM I'd better ask Jack.

She begins to make tea.

BARNEY I must depart also. My caravan has a big bump to hammer out. You feel not too bad now, Nora?

NORA Not too bad surely, Barney.

BARNEY Good. I come to see you in the morning. (*To* JACK) Thank you for the vodka. I leave this (*cup*) on the gulder. Goodnight, Evette — and Evette — Ha-ha-ha. Goodnight, Herr McNeilis (*Tim*) and your house guest (*Jack*). (*To* TIM) I come to talk with you tomorrow. (*To* JACK) And you must visit handsome Ballybeg soon again — *ja*?

JACK That's very kind of you.

BARNEY You are welcome (*the gesture*). (*To* ALL) Goodnight — goodnight. *Auf Wiedersehen.*

As he exits:

CLAIRE Mind the lamp!

NORA A grand man that, Barney; a great neighbour to all of us about here.

JACK How's the ankle?

NORA Fair to middling. The Doctor says I'm to put no weight on it for a week at least.

JACK Nora, what he said was —

NORA So would it be all right with you if I just lay here until I get my strength back?

JACK Elizabeth's arriving tomorrow.

NORA Isn't that providential! Sure wee Elizabeth and me get on powerful well together. And I'll have Claire till Wednesday — for all the attention I'll need — just a cup of tea now and again to keep me going. Sure between yous all yous'll have me spoiled.

JACK Nora —

NORA I'll take another sup of that whiskey now and maybe I'd sleep for a while.

CLAIRE Will I pull the curtains?

NORA Pull the curtains surely. And goodnight to yous all.

CLAIRE Sleep well, Nora.

JACK Bitch!

SUSAN *(To* JACK) Are you ready? I want away from this place.

JACK All right. *(To* TIM) Where's the bike?

TIM It's lying at the back of the caravan.

JACK Are you sure it's not damaged?

NORA *(From behind curtains)* Sure if it is, Barney's the man'll fix it for you.

TIM Susan, I —

SUSAN *(Ignoring him)* Will you be able to take my case?

JACK We'll manage.

SUSAN I'll go and change.

JACK You'll need a candle up there.

SUSAN I'm all right.

CLAIRE Anybody want tea?

JACK I need a drink.

CLAIRE Tim?

TIM Please.

SUSAN *is about to take her case upstairs.*

Let me carry that for you.

Again she ignores him. She rushes upstairs. JACK *pours himself a drink and drifts over to the posts and chains.*

JACK What a bloody day! A total disaster in every respect. You were right, professor — it was stupid and dangerous. But I had one second of absolute pleasure: just after I had come in the door and someone had lit the lamp — and there was Dr Bollocks on his hands and knees, lamenting like a stuck pig! That almost compensated for everything. My God, if we'd got a picture of that! 'Senator Donovan Worships the Ancestral Pieties'! Stupid bloody bastard.

CLAIRE *hands* TIM *a cup of tea.*

TIM Thanks.

CLAIRE Biscuit?

TIM　No, thanks. Amn't I all right?

CLAIRE　What do you mean?

TIM　Just that the Doctor said . . . maybe he noticed something about me. When I came off the bike I think I
landed on my head.

CLAIRE　You're as right as you ever were.

He puts the cup down and catches her hand.

JACK　(*Looking at the chain*) There's nothing wrong with that
clasp. What's he mouthing about? The clasp's working perfectly.

TIM *now takes* CLAIRE's *other hand in his.*

CLAIRE　Are you staying?

TIM　Yes. Are you glad?

JACK　I suppose he was showing you how cows used to be
chained?

CLAIRE　Yes. A very large quantity of glad.

JACK　As if he would know.

TIM　Did I say that?

JACK　Absolutely.

CLAIRE　Yes.

TIM　God. A response cry.

JACK　'You see, what you do is this. You put the chain round
the cow's neck — like this — and fasten it with this
clasp here. Right?'

CLAIRE　It's been a long time, Tim.

TIM　Seven and a half years. The very week I began working on the thesis.

CLAIRE　Tim the Thesis.

JACK　Pompous bloody idiot.

CLAIRE　It's on conversation, isn't it?

TIM　Language as a ritualized act between two people.

CLAIRE　Yes.

TIM　The exchange of units of communication through an
agreed code.

CLAIRE　Yes.

TIM   Fundamental to any meaningful exchange between individuals.

CLAIRE   Is it?

TIM   That's the theory.

JACK   (*Tentatively*) Tim . . . ?

CLAIRE   Chat, really.

TIM   Yes.

CLAIRE   What we're doing now.

TIM   But I think that after this I may have to rewrite a lot of it.

CLAIRE   Why?

TIM   All that stuff about units of communication. Maybe the units don't matter all that much.

CLAIRE   I think that's true.

JACK   Can you come here for a minute, Tim?

TIM   We're conversing now but we're not exchanging units, are we?

CLAIRE   I don't think so, are we?

TIM   I don't think we can because I'm not too sure what I'm saying.

CLAIRE   I don't know what you're saying either but I think I know what's implicit in it.

JACK   Tim, I think I'm in a bit of trouble.

TIM   Even if what I'm saying is rubbish?

CLAIRE   Yes.

TIM   Like 'this is our first cathedral'?

CLAIRE   Like that.

TIM   Like 'this is the true centre'?

CLAIRE   I think I know what's implicit in that.

TIM   Maybe the message doesn't matter at all then.

JACK   Tim!

CLAIRE   It's the occasion that matters.

TIM   And the reverberations that the occasion generates.

> *They have now drifted across the stage together and end up leaning very gently against the upright supporting the loft.*

CLAIRE   I feel the reverberations.

TIM I feel the reverberations.

CLAIRE And the desire to sustain the occasion.

TIM And saying anything, anything at all, that keeps the occasion going.

JACK Tim!

CLAIRE Maybe even saying nothing.

TIM Maybe. Maybe silence is the perfect discourse.

CLAIRE Kiss me then.

TIM I can scarcely hear you. Will you kiss me, Claire?

They kiss and hold that kiss until the play ends. As they kiss they lean heavily against the upright.

JACK I'm stuck, Tim! Will you for God's sake come here and —

The upright begins to move. Sounds of timbers creaking.

Get away from the upright, Tim! You'll bring the roof down!

SUSAN *(Off)* Jack?

JACK D'you hear me, Gallagher?! Get away from the upright! Susan!

SUSAN, *now dressed as in her first appearance, appears at the top of the stairs.*

SUSAN What's happening, Jack?! The floor's shaking!

She staggers down the shaking stairs.

JACK The upright, Tim! Get away from it!

The curtains are pulled back. NORA*'s head appears.*

NORA Jesus, Mary and Joseph, what's the noise?!

SUSAN Jack!

The big door blows open. The lamp flickers — almost dies — survives — almost dies. The sound of cracking timbers increases.

JACK Watch the lamp!
SUSAN Jack, where are you, Jack?!
NORA What's happening?
JACK Help! I'm trapped!
NORA Jesus, Mary and Joseph, the house is falling in!
SUSAN Jack, the place is . . . oooh!
JACK Oh my God.

The lamp dies. Total darkness.

FATHERS
AND SONS

after Turgenev

Music

Characters

ARKADY NIKOLAYEVICH KIRSANOV (22), student
YEVGENY VASSILYICH BAZAROV (22), student
NIKOLAI PETROVICH KIRSANOV (44), Arkady's father; estate owner
PAVEL PETROVICH KIRSANOV (45), Arkady's uncle; retired
  guardsman
VASSILY IVANYICH BAZAROV (60s), Bazarov's father; retired
  army doctor
ARINA VLASSYEVNA BAZAROV (50s), Bazarov's mother
FENICHKA FEDOSYA NIKOLAYEVNA (23), Nikolai's mistress
ANNA SERGEYEVNA ODINTSOV (29), estate owner; widow
KATYA SERGEYEVNA (18), Anna's sister
PRINCESS OLGA (70s), Anna's aunt

Servants in Kirsanov home
DUNYASHA (20s)
PROKOFYICH (60s)
PIOTR (19)

Servants in Bazarov home
TIMOFEICH (60s)
FEDKA (16)

Time and Place

Mid-nineteenth century. Rural Russia.

Fathers and Sons was first produced at the Lyttelton Theatre, South Bank, London, on 8 July 1987, with the following cast:

ARKADY NIKOLAYEVICH KIRSANOV	Ralph Fiennes
YEVGENY VASSILYICH BAZAROV	Robert Glenister
NIKOLAI PETROVICH KIRSANOV	Alec McCowen
PAVEL PETROVICH KIRSANOV	Richard Pasco
VASSILY IVANYICH BAZAROV	Robin Bailey
ARINA VLASSYEVNA BAZAROV	Barbara Jefford
FENICHKA FEDOSYA NIKOLAYEVNA	Lesley Sharp
ANNA SERGEYEVNA ODINTSOV	Meg Davies
KATYA SERGEYEVNA	Robin McCaffrey
PRINCESS OLGA	Joyce Grant
DUNYASHA	Hazel Ellerby
PROKOFYICH	Antony Brown
PIOTR	Jay Villiers
TIMOFEICH	Peter Halliday
FEDKA	Jim Millea

Directed by	Michael Rudman
Designed by	Carl Toms
Music by	Matthew Scott

for Tom and Julie

ACT ONE

Scene One

Before the scene begins bring up the sound of Beethoven's Romance in F-major, Op.50, *played by* NIKOLAI *on the cello. Early afternoon in May, 1859. The garden lawn in front of the Kirsanov home. We can see into the living room. A verandah runs across the front of the house with two steps leading down to the garden. Some potted plants in front of the verandah. Downstage left there is a gazebo/summer house. Various summer seats and stools (left and right from the point of view of the audience). Characters enter from the left — i.e. the yard, outhouses, servants' quarters off — or from the house.*

NIKOLAI *is playing the cello in the living room.* FENICHKA *is sitting in the gazebo knitting a garment for her baby who is sleeping in a pram at her side. She is an attractive young woman with innate dignity and confidence; but because she is no longer a servant and not yet mistress in the house she is not fully at ease in her environment. Occasionally she glances into the pram. She leaves aside her knitting, closes her eyes and sits listening to the music.*

DUNYASHA *enters left carrying a laundry basket full of clothes. She is a plump, open-natured, open-hearted, practical-minded girl who loves to laugh.*

DUNYASHA Oh my God, this heat has me destroyed. How do you stick it?

FENICHKA You should have something on your head.

DUNYASHA I met the new estate manager over there at the clothes line. Do you know him?

FENICHKA Only to see.

DUNYASHA He is just so beautiful — isn't he? I could spend my days just gazing at him, with that glossy black moustache and those sleepy brown eyes. Did you notice that beautiful black 'tash?

FENICHKA Dunyasha!

> DUNYASHA *flops down beside her.* FENICHKA
> *resumes her knitting.*

DUNYASHA Honestly. All he'd have to do is raise his little finger
and I'd kiss his feet. Anyhow, he looked at me and
he said, 'Are you going to faint, little one?' All the
same that was nice, wasn't it? — 'little one'. And I
said, 'What d'you mean — am I going to faint?'
'Oh,' he said, 'your face is all bloated and red.'

FENICHKA (*Laughing*) He did not. That's another of your
stories.

DUNYASHA Cross my heart. (*Into pram*) Hello, Mitya. How are
you today, my little darling? Are you well?

> *She spreads out under the sun.*

Beautiful. This must be the hottest May ever. (*Eyes
closed*) Is that the big fiddle he's playing?

FENICHKA You know very well it's called a cello.

DUNYASHA Sort of nice, isn't it? Bit lonely — like himself.

FENICHKA Is he lonely?

DUNYASHA You should know. Not much good for dancing.

FENICHKA I heard you were dancing last night.

DUNYASHA Five this morning. Oh, that heat's lovely.

FENICHKA Any good?

DUNYASHA You mean did I click? (*She sits up*) Tell me this,
Fenichka: remember all those young fellows used
to be at the dances when you and I went together
— all that laughing and all that fun — remember?

FENICHKA Yes.

DUNYASHA Well, where in God's name have they gone to,
those boys? Or haven't they young brothers? All
you see now are half-drunk louts that say things
like, 'My God, girl, but you're a powerful armful
of meat.' (FENICHKA *laughs*) It's true. That's what a
big clodhopper said to me last night. And if it's
not the clodhoppers it's the usual old lechers with

their eyes half closed and their hands groping your bum.

> *She sees* PAVEL *entering left with a book under his arm. She gets quickly to her feet.* PAVEL *is the typical 'Europeanized' Russian of the nineteenth century — wears English clothes, speaks French. His manner is jaded but his emotions function fully and astutely.*

Jesus, here comes the Tailor's Dummy! He must have spotted you.

FENICHKA Don't go, Dunyasha. Stay with me.

DUNYASHA You're well fit to handle that old goat. And Dunyasha's place is in the kitchen.

FENICHKA Please.

DUNYASHA You're too gentle. Tell him straight out to bugger off.

> *She rises, makes a curtsy to* PAVEL *and exits quickly left, leaving her basket behind her. The relationship between* PAVEL *and* FENICHKA *is uneasy. He looks into the pram and then at* FENICHKA.

PAVEL Am I intruding?

FENICHKA No. Not at all.

PAVEL Will you be sending into town for groceries today?

FENICHKA Yes.

PAVEL Would you order something for me?

FENICHKA What do you want?

PAVEL Tea. Green tea. If you would.

FENICHKA Of course.

PAVEL Half a pound would suffice.

FENICHKA I'll see to that.

PAVEL *Merci bien.* (*Into pram*) Hello-hello-hello-hello. He has very strong fingers. Maybe he'll be a cellist like his father. How do you like your new bedroom, Fenichka?

FENICHKA I love it. It gets the sun in the early morning.

PAVEL I see your light on very often in the middle of the night.

She rises and gathers her things.

FENICHKA That's his lordship — cutting a new tooth. (*Into pram*) Aren't you cutting a new tooth, you rascal, and keeping your mother awake at night?

PAVEL *Tu es très belle.*

FENICHKA Sorry?

PAVEL Look — he won't let me go.

FENICHKA Let your uncle go, Mitya.

PAVEL Fenichka —

FENICHKA I think I'll take him inside. This sun's a bit hot for him.

PAVEL All I want to say is —

He gets no further because PROKOFYICH *enters left. He is an elderly retainer, excessively dignified and formal in manner; but now he is so excited, indeed so confused, that he almost runs across the stage and proclaims too loudly to nobody in particular:*

PROKOFYICH The carriage has arrived! He's back! Master Arkady is back!

PAVEL That's early. They must have made good time.

PROKOFYICH The carriage is here! He has arrived! He has arrived!

PAVEL A bit of life about the place.

FENICHKA Yes.

PAVEL Fenichka, forgive me if —

PROKOFYICH Master Arkady is back! The carriage is here! Arkady's home from Petersburg!

PROKOFYICH *is now on the verandah and calling into the living room.* NIKOLAI *emerges with the cello bow in his hand. He walks with a slight limp. He is a kind, decent, generous-spirited man,*

> *vague and bumbling at times but always fully*
> *alert to what is happening around him.*

The carriage is here! Arkady's home! He's back!
He's back!

PAVEL All right, Prokofyich, we hear you.

NIKOLAI Did you hear the news?

PAVEL I think so, Nikolai.

NIKOLAI Arkady has arrived from Petersburg. Wonderful!
Where's Piotr? Piotr! Somebody help him with the
luggage. Go and meet him, Pavel. (*To* FENICHKA)
He'll probably want something to eat, won't he?
Everything's in such confusion. This is no welcome.
Piotr! I'm really going to have to reprimand that
young scamp.

> *General confusion and excitement.* PROKOFYICH
> *rushes off left.* DUNYASHA *rushes on and picks*
> *up her basket.*

DUNYASHA (*Privately to* FENICHKA) He has a friend with him!
Get out your smelling salts! Oh sweet Saviour!

FENICHKA Take the pram inside, Dunyasha, will you?

DUNYASHA Wait till you see *him*! A dark god! Jesus, could this
be my lucky day?!

PAVEL Who is he bringing with him, Nikolai?

NIKOLAI Dunyasha, tell Piotr I want him — immediately!

> *She dashes off with the pram and basket.*

Yes, he's bringing a friend with him — a young
man called — called — I'm sorry, I've forgotten,
Pavel. I'm really going to sack that boy.

> ARKADY *enters.*

Ah! There he is! Arkady! Arkady!

ARKADY Father! How are you!

*Father and son embrace with great warmth.
Already* ARKADY *is beginning to resemble his
father.* PROKOFYICH, *cases in his hands, stands
in the background and beams.*

NIKOLAI   Welcome home! Welcome home, graduate!
ARKADY   Thank you.
NIKOLAI   Let me look at you. You're different. Have you lost
weight? You're altogether different. Have you eaten?
You're pale — that's it — you're very pale —
ARKADY   All that study and all those exams. What I need is
a long rest. Uncle Pavel!
PAVEL   Welcome back, Arkady.
ARKADY   It's great to see you.

They embrace warmly.

And . . . Fenichka. It *is* Fenichka, isn't it?
FENICHKA   It is.
NIKOLAI   Of course it is.
ARKADY   Indeed. Good to see you, Fenichka.
FENICHKA   And you, Arkady.

They shake hands and she leaves.

NIKOLAI   Prokofyich usually drives so slowly, we didn't ex-
pect you until much later. Had you a good journey?
ARKADY   It was all right. I've brought a friend with me,
Father.
NIKOLAI   You mentioned that in your last letter. Great.
ARKADY   His name is Bazarov.
NIKOLAI   Wonderful. We'll have a full house again. And wait
till you see your bedroom — we've had it all re-
papered. Pavel chose the colour scheme.
PAVEL   That was a major row.
NIKOLAI   No, it wasn't — was it?
PAVEL   A minor row.
ARKADY   His name is Bazarov — Yevgeny Vassilyich Bazarov.
I would like you to make him very welcome.

226

Fathers and Sons

NIKOLAI Naturally we'll make him very welcome. Won't we, Pavel?

ARKADY Our friendship is very important to me.

PAVEL Did he graduate, too?

ARKADY Next year. He's doing Natural Science and Medicine. He's probably the most brilliant man I've ever met.

NIKOLAI Well, the brilliant Bazarov is every bit as welcome as you are . . . well, almost.

ARKADY Would you go and meet him, Uncle Pavel?

PAVEL (*To* ARKADY) See? Still the message-boy. *Plus ça change* . . .

PAVEL *goes off and* PROKOFYICH *is about to follow him.*

NIKOLAI And isn't Prokofyich looking well?

ARKADY Prokofyich never changes. Thank you for picking us up.

PROKOFYICH My pleasure. We'll go out looking for birds' nests tomorrow morning.

ARKADY First thing. We'll show Bazarov all the good spots.

PROKOFYICH Maybe you and I should go by ourselves first and then we —

PAVEL (*Off*) Prokofyich!

PROKOFYICH Coming, sir. (*To* ARKADY) It's good to have you back, Arkady.

ARKADY Thank you.

PROKOFYICH *exits left.*

Bird-nesting! He thinks I'm still a schoolboy.

NIKOLAI In a way so do I.

ARKADY And I deliberately mentioned Bazarov because they didn't get on very well on the journey. Prokofyich prefers the old ways, the old formalities. (*Embraces* NIKOLAI *again*) It's great to see you, Father.

NIKOLAI Thank you.

ARKADY And you're looking very fresh.

NIKOLAI Fresh? At my age?

ARKADY And so is Uncle Pavel. What's he doing with himself these days?

NIKOLAI Oh, you know Pavel — killing time, as he says himself — walking — reading — (*whispers*) going to his English tailor and his French barber — thinking his own very secret thoughts . . . (*After a quick look round*) Arkady, there's one little matter before the others join us — I'm really a bit embarrassed mentioning it —

ARKADY It's about Fenichka.

NIKOLAI Shhh. How did you know?

ARKADY Intuition.

NIKOLAI Yes, it's about Fenichka. You know Fenichka, don't you? What am I talking about — of course you do! Well, as you know, Arkady, I've been very fond of her for a long time now. Her mother was the best housekeeper we ever had here and Fenichka has taken on those responsibilities with great assurance and skill, considering she's only twenty-three, just a year older than yourself; so I'm old enough to be her father, too, amn't I? Ha-ha. Anyhow, as I say, I've been very attached to her for a long time now; and indeed I have asked her — I have insisted — that she move out of that damp flat above the laundry and come into the main house. And I mention this now, Arkady, partly because I — I — because she's afraid you might . . . well, disapprove of her.

ARKADY I might disapprove of Fenichka?

NIKOLAI I hope you don't mind too much, Arkady.

ARKADY Mind? Why in God's name should I mind?

NIKOLAI Well, because . . . well, I just thought that . . . Anyhow, anyhow, the real reason I brought her into the house — and I want you to know that I do, I do care very much for the girl, Arkady — I thought it only proper and correct that she ought to be in the house after — (*pause*) — she'd had the baby.

ARKADY Baby?

NIKOLAI Hers and mine.

ARKADY You mean — ?

NIKOLAI A boy.

ARKADY You and — ?

NIKOLAI Six months old.

ARKADY I have a new brother.

NIKOLAI Half-brother.

ARKADY Half-brother.

NIKOLAI Mitya.

ARKADY Mitya!

NIKOLAI Mitya. Now you know it all. Actually he's the image of me.

> ARKADY *suddenly laughs, throws his arms around his father.*

ARKADY Father, that is the best news ever!

NIKOLAI Is it?

ARKADY Of course it is! You're a sly old rascal but I think you're great. Congratulations!

NIKOLAI You're not angry?

ARKADY Angry? For God's sake, Father, I'm delighted for you!

NIKOLAI Thank you, son. Thank you. We'll not talk about it before Pavel. I'm not sure he quite approves of the whole thing. You know Pavel, with his silly notions of class and public decorum.

> PAVEL *and* BAZAROV *enter left.*

We can talk later.

> BAZAROV, *a student, dark, lean, intense. He senses that he is an outsider politically and socially in this house — hence the arrogance and curt manner.*

ARKADY There he is! Come on, Bazarov! Come over here. Uncle Pavel you've obviously met — Pavel Petrovich Kirsanov. And this is my father, Nikolai

Petrovich Kirsanov. Yevgeny Vassilyich Bazarov.

BAZAROV *bows formally.*

NIKOLAI You are most welcome to this house, Yevgeny Vassilyich. I hope you can stay with us for most of the summer and I hope you don't find us very dull company.

PAVEL Do you remember a Doctor Bazarov in Father's old division? That's his father, he tells me.

NIKOLAI Really? My goodness, it's a small . . . it's a . . .

PAVEL *Extraordinaire, n'est ce pas?*

NIKOLAI Indeed. And you're going to be a doctor, too? Great. Splendid. Sit down. Sit down. You must be tired after your journey.

BAZAROV I'd prefer to stand.

NIKOLAI Of course. Stand. Naturally. Stretch your legs. By all means — stand . . . Now to organize our lives. Let's have tea out here. Then you young men can have a rest and we'll eat about seven o'clock. All right? Piotr! He deliberately hides on me, you know. It's gone far beyond a joke. Dunyasha! Oh, you've no idea how difficult things are becoming. I'm not exaggerating, Pavel, am I? The old system — of course it had its failings. But now? — now I give all my land to the peasants to farm — *give* it to them. Will they even farm it for themselves? I wish you'd take an interest in it all, Arkady. It's becoming too much for me at my time of — sorry. (*To* DUNYASHA) Ah, Dunyasha. Bring the samovar out here.

PAVEL Cocoa for me, *s'il vous plaît.*

NIKOLAI And a bottle of that black sherry in the sideboard. The young men may wish to — to — to dissipate!

DUNYASHA *is staring at* BAZAROV.

ARKADY Do you wish to dissipate, Bazarov? We would love to dissipate, Father.

NIKOLAI Dunyasha!

DUNYASHA Sorry, sir?

NIKOLAI Black sherry. In the sideboard. And glasses.

She goes into the house.

What's the matter with that girl? And how is your father, Yevgeny Vassilyich?

BAZAROV *looks blankly at him. Pause.*

Your father — is he well?

BAZAROV I suppose so. I haven't seen him for three years.

NIKOLAI He has been away — has he? — travelling?

BAZAROV Not that I know of.

NIKOLAI Ah.

BAZAROV I haven't seen him for three years because I haven't been home since I went to the university.

Silence.

ARKADY (*Quickly*) Let me tell you about this character. He won the gold medal for oratory again this year — the third year in succession.

NIKOLAI Wonderful!

ARKADY And he is also — (*to* BAZAROV) — no, don't try to stop me — he is also president of the philosophical society and editor of the magazine. It's an astonishing radical publication — the college authorities banned both issues this year! We were brought before the disciplinary council — remember? 'Revolutionaries! Damned revolutionaries!'

NIKOLAI Oratory is an excellent discipline; excellent. I approve very strongly of — of — of — of oratory.

PAVEL On what do you . . . orate?

BAZAROV Politics. Philosophy.

PAVEL They have something in common, have they?

ARKADY Come on, Uncle Pavel. You know they have.

PAVEL (*To* BAZAROV) And your philosophy is?

ARKADY Nihilism.

PAVEL Sorry?

ARKADY Nihilism, Uncle Pavel. Bazarov is a Nihilist. So am I.

NIKOLAI Interesting word that. I imagine it comes from the Latin — *nihil* — nothing. Does it mean somebody who respects nothing? No, it doesn't.

ARKADY Someone who looks at everything critically.

PAVEL If there's a difference.

ARKADY There's a significant difference, Pavel. Don't be so precious.

PAVEL Me? — Precious? Good Lord.

ARKADY Nihilism begins by questioning all received ideas and principles no matter how venerated those ideas and principles are. And that leads to the inevitable conclusion that the world must be made anew. (*To* BAZAROV) That's a fairly accurate summary of our stance, isn't it?

>   BAZAROV *shrugs indifferently and spreads his hands.*

PAVEL So you believe only in science?

ARKADY We don't *believe* in anything. You can't believe in science any more than you can believe in the weather or farming or swimming.

NIKOLAI I can tell you farming isn't what it used to be. In the past five years the advances I've seen in farming techniques —

ARKADY I wish you would stop trying to divert me with your juvenile asides, Father.

NIKOLAI I am sorry.

PAVEL A simple question: if you reject all accepted principles and all accepted precepts, what basis of conduct have you?

ARKADY I don't understand what the simple question means.

PAVEL On what basis do you conduct your life?

ARKADY If something is useful — keep it. If it is not useful — out it goes. And the most useful thing we can do is repudiate, renounce, reject.

PAVEL Everything?

ARKADY Everything without use.

PAVEL All accepted conventions, all art, all science?

ARKADY What use are they? Out.

PAVEL Civilization has just been disposed of, Nikolai.

NIKOLAI But surely, Arkady, surely rejection means destruction; and surely we must construct, too?

ARKADY Our first priority is to make a complete clearance. At this point in our evolution we have no right to indulge in the gratification of our own personal whims.

NIKOLAI I don't think I had whims in mind, Arkady.

ARKADY At times it's difficult to know what you have in mind, Father.

PAVEL And when do you begin to preach this gospel publicly?

ARKADY We're activists. We aren't preachers, are we, Bazarov? We are not going to —

PAVEL Aren't you preaching now? (*To* NIKOLAI) This is all nonsense; weary old materialistic nonsense I've heard a hundred times.

ARKADY We know there is starvation and poverty; we know our politicians take bribes; we know the legal system is corrupt. We know all that. And we are tired listening to the 'liberals' and the 'progressives' —

PAVEL So you have identified all society's evils —

NIKOLAI Let him finish, Pavel.

PAVEL I would prefer Yevgeny Vassilyich would do his own talking. (*To* ARKADY) But you intend to do nothing constructive yourselves?

BAZAROV We intend to do nothing constructive ourselves.

PAVEL Just abuse people who do.

BAZAROV Just abuse people who do.

PAVEL And that's called Nihilism.

BAZAROV And that's called Nihilism. Is this riveting discussion nearly over?

PAVEL *Incroyable!* Let me see, have I got it right —

NIKOLAI I'm sure you've got it right, Pavel. Let's leave it for now.

PAVEL First our saviours will demolish the country and then they will remake the country. But suppose some simple person were to suggest that our saviours were just bletherskites — gold-medal bletherskites?

BAZAROV My grandfather was a serf, Pavel Petrovich. I believe I have some knowledge of the Russian people.

PAVEL I'm sure you have a very —

BAZAROV Indeed I believe I have at least as accurate and as sympathetic an understanding of their needs and of their mute aspirations as those absurd provincial aristocrats who affect English clothes and English customs; who believe they are civilized just because they speak cliché French; who talk endlessly about Mother Russia but who sit on their backsides and do sweet nothing for the '*bien public*' as they call it.

PAVEL I suspect you're deliberately trying to —

BAZAROV Words that come so easily to lips like yours — liberalism, progress, principles, civilization — they have no meaning in Russia. They are imported words. Russia doesn't need them. But what Russia does need — and action will provide it, Pavel Petrovich, action, not words — what Russia does need is bread in the mouth. But before you can put bread in the mouth, you have got to plough the land — deep.

NIKOLAI He's right, you know: ploughing is a very important part of the farming cycle. (*To* ARKADY) Sorry. I didn't —

PAVEL So the two of you are going to reform Russia.

BAZAROV Remake Russia. Yes.

PAVEL By force?

BAZAROV (*Shrugging*) If necessary.

ARKADY All that's needed is a few people with total dedication. It was a penny candle that burned Moscow down, Uncle Pavel.

NIKOLAI That's quite true, you know.

PAVEL For God's sake, Nikolai, you know nothing about it!

NIKOLAI I beg your pardon, Pavel — it *was* a penny candle burned Moscow down. That is an historical fact. Father was able to quote chapter and verse on it.

To FENICHKA *and* DUNYASHA *who have entered with a tray and samovar.*

Ah! Fenichka! Good! Great! Splendid! And beautifully timed — just when we had all come to a close understanding of one another's position. Have you the sherry? Excellent. (*To* DUNYASHA) Just leave the tray there. Thank you. Thank you. You haven't met Arkady's friend, have you, Fenichka? Yevgeny Vassilyich Bazarov.

BAZAROV Pleased to meet you.

FENICHKA You're welcome.

BAZAROV Thank you.

ARKADY Dr Bazarov — almost.

FENICHKA Welcome, Doctor.

NIKOLAI (*To* DUNYASHA *who is staring at* BAZAROV) Dunyasha, will you put the tray down on the seat, please?

DUNYASHA Oh yes — yes, yes, yes.

NIKOLAI I think this is yours, Pavel (*cocoa*).

PAVEL Thanks.

As the cups are being passed round ARKADY *has a private word with* FENICHKA.

ARKADY Congratulations. (*She looks puzzled*) On the baby.

FENICHKA Oh. (*She looks quickly towards* NIKOLAI)

ARKADY He's just told me.

FENICHKA He wasn't sure how you'd react.

ARKADY I'm pleased for you both.

FENICHKA Thank you.

NIKOLAI *is aware of this private conversation.*

NIKOLAI   You're sitting with us, Fenichka, aren't you?
FENICHKA Not just now. I've got to bath Mitya and put him
          to bed. I'll join you later.
NIKOLAI   Please do.

          FENICHKA *leaves.*

DUNYASHA Can I get you anything else?
NIKOLAI   That's everything, I think, Dunyasha.

          She is gazing at BAZAROV *and does not move.*

          Thank you.

          She goes.

          There's something the matter with that girl today.
          Now to organize our lives. Let me tell you what
          plans we have in store for you. The first formal
          engagement is on Monday week. It's a rather long
          and convoluted story that —
PAVEL   It's quite simple: he's having a welcome-home
          party for you.
ARKADY   Great.
NIKOLAI   Some weeks ago quite out of the blue I had a visit
          from a young lady called Anna Sergeyevna
          Odintsov. (*To* BAZAROV) An unusual name, isn't it?
          — Odintsov. Are you familiar with it?
BAZAROV   (*Not listening*) No.
NIKOLAI   It was unknown to me, too, I must confess. Any-
          how it transpires that the young lady's mother,
          may she rest in peace, and my good wife, may she
          rest in peace, were very close friends when they
          were young girls. But, as so often happens, they
          lost touch with one another shortly after they
          got married. But to cut a long story short, Anna
          Sergeyevna was rummaging in an attic in her
          home —
PAVEL   Could I have sugar?

NIKOLAI (*To* ARKADY) — and she came across a bundle of
letters written by your good mother, Maria, to her
old friend — well, her young friend then. And
Anna Sergeyevna had the kind thought that I
might like to have these letters since they contain
many references to myself. (*To* BAZAROV) Arkady's
mother and I were, as we say, walking out at the
time.

BAZAROV (*Not listening*) Yes?

PAVEL Cream, please.

NIKOLAI I'd be delighted to have the letters, I said. So the
following week Anna Sergeyevna Odintsov called
on us again and handed over Maria's epistles and
spent a very agreeable couple of hours with us —
didn't she, Pavel?

PAVEL I found her very . . . measured.

NIKOLAI Did you think so?

PAVEL And emotionally dehydrated.

ARKADY Uncle Pavel!

PAVEL Oh yes.

NIKOLAI Well, I liked her very much.

ARKADY What age is she?

NIKOLAI I'm very bad at that sort of thing. I would imagine
she might —

PAVEL Twenty-nine.

ARKADY Interesting.

NIKOLAI Oh yes, an interesting lady.

PAVEL Enormously wealthy. With a huge estate. And a
widow.

ARKADY *Very* interesting.

NIKOLAI Very . . . ? Oh, I see what you mean now. Very
good. Very good. What else do we know about
her? She lives with an eccentric old aunt, Princess
Something-or-Other.

PAVEL Olga.

NIKOLAI Olga. And she has a young sister called — what's
the young sister's name?

PAVEL Katerina.

NIKOLAI That's it — Katya. All three are coming on Monday

week. (*Pause*) And we'll have a wonderful party. (*Pause*) And we'll all have a wonderful time. (*Pause*) Won't we?

PAVEL   If you'll excuse me. I get a headache when I sit too long in the sun.

NIKOLAI   We have a meeting with the new estate manager in half-an-hour, Pavel.

PAVEL   I'll be in my room.

NIKOLAI   I'll join you in a few minutes.

As he exits PAVEL *puts his hand on* ARKADY's *shoulder and pats it. Then he leaves.*

Nothing Pavel likes better than a vigorous discussion, plenty of thrust and parry. We're inclined to go to seed here in the wilds, Yevgeny.

BAZAROV   Yes.

ARKADY   (*Quickly*) What were the letters like?

NIKOLAI   Letters?

ARKADY   The letters Mother wrote to her friend about you.

NIKOLAI   Oh, they were . . . oh-ho, I'm afraid they were a bit naughty in places . . . very naughty in fact . . . in fact a few of them were very naughty indeed . . . You never really know what people are like, do you? We all have our codes. We all have our masks.

PIOTR *enters left. He is nineteen, exceedingly cocky and self-assured. He knows* NIKOLAI *is fond of him and he plays on that. He wears a single earring and his hair is done in various vivid colours.*

PIOTR   You wanted me, sir?

NIKOLAI   Yes, Piotr?

PIOTR   You sent for me, sir.

NIKOLAI   I did?

PIOTR   Dunyasha said you wanted me.

NIKOLAI   I'm sure I did, Piotr; and I'm sure you didn't hear me. (*To* BAZAROV) Piotr's hearing is erratic.

PIOTR   (*Aggrieved*) My hearing is perfect, sir. I was slaving

NIKOLAI in the stables. You could scream and I wouldn't hear you there, sir.

NIKOLAI Never mind now, Piotr. Look who's here.

PIOTR I know. I saw the carriage. Welcome home, Arkady.

ARKADY Thank you, Piotr.

NIKOLAI And this is another young graduate — well, almost a graduate — Yevgeny Vassilyich.

PIOTR Sir.

BAZAROV Hello.

NIKOLAI Do you like his multicoloured hair?

ARKADY It's what all the young dudes in Petersburg are wearing, Piotr.

PIOTR I know that. But nobody around this place does.

NIKOLAI And his single blue earring?

PIOTR Pardon me, sir — turquoise.

NIKOLAI Forgive me, Piotr — turquoise. I beg your pardon. (*Waving him away*) No, I don't want you now. Yes, I do. Take this tray away with you. And get the carriage out and bring it round to the back.

PIOTR Certainly, sir. No sooner said.

NIKOLAI 'No sooner said'! He has my heart broken.

PIOTR *exits.*

And I'm very fond of him — he's so cheeky. (*Looks at watch*) Five-thirty. I must run. Show Yevgeny where the guest room is. Have a wash. Walk around. Take a rest. Do whatever pleases you. We'll eat at seven. And welcome again — both of you.

He leaves. ARKADY *is annoyed with his friend; he thinks his exchange with* PAVEL *was too personal.* BAZAROV *is unaware of this. He goes to the samovar.*

BAZAROV How did your father get that limp?

ARKADY Broken leg when he was young. Badly set.

BAZAROV I like him. He's a decent man. An astute bird, too. What's the relationship between him and the blonde woman?

ARKADY Fenichka. She's his mistress.

BAZAROV Ah. I got a whiff of something there.

ARKADY I suppose that's one way of putting it.

BAZAROV Have they known each other long?

ARKADY She has a child by him.

BAZAROV Good-looking woman. A nice self-awareness about her. Fenichka.

ARKADY He should marry her.

BAZAROV Who needs marriage? Your father's a lot more progressive than you, my friend. I suspect — just glancing round the yard — I suspect he's not the most organized landowner in Russia. But his heart's in the right place. Tea?

ARKADY I thought you were a bit severe on Uncle Pavel.

BAZAROV God, what a freak that is!

ARKADY It sounded like a personal attack — cliché French — all that stuff.

BAZAROV Have you any idea of the shock it is to walk into a place like this, miles from anywhere, and to be confronted by that — that decaying dandy? And all those archaic theories about 'civilization' and a 'basis of conduct'! He's a bloody absurdity!

ARKADY He was considered to be the most handsome officer in the army in his day; and the best gymnast.

BAZAROV No, he's not absurd — he's grotesque.

ARKADY He was made a captain when he was only twenty-one. Women just threw themselves at him. And he has travelled everywhere and read everything. And he speaks three or four languages. And he dined once with Louis Philippe; and he and the Duke of Wellington corresponded on and off for years.

BAZAROV (*Imitating* PAVEL) Good heavens.

ARKADY And then, when he was in his mid-twenties, he fell in love — one of those passions that consumes totally. I remember hearing the story when I was very young. She was a princess; married; with a child.

DUNYASHA *appears on the verandah and shakes out a tablecloth.* BAZAROV *pretends to think she is waving at him and waves back at her.* DUNYASHA *withdraws coyly.*

BAZAROV That Dunyasha lady has a sporty eye.

ARKADY And she had this radiant golden hair and when she let it down 'it fell to below her knees', like Rapunzel in the fairy story. They lived together for a while. Then she got tired of him. Cleared off to Germany, France, somewhere. Just disappeared. He followed her, of course; pursued her frantically for ten years all over Europe. Then he got word that she had died, apparently in some kind of demented state, in some shabby boarding-house in Paris.

BAZAROV Where else.

ARKADY Oh yes, there was another detail.

BAZAROV *(Pretending eagerness)* What was that?

ARKADY Early in their affair he gave her a ring with a sphinx engraved on the stone. And the family legend has it that she said to him, 'Why the sphinx?'

BAZAROV 'You are that sphinx.'

ARKADY That's right! That's what he said! And exactly seven weeks after she died a package was delivered to his club. He opened it up and inside —

BAZAROV — was the ring.

ARKADY Yes. That was in 1848, the year Mother died. Father was alone here then, lost without his Maria. He asked Uncle Pavel to join him. And he came. And he has lived here, really like a recluse, ever since, in a sort of profound and perpetual melancholy ... I'm very fond of him. I think he's a good man, Uncle Pavel.

Pause.

BAZAROV You astonish me at times, Arkady. I tell myself that you *are* maturing politically, intellectually, emotionally. And then you come out with the greatest load of romantic hogwash that quite honestly alarms me. Rapunzel — radiant golden hair — passions that consume totally —

ARKADY If you knew Pavel as well as I —

BAZAROV Look at him dispassionately. The shape and character of his entire life was determined by a single, ridiculous passion. And when that ridiculous passion wasn't reciprocated — what happens? He sinks into a 'profound and perpetual melancholy'! For the rest of his life! Because of a crazy woman! That's the behaviour of an imbecile! (*Beginning to win* ARKADY *over*) Let me give you Dr Bazarov's Principles Concerning the Proper Ordering of the Relationships between Men and Women.

ARKADY I must write these deathless words down.

BAZAROV One. Romantic love is a fiction. Two. There is nothing at all mysterious between the sexes. The relationship is quite simply physical. Three. To believe that the relationship should be dressed up in the trappings of chivalry is crazy. The troubadours were all lunatics. Four. If you fancy a woman, any woman, always, always try to make love to her. If you want to dissipate, dissipate.

ARKADY Poor old Father — I was a bit sharp with him.

BAZAROV And if you can't make love to that particular woman, so what? Believe Dr Bazarov — there are plenty more fish in the sea.

ARKADY You're a bastard, Bazarov. You know that?

BAZAROV Admit it. Am I not right?

ARKADY (*Thawing*) A perverse bastard — that's what you are.

BAZAROV Draw up a list of all the women you'd like to make love to — no commitment, no responsibilities — just for the sheer pleasure of it.

ARKADY Keep your voice down, man.

BAZAROV No complications of 'love', romance, none of that rubbish.

ARKADY That's a game for undergraduates. I'm a graduate

BAZAROV — remember?

BAZAROV A quick roll in the hay — great fun — goodbye.

ARKADY All gross pigs, you medicals.

BAZAROV I'll start you off. Natasha Petrova.

ARKADY Natasha who?

BAZAROV The inconstancy of the man! Your first year in Petersburg — the landlady's big red-headed daughter — Natasha the Greyhound!

ARKADY Come on, Bazarov. There was nothing at all to that.

BAZAROV You wrote a sonnet to her.

ARKADY I never did!

BAZAROV 'Could I outstrip the beauty of that form
That haunts these dark and wretched hours
    called life — '

ARKADY All right — all right! That was just a passing —

BAZAROV Exactly. Quick roll — great fun — goodbye. She's number one. Dunyasha?

ARKADY Dunyasha? — Here?

BAZAROV On the list or not?

ARKADY I never really thought about her in that —

BAZAROV A sporty eye, an open heart, a great armful.

ARKADY Now that you mention her, I suppose she —

BAZAROV She's elected; number two. Anna Sergeyevna?

ARKADY Who's she?

BAZAROV The woman who's coming for the party on Monday week.

ARKADY We've never seen her.

BAZAROV Who cares?

ARKADY She's wealthy.

BAZAROV Twenty-nine years of age.

ARKADY A huge estate.

BAZAROV And a widow.

ARKADY Is that important?

BAZAROV The experience, man.

ARKADY Good point. What do you say?

BAZAROV If only for the experience — number three. And her young sister — Katya?

ARKADY I think so.

BAZAROV Vote. Yes or no.

ARKADY Katya? I like Katya. I fancy Katya. Yes.

BAZAROV Elected. Good. Four so far.

FENICHKA appears on the verandah.

FENICHKA Yevgeny Vassilyich!

BAZAROV Hello.

FENICHKA The baby has some kind of a rash on the back of his neck. Would you take a look at it for me?

BAZAROV It would be a pleasure. Where is he?

FENICHKA He's back here in the kitchen.

BAZAROV I'm on my way. (*To* ARKADY) My first professional job.

ARKADY I'd be sure to get a second opinion, Fenichka.

BAZAROV (*Softly*) Would you say that Fenichka is a possible number five?

ARKADY Bazarov, you — !

BAZAROV In jest, my friend, in jest.

He goes towards the verandah where FENICHKA is waiting for him.

ARKADY (*Calls*) Even in jest! Bazarov, for God's sake, man.

BAZAROV turns at the steps and smiles back at him. Then he and FENICHKA go into the house.

ACT ONE

Scene Two

Early June. After dinner. NIKOLAI *and* KATYA *are playing duets on the piano in the living room.* KATYA *is eighteen, open, spirited, garrulous.* FENICHKA *is standing beside the piano turning the pages on* NIKOLAI's *instructions.* BAZAROV *is outside on the verandah, leaning across the rail, slowly eating a dish of ice cream.* PAVEL *is sitting alone and remote downstage right; reading.* ANNA *is sitting downstage left, listening to the music. She is an elegant, carefully-groomed, circumspect woman. She deliberately lives within certain emotional limits and is wary of any intrusion inside them or any excursion outside them. The* PRINCESS *is sitting upstage right, beneath an enormous parasol which partly conceals her. Now and then she emerges from behind it. She is very old, very eccentric, very energetic. She constantly and vigorously masticates imaginary food and every so often brushes imaginary crumbs from her sleeve and skirt. Just before the music comes to an end* NIKOLAI *calls:*

NIKOLAI Wonderful, Katya. Terrific. Don't stop. Let's do it again from the beginning. Splendid. Two-and-three-and —

> *They begin the piece again and keep playing throughout the early part of the scene.* ARKADY *rushes through the living room and out into the garden, carrying a dish of ice cream. He is very elated.*

ARKADY (*As he passes behind* BAZAROV) Get yourself some more ice cream before it all melts.

> *He leaps down the steps.*

BAZAROV (*As* ARKADY *crosses before him*) I think the dehydrated widow fancies you.

ARKADY Doing well, amn't I?

BAZAROV Give her a message for me.

ARKADY What?

BAZAROV Tell her I'd like to do my anatomy practical on her.

ARKADY Cut that out, Bazarov.

BAZAROV I'm sure she'd agree.

ARKADY *crosses over to the* PRINCESS.

ARKADY Can I get you anything, Princess Olga?

PRINCESS (*Emerging*) Cat.

ARKADY Sorry?

PRINCESS I smell cat.

ARKADY Cat?

PRINCESS Cat-cat-cat. Damn place must be overrun with
them. Shoot them all! Shoot them! Shoot them!
They'll overrun you if you don't. My father told
me that.

She vanishes behind the parasol. He goes to ANNA.

ANNA It's best to pay no attention to her.

ARKADY She sounds so furious.

ANNA Ignore her. She lives quite contentedly in her own
world.

ARKADY There you are. (*Offers her ice cream*) I'm afraid it's
gone a bit soft.

ANNA You have it.

ARKADY I've had enough. Go ahead. There's plenty more.
Loads of it. We eat it all the time here. In the summer. God, she's really a magnificent pianist, Katya.

ANNA She's very competent; no more than that.

ARKADY And she can sight-read brilliantly. I love that piece.
I remember Father and Mother playing it together
when I was very small. I'm sure you play, too?

ANNA No.

ARKADY Yes, you do. You're being modest.

ANNA I don't, Arkady.

ARKADY I'm sure you're a brilliant pianist.

ANNA No.

ARKADY I don't believe you. And I'm told you're a painter. (*She shakes her head*) Yes, you are. Katya told me. She says you're terrific with watercolours.

ANNA Katerina exaggerates.

ARKADY Bazarov and I are going to visit his parents soon, maybe at the end of next week. I was wondering if we could call on you on our way there?

ANNA We'd be glad to see you.

ARKADY Great! Tomorrow, maybe? Are you sure that's all right?

ANNA He looks like a painter. Is he artistic?

ARKADY Uncle Pavel?

ANNA Your friend — who believes in nothing.

ARKADY Bazarov? He's a total philistine! (*Calls*) We're talking about you!

BAZAROV *points to his ears, then into the living room: he cannot hear above the music. Shouting:*

Anna Sergeyevna wants to know — (*He gives up*) It doesn't matter.

ANNA (*Beckoning*) Come and join us.

ARKADY Keep him off politics or he'll give you a boring lecture. I'm a Nihilist, too, you know; like Bazarov.

ANNA (*Watching* BAZAROV *approach*) Really?

ARKADY We've a very active cell in Petersburg. There aren't all that many of us but we're absolutely, totally dedicated. (*To* BAZAROV) Anna wants to know if you're artistic!

ANNA Arkady says you're a philistine.

ARKADY He's the worst kind of philistine — he's a scientist.

BAZAROV What is art for?

ARKADY (*To* ANNA) I told you.

BAZAROV Is it necessary?

ANNA*'s attention has switched to* BAZAROV. *In an*

attempt to hold her ARKADY *launches into his monologue. While he lectures* ANNA *and* BAZAROV *conduct a mute dialogue; 'Sit here' — 'No, thanks' — 'There's a stool' — 'I'd prefer to stand' — 'There's a chair' — 'I'm fine' — etc.*

ARKADY   And the answer to that is: what does the word 'necessary' mean in that context? Is that dish necessary? — that tree? — that cloud formation? We're not exactly in unison on this issue, Bazarov and I. He believes that Nihilism and art are seldom compatible. I don't. But I believe that at this point in our history and in our sociological development it would be wrong for us now to channel our depleted energies into artistic endeavour, not because there is anything intrinsically wrong, or indeed right, with artistic endeavour — but I believe that whatever energies we can muster now have got to be poured into the primary and enormous task of remaking an entire society and that imperative is not only a social obligation but perhaps even a moral obligation and indeed it is not improbable that the execution of that task may even have elements of . . . of artistic pursuit . . . or so it seems to me . . .

He tails off in some confusion, unsure that he has made his point, any point, unsure that he has impressed ANNA, *unsure that she has even listened to him. Pause.*

PRINCESS   (*Suddenly emerging*) My father always said that the quickest and most efficient way to break in a difficult young horse was to hit him over the head with a crowbar. (*She demonstrates*) Bang between the ears! Ha-ha. He was right, you know. I've done it myself. And it works! It works! It works!

She vanishes again. Pause.

BAZAROV Lively music, isn't it?

ANNA So you're not a total philistine. (BAZAROV *shrugs*)

BAZAROV Silly word.

ARKADY What word?

BAZAROV Philistine.

ARKADY No, it's not. It's a precise word.

ANNA Art can at least help us to know and understand people, can't it?

BAZAROV Living does that. (*Laying down ice cream dish*) That was good.

ANNA Not to the same extent; not in any depth.

> DUNYASHA *enters and picks up various dishes around the lawn.*

BAZAROV What is there to understand in depth? All men are similar physically and intellectually. Each has a brain, a spleen, heart, lungs. Intellectually? — darker and lighter shadings, that's all. We're like trees in the forest. Ask any botanist. Know one birch, know them all.

> DUNYASHA *is about to pick up the dish beside* ANNA.

ANNA I'm not finished yet.

DUNYASHA Sorry, miss.

BAZAROV And Dunyasha is the most wholesome and un-complicated birch tree in the whole of Russia.

DUNYASHA What does that mean?

BAZAROV It means that you're beautiful and desirable.

ARKADY Don't listen to him, Dunyasha. Uncle Pavel says he's a bletherskite.

> DUNYASHA *loves this. She gives a great whoop of laughter.*

DUNYASHA He did not, did he? A bletherskite! That's great! That's what he is all right!

249

She goes off, laughing.

BAZAROV (*Calling*) I still think you're beautiful.

ANNA So there is no difference between a stupid person and an intelligent person, between a good person and a bad person?

BAZAROV Of course there is, just as there is a difference between a sick person and a healthy person. The man with tuberculosis has the same *kind* of lungs as you and I but they are in a different condition; and as medicine advances we know how to correct that condition. Moral disease, moral imbalance has different causes — our educational system, religious superstition, heredity, the polluted moral atmosphere our society breathes. But remake society and you eradicate *all* disease.

ANNA Physical and moral?

BAZAROV All.

ANNA (*To* ARKADY) Does he believe that? (*To* BAZAROV) That if you reform society —

BAZAROV Remake.

ANNA Then all illness, all evil, all stupidity disappear?

BAZAROV Because in our remade society the words stupid and clever, good and bad, will have lost the meaning you invest them with, will probably come to have no meaning at all. Do they not play polkas in the houses of the gentry?

ANNA (*To* ARKADY) What do you think?

ARKADY I agree with Bazarov. Bazarov's right. (ANNA *looks keenly at* BAZAROV)

ANNA (*Suddenly to* ARKADY) Could I have some more of that ice cream?

ARKADY (*Jumping to his feet, eager to serve*) Wonderful, isn't it? I made it myself. Ice cream, Uncle Pavel?

PAVEL What's that?

ARKADY Ice cream — do you want some?

BAZAROV 'Good heavens, no'.

PAVEL Good heavens, no.

ARKADY (*Coldly to* BAZAROV) What about you?

BAZAROV Not for me.

ARKADY goes to the PRINCESS.

ARKADY Princess, would you like —

She emerges momentarily and scowls at him.

PRINCESS Would I like what? What would I like?
ARKADY Sorry.

He flees, tripping on the verandah steps.

ANNA He's such a nice young man.
BAZAROV You have unbalanced him.
ARKADY (*Calling above the piano music*) Anybody for ice cream?
KATYA Me, Arkady. Please.
ARKADY Fenichka?

She signals 'no'. He goes to her and dances her round the room in time to the music. ANNA *claps.*

ANNA (*Calling*) Very good, Arkady! Lovely!
BAZAROV Exquisite.
ANNA He's a very good dancer.
BAZAROV (*Sharply*) Altogether he's such a nice young man.
ANNA (*Calling*) Beautiful, Arkady. Very elegant.
ARKADY Can't hear you.
BAZAROV He can't take his eyes off you.
ANNA Do you dance?
BAZAROV No.
ANNA I love dancing.
BAZAROV Naturally. All aristocrats love dancing.
ANNA I've told you, Yevgeny — I'm not an aristocrat.
Tell me more about your Nihilism.
BAZAROV It's not mine. I don't possess it like an estate. Tell
me what you believe in.
ANNA Routine; order; discipline.
BAZAROV That's how you conduct your life, not what you

believe in.

ANNA It's adequate for me.

BAZAROV Because you have no beliefs or because your beliefs have no passion?

ANNA Passion is a luxury. I make no excursions outside what I know and can handle.

BAZAROV These new psychiatrists would say that you avoid belief because belief demands commitment and you're afraid of commitment. And you're afraid of commitment because it would demand everything of you. And because you're not prepared to give everything you give nothing. And you excuse yourself by calling passion a luxury but you know in your heart that your excuse is a lie.

ANNA I'm not a liar, Yevgeny Vassilyich.

BAZAROV I haven't met all that many aristocrats like you in my life —

ANNA I am not an —

BAZAROV — but I've noticed that their brain is divided into two equal parts. One part is totally atrophied — the part that might be capable of generosity, enthusiasm, of a thirst for social change, of the desire for risk, for the big gamble, for that dangerous extreme. So they function, these aristocratic cripples, they function with the portion that is left to them; and like some mutilated organ it becomes unnaturally developed and unnaturally active. Hence your aristocrat's irrational obsession with wheat yield and good management and productivity and efficiency —

ANNA And routine and order and discipline. Why are you being so difficult?

BAZAROV Perhaps I haven't the grace for aristocratic ladies like you.

ANNA My father, my handsome, gambling, risking, reckless father died when I was twenty. Katerina was only nine. For two years we lived in penury, the kind of grinding poverty I suspect you have never known, Yevgeny. Then I met a man who was

twenty-five years older than me. He was very
wealthy, eccentric, a hypochondriac, enormously
fat. He had no illusions about himself. He asked
me to marry him. I thought about it very carefully
and then I said yes. We had six years together. I
still miss him. He was a kind man.

BAZAROV So?

ANNA So that's all. I suppose I'm trying to — Oh I don't
know why I told you that.

BAZAROV I'm afraid I'm lost here. I mean — am I to applaud
your circumspection in netting a rich old eccentric
— or commiserate with you on your bereavement
— or congratulate you on your sudden wealth?

ANNA Let's not talk about it anymore.

BAZAROV Or are you just teasing my appetite for the full
biography? Because if you are I'm afraid I find it
less than gripping. But it does have the makings
of the kind of rags-to-riches novelette that someone like Dunyasha, or indeed the very nice young
Arkady, would probably find irresistible.

> ANNA *jumps to her feet and would leave but*
> BAZAROV *catches her by the arms.*

Oh my God, Anna — forgive me — I'm sorry —
I'm sorry — please, please forgive me —

> *The music has stopped. Everybody is aware of*
> *the scene, of the raised voices. Everybody is*
> *staring at them.* BAZAROV *realizes he is hold-*
> *ing her and lets her go.*

(*Lowering his voice*) I've no idea why I said that —
it was unpardonable, unpardonable — I'm sorry
— I'm deeply sorry — please forgive me — please.

> *Silence.* PAVEL, *the only person unaware of the*
> *scene, closes his book and walks slowly across*
> *the stage towards* ANNA.

PAVEL   (*Applauding the pianists*) Bravo! Well done! Lovely! Thank you. Your sister is a very talented pianist.

ANNA   What are you reading, Pavel Petrovich?

PAVEL   This? *Ne vaut pas la peine d'être lu. The Romance of the Forest* by an English novelist called Mrs Ann Ward Radcliffe. A simple lady. But it kills time. Harmlessly.

> As PAVEL *goes into the living room* ARKADY *enters carrying two dishes of ice cream — one for* KATYA *and one for* ANNA.

(*With distaste*) Good Lord.

ARKADY   Good Lord, it's lovely, Uncle Pavel. Here we are! Who ordered what? Katya — there you are — one vanilla ice cream coated with chocolate dressing and topped with a single glistening cherry.

KATYA   Thank you, Arkady. Oh, lovely!

BAZAROV   (*Softly to* ANNA) Please forgive me. I'm deeply sorry.

> *He exits quickly left.*

ARKADY   (*To* KATYA) My great pleasure. (*Coming outside*) And one without dressing for Anna Sergeyevna Odintsov.

> KATYA *comes down beside him.*

KATYA   Did you really make it yourself?

ARKADY   Why the surprise? I'm an expert at all foods, amn't I, Bazarov? Where's Bazarov? In the flat we shared I did all the cooking and he did all the washing and cleaning.

KATYA   (*To* ANNA) You're pale. Are you all right?

ANNA   I'm fine — fine — we'll soon have to go, Katerina.

KATYA   No, we're not leaving for some time. I like it here.

> NIKOLAI *and* FENICHKA *come down.*

NIKOLAI I really enjoyed that. I haven't played piano duets since Maria and I used to sit in there and — (*recovering*) — oh, not for years and years. Did we go on too long?

ANNA Not long enough. We had a lovely evening.

NIKOLAI I hope it's the first of many. It's beginning to get cold. Do you think the Princess is warm enough?

ANNA She's all right. Anyway it's time we got the carriage ready.

NIKOLAI Piotr! Piotr! He must be somewhere around. Ah, Prokofyich, would you see to Madam Odintsov's carriage?

PROKOFYICH Certainly, madam.

ANNA *pushes the parasol aside.*

ANNA Time to move, Auntie Olga. We have a long journey before us.

PRINCESS Long journeys — short journeys — my father always said they all end up in the same place: nowhere, nowhere, nowhere.

ANNA *takes her arm and together they go into the living room.* ARKADY *watches* ANNA *as she goes.*

KATYA You were to show me the litter of pups, Arkady.

ARKADY Sorry?

KATYA The litter of pups — you were to show me them.

ARKADY So I was. We'll go just now. They're in the stable.

KATYA How many are there?

ARKADY Four. Would you like one?

KATYA What do you mean — would I like one? We talked about this all morning and you said I could have the pick of the litter. Don't you remember?

ARKADY Of course I remember. And it's the pick of the litter you'll get, Katerina.

KATYA Katya! Katya! Katya! We talked about that, too! I told you I loathe Katerina. Anna's the only one who calls me Katerina.

ARKADY   Sorry, Katya. The pick of the litter — your choice — whatever one you want. Or take two of them. Or three of them. Or take them all.

KATYA   'Take them all'! You're an awful clown, you know.

ARKADY   Why?

KATYA   Just the way you go on. If you want my honest opinion, I think you're not a very mature person yet.

ARKADY   Really?!

KATYA   But that will come in time.

ARKADY   Oh, good. Then I'll be like you.

KATYA   No, no — always a little behind. But close enough. Come on — Anna wants to leave soon.

> *She leads him off left.* NIKOLAI *and* FENICHKA *move downstage.* DUNYASHA *comes into the living room and tidies around. She is singing.*

NIKOLAI   I wouldn't be at all surprised if Arkady has fallen for young Katya. I noticed, when we were playing the piano, she kept watching him.

FENICHKA   I think it's Anna Sergeyevna he likes.

NIKOLAI   Do you think so? Oh, I would hope not. Anna Sergeyevna is a splendid young woman but much too sophisticated for Arkady. Sit down beside me. You must be tired. You had a busy day.

FENICHKA   I was tired earlier but I'm fine now. When are the boys leaving?

NIKOLAI   The end of next week, I believe. And I'm glad — no, not that they're leaving — (*whispers*) — but that Bazarov is finally going to his parents. Hasn't seen them for three whole years! Can you imagine — not since he started college!

FENICHKA   Some people live like that. It doesn't mean he doesn't care for them.

NIKOLAI   That's true. Maybe it's just a matter of being alert to certain sensibilities. He's fond of you — Bazarov.

FENICHKA   Is he?

NIKOLAI   Oh, yes. He's more relaxed with you than with

anybody else in the house.

FENICHKA I like him, too. Strange man.

NIKOLAI And Arkady's also fond of you, thank heaven!

FENICHKA I'm very fond of Arkady.

DUNYASHA *exits. They are alone.*

NIKOLAI And of Mitya. Calls him 'little half-brother'.

FENICHKA I've heard him. It's funny to see them playing together.

NIKOLAI We had a long talk the other day. We were alone in the garden here. It was like old times — just the two of us. And then do you know what he did out of the blue? He scolded me!

FENICHKA Arkady?

NIKOLAI Quite severely. He said I shouldn't have allowed you to live above that laundry for so long.

FENICHKA (*Becoming embarrassed*) What Arkady doesn't know is that the room above the laundry is the warmest room in the house.

NIKOLAI It is also damp. Anyhow, his point was that you were pregnant and you should have been in the main building; that it was most insensitive of me. And he's right.

FENICHKA That's all over, Nikolai. I'm in the main house now. You're right — it is getting cold.

NIKOLAI He said, too, that we should be married. Yes. He had no doubts whatever. He thinks it's ridiculous we're not married. Remarkable, isn't it?

FENICHKA What is?

NIKOLAI That that is his attitude. And I found it very re-assuring. More than reassuring — encouraging, most encouraging. Wouldn't you agree?

FENICHKA Oh, yes; most encouraging.

NIKOLAI And of course Pavel would be in favour. No question about his attitude.

FENICHKA Has he said that to you?

NIKOLAI He doesn't have to say it — I know Pavel. Con-vention — decorum. Oh, yes, Pavel will want the proprieties observed. So, since I now know what Arkady thinks — and unlike his dithering old father he hadn't a moment's hesitation — and since I've always known that Pavel would be in favour —

FENICHKA *buries her face in her handkerchief and cries.* NIKOLAI *watches her in alarm and bewilderment.*

Fenichka? Fenichka, what's the matter with — ? My God, what have I done wrong? Did I do anything? — Did I say anything? Did somebody hurt you? Who hurt you? Please don't cry, Fenichka. Please. Tell me what's the matter with you. Fenichka? Fenichka?

She continues to cry. He continues to watch her in bewilderment.

ACT ONE

Scene Three

End of June. ARKADY *and* BAZAROV *are sitting at the dining-room table in Bazarov's home. With them are Bazarov's father,* VASSILY IVANYICH BAZAROV, *and his mother,* ARINA VLASSYEVNA. VASSILY IVANYICH *is in his early sixties, a tall, thin, pipe-smoking man dressed in an old military jacket. He is very ill-at-ease in the presence of his guests and talks too much — and is aware that he is talking too much — to hide his unease.*

ARINA VLASSYEVNA *is a small, plump woman in her fifties. The first impression is of a quiet, simple country woman. But she is alert to every nuance in the conversation and watches her son and his friend to gauge their reaction to her husband's compulsive talking.*

Two servants attend the table — TIMOFEICH, *an old retainer, almost decrepit, and* FEDKA, *a very young boy who is employed only because of the visitors.* FEDKA *is barefooted.*

Lunch has just finished.

VASSILY Very good question, Arkady Nikolayevich: how do I pass the time? Excellent question. And I will tell you the answer to that question. Timofeich, more blackcurrant tea for our guest.

ARKADY Just a little. (*To* ARINA) That was a very nice lunch. Thank you.

ARINA You're welcome.

> BAZAROV *gets to his feet and paces round the room.*

VASSILY Yevgeny?

BAZAROV None for me.

ARINA (*Privately to* BAZAROV) Take another biscuit.

BAZAROV (*Playfully shaking his head*) Shhh!

ARINA I'm going to have to fatten you up over the next two months.

> BAZAROV *responds by puffing out his cheeks and his chest and miming a fat man.*

VASSILY How do I pass the time? I'm a bit like ancient Gaul: I'm divided into *tres partes*, as our friend Caesar might put it. One part is the reader. Another part is the gardener. And the third part is the practising doctor — even though I'm supposed to have retired years ago. Not a day passes but there's a patient at my door. (*To* ARINA) That wouldn't be incorrect, my pet, would it? And interestingly enough all of those three parts add up to one complete integer. My reading is all medical reading. My gardening is all medical gardening — I believe I have the best garden of medicinal herbs in the whole province. That wouldn't be inaccurate, my pet, would it? Nature itself as healer — it's the answer, you know. As our friend Paracelsus puts it: I trust *in herbis, in verbis et in lapidibus*.

BAZAROV (*To* ARKADY) Father was a great classical scholar in his day.

VASSILY Great? I wouldn't say I —

BAZAROV Won a medal for Latin composition. Silver. When he was only twelve.

VASSILY I suspect he's mocking me. Are you mocking me?

BAZAROV Me?

ARINA Finish your story, Vassily.

VASSILY Where was I?

BAZAROV *In herbis, in verbis et in lapidibus.*

VASSILY Tending to my garden, attending my patients, and in my spare time looking after my modest farm. (*To* ARKADY) I shouldn't say 'my modest farm' — I'm a plebeian, a *homo novus* — Yevgeny's mother is the patrician.

ARINA Vassily!

Fathers and Sons

BAZAROV *bows to his mother and kisses her hand.*

BAZAROV   Her serene highness, Arina Vlassyevna Bazarov.

ARINA   Behave yourself.

VASSILY   For God's sake, Fedka, will you put something on your feet. Timofeich, take this little urchin away and dress him correctly. Arkady Nikolayevich will think he's staying with some sort of primitives.

BAZAROV   Isn't that what we are?

VASSILY   You're very facetious today, young man. But where was I? Yes, talking of medicine. You'll enjoy this. I hear that a retired major about six miles from here is doing a bit of doctoring. So one day, when we meet at the market, this major and I, I said, 'I hear you're in practice, Major?' 'Yes,' he said. 'Where did you qualify?' 'I never qualified,' he said. 'Never? But where did you study your medicine?' 'I never studied medicine.' 'But you practice medicine, Major?' 'Oh, yes. But not for money — just for the good of the community.'

VASSILY *alone laughs at this.* ARKADY *smiles politely.*

I love that — 'just for the good of the community' — I really love that. Wonderful man to have around in a typhus epidemic. Incidentally there's a lot of it around . . . typhus . . .

Pause.

ARINA   (*To* ARKADY) How long did you stay with this — this Madam Odintsov?

ARKADY   A week — (*to* BAZAROV) — wasn't it? I've lost track of time.

BAZAROV   Eight nights.

ARINA   (*To* ARKADY) And you had a nice time there?

ARKADY   It was sheer luxury. We were a bit overwhelmed at first, weren't we?

BAZAROV Were we?

ARKADY Well, I was.

BAZAROV Yes, you were.

ARKADY A butler in black tails, footmen in livery, scores of maids and servants all over the place. It's really a miniature empire she has there.

ARINA And she lives with an old aunt and a young sister, this Madam Odintsov?

ARKADY The old aunt's as mad as a hatter.

ARINA And the young sister?

ARKADY Katya is — (*to* BAZAROV) — how would you describe Katya?

BAZAROV You should have no difficulty. You voted her on your list.

ARINA List? What list?

ARKADY (*Embarrassed*) Oh, we made a list, Yevgeny and I — a sort of silly list of — of — of all the pretty girls we know.

ARINA Ah. And Katya is on that list?

ARKADY She *was* on the list — at the beginning. She was on the first list.

ARINA I see. She was pretty but she's not pretty now.

ARKADY Oh, she's pretty, very pretty, isn't she?

BAZAROV You're not alert to Mother's subtleties, Arkady. When she inquires about 'this — this Madam Odintsov', can't you hear the disapproval in her voice? She has already made up her mind that This Madam Odintsov is what novelists call an adventuress.

ARINA That's not true.

BAZAROV (*Hugging her affectionately and laughing*) You're suspicious of her.

ARINA Don't be silly, Yevgeny.

BAZAROV You dislike her intensely.

ARINA I never even heard of the woman until yesterday. He's trying to annoy me.

BAZAROV In fact you hate The Woman. I know exactly what it means when that little nose twitches like that. It always gives you away.

ARINA   And you? What do you think of her?

> BAZAROV *hugs her again and laughs.*

BAZAROV   Oh no, no, no, no, no, no, no; you're not going to
turn the tables like that, Arina Vlassyevna. Isn't
she a cunning little squirrel?

VASSILY   (*To* ARKADY) They're well met, the pair of them.

BAZAROV   The question you really want to ask, Mother — it
has tormented you since we arrived yesterday —
what you want to ask straight out is: am I in love
with This Madam Odintsov? And the answer is:
I don't believe in love, in falling in love, in being
in love. Arkady and I spent a pleasant week with
Katya and Anna. They're good company. I'm fond
of them both. And that's it — *finis fabulae* — (*to*
VASSILY) — correct?

VASSILY   Very good, Yevgeny.

BAZAROV   If there is such a thing as a *maladie d'amour* — as
the Tailor's Dummy would put it — I'm immune
to it. Why don't you direct your loaded questions
to Arkady? You're not immune, are you?

ARINA   You're too smart for your own good. (*To* TIMOFEICH
who has entered) Clear the table, will you.

TIMOFEICH   Excuse me, sir. A patient here to see you — a
woman.

VASSILY   Can't you see we're still eating, Timofeich? Tell
her to come back tomorrow.

> *To* FEDKA *who has entered wearing boots that are
much too big for him.*

That's more like it. Good boy, Fedka.

BAZAROV   What's wrong with the woman?

TIMOFEICH   She's holding herself as if she was in pain. I think
she has the gripes.

VASSILY   Dysentery — that's what she has. They call it the
gripes about here. *Torminum*, Pliny calls it. Cicero
uses the plural — *tormina*. (*To* TIMOFEICH) Tell her

to come back tomorrow morning.

BAZAROV Let me have a look at her, Father.

VASSILY No, no; you're on your holidays and —

BAZAROV Please. I'd like to.

VASSILY If you'd like to. Very well. Certainly. We'll only be a few —

BAZAROV I'd prefer to see her by myself.

VASSILY Off you go. Give her a good shot of opium — you'll find it in my bag on the desk in the study. She'll be most grateful — probably want to pray over you.

BAZAROV has gone. VASSILY calls after him.

And she'll offer you four eggs as payment. (*To* ARKADY) Do you know how many eggs I was given last week? One hundred and seventy nine! That's no exaggeration, my pet, is it?

TIMOFEICH is clearing the table. FEDKA helps him.

ARINA (*Sitting again*) Leave the table for the moment, Timofeich. Fedka, put those raspberries out in the pantry.

Both servants leave.

Are you an only child, too, Arkady?

ARKADY Yes. No — no — I have a half-brother, Mitya.

ARINA Is he at college?

ARKADY He's eight months old.

VASSILY He has a few weeks to wait yet. (*Raising his glass*) Welcome again, Arkady. It's a great pleasure for us to have you here.

ARKADY Thank you.

VASSILY A very great pleasure. Isn't that correct, my pet?

ARINA You're most welcome.

Now that they have ARKADY alone both parents

*want desperately to ply him with questions about
their son. They move physically closer to him.*

VASSILY And I hope you can stay with us until you go
back to college.

ARINA You've forgotten, Vassily — Arkady has graduated.

VASSILY Forgive me. Of course.

ARINA And I'm sure he has hundreds of plans for the
rest of the summer.

ARKADY I haven't a plan in the world. I'm — at large!

VASSILY Then you'll stay. Excellent. It's a delight for us to
have Yevgeny's student friends. He usually brings
somebody home with him every holiday. Fine
young men all of them. And we love the company.

ARINA Have you known Yevgeny long?

ARKADY For about a year. We met at the philosophical
meetings.

VASSILY A philosopher, too, is he? Aha! That's a little detail
we didn't know, did we?

ARINA Has he got a girl in Petersburg?

ARKADY Not that I know of.

VASSILY I'm sure you have, Arkady; dozens of them.

ARINA But nobody special?

ARKADY Yevgeny? No; nobody special.

ARINA He ate hardly any lunch. Is his appetite always as
bad?

ARKADY He's not very interested in food — maybe because
I do the cooking!

ARINA In this flat you share?

ARKADY Yes.

ARINA How many rooms do you have?

ARKADY Three: bedroom, kitchen, washroom.

ARINA And how long have you been together?

ARKADY Oh, for the past year.

ARINA What does he do about his laundry?

ARKADY He does it himself. Mine, too. That's the arrangement.

VASSILY Does he take any exercise?

ARKADY He walks to lectures. And back. That's about it.

VASSILY No good. He was always lazy about exercise. Not enough. Not nearly enough.

ARINA How do you know when you don't know how far it is from the flat to the university? You just don't know. (*To* ARKADY) And that hotel he mentioned — how many hours a week does he work there?

ARKADY It varies. Sometimes twenty. Maybe up to thirty.

ARINA And does he really make enough to feed and clothe himself?

ARKADY Just about.

ARINA And pay his fees?

ARKADY We all live fairly frugally.

ARINA You know he has never accepted any money from us, never since the first day he —

VASSILY Arkady Nikolayevich is not interested in our domestic affairs, my pet. Tell me about this revolutionary stuff he was spouting last night, this — this — this —

ARKADY Nihilism.

VASSILY That's it. He's not really serious about that, is he? All that rubbish about —

ARKADY We both are. Deadly serious.

VASSILY Well, of course it is always valuable — and important, very important — most important to keep reassessing how we order our society. That's a very serious matter.

ARINA I hope he wasn't serious when we were talking about that Madam Odintsov. He said I disliked her — that I hated her for some reason or other! That was very naughty of him.

ARKADY He was only joking.

ARINA I hope so.

ARKADY You know he —

ARINA (*Rapidly*) Is he in love with her?

ARKADY (*Deeply confused*) With Anna? . . . Yevgeny? . . . I — I — how would I know? How do you tell? Maybe. I wouldn't know. I really wouldn't know.

VASSILY And if he is, that's his own business, Arina. There's just one question I'd like to ask you, Arkady —

ARINA You've asked Arkady far too many questions. Let him finish his tea.

VASSILY With respect, my pet, it's you who have asked the questions. My one question is this. In Petersburg — in the university — in the circles you move about in — how would he be assessed academically? What I mean is, would he be considered run-of-the-mill, average, perhaps below average — ?

ARKADY Yevgeny?! Below average?!

VASSILY Yes?

ARKADY Yevgeny is — well, he's the most brilliant student in the university at present, probably one of the most brilliant students ever there.

VASSILY Yevgeny?

ARKADY But you must know this yourselves. Yevgeny Vassilyich is unique.

VASSILY Unique?

ARKADY Yes. Yes — yes — yes; absolutely unique. And whatever he chooses to do, he's going to have a dazzling future.

VASSILY Are you listening, Arina?

ARKADY Oh, yes. You have an extraordinary son.

> ARINA *cries quietly.* VASSILY *cries quietly at first but then his emotion gets the better of him. Unable to contain himself he grabs* ARKADY's *hand and kisses it repeatedly.*

VASSILY Thank you. (*Kiss*) Thank you — thank you — thank you. (*Kiss*) You have made me the happiest man in Russia. (*Kiss*) And now I'm going to make a confession: I idolize my son. So does his mother. We both do. Worship him. That's not incorrect, my pet, is it? And yet we daren't offer him even the most simple gesture of love, even of affection, because we know he detests any demonstration of emotion whatever. When you arrived here yesterday I wanted to hold him, to hug him, to kiss him all over. But I daren't. I daren't. And I respect that attitude. It's my own attitude. What we must never forget is that we are talking here about an extraordinary man. And an extraordinary man cannot be judged by ordinary standards. An extraordinary man creates his own standards. Do you understand what I'm trying to say to you, Arkady?

ARKADY Yes, I do.

VASSILY A dazzling future — did you hear that, Arina?

ARINA (*Now recovered*) It's a beautiful day now.

VASSILY There's no doubt in your mind?

ARKADY None at all.

ARINA We should all be out in the garden.

ARKADY What area he'll move into I can't guess — science, philosophy, medicine, politics — he could be outstanding in any of them. But I do know he's going to be famous.

VASSILY 'Going to be famous'. *Non superbus sed humilis sum.* Because some day, Arkady, some day when his biography is written, the following lines will appear: 'He was the son of a simple army doctor who from the beginning recognized his extraordinary talents and who despite every discouragement devoted his entire life and every penny he earned to his boy's education.'

> BAZAROV *enters. He is instantly aware of the changed atmosphere and notices* VASSILY *putting away his handkerchief.* ARINA *gets quickly to her feet.*

ARKADY Ah, Dr Bazarov on call!

ARINA It didn't take you long.

ARKADY Where are the eggs? Did you not deserve a fee?

BAZAROV The woman had a sprained wrist. All I had to do was strap it.

ARINA Timofeich!

BAZAROV What's been happening here?

ARINA You boys are about to go out and get a bit of colour in your faces. (*To* BAZAROV) Take Arkady round by the acacia plantation and down to the old mill.

VASSILY I want to show them my herb garden first.

ARINA I need you to help me put up new curtains in the study, Vassily.

BAZAROV There's something going on here.

VASSILY (*Unable to contain his excitement any longer*) There certainly is something going on here. *Primo*: Arkady Nikolayevich has just decided to spend the rest of the summer here with us. *Secundo*: I have just decided to invite Anna and Katya Odintsov to come and have dinner here with us next Sunday.

ARINA None of this has been —

VASSILY Please. Allow me. And *tertio*: I have had a bottle of champagne in my study for the past three years — and now is the time to open it.

ARINA We'll celebrate later, Vassily. We'll have your champagne at dinner tonight. Can you come into the study now?

VASSILY Your curtains are much less important —

ARINA Now. (*To* BAZAROV *and* ARKADY) We'll eat at seven. Have a nice walk.

She catches VASSILY *by the elbow and leads him quickly and firmly out.*

BAZAROV What's this all about?

ARKADY What's what all about?

BAZAROV You know damn well what I mean.

ARKADY Just a moment, Bazarov. Just calm down. Your mother asked me what plans I had. I said none. Your father then said — excellent, spend the summer here.

BAZAROV Fine — fine — fine. Spend the summer here. But you'll spend it here alone. And what's this about inviting Anna over here next Sunday?

ARKADY You're shouting, Bazarov.

BAZAROV How did that come up? Whose brilliant idea was

that?

ARKADY Your father's.

BAZAROV Who else! The moment you used the words miniature empire I could see the peasant eyes dilate. Well, that is not going to happen!

VASSILY *puts his head around the door.*

VASSILY A patient outside. Sorry — am I intruding? Suffering from icterus. I have him on a diet of centaurion minus, carrots and St John's wort. Now, I know you don't believe in medicine, Yevgeny, but I'd welcome your opinion on this. Not now, of course. Later. Later. Sorry.

He withdraws.

BAZAROV A whole summer of that? Icterus — do you hear him! — icterus! He couldn't say bloody jaundice, simple bloody jaundice like anybody else. And he's prescribing bloody cabbage water and bloody carrots! For jaundice! The man's a fool! That's what he is — a fool, a fool, a fool! And he's killing that poor bugger out there!

ARKADY I like him.

BAZAROV You like him.

ARKADY He's a nice man.

BAZAROV My mother's nice. My father's nice. The lunch was nice. Your Uncle Pavel is nice. I've no idea what the word means. Let's look at my father's life and see can we not find a more exact word. What does he do all day? Fusses about his garden. Dabbles in medicine. Bores my mother to death with his endless and pointless prattle. And he'll go on fussing and dabbling and boring until the whole insignificant little episode that was his trivial life is over. We can hardly call that nice, can we? What about futile? — fatuous? — would you risk ridiculous?

ARKADY   And your life is so meaningful, Bazarov, so significant?

BAZAROV   When we were out walking this morning we passed
the new cottage that Father has just built for his
bailiff and you said, 'Only when every peasant has
a decent place like that to live in, only then will
Russia be close to perfection. And it's our responsibility to bring that about.' And your face positively
glowed with . . . niceness. And I thought to myself,
I thought: there really is an unbridgeable chasm
between Arkady and me. He thinks he loves those
damned peasants. I know I hate them. But I know,
too, that when the time comes I will risk everything, everything for them, and I'm not at all sure if
Brother Arkady is prepared to risk anything. But of
course the ironic thing is that those same damned
peasants won't thank me — won't ever know of
my existence. So there they'll be, all nice and cosy
and smiling in their comfortable cottages and sending eggs up to Arkady in his big house; and
Bazarov will be feeding the worms in some
unmarked grave in the wilderness.

ARKADY   I don't know what your point is.

BAZAROV   That life is ridiculous and he doesn't know that it
is.

ARKADY   And your life?

BAZAROV   Equally ridiculous. Maybe more ridiculous. But
I'm aware that it is.

ARKADY   I'm going out for a walk.

BAZAROV   To be in good shape for the revolution or for
Anna Sergeyevna?

ARKADY   If I stay we'll fight, Bazarov.

BAZAROV   Then by all means stay. Let's have a fight, Arkady.
A fight between us is long overdue.

ARKADY   (*Flushed with anger*) I'm fond of you, Bazarov. But
there are times when I find your arrogance very
hard to take. Only Bazarov has the capacity for
real sacrifice. Only Bazarov is a fully authentic
revolutionary. Only Bazarov has the courage and

the clarity of purpose to live outside ordinary society, without attachments, beyond the consolation of the emotions.

BAZAROV   Yes, I have that courage. Have you?

ARKADY   I'm not as cleansed as you, Bazarov. I like being with people I'm fond of. I even love some people — if you know what that means.

BAZAROV   What what means?

ARKADY   Love — loving — do you know what loving means?

Pause.

BAZAROV   Yes, I know what loving means, Arkady. I love my mother. I love her very much. And I love my father very much. I don't think there are two better people in the whole of Russia.

ARKADY   You don't behave like that.

BAZAROV   How do you expect me to behave? Kiss them? Hug them? Paw over them? You're talking like an idiot. Uncle Pavel would be proud of you.

ARKADY   What did you call Uncle Pavel?

BAZAROV   An idiot. The Tailor's Dummy is an idiot.

ARKADY   Bazarov, I'm warning you —

BAZAROV   It's interesting, you know, how deep-seated domestic attachments can be. Six weeks ago — a month ago you were preaching the dismantling of the whole apparatus of the state, the social order, family life. But the moment I say your Uncle Pavel is an idiot you revert to the old cultural stereotype. We're witnessing the death of a Nihilist and the birth — no, the rebirth of a very nice, liberal gentleman.

ARKADY *goes rapidly and in sudden fury towards* BAZAROV. *He is almost certainly going to strike him when the door opens and* VASSILY *puts his head in. He speaks softly and is very embarrassed.*

VASSILY   There's something I — may I come in? — there's

something I want to talk about to both of you.

He comes in and closes the door behind him.

You're sure I'm not intruding?

ARKADY   No, not at all.

VASSILY   Well. Before we eat this evening, a local priest, Father Alexei, is going to call on us. At your mother's request. She's a very devout woman, as you know, Yevgeny. Unlike myself, as you know, too. And the purpose of his visit is to — to — to gather the family around — your mother, myself in all probability, Yevgeny if he chooses, Arkady if he chooses — you'd be most welcome — to gather us all around in one large domestic circle and — and — well, really to offer up some prayers of thanksgiving for your arrival home. A *Te Deum, Laudamus* 'We praise Thee, Lord'. The little informal service will be held in my study — hence the new curtains. If you'd like to attend, please do. I can't tell you how grateful your mother would be if you did. But if you don't — and that's an attitude I'd respect, I certainly would — then — then — then don't. And we'll all meet for our celebratory dinner at seven. With champagne. And that's it. All right?

BAZAROV   Yes, I'll be at the service, Father.

VASSILY   (*Delighted and relieved*) You will?!

BAZAROV   Why not. You and Mother would like me to be there.

VASSILY   Like you to?! We would —

BAZAROV   So I'll be there.

VASSILY   This is — this is just — just magnificent! Thank you, Yevgeny. Thank you from the bottom of my heart. You have no idea how much I appreciate that — how thrilled your mother will be!

BAZAROV   Not at all. (*To* ARKADY) You'll join us, won't you? But if you'd prefer not to —

ARKADY   I'll join you, of course. And sorry for losing my

temper just now, Bazarov. I mean that.

BAZAROV *catches his hand.*

BAZAROV We were both a bit hasty. But I don't withdraw anything I said.

ARINA *enters.*

ARINA Vassily, are you going to help me or are you not?
VASSILY Arina! Good news! Great news!
BAZAROV I'm just telling Father I'd be happy to attend the *Te Deum* service, Mother.
ARINA Vassily?
VASSILY Yes.
BAZAROV It's this evening, isn't it?
VASSILY Before we eat.
BAZAROV Fine. As long as it's today some time. You see I'm leaving first thing in the morning.
ARINA Leaving?
BAZAROV Yes. I've exams in September and I've a lot of work to catch up with.
ARINA But, son, you've only just arrived.
VASSILY And you can study here, can't you? Amn't I right, my pet? My study is —
BAZAROV My books are all at Arkady's home. I'll work there — if they will allow me. If they don't, I'll go back to Petersburg. But I'll come and see you for a night or two before next term begins. That's a solemn promise. Well. What time do you expect Father Alexei to arrive? When do we all sing the *Te Deum* together?

Quick black.

ACT TWO

Scene One

Late August. Just before noon. Scene as in Act One.

ANNA SERGEYEVNA and NIKOLAI have spent the morning looking at accounts and touring the Kirsanov estate. They have just returned. She is alone on stage, sitting at a table, examining estate maps and accounts with a quick and efficient eye. BAZAROV *enters. He is looking for* ANNA *but when he sees her he pretends to be surprised. He is very tense.*

BAZAROV Ah. So you're back.

ANNA Yes.

BAZAROV The grand tour's over?

ANNA Yes.

BAZAROV It didn't take you long.

ANNA A few hours.

BAZAROV Nice day for it.

ANNA Lovely.

BAZAROV Beautiful. (*Pause*) I think I left a book out here somewhere . . . (*He looks around*) Probably in the living room.

ANNA (*Just as he is about to exit*) How are the studies going?

BAZAROV Well. No, not well.

ANNA When do the exams begin?

BAZAROV Early September. I didn't hear you come back.

ANNA Oh, we're back about half-an-hour.

BAZAROV Really?

ANNA Yes. Maybe an hour.

BAZAROV I didn't hear you. Well, you couldn't have chosen a better day.

ANNA Lovely.

BAZAROV Beautiful.

> *Pause. Then he moves beside her and speaks softly and with intensity.*

We've got to have a talk before you leave, Anna. Last Wednesday in your house you said something I've thought a lot about —

> *He breaks off because* NIKOLAI *enters with another bundle of estate maps.*

NIKOLAI Leave a thing out of your hand for five minutes in this house and somebody's sure to lift it. D'you know where they were? In the pantry! Maps in the pantry! Bats in the belfry! Ha-ha! (*Seeing* BAZAROV) Do you know where Arkady is, Yevgeny?

BAZAROV Yes; he's gone for a swim with Katya.

NIKOLAI I'm glad Master Arkady's enjoying himself. He ought to have been with Anna and me all morning. This is all going to be his one day and the sooner he masters the very complicated business of running an estate — (*he drops one of the maps, picks it up quickly*) — firmly and efficiently, the better. Now let's organize our lives.

> *He sits at the table beside* ANNA. BAZAROV *goes off.* ANNA *watches him go.*

We had got the length of (*map*) number four. Where's five? — five? — five? — here we are. (*He spreads the fifth map across the table*) Now. That's where we crossed the river. And somewhere about here — yes, there it is — that's the old well. Remember? — I pointed it out to you. (*Aware that* ANNA *is not listening*) Are you sure you're not exhausted?

ANNA Not a bit.

NIKOLAI Some tea? Coffee? Perhaps a glass of — ?

ANNA   I'm quite fresh. (*Concentrating fully*) Let's carry on.

NIKOLAI   This is a tremendous help to me, Anna. I can't tell you how grateful I am. Now. We drove along that road there and that's the area that is under wheat. The estate manager's cottage would be about here; Adam's house.

ANNA   And that's where the new threshing machine is sunk in the quagmire.

NIKOLAI   Yes.

ANNA   But that's clearly marked as a swamp ground.

NIKOLAI   Yes, it is, isn't it?

ANNA   Why didn't Adam take all the heavy machinery in from the far side?

NIKOLAI   I suppose he just — just took the short cut.

ANNA   But he must have known he couldn't get across that swamp.

NIKOLAI   Do you think I should abandon it — the thresher?

ANNA   When your tenants have finished stripping it there won't be much of a thresher left.

NIKOLAI   That means I've lost the entire wheat crop.

ANNA   Where's the map of the land east of the river?

NIKOLAI   Here we are. These buildings are my new cheese and yogurt plant. I'm afraid I spent a great deal of money on those buildings. It hasn't been exactly an unqualified success, that plant.

ANNA   Did you sell any cheese at all last year?

NIKOLAI   Not a lot. Very little. None.

ANNA   Yogurt?

NIKOLAI   A few cases. But the cheese didn't go to loss. The poorer peasants were very grateful for it when —

ANNA   What map is that?

NIKOLAI   The stables — paddock — the area behind the house here —

ANNA   No, don't open it. I know that area.

She checks some detail in an account book. He waits. Pause.

NIKOLAI   The Kirsanov estate; all five thousand acres of it.

277

A bit of a mess, isn't it? What do you advise?

ANNA Right. We're now in the last week of August. What I'll do is this. My crops are ready for harvesting. With a bit of organization I may be able to begin next Monday. That means that in two weeks' time all my machinery will be available. It will take — say — two days to transport it over here. So you must be ready to start the moment it arrives, otherwise your wheat and corn and oats will have become too heavy and the thresher won't lift them.

NIKOLAI But I can't possibly —

ANNA I want to have another look at your cheese and yogurt accounts for the past year.

NIKOLAI Of course. Piotr! Piotr!

ANNA No, no; not now. Later. But from the quick look I had this morning it seems to me that the best thing you can do at this stage is cut your losses and close the dairy plant down.

NIKOLAI My new plant? But it's only —

ANNA I know you've spent a lot of money on the buildings but I think you can use them more profitably to store your wheat and oats and hay. You need more storage space anyway.

NIKOLAI You're right.

ANNA And finally you've got to sack that estate manager — what's his name? — Adam.

NIKOLAI Sack my Adam?! Oh Anna, I'm afraid that's something I just couldn't —

ANNA At best he's incompetent. And I suspect he may be corrupt. According to these records fifty foals were born last year and yet I counted only twelve yearlings this morning in the paddock.

NIKOLAI There's an explanation for that. Apparently last winter wolves got into the enclosure and —

ANNA That's his story. I've talked to Prokofyich. He says there have been no wolves around here for almost twenty years. You cannot run an estate this size unless you have a manager who is both competent and trustworthy.

PIOTR *enters, as usual breathless with haste and a bogus eagerness to serve.*

PIOTR You wanted me, sir?

NIKOLAI Yes, Piotr?

PIOTR You called me, sir.

NIKOLAI I did?

PIOTR No question about it, sir. I heard you myself.

NIKOLAI I'm sure I did, Piotr. And I'm sure you pretended you didn't. (*To* ANNA) Piotr's hearing is erratic.

PIOTR That's unfair, sir. With the deepest respect, sir, that's a bit unfair.

NIKOLAI I apologize, Piotr. Your hearing is perfect.

PIOTR I was carrying logs into the kitchen, sir. The moment I heard you I dropped everything.

NIKOLAI Very well, Piotr. I'm sure you did. Anyhow, I don't want you now. Here — take all this stuff with you. You know where to leave it.

PIOTR I certainly do, sir. Leave it to Piotr, the man in the gap.

He takes the maps and account books and exits.

NIKOLAI 'The man in the gap'! I don't know where he gets these expressions. Well. That's a splendid morning's work. Thank you again.

ANNA I hope it's some help.

NIKOLAI I really feel ashamed of — of — of my stewardship. I'm not trying to make excuses for myself but the whole place fell into my lap the year I graduated. I was the same age as Arkady is now. I knew nothing at all about the land . . . Anyhow. Invaluable. I do mean that. (*To* BAZAROV *who has entered as before*) Ah, Yevgeny, taking a break from the books, eh? (*To* ANNA) I keep telling him — he studies too much. Excellent. Splendid. I must tell Pavel about my plans. (*To* BAZAROV) Anna Sergeyevna has clarified my thinking wonderfully. I'm going to close down the cheese and yogurt plant and I'm going to get rid of Adam, the estate manager. He is neither competent nor trustworthy. I'll be back shortly.

He goes off. BAZAROV *is as awkward and ill-at-ease as before. Pause.*

ANNA   I don't think I clarified his thinking at all. (*Pause*) He sounds full of purpose now but I wouldn't be surprised if some of the resolution is gone before he talks to Pavel. (*Pause*) He thinks that his responsibilities ended when he gave the estate to the peasants to farm.

BAZAROV   I want to talk to you about a conversation you and I had last Wednesday at your house.

ANNA   Last Wednesday?

BAZAROV   It was just before dinner. We were sitting together in the conservatory. Somebody was playing a guitar in the distance. Katya's pup was lying between us and there was a circle of moisture where his nose rested on the tiled floor. You said I should offer him my handkerchief and I laughed very heartily because it sounded very, very funny . . . at that moment.

DUNYASHA *appears briefly to do some housekeeping and exits immediately.*

ANNA   For no reason at all that maid annoys me intensely.

BAZAROV   You were wearing a pale blue dress with a white collar and white lace cuffs. Anyhow, Katya and Arkady joined us at that point when I was just about to explain what I had meant a short time before when I had said that it seemed to me that we both appeared to act on the assumption that we talked to one another across some very wide chasm that seemed to separate us even though neither of us knew why that chasm was there, if indeed it was there; but because it seemed to both of us that it was, we behaved towards one another with a certain kind of formality that was more appropriate to people who had only just met . . . Probably none of this makes much sense to you. You probably don't remember any of it — do you?

ANNA Yes, I do.

BAZAROV Do you?

ANNA Bits . . . fragments . . . more your intensity than what you said . . .

BAZAROV It was a conversation of some importance to me and I'd just like to summarize it briefly — very briefly — if I may, and to say what I intended to say then if Katya and Arkady hadn't joined us and interrupted us . . . me . . .

ANNA Katya and Arkady are having a long swim, aren't they?

BAZAROV We were talking about relationships. We were talking about happiness. You said that for you happiness always seemed to be just that one step beyond your reach but that you still believed that some day you would grasp it. You said we had a lot in common; that you had been poor, too, and that you had been ambitious. You asked me what would become of me. I said I would probably end up a country doctor somewhere in the back of beyond and you said I didn't believe that for a minute but that I wasn't prepared to tell you what I really thought. You said you believed you could talk truthfully and openly about how you felt about things. I said I couldn't do that. You asked me why not. I said I always found it difficult to express exactly how I felt but that when I was with you I found it — found it even more difficult. And that's how the issue of a chasm between us came up. And how that chasm inhibited us — well, inhibited me. Because at the point when Katya and Arkady joined us I was about to say that that chasm had prevented me from saying to you what I have wanted to say to you for weeks, what I have wanted to say to you ever since that very first day when we met here away back last May just after I had come from Petersburg — that I'm mad about you, Anna Sergeyevna, hopelessly, insanely, passionately, extravagantly, madly in love with you.

ANNA Oh Yevgeny, Yevgeny —

BAZAROV Yes, I am, I am. You know I am. I can't eat. I can't sleep. I can't study. I'm obsessed with you. I'm besotted by you. Let me kiss you, Anna. Please. Please let me kiss you.

He takes her in his arms and kisses her. She does not free herself immediately. Then suddenly she pushes him away roughly.

ANNA Yevgeny! Please! Oh, my God! You shouldn't have done that.

BAZAROV Yes-yes-yes.

ANNA No, you shouldn't. You've misunderstood the whole situation. You've misread the whole thing.

BAZAROV No, I haven't, Anna. And you wanted me to kiss you. Admit that.

ANNA Yes, you have, Yevgeny. Oh, yes, you have. Misread it totally. Oh, my God . . .

She rushes into the house.

BAZAROV Anna — ! Anna, please — !

But she is gone. He is distraught. He does not know whether to run after her or to run away. Then he hears KATYA and ARKADY approach — they are laughing and calling to one another. He cannot escape that way. The only other hiding place is the gazebo. He rushes to it, sits down, pulls a book from his pocket, opens it at random and pretends to be immersed in it.

ARKADY (*Off*) Give that shoe back to me!

KATYA (*Off*) I will not!

ARKADY (*Off*) Katya, I'm warning you.

KATYA (*Off*) Come and get it yourself.

> *She runs on laughing, her hair wet, her towel flying, his shoe in her hand.*

Oh my God!

> *She looks round frantically for somewhere to hide the shoe. She sees* BAZAROV *in the gazebo.*

I've got his shoe! He's going mad! Can I hide it here?

ARKADY (*Off*) Katya! Katya?

> *She approaches* BAZAROV *and realizes at once that something is amiss. Pause.*

KATYA (*Quietly, seriously*) Yevgeny? Are you all right, Yevgeny?

ARKADY (*Off*) Katya! Where are you?

> *She gazes at him, hunched, tense, behind his book. She reaches out to touch him.*

KATYA Yevgeny?

ARKADY You're for it, madam — I'm telling you!

> ARKADY *is just outside. She withdraws her hand and runs out of the gazebo.*

KATYA I've hidden it in the gazebo, Arkady!

> *She runs into the living room and hides behind a door.* ARKADY *enters, limping; a limp similar to his father's.*

ARKADY I'm warning you, girl! You've crippled me — that's what you've done! (*To himself*) The gazebo . . .

He goes to the gazebo and searches it. As he does:

Was Katya here, Bazarov? Where did she hide my shoe? I'm going to kill that girl!

KATYA (*Appearing on the verandah*) Cold, Arkady. Very cold. Getting colder, much colder.

ARKADY Come on, Katya! Where is it? Where is it? My feet are wrecked with bloody thorns!

KATYA (*Holding up a shoe*) This isn't yours, is it?

She laughs and disappears into the living room. He runs/hops after her. As he does:

ARKADY You told me lies! You misled me! Just you wait there, madam! I'm going to twist your neck! Katya! Katya! Wait there! Wait!

He disappears into the living room. Their laughter dies away. BAZAROV *closes his book. He sits with his eyes shut tight, his shoulders tensed and hunched, his whole body rigid and anguished.* FENICHKA *enters carrying a large bunch of roses she has just cut. Just before she enters the house she glances over at the gazebo, thinks she sees somebody, looks again and recognizes* BAZAROV. *She approaches slowly and studies him for a few seconds before she speaks to him. She speaks softly.*

FENICHKA Yevgeny, is there something wrong?

He opens his eyes suddenly. He is startled.

BAZAROV Hello? — yes? — yes?

FENICHKA Are you all right, Yevgeny? Is something the matter?

He flashes a smile at her and speaks with excessive enthusiasm, almost in panic.

BAZAROV   Fenichka! It's you! How are you? I'm glad to see you — I'm delighted to see you! Yes, yes, I'm fine, I'm fine, I'm really fine, Fenichka. I mean that — I really do — honestly. It's all over and I'm still alive. In fact I'm perfectly well. But how are you? I haven't seen you for days and days and I've missed you. Where have you been hiding?

FENICHKA   You're the one who has been hiding — upstairs reading those books of yours.

BAZAROV   Sit down beside me. Talk to me.

She sits beside him.

FENICHKA   What about?

BAZAROV   It doesn't matter. About chasms and relationships and happiness — about your healing presence in this disturbed house — about those tranquil roses. They're beautiful roses.

Sound of Nikolai playing the cello in the distance: Beethoven's Romance *for violin and orchestra in G-major, Op.40.*

FENICHKA   They're past their best. But Nikolai likes to have flowers on the dining-room table.

BAZAROV   Nikolai is blessed. That's a strange word for me to use — blessed. Six months ago I would have said the word had no meaning. But it has — it describes the condition of someone, anyone, to whom the beautiful Fenichka turns her open face and on whom she smiles. Yes, I have missed you. It's not that we ever talk — this is probably the first time we've ever been alone together — but I'm always aware of your presence in the house, even when you're not there. I think it's because you generate goodness. That's another strange word for me. And suddenly it has meaning, too. You're equipping me with a new vocabulary, Fenichka!

FENICHKA Will you stop talking like that, Yevgeny! I don't understand a word you're saying!

BAZAROV Are you happy, Fenichka? I hope you are. Are you?

He takes her hand in his. PAVEL *enters from the living room. He is engrossed in a book. He pauses on the verandah and then moves slowly downstage.*

FENICHKA I don't think about things like that.

BAZAROV Then you are.

FENICHKA I'm young. I have my health. I have Mitya.

BAZAROV And you have Nikolai.

She withdraws her hand.

FENICHKA Nikolai is a kind man.

BAZAROV Yes, he is. Do you love him?

FENICHKA Do you remember those drops you gave me for Mitya? Three days ago — remember? — he was vomiting — you thought he had eaten something. Well, they worked miracles. He was as right as rain in a couple of hours.

BAZAROV I'm glad of that. So now you must pay me.

FENICHKA (*Unsure and embarrassed*) I — ?

BAZAROV Doctors have to be paid, don't they? Doctors are notoriously greedy people, aren't they?

FENICHKA You're right, Yevgeny. I'm sorry. I'll speak to Nikolai today and he'll —

BAZAROV No, no, no, no, no, no, Fenichka. I don't want money. It's not mere money I want. I want something personal — from you.

FENICHKA What is that?

BAZAROV Guess.

FENICHKA I'm no good at guessing, Yevgeny.

BAZAROV All right. I'll tell you what I want from you. I want . . . one of those roses.

*The cello music stops. She laughs with relief. He
laughs with her.*

FENICHKA What colour would you like, sir?
BAZAROV A red one. A small red one, Fenichka Fedosya.
FENICHKA There you are, Yevgeny Vassilyich — one small
red rose.

*Between them they drop it. Together they stoop
down to pick it up. Their hands meet on the ground.
They laugh briefly and then stop. They look at
one another. He kisses her on the lips.* PAVEL *is
now downstage and happens to look across at
them at the moment they kiss.* FENICHKA *looks over*
BAZAROV's *shoulder and sees* PAVEL *watching.*

PAVEL So this is how Nihilists betray hospitality.
FENICHKA (*Jumping to her feet and moving towards* PAVEL) There
is nothing, Pavel Petrovich — I swear before God
— there is nothing at all —

She rushes off.

BAZAROV Fenichka, your flowers —

He begins to pick them up.

PAVEL What are your views on duelling, Monsieur
Bazarov?
BAZAROV Sorry?
PAVEL I said what are your views on duelling?
BAZAROV I have no 'views' on duelling.
PAVEL Would you accept that it is a method by which
gentlemen can settle their differences?
BAZAROV I think it's just another method of killing — or
being killed.
PAVEL But if you were insulted you would demand satis-
faction?
BAZAROV I don't know. Maybe. I suppose so.

PAVEL Excellent.

> BAZAROV *has now gathered the scattered flowers and for the first time faces* PAVEL.

BAZAROV What's all this about?
PAVEL I wish to fight you.

> BAZAROV *now realizes that* PAVEL *is deadly serious.*

BAZAROV A duel? You want to fight a duel with me?!
PAVEL Tomorrow morning at six.
BAZAROV You're not serious!
PAVEL Behind the birch plantation.
BAZAROV But — but — but why would you want to fight with me?
PAVEL It is sufficient for you to know that I despise you — indeed, I detest you.
BAZAROV But that's no reason to *fight*, Pavel Petrovich!

> PAVEL *raises his walking stick as if to strike* BAZAROV.

PAVEL If you wish I'll give you a more immediate reason.
BAZAROV You're serious! Good God, the man's serious!
PAVEL We will use pistols at a distance of ten paces.
BAZAROV I can't shoot.
PAVEL Every gentleman can shoot.
BAZAROV I haven't got a pistol.
PAVEL We will use my pistols.
BAZAROV I'm not taking part in this, Pavel.
PAVEL We will dispense with seconds. I'll get Piotr to act as witness.
BAZAROV Why are you doing this? What is this all — ?
PAVEL Nobody else need be involved. Tomorrow morning at six, then.
BAZAROV Good God Almighty! What in Christ's name is the —

He stops because he suddenly knows the reason for the challenge.

You're jealous, Pavel Petrovich! You saw me kissing Fenickha and you thought —

PAVEL Behind the birch plantation. Be there.

He moves away. NIKOLAI *appears on the verandah. Neither* PAVEL *nor* BAZAROV *sees him nor hears him.*

NIKOLAI Ah, Pavel. We should both go and have a word with —

BAZAROV That's it! Of course! You're jealous, Pavel Petrovich! You're jealous because you're in love with Fenichka! Oh my God! (*Remembering the duel*) Oh my God . . .

NIKOLAI *retreats into the living room.* BAZAROV *drops into a seat.*

ACT TWO

Scene Two

The following morning. DUNYASHA *is gathering up dishes that are on a table downstage left close to the gazebo. She has only recently stopped crying — her face is red and she is snivelling.* PROKOFYICH *enters from the living room. He is carrying a case which he leaves upstage left. When* DUNYASHA *sees the case she sobs again.*

PROKOFYICH   Get a move on, Dunyasha. Don't spend all morning picking up a few dishes.

DUNYASHA   (*Sotto voce*) Shut up, you old get.

PROKOFYICH   I'm talking to you, miss.

DUNYASHA   (*Sotto voce*) Bugger off.

PROKOFYICH   The guest room is empty — at last. Change the sheets and the pillowcases and sweep the place out thoroughly.

DUNYASHA   Have I your permission to finish this job first, Prokofyich, sir?

PROKOFYICH   We'll do without your lip, missy. Then take the mattress and the floor mats and leave them out in the sun for the rest of the day. Maybe they should be fumigated. (*To* PIOTR *who has entered with another case*) Come on, boy! Move! Move! Move! The sooner this house gets back to normal the better.

> PROKOFYICH *goes back into the house.* PIOTR *leaves his case beside the first and goes downstage to join* DUNYASHA. *All the assurance, all the perkiness is gone. He is thoroughly wretched. He has to tell his story to somebody.* DUNYASHA *does not want to listen — she has her own grief. He holds out his hands. They are trembling.*

PIOTR   Look, Dunyasha — look — look — I can't stop
         them — look. And my whole body feels as if it's
         trembling, too. Give me your hand — put it there
         (*his heart*) — it's galloping like a bloody horse; and
         about every ten minutes or so it stops — dead.

         She ignores him and continues working and
         snivelling.

DUNYASHA Get out of my road, will you!
PIOTR   What — what — what's that?
DUNYASHA You're in my way, Piotr!
PIOTR   (*Almost in tears*) I don't hear a word you're saying,
         Dunyasha. As true as God's above. I'm as deaf as
         a post.
DUNYASHA So you've told me.
PIOTR   What happened was this —
DUNYASHA I don't want to hear about it.
PIOTR   Yevgeny was about there and I was about here and
         the Tailor's Dummy was about there — (*trembling*
         hands) — look! — didn't I tell you — there! —
         there! — there! God, the sight of this is going to
         break my Mammy's heart. Anyway, Yevgeny and
         the Tailor's Dummy had their backs to one another;
         and just when they were about to turn to face
         each other, Yevgeny called me to him and he
         whispered, 'How do you cock a gun, Piotr?' and
         the sweat's standing out on his forehead and he's
         holding the gun like this and his eyes are half
         shut and he's facing the other way. 'How do you
         cock a gun?' — for Christ's sake! And I'm stand-
         ing as close to him as I am to you now and I reach
         over to pull the hammer back and he sort of turns
         towards me and whatever messing we're both at,
         suddenly, suddenly there's this huge explosion
         right beside my cheek —
PROKOFYICH (*On the verandah*) Piotr!
PIOTR   — and I thought, my God, I thought, he's blown
         my head off —

DUNYASHA You're wanted, Piotr.

PIOTR — because I fell to the ground and I could hear nothing and see nothing and feel nothing. And then the smoke cleared and there, lying across a fallen birch tree, there's —

PROKOFYICH has come up behind PIOTR *and now grips him by the arm.*

PROKOFYICH Are you a guest here, boy?

PIOTR What's that, Prokofyich? I think my drums are ruptured.

PROKOFYICH (*Very loudly into his face*) Can you hear me now, Piotr?

PIOTR Shouting's no help, Prokofyich.

PROKOFYICH If you don't get back to work at once — at once! — I'll rupture your head, Piotr. Harness the carriage. Bring it round to the back. Now!

He pushes PIOTR *roughly.* PIOTR *goes off left.* PROKOFYICH *now turns to* DUNYASHA. *She is wiping the surface of the table.*

That's all right. Leave it now. No need to make a meal of it. Get upstairs and clean out that guest room.

As he is about to go off left:

DUNYASHA I'm thinking of leaving, Prokofyich.

PROKOFYICH (*Without hesitating*) Don't think about it, miss. Just leave.

DUNYASHA Well, if I do, I won't do it just because you would want me to do it. If I do it, I'll do it because I want to . . .

But he has already gone. She wipes her nose, lifts her tray and goes towards the house. Just as she approaches the verandah steps ARKADY, PAVEL *and*

NIKOLAI *come out of the living room.* PAVEL *is very pale and his arm is in a sling.* ARKADY *comes first, walking backwards.* NIKOLAI *holds* PAVEL's *'good' arm even though* PAVEL *has a walking stick.* ARKADY *and* NIKOLAI *fuss over him as if he were very ill. He is barely able to keep his temper.*

ARKADY Careful, Uncle Pavel, careful.
NIKOLAI Watch that step.
ARKADY Take it slowly. There's no rush.
NIKOLAI (*To* DUNYASHA) Watch, girl. Out of the way.
ARKADY Get a cushion, Dunyasha. Two cushions.

She goes into the house.

NIKOLAI Let me take that stick, Pavel, and you can hold on to my arm.
ARKADY (*Preparing a seat*) Here we are, Uncle Pavel.
NIKOLAI Turn it round. He doesn't like the direct sun. Splendid. Now get something for his feet.
PAVEL (*Groaning*) Oh my God . . .
NIKOLAI (*Misunderstanding the groan*) I know you're in pain. Hang on for another second. That's it now, Pavel — here we are. Sink back into that — gently — gently — that's it — lovely. Can you lean forward a little? (*He slips a cushion behind* PAVEL) Excellent.

At the same time ARKADY *puts the second cushion, which* DUNYASHA *has brought, on a stool and slips the stool under* PAVEL's *feet.*

Thank you, Arkady. Now we're comfortable, aren't we?

DUNYASHA *leaves.*

ARKADY Should I get a lower stool?
NIKOLAI I think that's about right. (*To* PAVEL) That bandage isn't too tight, is it?

ARKADY He lost a lot of blood, you know.

NIKOLAI As long as the fingers are free to —

PAVEL (*Almost a shout*) Please! (*Now softly and controlled*) *S'il vous plaît*. I got a superficial cut. I lost a few drops of blood. I am properly bandaged. I am in no pain.

NIKOLAI Pavel, you have been through a shocking —

PAVEL I am perfectly well and perfectly comfortable, thank you very much, and I would be very grateful if both of you would leave me alone now. There's a green-backed book sitting on the couch in the conservatory, Arkady. Would you bring it to me?

ARKADY *goes into the house. Pause.*

I owe you an apology, Nikolai. I am sorry to have caused all this . . . upset. I apologize. I won't mention it again.

Pause. PAVEL *puts perfume on his hands.*

If anybody's going into town today I'd be grateful if they'd get me some eau de cologne. (*Pause*) I overheard young Katya talking to her sister yesterday afternoon. She referred to me as 'beau de cologne'. Not bad, I thought. I like that little lady. Spirited. (*Pause*) And I understand Bazarov is leaving us.

NIKOLAI Why did you have the duel with him, Pavel?

PAVEL It was my fault entirely.

NIKOLAI What did you fight about?

PAVEL We had a political disagreement.

NIKOLAI What about?

PAVEL I don't wish to discuss it further, Nikolai.

NIKOLAI I would like you to tell me exactly what the disagreement was about, Pavel.

ARKADY *returns with the book.*

ARKADY *The Castles of Athlin and Dunbayne* — is this it?

PAVEL Set in Scotland. The wonderful Mrs Ann Ward Radcliffe. She's charming — she understands nothing.

ARKADY There's something I'd like to say, Uncle Pavel. Formally. In my father's presence.

PAVEL Oh dear — a manifesto.

ARKADY Because I brought Bazarov to this house I feel at least partly responsible for whatever happened this morning — I know now I shouldn't have brought him here in the first place but —

NIKOLAI Nonsense, Arkady. This is your home.

ARKADY I'm trying to be rational and fair, Father. Our friendship was very important to me. It still is. So I want to be fair to that friendship and at the same time I don't want to judge anybody quickly or rashly. So I'm afraid I must ask you, Uncle Pavel, to tell me exactly, if you would, please, exactly what —

PAVEL Exactly — exactly — exactly! Why this sudden passion for exactitude? Very well. Let's get the damned thing said once and for all. But first I want a promise from you both that what I'm going to tell you will not be repeated by either of you to anybody. Do I have that assurance?

They both nod.

ARKADY Of course you do.

PAVEL Well. Monsieur Bazarov and I were talking about English politicians. About Sir Robert Peel, to be exact, and his family background. I said Peel's father was a wealthy landowner. Bazarov said he was a cotton manufacturer. I've looked it up since. I was wrong. Bazarov was in the right. Not that that matters — the issue itself was trivial. But one word, as they say, borrowed another. Tempers, as they say, too, flared. In a moment of irrationality I challenged him to a duel. He was astonished — naturally. And he met me this morning merely to flatter my pathetic pride. All in all he behaved admirably. His gun went off accidentally. I fired into the air. I have acquired some respect for Monsieur Bazarov. Some modest respect. (*Pause*) I will never mention that episode ever again. Now will somebody please tell me why Prokofyich is stumping about the house like an enraged beast?

ARKADY He disliked Bazarov from the beginning. Now he believes he has a reason to hate him.

PAVEL Isn't he a loyal soul? Life must be very simple for him.

PIOTR enters from the left, exactly as we saw him at the beginning of the scene.

PIOTR The carriage is waiting in the yard, sir.

Immediately after he makes his announcement PIOTR turns and goes off left.

NIKOLAI Thank you, Piotr. Oh, Piotr — my straw hat's in the hall. Would you bring it to — Piotr! Piotr! My God, did you see that! He ignored me! The insolent pup ignored me! Oh-ho, Master Piotr is certainly going to go. There are going to be changes about here. I'm not going to be insulted in my own house by a servant or by anybody else.

PAVEL I don't think he heard you, Nikolai.

NIKOLAI (*Violently*) That's a damned lie! And you know that's a damned lie! The bastard never hears me! Never! Never! I'm sick of him never hearing me! Sick to death of it! (*Quickly recovering*) Forgive me . . . I'm sorry . . . That was unpardonable. I think I'll play the cello for a while . . . The cello, I find, is very . . . healing . . .

He goes into the house. ARKADY is astonished at the outburst. PAVEL has some idea why it happened.

PAVEL Good Lord. What was that all about?

ARKADY He never really warmed to Bazarov either.

PAVEL Perhaps.

ARKADY I know Bazarov likes him very much but he can't show affection easily.

PAVEL What are his plans?

ARKADY He intended going to Petersburg to study. But when he was packing this morning he got a message that there's a typhus epidemic in his home province; so he's going there first to help his father out.

PAVEL Ah. Very worthy. I'm thinking of moving out myself.

ARKADY What do you mean?

PAVEL Just going away. Leaving.

ARKADY Where to?

PAVEL Germany. France. England. Maybe Scotland! Perhaps I should buy the castle of Dunbayne?

ARKADY You don't mean leaving for good, Uncle Pavel, do you?!

PAVEL We'll see. But certainly not until after the harvest is saved. They couldn't save the hay without my muscle, could they? Ah, Monsieur Bazarov. I hear you're going home?

> BAZAROV *enters left with a book in his hand. He is dressed for travelling. He leaves his jacket beside his cases and comes down to* ARKADY *and* PAVEL. *This is now a fully mature young man — neither in his clothes nor in his demeanour is there any trace of the student. His manner is brisk, efficient, almost icy.*

BAZAROV How is the arm?

PAVEL Fine, thank you. You dressed it well.

BAZAROV Take the bandage off after three days and let the fresh air at the wound.

> *The sound of* NIKOLAI *playing the cello.* Romance in F-major, Op.50.

PAVEL   *Le malade n'est pas à plaindre qui a la guérison en sa manche.*

BAZAROV   I don't speak French.

PAVEL   Montaigne. It means: don't pity the sick man who —

BAZAROV turns abruptly away from him.

BAZAROV   (*To* ARKADY) I must say goodbye to your father.

> *He goes towards his cases.* ARKADY *follows him, takes his arm and speaks to him quietly, privately, in an attempt to restore the old intimacy.* PAVEL *goes off to the far side of the garden and reads.*

ARKADY   I have a plan, Bazarov. I'll go to Petersburg at Christmas; back to the old flat; and we'll —

BAZAROV   No, you won't do that, Arkady. By Christmas you and Katya will probably be married.

> *They continue this conversation as* BAZAROV *opens a case and puts his book into it.*

ARKADY   Married?! Me?! For God's sake, man, we Nihilists don't believe in —

BAZAROV   And I'm pleased for you. She'll take you in hand and you want to be taken in hand. You're naturally complementary. And natural elements that complement one another tend to create a balanced and stable unit.

ARKADY   Cut that out, Bazarov! Stop addressing me, man! This is your old matie, Arkady, your old cook and bottle washer. And what I'm going to do is fix a date for a big reunion. Immediately after you finish your exams! — Mid-September! I'll go to Petersburg. We'll get a keg of beer. We'll get all the boys from the old cell together and —

BAZAROV   We won't be getting together again, Arkady. We both know that. We are saying goodbye now.

From your point of view you're making all the sensible choices because instinctively you know you're not equipped for our harsh and bitter and lonely life.

ARKADY Who the hell do you mean by 'our', Bazarov? I'm a Nihilist, too, remember?

BAZAROV When you were a student. But your heart never really forsook the gentry and the public decencies and the acceptable decorum. Of course you have courage and of course you have your honest passion. But it's a gentleman's courage and a gentleman's passion. You are concerned about 'difficult issues' but you believe they are settled by rational, gentlemanly debate and if that doesn't work, by gentlemanly duels. But that's not how real change, radical change is brought about, Arkady. The world won't be remade by discussion and mock battles at dawn. As you told your uncle a long, long time ago we're long past the stage of social analysis. We are now into the era of hostilities — of scratching, hurting, biting, mauling, cutting, bruising, spitting. You're not equipped for those indecencies. When it would come to the bit you would retreat into well-bred indignation and well-bred resignation. Your upbringing has provided you with that let-out. Mine didn't. I am committed to the last, mean, savage, glorious, shaming extreme.

ARKADY I see.

BAZAROV To be blunt with you, Arkady: you are not good enough for us.

ARKADY Was it that savage, shaming side of you that frightened Anna Sergeyevna off? I shouldn't have said that. Forgive me, Bazarov.

BAZAROV *responds as calmly and as coldly as before.*

BAZAROV No need to apologize. I may very well have frightened Anna Sergeyevna. But if that is what happened I have no regrets. Miniature empires have no appeal to me. My sights are trained on a much, much larger territory. We had a good year together, Arkady. Thank you for that.

ARKADY Bazarov, I still think we should —

He stops because FENICHKA *has come from the living room and joins them. She is carrying a package of sandwiches for* BAZAROV.

FENICHKA So you're all set.

BAZAROV Yes.

FENICHKA Did someone say something about a typhus epidemic?

BAZAROV My father. He likes dramatic language. It's all probably a ruse to get me home.

FENICHKA Well, don't take any unnecessary risks, Doctor. I made a few sandwiches for the journey. I know you like cold lamb.

BAZAROV Thank you very much.

The conversation is punctuated by the awkward silences that farewells create.

ARKADY Who's driving you?

BAZAROV Prokofyich. He volunteered.

FENICHKA You're honoured. He doesn't drive me.

BAZAROV He's just making sure he's getting rid of me. (*Brief laughter. Silence*) I must say goodbye to your father.

ARKADY Yes.

FENICHKA He told me he prefers playing piano duets with Katya to playing the cello by himself.

ARKADY Yes, I think he enjoys the duets.

FENICHKA He says Katya is as good as your mother.

ARKADY Did he say that?

DUNYASHA *appears at the living-room door.*

DUNYASHA (*Calling*) Fenichka.

FENICHKA Yes? (DUNYASHA *beckons*) What is it?

> FENICHKA *goes to* DUNYASHA.

ARKADY Dunyasha's suddenly very coy.

> DUNYASHA *gives the bottle of milk to* FENICHKA.
> *They exchange a few words.* DUNYASHA *keeps her
> face averted.*

BAZAROV (*Calling*) Goodbye, Dunyasha.

> DUNYASHA *disappears.* FENICHKA *returns.*

FENICHKA She has a very bad head cold. This is a bottle of
milk for the journey. She says to say goodbye.

BAZAROV Thank her for me, will you?

FENICHKA I will.

BAZAROV I think she thought I wasn't sticking at the books
enough: she kept bringing cups of tea up to my
room.

> *Silence.*

ARKADY He's talking about going away, too. Uncle Pavel.
France. Germany. Scotland, maybe!

FENICHKA For a holiday?

ARKADY For good, he says.

BAZAROV You'll have an empty house.

FENICHKA He's not serious, is he?

ARKADY I think he is.

FENICHKA When is he leaving?

ARKADY After the harvest is in. He wants to do his share of
the scything.

FENICHKA Pavel?!

ARKADY Yes!

FENICHKA You're joking!

ARKADY No, I'm not. Yes, of course I am.

FENICHKA Pavel scything! Can you imagine? Shhh . . .

Again the brief laughter. The cello stops. Silence.
PAVEL *moves towards them.*

PAVEL Are the beautiful Katya and Anna joining us for dinner tonight?

ARKADY Great! (*Recovering*) Are they? That's news to me.

PAVEL Am I wrong?

FENICHKA It's tomorrow night.

ARKADY I thought it was Sunday.

PAVEL (*Looking straight at* FENICHKA) Ah. Then I was wrong. Yet again.

FENICHKA They're coming straight here after church. That was the arrangement.

PAVEL (*Still looking straight at* FENICHKA) My mistake. I get things wrong, Fenichka. Sorry.

FENICHKA Tomorrow night.

PAVEL I see. *Bon. Bon.*

BAZAROV I think I should call Prokofyich.

ARKADY (*Holding on*) Katya has finally chosen a name for her pup, Pavel.

PAVEL Pup? What pup?

ARKADY The borzoi pup she got from us at the beginning of the summer! She's going to call it Pavel!

Brief laughter. NIKOLAI *joins them.*

PAVEL I suppose it's one way to be remembered?

NIKOLAI We're all ready for departure, are we, Yevgeny? Good. Great. And Piotr's driving you, is he? Good. Excellent. (*Calling*) Piotr!

ARKADY Prokofyich's taking him, Father.

NIKOLAI Prokofyich? (*Softly*) Much better. Much more reliable. You should be in Petersburg well before night.

BAZAROV I'm not going to Petersburg. I'm going home.

NIKOLAI Good. Good. Excellent in fact. I'm sure your parents will be delighted to have you. Indeed. Just as we were.

BAZAROV Thank you for all your hospitality, Nikolai Petrovich.

NIKOLAI   It was my pleasure. It was our pleasure. We'll all miss you — won't we? I'll miss all those early morning walks we had — occasionally. And Pavel will miss those — those — those stirring political discussions. And Arkady will miss the student banter. And Fenichka — Fenichka — Fenichka will miss your excellent medical advice — won't you? And —

> PROKOFYICH *appears left. Absurdly stiff-backed and formal. He stares at a point above every-body's head.*

PROKOFYICH   (*Loudly*) I beg your pardon.
NIKOLAI   What is it, Prokofyich?
PROKOFYICH   The carriage is about to depart.
NIKOLAI   Yes, we know, Prokofyich. Thank you.
PROKOFYICH   I merely mention the fact in case any person wishes to travel in it.

> *He lifts the cases and exits stiffly. They stare after him in astonishment and amusement. A quick, stifled giggle from* FENICHKA. *One from* ARKADY. *Then* FENICHKA *explodes. Then they all laugh, excessively, in relief.* BAZAROV *only smiles. He observes the happy family group from the out-side.*

NIKOLAI   Shhh! He'll hear you.
ARKADY   He couldn't — he couldn't even look at us!
NIKOLAI   I know — I know —
ARKADY   In case any person — any person wishes to travel in it!
FENICHKA   It's going to be a — a — a — (*breaking down again*)
PAVEL   A what?
FENICHKA   Can't say it.
NIKOLAI   Shhh!
ARKADY   I know what she's trying to — (*breaking down*)
PAVEL   A what?

FENICHKA It's going to be a very chatty journey!

Again they explode. Then as suddenly the laughter dies. Silence.

NIKOLAI Oh dear — oh dear — oh dear.
ARKADY It was that eye fixed on the sky.
FENICHKA I know. And the shoulders back.
NIKOLAI Poor old Prokofyich. But we mean no harm, do we? No, no; we mean no harm at all.
ARKADY About to depart. Oh, I'm sore. Very sore.

Silence. BAZAROV *goes to* NIKOLAI.

BAZAROV Again, thank you for everything.
NIKOLAI You'll come and stay with us again — perhaps.

They shake hands. BAZAROV *now goes to* PAVEL.

BAZAROV (*Bowing*) Pavel Petrovich.

They shake hands.

PAVEL Thank you. *Adieu.*

BAZAROV *goes to* FENICHKA. *He takes her hand.*

BAZAROV I wish you every happiness, Fenichka. Take care of yourself.
FENICHKA You, too, Yevgeny.

He goes to ARKADY *and holds out his hand.*

BAZAROV Arkady.

ARKADY *hesitates and then impulsively embraces him.*

ARKADY I don't give a damn what you say! Mid-September!

After the exams! That's settled. And make it two kegs.

He releases BAZAROV. *He is crying.*

Come, you twisted, perverse bastard! Clear out to hell! Move! Move!

He pushes BAZAROV *in front of him. They exit.* NIKOLAI *follows them, then* PAVEL.

He's coming, Prokofyich! Here's your passenger!

FENICHKA *is alone on stage. She listens to the voices off. The lines overlap.*

NIKOLAI (*Off*) Put the bags at your feet.
ARKADY (*Off*) Where's your jacket?
PAVEL (*Off*) Good luck, Yevgeny.
BAZAROV (*Off*) Thank you very much.
ARKADY (*Off*) All set?
BAZAROV (*Off*) I left a book somewhere.
ARKADY (*Off*) It's in your hand. Fool.
BAZAROV (*Off*) Thank you again.
NIKOLAI (*Off*) Good luck with the exams.
ARKADY (*Off*) Mid-September. That's settled.
PAVEL (*Off*) Have a good journey.
ARKADY (*Off*) Give my love to your father and mother.
BAZAROV (*Off*) Goodbye.
ARKADY (*Off*) Write me, Bazarov.
BAZAROV (*Off*) I will.
NIKOLAI (*Off*) Goodbye.
PAVEL (*Off*) Goodbye.

A chorus of goodbyes. FENICHKA *waves tentatively and says 'goodbye' quietly.* DUNYASHA, *who has been watching from the living room, now comes down and stands behind* FENICHKA. FENICHKA *turns and sees her. She is sobbing helplessly.*

DUNYASHA All he had to do, Fenichka — all he had to do was raise his little finger and I'd have kissed his feet.

FENICHKA Oh, Dunyasha —

DUNYASHA Oh God, I would have, Fenichka. Just raise his little finger.

She throws her arms around FENICHKA *and sobs.* FENICHKA *holds her.*

FENICHKA Shhh. I know, Dunyasha. I know. I know.

ACT TWO

Scene Three

Early September. Afternoon. The dining room in the Bazarov home. VASSILY *is standing at the head of the table, always on the point of lighting his pipe.* ARKADY *is sitting at the bottom of the table, immobile, staring at the ground. (This is not where he sat in Act One, Scene Three.) He is scarcely aware that* VASSILY *is speaking.* VASSILY *is smiling as fixedly as in Act One and is even more breezy and energetic. But the energy is spurious and it is soon apparent that occasionally he forgets what he is saying — hence the repetitions in his speech — and that he is on the point of breakdown.*

VASSILY   Yes, yes, that was a memorable lunch. I recall every detail of that lunch with total clarity. Oh yes, that was one of the happiest occasions ever in this house. We'd been expecting you for so long, you see — for years, for heaven's sake! And now here you were, in this very room, around this very table. And all I can say now — and I was aware of it then, too — is that your presence alone quickened these ancient bones again. *Omnia animat, format, alit*, as Cicero says . . . *omnia animat* . . . That doesn't sound like Cicero, does it? . . . Oh yes, that was a lunch to remember. That's the event that furnished us with the richest and warmest memories — that's not inaccurate, my pet, is it? . . . (*He looks around and realizes she's not there*) Where had she placed us? I was here. And she was there. And you were sitting where you're sitting now. And Yevgeny was over there. And I have one particularly vivid recollection. I had just told you that story of the retired major who practises medicine

307

'just for the good of the community'; and the two of you gazed at me for a second and then suddenly collapsed with laughter; and there you both are, spread across the table, convulsed, unable to speak! Oh, that's a particularly vivid memory. 'Just for the good of the community.' Couldn't move. Couldn't speak.

> TIMOFEICH *shuffles in. He seems even more decrepit than before. He begins pottering aimlessly with the dishes on the table.*

And Timofeich was looking after us as usual, weren't you, Timofeich?

TIMOFEICH She's awake.

> VASSILY, *suddenly alert, leads* TIMOFEICH *to the side so that* ARKADY *will not hear the conversation.* ARKADY *is scarcely aware that* TIMOFEICH *is there.*

VASSILY Well?

TIMOFEICH No change.

VASSILY Did she speak?

TIMOFEICH Not a word.

VASSILY Is she still in bed?

TIMOFEICH She's in the study.

VASSILY What's she doing there?

TIMOFEICH Sitting.

VASSILY On the couch?

TIMOFEICH On the swivel chair. You should comb her hair for her.

> TIMOFEICH *returns to the table.*

VASSILY Leave that stuff, Timofeich. And stay with her, will you?

TIMOFEICH She can't go on without food in her. You should get her to eat.

VASSILY   (*Suddenly fearful*) Where's my medicine bag, Timo-
           feich?

           TIMOFEICH *points to a high shelf where the bag is
           almost hidden.*

           Ah! Good man. Thank you. Thank you.
TIMOFEICH What are you thanking me for? You hid it there
           yourself.

           TIMOFEICH *exits.* VASSILY *assumes the smile again
           and the breezy manner.*

VASSILY   He's been a tower of strength to me, old Timofeich.
           I don't know what I'd have done without him.
ARKADY   How is Arina Vlassyevna?
VASSILY   She'll be with us in a while. Arina Vlassyevna is
           — what's the cliché? — she is as comfortable as can
           be expected — everything considered — consider-
           ing everything. But we were discussing that lunch,
           weren't we? Oh, that was a memorable occasion.
           Do you happen to remember a boy who helped at
           table that day? — a very young boy? — in his
           bare feet? — Fedka? I have a confession to make
           about Fedka: Fedka wasn't a servant of ours at all.
           We hired Fedka for that occasion. To impress you,
           my friend. To give Yevgeny's background that
           tiny bit of extra weight. *Vanitas vanitatum et omnia
           vanitas.* Ecclesiastes, I think. But don't trust me on
           that. I can still quote with some accuracy but the
           attribution . . . the attribution seems to . . . That
           lunch, yes. And Fedka. I had asked Father Alexei
           could he recommend somebody. And what did he
           present us with? — the butcher's second son with
           the running nose and not a shoe to his name —
           in a manner of speaking. Serving at the table, bare-
           foot! Good Lord. I can laugh at it now. I remember
           I said, 'Arkady Nikolayevich will think he's stay-
           ing with some sort of primitives.' And Yevgeny

lifted his head — you know how he lifts his face
and turns it slightly sideways — and gave me that
sharp, quick eye of his — and he said — he said
— and nobody's wittier than Yevgeny as you well
know — he lifted his head and he gave me — gave
me —

He breaks down: sudden, uncontrollable sobbing.
He recovers almost immediately.

I should pray to God, they say. How can I go on?
— that's what I say to God. How do you expect
me to go on? — I say. What do you think we're
made of? — I say.

Pause.

ARKADY It was very late when I got back from Petersburg.
My father was waiting up for me. 'I've got very
bad news for you, son. I can't tell you how bad
the news is.' 'It's Bazarov,' I said. 'Yes,' he said.
'It's Bazarov.'

Pause.

VASSILY At the end of that first week there were so many
people sick and dying that we decided to split up:
he took the whole town and the region to the
north and west. I had the south and east. Some
nights he didn't get home at all. And when the
epidemic spread to the neighbouring province
we didn't see him for days on end. 'All for the
bloody peasants,' he said to me. 'Everything for
the bloody peasants, damn them!' And then I
came in this night — it was Friday — amn't I correct, my pet? There was a light under his bedroom door. And I was tiptoeing past when he
called me. He was sitting up in the bed, propped
up against the pillow; and even though the candle

was behind his head the first thing I noticed was how bright, how bright his eyes shone. And he said in that ironic tone of his, 'Father,' he said, 'I'm going to make you a present of a much larger practice. I'm going to present you with the town and the region to the north and west.' 'What does that mean?' I said. (*His voice begins to waver*) 'It means,' he said — 'It means,' he said — 'It means that I'm considering retiring. What's your opinion of this, Dr Bazarov? Does it look like typhus?' And he pulled up the sleeve of his nightshirt and held his bare arm over to the candle and there were the purple blotches. (ARKADY *is now crying quietly*)

ARKADY I'm sorry for behaving like this . . .

VASSILY There was nothing we could do. His mother made him lime-flower tea and she tried to feed him spoonfuls of beetroot and cabbage soup. But he was too weak to swallow anything. And the next morning — that was Sunday — amn't I right, my pet? — yes, I am — that was Sunday — he opened his eyes and said, 'Do something for me, Father. Send a messenger to Anna Sergeyevna Odintsov and tell her that Yevgeny Vassilyich Bazarov is dying.'

ARKADY All Katya knew was that a messenger came to the house and that within five minutes Anna was gone.

VASSILY And late that same evening a grey carriage with red wheels and drawn by four horses drew up at our door and a footman in dark green livery opened the carriage door and this lady in a black veil and a black mantle got out. She told me she was Anna Sergeyevna Odintsov and asked to see my son. I argued with her. I said it was too dangerous. But she was determined. So I brought her to him. I left them together. She stayed with him for half-an-hour. He was too weak to talk. She just sat with him and held his hand.

ARKADY Nobody has seen her since. She didn't go home when she left here. She sent the carriage home and she went on to Moscow. She probably wants to be by herself for a while.

VASSILY He passed away that same evening. His mother sent for Father Alexei. He was dead by then but Father Alexei gave him the last rites anyway.

ARKADY My father didn't know what to do. I was somewhere in the Petersburg area buying a new thresher — that's all he knew. But where I was staying — how to get in touch with me — he was at his wits' end. Finally he sent Piotr to look for me — just to walk the streets of Petersburg and look for me. And all the time I was in our old flat. That never occurred to them.

VASSILY We tried to get word to some friends. Timofeich did the best he could. I thought it best to have a short wake because of the nature of the illness and because his mother was a little . . . *perturbata*. So we buried him on Monday morning, early. A quiet funeral; his mother, Father Alexei, Timofeich, myself. And Fedka, the worthy Fedka, properly shod. It was nice of him to come. And brave. A few prayers. Flowers. The usual. I'll take you there if you wish. It's only a ten-minute walk. But if you prefer not . . . some people find cemeteries . . . difficult. There's something not right about a father burying his son, isn't there? Some disorder in the proper ordering of things, isn't it? It's not the way things should be, is it?

ARKADY He was the best friend I ever had, Vassily Ivanyich.

Pause.

VASSILY (*Almost in a whisper but with a sudden and astonishing passion*) Damn you, Almighty Father! I will not stand for it! I certainly will not stand for it!

ARKADY He was the only real friend I ever had.

VASSILY What's that?

ARKADY (*Suddenly resolute*) I'm going to carry on his work, Vassily Ivanyich! I'm going to dedicate myself to his memory and to the work he was so involved in! I have none of his brains and none of his talent. But whatever talent I have and whatever energy I have I will give to the revolution, to Bazarov's revolution.

VASSILY (*Dreamily*) Oh, yes. Politics are very important.

ARKADY He never thought I was capable of much. But I am! I am! And I am now more than ever because I'm doing it for him! (VASSILY *pats him on the shoulder*)

VASSILY Every so often he would regain consciousness. One time he opened his eyes and he said, 'I am no loss to Russia. A cobbler would be a loss to Russia. A butcher would be a loss. A tailor would be a loss. I am no loss.' It never occurred to him the loss he'd be to his mother and me.

ARKADY If you would take me to the cemetery, I'd like to make my solemn promise to him there.

> ARINA *enters, her hair dishevelled, wearing slippers and an odd assortment of clothes. When she enters her face is vacant. Then she sees* VASSILY *and she smiles.* VASSILY *greets her with great warmth and enthusiasm.* ARKADY *gets to his feet.*

VASSILY Ah — Arina! Now that's an improvement! Now you're looking really well, my pet! Do you know that you slept for almost three hours? And who's going to do the housework if my wife lies in bed and spends the day sleeping? Tell me that, my sweet and beautiful wife? And look who's here! Look who's come to see us!

> *She looks blankly at* ARKADY.

Yes! It's Arkady, my pet! It is, indeed! Arkady

Nikolayevich! The very moment he heard he came straight over. He was afraid he'd have to leave without seeing you.

ARKADY All I can say, Arina Vlassyevna — (*he begins to cry again*) — all I can say is that — that — that — that I'm shattered, just shattered.

VASSILY (*To* ARINA) We've looked after ourselves, as you can see. But what we've got to do now is get you something to eat. What can I offer you? What would tempt you? I have it! Arina Vlassyevna is partial to a cup of blackcurrant tea! The very thing!

ARKADY I'll never forgive myself that I wasn't here. I was away in Petersburg. I didn't hear a thing until late last night.

VASSILY (*Breezy, busy*) One small cup of blackcurrant tea and two very tiny but very appetizing homemade biscuits — that's what this aristocratic lady requires and that is what she is going to eat. What does Cicero say? *Tantum cibi et potionis* — we should drink and eat just enough to restore our strength — no more, no less.

ARKADY I can't tell you how devastated I am. I know I'll never get over it.

> ARINA *now sits. Pause. She looks at* ARKADY *as if she were trying to remember him, as if she were going to speak to him. Her face is placid, childlike, almost smiling. And when she sings it is the gentle, high-pitched voice of a very young girl.*

ARINA (*Singing*)
> 'Te Deum, laudamus: te Dominum, confitemur.
> Te, aeternum Patrem, omnis terra veneratur.'

> *As soon as she begins singing* ARKADY *looks in alarm at* VASSILY. VASSILY *responds by putting his finger to his lips and shaking his head as if to say — Say nothing; don't interrupt. Then he sits beside his wife, puts both arms round her, and sings*

with her and directly to her:

VASSILY ⎱ *'Tibi omnes Angeli; tibi Caeli et universae Potestates.'*
ARINA ⎰ *'Tibi Cherubim et Seraphim incessabili voce proclament:*
Sanctus, Sanctus, Sanctus, Dominus Deus Sabaoth.'

Slowly bring down the lights as they sing together.

ACT TWO

Scene Four

After dinner. Early October. The lawn/garden in front of the Kirsanov home. ARKADY *is standing at the piano and singing 'Drink to me only'. He sight-reads the words.* KATYA *accompanies him.* ANNA *sits by herself in the living room, listening to the music.* PAVEL *stands on the verandah.*

PAVEL　(*Singing very softly*)
　　　'But might I of Jove's nectar sup,
　　　I would not change for thine.'
FENICHKA　Very nice, Pavel.

> PAVEL, *realizing that he has been overheard, wags his finger in admonition. He then lapses into his own private thoughts. Two or three times we hear the faint sound of dance music played on the piano accordion some distance away. These brief coincidences of the two sounds — the piano and the piano accordion — produce an almost eerie noise. The* PRINCESS *is sitting alone downstage right, partly concealed behind her unnecessary parasol, vigorously masticating and every so often brushing her sleeve and skirt.* PROKOFYICH *and* PIOTR *have assembled a large trestle table in the centre of the lawn. They now cover it with a white cloth and arrange chairs around it.* FENICHKA *oversees this work with a proprietorial eye. She is now very much mistress of the house and fully at ease in* PAVEL's *presence.* PIOTR, *slightly intoxicated, is completely restored to health and cockiness and jaunty self-assurance. He nips down behind the*

> *gazebo on the pretext of getting a chair and tosses
> back a quick, secret drink from a hip flask. He is
> about to pour a second drink when the* PRINCESS
> *calls him:*

PRINCESS   You, boy! Come here! Come here! Come here!

> *He quickly hides his flask and does a little dance
> as he goes to her.*

PIOTR   Princess, can I help you?

PRINCESS   What's that noise?

PIOTR   That noise, Princess, is Arkady singing and Miss
Katya playing the piano for —

PRINCESS   The noise! The damn noise! There — d'you hear
that?

PIOTR   My apologies. That is the musician getting ready
for tonight — the annual harvest dance. We hold
it in the granary.

PRINCESS   Musician? What musician?

PIOTR   A piano-accordion player, Princess. He comes from
the town of Orel.

PRINCESS   My brother, Josef, had the first accordion ever
brought into Russia. My father lit a bonfire in the
yard and burned the damn thing before the whole
household. Then he whipped Josef with his own
hunting crop until he apologized publicly to everybody — family and servants. Ha-ha. That ended
damn accordions in our house!

PIOTR   I'm sure it did.

PRINCESS   Josef was black and blue for a month. Tell your
friend from Orel that story. Ha-ha. Whipped him!
Whipped him! Whipped him!

PIOTR   I'll tell him, Princess.

> *She withdraws.* PIOTR *returns to his work.* PAVEL
> *comes down and joins* FENICHKA.

PAVEL   I bought that songbook in London — oh, it must

be twenty-five years ago. (*Suddenly remembering*) I know exactly when I bought it — the day they made Arthur Wellesley Foreign Secretary. We were out on the town, celebrating!

FENICHKA Who was that, Pavel?

PAVEL Arthur? The 1st Duke of Wellington. Good man. Good fun. We had a lot of laughs together . . . Nice time of the day, this.

FENICHKA Lovely.

PAVEL Nice time of the year. Do you like October, Olga?

PRINCESS I detest every month — for different reasons.

PAVEL It's my favourite season, the autumn. I tell myself it's the one time of the year when the environment and my nature are perfectly attuned.

PRINCESS It seems to me you tell yourself a lot of rubbish. And you'd need to be careful — the way you carry yourself — you could be mistaken for an accordion player.

PAVEL I beg your pardon?

PRINCESS You look very like one to me, with your shoulders so far back.

PAVEL (*To* FENICHKA) I didn't catch what she said. I could be a — ?

FENICHKA An accordion player.

PAVEL Me?!

PRINCESS They all carry their shoulders back. That's because the weight is all down the front here. Ha-ha, you could end up being whipped by mistake!

PAVEL Good heavens, could I? (*To* FENICHKA) Why do they whip accordion players?

FENICHKA I don't know. Do they?

PAVEL So it seems.

FENICHKA (*To* PIOTR) There's a vase of dahlias and a vase of chrysanthemums outside the pantry door. Put the dahlias here and the chrysanthemums there.

PIOTR Anything the lady wishes.

PAVEL Arkady has a pleasing voice. From the mother's side of the house. Maria had a sweet voice.

FENICHKA (*To* PIOTR *as he dances off*) And napkins from the

	linen press. On the top shelf. (*To* PAVEL) What is that song?
PAVEL	'Drink to me only.'
FENICHKA	I never heard him singing that before.
PAVEL	(*Speaks*)

> 'I sent thee late a rosy wreath,
> Not so much honouring thee
> As giving it a hope that there
> It could not withered be . . . '

FENICHKA *has been counting the chairs.*

FENICHKA	Sorry, Pavel — what was that?
PAVEL	Nothing. Just mumbling to myself.

DUNYASHA *enters left.*

FENICHKA	I've noticed you doing that a lot recently. You're not beginning to dote, are you? There are only wine glasses here, Dunyasha. Bring out the champagne glasses, will you?

> PAVEL, *wounded, moves away.* DUNYASHA *is so excited she can scarcely keep her voice down.* FENICHKA *continues moving around the table, adjusting the settings.* DUNYASHA *follows her.* FENICHKA *listens with interest but her manner hints that the days of confidences are over.*

DUNYASHA	Brilliant news, Fenichka! Absolutely brilliant! The aunt died at half-past-three this morning! Can you believe it!
FENICHKA	Who?
DUNYASHA	The aunt — the old aunt — the old bitch that reared Adam!
FENICHKA	Oh, I'm sorry to hear —
DUNYASHA	He'll be able to sell her cottage. And she has left him about two hundred roubles. And he wants to get married, Fenichka.

FENICHKA To you?

DUNYASHA Jesus, you don't think he fancies the Tailor's Dummy, do you?!

FENICHKA Dunyasha, I —

DUNYASHA Of course it's to me! At five this morning — the old cow couldn't have been right stiff — he was up banging on my bedroom door: 'Little one, will you make me the happiest man in Russia?' That's what he said! Can a duck swim, says I to myself. He didn't go back to the corp-house till well after nine. Jesus, you should have seen that glossy black 'tash of his twitching! D'you know what we should do, Fenichka? — you hang on for another couple of months and we'll get married together! Wouldn't that be a howl! A double wedding! Drive the poor old Tailor's Dummy astray in the head altogether!

FENICHKA I don't want you to call Pavel Petrovich by that name again, Dunyasha.

DUNYASHA The Tailor's Dummy? Between ourselves, for God's sake; it's only to you and Piotr and —

FENICHKA I never want to hear it again.

DUNYASHA Are you — ?

FENICHKA Is that clearly understood? Good. I'm sorry about the old aunt. But Adam should have no regrets: he was more than attentive to her. I'll take those napkins from you, Piotr; thank you. You arranged those flowers beautifully, Dunyasha. I'm glad you're thinking of marrying him. He'll make a very reliable husband. Now — what's missing? The champagne glasses. (*To* DUNYASHA) Would you get them for me?

DUNYASHA *stumps off.*

No, the other way round, Piotr — the dahlias on this side. Don't you think so?

PIOTR I'm sure you're right. The dahlias are left-handed. (*While he was out* PIOTR *has had a few more drinks*)

What else can I do for you, Fenichka? You just tell Piotr.

FENICHKA That's all for now.

PIOTR Have you enough chairs?

FENICHKA I think so.

PIOTR What about some stools?

FENICHKA They won't be needed.

PIOTR Stools are a very efficient means of seating large numbers of guests in an outdoor environment, Fenichka.

FENICHKA We haven't got large numbers, Piotr.

PIOTR Once again you are right. Another few bottles of wine, perhaps?

FENICHKA (*Dismissing him*) Thank you, Piotr.

PIOTR I know a poem. Would you like me to recite it?

FENICHKA Not now, Piotr.

PIOTR Later perhaps. I could spell chrysanthemum for you.

FENICHKA That is all for the time being, Piotr.

PIOTR Well, as soon as the time being is up, Piotr will be at your elbow and at your command.

He bows formally and goes off left.

FENICHKA The harvest party has begun early. (*She holds up an empty bottle*) Since lunchtime. (*To* ANNA *who comes out*) Come and join us, Anna.

ANNA The days are shortening already, aren't they? (*She pauses beside the* PRINCESS) Are you all right, Auntie?

PRINCESS Why do you always ask that absurd question when you know the answer. No, I am not all right. There's a constant buzzing in my head. I can scarcely walk with arthritis. That meal they gave us was inedible. And I am about to be sick with the smell of cat in this damn place.

She rises and leaves left.

When you're ready to leave you'll find me in the

paddock. There's a black filly there that needs to be broken.

ANNA She gets great comfort from her misery.

PAVEL I'm studying her carefully. We could have a lot in common.

FENICHKA You don't have her vigour, Pavel.

PAVEL I could simulate that, too, couldn't I?

FENICHKA Nikolai tells me you had a good harvest.

ANNA I was away for most of it. Yes, it was a good harvest. (*She gestures her indifference*) The best I've ever had . . . It's good to hear Arkady singing.

FENICHKA Yes.

ANNA And Katerina tells me he's out and about again.

FENICHKA He hadn't much choice. The estate's his now. He was needed on the land.

ANNA They're a handsome couple.

PAVEL Aren't they.

ANNA A pity you'll miss the wedding, Pavel.

FENICHKA The weddings, Anna.

ANNA Of course.

PAVEL Yes, I'm sorry about that. I'm due to arrive in Zurich that day.

FENICHKA *waters the plants in front of the verandah.*

Any news of the epidemic? — The typhus epidemic?

ANNA I'm told it's almost died out.

PAVEL Has it?

ANNA So I've heard.

PAVEL Ah. Good.

ANNA Yes.

PAVEL So it's over now?

ANNA Almost. Not quite.

PAVEL Good. They cause great devastation, those things. But they pass — they pass.

ANNA That's true.

PAVEL And the world carries on.

ANNA   I suppose so. Yes, of course it does.

Pause.

PAVEL   I got to know him slightly just before he left here. I hadn't understood him at all before that. In my stupidity. He was a fine man.

ANNA   He was also a . . . difficult man.

PAVEL   He was that, too.

ANNA   He wanted to marry me.

PAVEL   I gathered that.

ANNA   (*Crying quietly*) I should have married him, Pavel . . .

PAVEL   Perhaps — perhaps.

ANNA   Oh, yes, I should. Oh, yes. It would have been a difficult marriage but I should have married him. It's very hard to carry on when you know you've made so enormous a mistake, Pavel. How do you carry on?

PAVEL   I wish I could help you, Anna. I very much wish I could help you. I have no answers to anything. We all want to believe at least in the possibility of one great love. And when we cannot achieve it — because it isn't achievable — we waste our lives pursuing surrogates; at least those of us who are very foolish do.

FENICHKA   Soon be time to bring them inside.

PAVEL   And that's no life, no life at all. (*He puts his hands on* ANNA's *shoulders*) A kind of contentment is available, Anna: in routine, acceptance, duty.

ANNA   I had that life.

PAVEL   It has its consolations. Is that a terrible thing to say?

ANNA   He thought so.

PAVEL   I know. But it's the only threadbare wisdom I have for you. I don't believe a word of it myself.

DUNYASHA *enters with the glasses. She barely conceals her fury.*

DUNYASHA Miss, the champagne glasses, miss.

FENICHKA (*Very calm*) Thank you, Dunyasha. Put them on the table.

DUNYASHA Is there anything else I can get you, miss?

FENICHKA That will be all for now, Dunyasha.

DUNYASHA Sir, what about you, sir?

PAVEL Sorry?

DUNYASHA Sir, can I get you anything, sir?

PAVEL (*Alarmed at this attention*) Me? No . . . nothing . . . nothing, thank you.

> DUNYASHA *stumps off into the house.* NIKOLAI *enters from the left. He is wearing a very brightly coloured jacket — a jacket for a much younger man. Now and again bring up the sound of distant piano-accordion music.*

NIKOLAI I've held you all up, have I?

FENICHKA I thought you'd gone dancing by yourself.

NIKOLAI Ha-ha. Just saying a word of formal thanks and encouragement to the workers for their sterling efforts over the past weeks. (*Quick kiss and embrace for* FENICHKA) This looks splendid! Excellent! I love those dahlias.

FENICHKA These are the dahlias.

NIKOLAI Are they? I never get them right. They're beautiful anyhow. (*To* ALL) Incidentally some time later on it would be greatly appreciated if we all put in a brief appearance at the dance; just to — you know — just to — to pass ourselves. No obligation whatever to — to participate — not that some of us could — (*indicates his lameness*) even if we wished to. I'll ask Arkady to dance with you on my behalf — just once!

PAVEL You'll have to let me have one dance, too, Nikolai.

NIKOLAI Yes?

PAVEL Of course. The brother-in-law to be. I was an excellent dancer once upon a time. (*To* FENICHKA) That's agreed, then.

NIKOLAI Good. Good. Yes. Fine. Anyhow. Now to organize
our lives. Is everybody here?

> *He looks into the living room where* KATYA *and*
> ARKADY *are talking heatedly.*

Look at those two lovebirds.

> KATYA *bangs the piano lid shut.*

FENICHKA Squabbling lovebirds.

NIKOLAI Arkady! Katya! Come out here at once! Where's
the Princess?

ANNA She's walking around somewhere.

NIKOLAI I'll go and get her.

ANNA No. Leave her. She's happier by herself.

> KATYA *and* ARKADY *join the others.*

ARKADY Well — well — well — well! (*Ironic clapping*) Feast
your eyes on that wonderful sight!

NIKOLAI What's the matter?

ARKADY Just look at that astonishing jacket! Where did that
come from?

NIKOLAI I agree with you, Arkady. I think myself it's much
too young for a man of —

FENICHKA I chose it, Arkady.

ARKADY Did you now?

FENICHKA And I think he's very handsome in it.

KATYA So he is. And it's a wonderful jacket. (*To* ARKADY)
We all agree.

ARKADY I'm sure you do. I still think it's remarkable.

> NIKOLAI *does a mock pirouette.*

NIKOLAI What do you think, Anna?

ANNA (*In a reverie*) Sorry — sorry?

NIKOLAI Do you approve of it?

ANNA Approve of — ?

PAVEL (*Quickly*) We all think you're gorgeous, Nikolai.
And I'm madly jealous. One Tailor's Dummy in
the house is sufficient.

NIKOLAI Who is the Tailor's Dummy?

PAVEL Didn't you know? That's what the servants call me.

NIKOLAI I never heard that, Pavel.

PAVEL I don't mind in the least. It's not without affection, is it?

FENICHKA Show them the lining, Nikolai.

NIKOLAI I certainly will not!

FENICHKA Go on! For my sake.

> With mock coyness NIKOLAI unbuttons the jacket
> and opens it to reveal an even more brilliant lining.
> Applause and laughter.

NIKOLAI And this, of course, is the real Nikolai Petrovich.

FENICHKA Feast your eyes on that!

KATYA Yes — yes — yes — yes!

ARKADY Ridiculous.

FENICHKA And when he's tired of it, I'm going to wear it —
inside out.

NIKOLAI Enough of this. I'm not sure you're all not taking
a hand at me. Let's all gather round the table and
get a glass. There's going to be no formality. And
no speeches. Just an exchange of congratulations
and good wishes between friends. Come over here
beside me, Fenichka. Has everybody got something in his glass?

KATYA (*Filling her glass*) Just a second, Nikolai.

NIKOLAI Give me your hand, Katya. Good. Splendid. Well.
The harvest is saved. It has been a good, an especially good, year. And first of all we want to thank
you most warmly, Anna — don't we, Arkady? —
most warmly indeed for all the tremendous help
you have been to us not only in your advice and
wisdom over the past months but more particularly, indeed most particularly, for your spontaneous and generous offer of your machinery —

an offer, may I say —

ARKADY You said no speeches.

NIKOLAI And there'll be none.

ARKADY Good. Thank you, Anna.

NIKOLAI Thank you most sincerely, Anna. And if the situation is ever —

ARKADY Father!

NIKOLAI Sorry — sorry. Thank you. We all thank Anna — don't we?

Clapping. Raising of glasses.

FENICHKA Incidentally did you hear that Adam's old aunt has died?

NIKOLAI Somebody did mention that. When did it happen?

FENICHKA Early this morning. Are you still thinking of sacking him?

NIKOLAI Yes. No. He worked like a Trojan this past month. But this is a matter for you, Arkady. You're master of the estate now.

ARKADY I'll think about it. I'll watch him. He knows he's on probation.

NIKOLAI Why do you ask?

FENICHKA No reason. Just wondering. Who's for more wine?

KATYA Me, please. We're all going to miss you very much, Uncle Pavel.

PAVEL For all of two minutes.

ARKADY I think you've had enough wine, Katya.

KATYA (*Dismissively*) I'll make that decision. (*To* PAVEL) Yes, we will. A whole lot.

PAVEL (*To* KATYA) Did I hear you playing 'Drink to me only'?

KATYA And Arkady was singing. Weren't you?

ARKADY *ignores her.*

NIKOLAI That used to be my song . . . long ago. Shakespeare wrote the words — did you know that?

PAVEL No.

NIKOLAI Yes, he did.

PAVEL Jonson.

NIKOLAI What's that, Pavel?

PAVEL A contemporary of Shakespeare.

NIKOLAI Yes?

PAVEL Ben Jonson.

NIKOLAI What about him?

PAVEL He wrote the words.

NIKOLAI What words?

PAVEL Ben Jonson.

NIKOLAI Who is this Ben Jonson, Pavel?

PAVEL Nothing — nothing — just that you said that Shakespeare wrote the words of —

ARKADY (*Shouting*) Who cares! (*Controlled*) Who cares who wrote the bloody words! Who gives a damn! Exactly four weeks ago today Bazarov died — and who cares about that? Who even remembers? Not even one of you! All you care about is stupid jackets and big harvests and stupid bloody songs! Well, I care. And I remember. And I will always remember. And in the coming years I'm going to devote my life to his beliefs and his philosophy — to our philosophy — to carrying out his revolution. That's what I'm going to do for the rest of my life. And nothing in the world — absolutely nothing — is going to stop me!

He breaks down and cries. There is a long, embarrassed silence. KATYA *pours another drink.* NIKOLAI, *unable to endure the silence, begins to hum but tails off quickly. Silence again. Then* FENICHKA *goes to* NIKOLAI *and whispers in his ear.*

NIKOLAI Sorry? What's that?

FENICHKA The books.

NIKOLAI Books? What books? Oh the books! Of course! Piotr'll get them for me. P-

He is about to shout 'Piotr!' and miraculously
there is PIOTR, *now very drunk, at his elbow.*

Ah. There you are, Piotr. Isn't that remarkable?
PIOTR Sir?
NIKOLAI I didn't call you, did I?
PIOTR Yes, sir, you did.
NIKOLAI Did I?
PIOTR With great clarity. Twice. And here I am.
NIKOLAI Well, if you say so, Piotr. Splendid. Run up to my
bedroom and on the table beside my bed you'll
find two books. Bring them here to me, will you?

Pause.

PIOTR C-h-r-y-s-
NIKOLAI Sorry? What's that?
PIOTR C-h-r-y-s-a-n-t-
NIKOLAI What's he saying?
PIOTR -r-y-s-a-n-t-m-t-m-r-s-y-

The others laugh. PROKOFYICH, *stiff and stern,*
enters.

NIKOLAI You're not intoxicated, Piotr, are you?
PIOTR I know it. I'm telling you I know it. Let me try
again. C-h-r-s-y-

PROKOFYICH *leads* PIOTR *off left.*

PROKOFYICH Come on, boy. You're for bed. (*To* ALL) Sorry about
this. It won't happen again. Come on. Move, boy.
(*To* ALL) You know you are all cordially invited to
the dance later on.
NIKOLAI Thank you, Prokofyich. We'll go for a short time.
PROKOFYICH Very good. I'm sorry about this.

They exit. PIOTR *still trying to spell.*

KATYA   I'll get those books, Nikolai.

NIKOLAI   Poor old Piotr. Poor boy must be suffering terribly.

FENICHKA   He's been at it since lunchtime.

PAVEL   And it's time I went and got some packing done. I hope the wedding — no, weddings — will be a great success. I'm sure they will. (*Produces a tiny box*) I have ordered a proper present — it's due to arrive at the end of the week. In the meantime — it's only a token. (*He hands the box to* FENICHKA)

FENICHKA   Thank you very much, Pavel.

NIKOLAI   What is this?

FENICHKA   It's a ring. It's beautiful, Pavel, really beautiful. Thank you.

NIKOLAI   Let me see.

FENICHKA *kisses* PAVEL *on the cheek.*

PAVEL   Make it two dances.

NIKOLAI   Lovely, Pavel. Thank you very much. What's engraved on the stone? Is it a sphinx?

PAVEL   Is it? It's only a token. No value whatever.

FENICHKA   I don't believe that.

NIKOLAI   Put it on.

FENICHKA   I love it. I'll think of you every time I wear it.

NIKOLAI   It'a a beautiful memento, Pavel.

PAVEL   *Magnifique!* That's two occasions I'll be recalled: whenever you wear that ring; and every time borzoi fanciers get together and Katya's damned pup is discussed. (*To* ARKADY) I've ordered something for you and Katya, too. I hope you'll like it.

ARKADY   Thank you — from both of us.

KATYA *returns with two books.*

KATYA   Here you are.

NIKOLAI   Thank you, Katya. And these are for you, Pavel. Something to read on your journeyings.

PAVEL   What's this?

NIKOLAI   Fenichka chose them. We hope you like them.

PAVEL   Mrs Ann Ward Radcliffe! Never! *A Sicilian Romance* and *The Mysteries of Udolpho.* Wonderful! Where did you get them? They've been out of print for years!

FENICHKA   Piotr hunted them out when he was in Petersburg last month.

PAVEL   Absolutely wonderful! You couldn't have given me greater pleasure! Darling, innocent Mrs Ann Ward Radcliffe. And the two I'm missing. Can I bear so much intellectual stimulation?

> *General laughter. He kisses* FENICHKA *and then* NIKOLAI.

FENICHKA   Brother — brother Pavel.

PAVEL   I'll carry them with me wherever I go. *Merci. Merci beaucoup.*

NIKOLAI   (*Wiping away his tears*) Now. One final toast. Yes, I'm sorry, Arkady. I'm going to make a short speech — a very short speech.

KATYA   I would like to hear a very long speech.

NIKOLAI   What I just want to say is that this house, this home, is about to suffer a permanent and irreparable loss. Pavel is leaving. We will miss him terribly. And I want him to know that wherever he goes, our love will accompany him always, everywhere. But there is a silver lining to — to — to every — We do have a compensation, indeed a very substantial compensation. Fenichka Fedosya has consented to be my wife and for that — that — that benediction I am profoundly grateful. And on the same day — this day two weeks, amn't I correct? — and on this very lawn another marriage will be celebrated between Katya Sergeyevna and my son, Arkady. And by that union, too, I am profoundly gratified. Some people might think that there is something inappropriate about a father and a son getting married on the same day, some disorder in the proper order of things. But I know that for both of us it will be an occasion of great joy and great fulfilment. And who is to determine what is the proper ordering of things?

Bring up the accordion playing 'Drink to me only'.

FENICHKA Listen, Nikolai.
NIKOLAI (*To* KATYA) That clever musician — he picked it up from you.

They all listen for a few seconds.

That was our song, long ago. Maria and I. I sang the melody and she sang the seconds. Our party piece. Her eyelids fluttered when she sang. Shakespeare wrote the words — did you know that?

He begins to sing. FENICHKA *watches him with a strained smile. He puts his arm around her and hugs her.*

Sing!

She gives him an uncertain smile but does not sing. KATYA *moves beside* ARKADY. *She catches his hand. She begins to sing and sings the words directly into his face. He does not sing.* PAVEL *moves across to* ANNA *who is sitting away from the others. He catches her hand.*

PAVEL Do you sing?
ANNA Occasionally. When I'm alone.
PAVEL Yes. *Je comprends . . .*
NIKOLAI ⎱ 'Drink to me only with thine eyes,
KATYA ⎰ And I will pledge with mine;
Or leave a kiss but in the cup
And I'll not look for wine.
The thirst that from the soul doth rise
Doth ask a drink divine;

But might I of Jove's nectar sup,
I would not change for thine.'

MAKING HISTORY

Characters

HUGH O'NEILL, Earl of Tyrone
HARRY HOVEDEN, O'Neill's private secretary
HUGH O'DONNELL, Earl of Tyrconnell
PETER LOMBARD, Titular Bishop of Armagh and Primate of
    All Ireland
MABEL, Countess, O'Neill's wife
MARY BAGENAL, Mabel's sister

Time and Place

Act One: *Before Kinsale*
Scene One: O'Neill's house in Dungannon
Scene Two: The same

Act Two: *After Kinsale*
Scene One: The Sperrin mountains
Scene Two: Penitenzieri Palace, Rome

Making History was first produced by Field Day Theatre Company at the Guildhall, Derry, on 20 September 1988, with the following cast:

HUGH O'NEILL	Stephen Rea
HARRY HOVEDEN	Niall O'Brien
ARCHBISHOP LOMBARD	Niall Toibin
HUGH O'DONNELL	Peter Gowen
MABEL (BAGENAL) O'NEILL	Clare Holman
MARY BAGENAL	Emma Dewhurst
Directed by	Simon Curtis
Designed by	Julian McGowan
Lighting by	Rory Dempster

for Basil and Helen

ACT ONE

Scene One

A large living room in O'Neill's home in Dungannon, County Tyrone, Ireland. Late August in 1591. The room is spacious and scantily furnished: a large, refectory-type table; some chairs and stools; a sideboard. No attempt at decoration.

O'NEILL moves around this comfortless room quickly and energetically, inexpertly cutting the stems off flowers, thrusting the flowers into various vases and then adding water. He is not listening to HARRY HOVEDEN who consults and reads from various papers on the table.

O'NEILL is forty-one. A private, sharp-minded man, at this moment uncharacteristically outgoing and talkative. He always speaks in an upper-class English accent except on those occasions specifically scripted. HARRY HOVEDEN, his personal secretary, is about the same age as O'NEILL. O'NEILL describes him as a man 'who has a comforting and a soothing effect'.

HARRY   That takes care of Friday. Saturday you're free all day — so far. Then on Sunday — that'll be the fourteenth — O'Hagan's place at Tullyhogue. A big christening party. The invitation came the day you left. I've said you'll be there. All right? (*Pause*) It's young Brian's first child — you were at his wedding last year. It'll be a good day. (*Pause*) Hugh?

O'NEILL   Yes?

HARRY   O'Hagan's — where you were fostered.

O'NEILL   Tell me the name of these again.

HARRY   Broom.

O'NEILL   Broom. That's it.

HARRY   The Latin name is *genista*. Virgil mentions it somewhere.

339

O'NEILL Does he really?

HARRY Actually that *genista* comes from Spain.

    O'NEILL looks at the flowers in amazement.

O'NEILL Good Lord — does it? Spanish broom — magnificent name, isn't it?

HARRY Give them plenty of water.

O'NEILL Magnificent colour, isn't it?

HARRY A letter from the Lord Deputy —

O'NEILL They really transform the room. Splendid idea of yours, Harry. Thank you.

    O'NEILL silently mouths the word genista *again and then continues distributing the flowers.*

HARRY A letter from the Lord Deputy 'vigorously urging you to have your eldest son attend the newly established College of the Holy and Undivided Trinity in Dublin founded by the Most Serene Queen Elizabeth'. That 'vigorously urging' sounds ominous, doesn't it?

O'NEILL Sorry?

HARRY Sir William Fitzwilliam wants you to send young Hugh to the new Trinity College. I'm told he's trying to get all the big Gaelic families to send their children there. He would like an early response.

O'NEILL This jacket — what do you think, Harry? It's not a bit . . . excessive, is it?

HARRY Excessive?

O'NEILL You know . . . a little too — too strident?

HARRY Strident?

O'NEILL All right, damn it, too bloody young?

HARRY (*Looking at his papers*) It's very becoming, Hugh.

O'NEILL Do you think so? Maybe I should have got it in maroon.

    He goes off to get more flowers.

HARRY A reminder that the Annual Festival of Harpers takes place next month in Roscommon. They've changed the venue to Rooskey. You're Patron of the Festival and they would be very honoured if you would open the event with a short —

He now sees that he is alone. He looks through his papers. Pause. O'NEILL *enters again with an armful of flowers.*

O'NEILL *Genista.*

HARRY Yes.

O'NEILL Spanish broom.

HARRY Really?

O'NEILL They need plenty of water.

HARRY A bit of trouble. O'Kane of Limavady says he can't pay his tribute until the harvest is saved but in the meantime he's sending ten firkins of butter and twenty casks of beer. As usual he's lying. It might be an idea to billet fifty extra gallowglass on him for the next quarter. That'll keep him in line. Sir Garret Moore invites you down to Mellifont Abbey for a few days' fishing on the Boyne. He says it's the best salmon season he's ever had. The Lord Chancellor'll be there. And Sir Robert Gardener. You knew him when you were in England, didn't you?

O'NEILL Who's that?

HARRY Sir Robert Gardener, the Lord Chief Justice.

O'NEILL Oh, that was twenty-five years ago. Haven't seen him since.

HARRY Might be worth renewing that friendship now.

O'NEILL *(Tyrone accent)* Just to show him I haven't reverted completely to type — would that be it?

HARRY For political reasons.

O'NEILL We'll see. Have the musicians arrived?

HARRY Yes.

O'NEILL And the rhymers and the acrobats?

HARRY I've told you — everything's ready.

O'NEILL   And you're sure nobody has heard a whisper?

HARRY   I've said you were in Dublin at a meeting of the Council. Everything's in hand.

O'NEILL   Good. (*He continues with his flowers*)

HARRY   And more trouble: the Devlins and the Quinns are at each other's throats again. The Quinns raided the Devlins' land three times last week; killed five women and two children; stole cattle and horses and burned every hay field in sight. The Devlins remind you — once more they say — that they have the right to expect protection from their chieftain and that if Hugh O'Neill cannot offer them safety and justice under the Brehon Law they'll have to look for protection under the new English Law. And they will, too.

O'NEILL   I know what I'll do, Harry.

HARRY   That's a squabble needs to be sorted out quickly.

O'NEILL   I'll make the room upstairs into our bedroom! And I'll shift that consignment of Spanish saddles down to the back room. They should be closer to the stables anyway. The room upstairs faces south and there's a good view down to the river. Yes — that's a good decision. Don't you agree?

HARRY   Why not?

O'NEILL   Excellent. (*He returns to his flowers*)

HARRY   Bad news from London. Young Essex's been arrested and thrown in the Tower.

O'NEILL *stops working.*

O'NEILL   What for?

HARRY   There's a list of charges. One of them is treason.

O'NEILL   Damn it.

HARRY   'For conferring secretly with the basest and vilest traitor that ever lived, Hugh O'Neill, in a manner most disloyal to Her Majesty, Queen Elizabeth.'

O'NEILL   Damn it.

HARRY   He was fond of you.

O'NEILL   I was fond of him — despite everything.

HARRY I know.

O'NEILL Crazy man.

Short pause.

HARRY What else is there? Hugh O'Donnell and Peter Lombard want to see you.

O'NEILL All right. Some day next week.

HARRY They're here, Hugh.

O'NEILL Now?!

HARRY Waiting outside.

O'NEILL Oh, come on, Harry! I'm scarcely in the door —

HARRY O'Donnell knows you're home. And the Archbishop's been waiting here four days for you. And he has done an enormous amount of work. (*He points to a large pile of papers*) That's only half of his file.

O'NEILL Oh, my God. All right — I'll give them ten minutes and that's all.

HARRY Did you know that he's begun writing a book on you?

O'NEILL (*Suddenly alert*) Lombard?

HARRY So he told me.

O'NEILL We have our own annalist.

HARRY He knows that.

O'NEILL What sort of book?

HARRY He said something about a history — I don't know — *The Life and Times of Hugh O'Neill*, I imagine.

O'NEILL He might have told me about that.

HARRY He spent all Tuesday checking dates with me.

O'NEILL I don't think I like this idea at all.

HARRY Maybe I got it all wrong. Ask him yourself. And this (*letter*) — you'll want to read this yourself. It arrived a few hours ago.

O'NEILL What's that?

HARRY From Newry.

He reaches the letter towards O'NEILL. O'NEILL *stretches out to take it — and then withdraws his hand.*

O'NEILL Bagenal?

HARRY Bagenal.

O'NEILL Her father or her brother?

HARRY Brother.

O'NEILL Give me that! No, no, read it to me.

HARRY 'From Sir Henry Bagenal, Queen's Marshal, Newry, to Sir Hugh O'Neill, Earl of Tyrone, Dungannon — '

O'NEILL clicks his fingers impatiently.

(*Reluctantly*) It's a — it's just a catalogue of accusation and personal abuse. Your first marriage was never properly dissolved. So your second marriage was ambiguous. And of course this third.

O'NEILL Bastard.

HARRY He's threatening to bring a charge of abduction against you.

O'NEILL What's he talking about?

HARRY Because she's under twenty-one.

O'NEILL 'Abduction'!

HARRY He's threatening to come and take her back by force.

O'NEILL She's not exactly Helen of Troy, for Christ's sake! (*He regrets this instantly*) And what's that?

HARRY We got our hands on a copy of a letter he's written to the Queen: 'I am deeply humiliated and ashamed that my blood, which my father and I have often shed in repressing this rebellious race, should now be mingled with so traitorous a stock.'

O'NEILL 'My blood'! Staffordshire mongrel!

HARRY He's going to be troublesome, Hugh.

O'NEILL No wonder our poets call them Upstarts. That's all he is — a bloody Upstart! Ignore him. He'll bluster for a few days. I'm going to see about that bedroom.

As he is about to exit O'DONNELL *and* LOMBARD *enter.*

O'DONNELL is a very young man in his early twenties. He is impulsive, enthusiastic and generous.

He has a deep affection for O'NEILL. ARCHBISHOP
LOMBARD is a contemporary of O'NEILL. By profession he is a church diplomat and his manner is
careful and exact. But he is also a man of humour
and perception and by no means diminished by his
profession. He now carries a large candelabra and
an elegant birdcage.

O'DONNELL I knew I heard the voice!
O'NEILL Young O'Donnell!
O'DONNELL How are you, man?
O'NEILL Good to see you, Hugh. You're welcome.
O'DONNELL Good to see you, too.

They embrace with great affection.

I haven't seen you since the horse-swimming at
Lough Owel, the day you rode the — ! (*He breaks
off*) Jesus, lads, what about that — eh? Is that not a
sight for sore eyes!
O'NEILL Do you like it?
O'DONNELL I bet you that's a London job — eh?
O'NEILL Of course.
O'DONNELL And the smell of perfume off him!
O'NEILL Peter.
LOMBARD How are you, Hugh?
O'NEILL Welcome back to Dungannon.
LOMBARD Thank you.
O'DONNELL My poor sister's not seven months dead and I bet
you the bugger's on the prowl again! (*To* HARRY)
Am I right?

HARRY *spreads his hands.*

LOMBARD Gifts for you, Hugh. From the Pope.
O'NEILL What's all this?
LOMBARD A silver birdcage and a gold and silver candelabra.
O'DONNELL Look at that for craftsmanship.
O'NEILL Lovely. Indeed. Beautiful.

O'DONNELL He sent me a present, too. Guess what I got — a papal blessing!

LOMBARD (*To* O'NEILL) With his warmest good wishes.

O'NEILL I'm not being paid off, am I?

LOMBARD He's solidly behind you in principle.

O'NEILL He always is. But no money?

LOMBARD These things take time, Hugh. I've a letter from him for you, too.

O'NEILL (*Aside to* HARRY) See about that room now. (*To* LOMBARD) So you're just back from Rome?

LOMBARD Home a week last Sunday. Came via Spain. I've a lot to report.

O'NEILL Good. Will you sit here, Peter?

> HARRY *exits.* O'DONNELL *goes to the sideboard*
> *where there are bottles, wine and glasses.*

LOMBARD (*Sitting*) Thank you.

O'DONNELL Can we help ourselves, Hugh?

O'NEILL Of course. Sorry. Peter?

LOMBARD Not for me, thanks. I have copies here for everybody.

O'DONNELL Do you know that the floor in the hall out there is going to cave in with dry rot?

LOMBARD This is all the recent correspondence with Spain — our case to Philip II and his responses, including his last reply which you haven't seen yet.

O'DONNELL We had dry rot in the house at Ballyshannon and my mother had to tear out every piece of timber in the place.

LOMBARD And this is a résumé of my *Commentarius* — a thesis I'm doing on the Irish situation. Briefly my case is this. Because of her mismanagement England has forfeited her right to domination over this country. The Irish chieftains have been forced to take up arms in defence of their religion. And because of your birth, education and personal attributes you are the natural leader of that revolt. I'll go into it in detail later on.

O'DONNELL Do you know what my mother did? She got oak off

those Armada wrecks lying about the coast and replaced every floor and window in the house. It's a terrific job. You could gallop a horse across those floors now. You should do the same here, Hugh.

O'NEILL   And I hear you're writing our history, Peter?

LOMBARD   Ah. Harry has been talking.

O'NEILL   Have you begun?

LOMBARD   No, no; only checking some events and dates.

O'NEILL   And when your checking is done?

LOMBARD   Then I suppose I'll try to arrange the material into a shape — eventually.

O'NEILL   And interpret what you've gathered?

LOMBARD   Not interpret, Hugh. Just describe.

O'NEILL   Without comment?

LOMBARD   I'll just try to tell the story of what I saw and took part in as accurately as I can.

O'NEILL   But you'll tell the truth?

LOMBARD   I'm no historian, Hugh. I'm not even sure I know what the historian's function is — not to talk of his method.

O'NEILL   But you'll tell the truth?

LOMBARD   If you're asking me will my story be as accurate as possible — of course it will. But are truth and falsity the proper criteria? I don't know. Maybe when the time comes my first responsibility will be to tell the best possible narrative. Isn't that what history is, a kind of storytelling?

O'NEILL   Is it?

LOMBARD   Imposing a pattern on events that were mostly casual and haphazard and shaping them into a narrative that is logical and interesting. Oh, yes, I think so.

O'NEILL   And where does the truth come into all this?

LOMBARD   I'm not sure that 'truth' is a primary ingredient — is that a shocking thing to say? Maybe when the time comes imagination will be as important as information. But one thing I will promise you: nothing will be put down on paper for years and years. History has to be made — before it's remade.

HARRY *returns.*

HARRY   That's being looked after.

O'NEILL   Good. Now, let's make this short and brisk, shall we? What's on the agenda?

HARRY   Hugh has got information that the English are planning new fortifications along the —

O'DONNELL   Do you know what the hoors are at? They're going to build a line of forts right across the country from Dundalk over to Sligo. That'll cut us off from the south. (*He illustrates this by tearing a sheet of paper in two*) The second stage is to build a huge fort at Derry so that you and I will be cut off from each other. (*He illustrates this by cutting the half-page into quarters*) Then, when Donegal and Tyrone are isolated, then they plan to move in against each of us.

HARRY   And the Archbishop has news about help from Spain.

LOMBARD   I have letters from both the King and —

O'DONNELL   But their first move is to strengthen the forts they already have: Bagenal's place at Newry; Armagh; and the Blackwater.

LOMBARD   (*As he passes papers around*) I've spent a lot of time in Madrid recently, Hugh, and I can tell you that Europe is looking more and more to us as the ideal springboard for the Counter-Reformation.

O'DONNELL   And another thing I want to talk about: the shit O'Doherty up in Inishowen. Do you know what the wee get's at, Hugh? Nipping down as far as Killybegs, stealing our sheep and shipping them off to France! Running a bloody big export business — with my sheep!

LOMBARD   The initial shock of the Reformation is over. Catholic Europe is now gathering itself together for a Counter-Reformation. And the feeling is that culturally, geographically and with some military assistance we could be the spearhead of that counterattack.

O'DONNELL   Now I can go in today and snatch the bastard and chop his head off. But if I do that all Inishowen's up in arms and already I have O'Rourke of West Breffni threatening to quarter me.

He now joins the others at the table.

Did you hear what we did to O'Rourke last week? Jesus, you'll love this, Hugh. We got word that he was away down in Clare at a funeral. So we slipped down to Lough Allen and took away every horse and foal he owns! Six hundred prime animals! Jesus, he's going mad! Because he can't come after us! Because he has no transport! Good one, Hugh — eh?

HARRY Let's begin with the Archbishop, shall we?

O'DONNELL You'll help me against the shit O'Doherty, won't you? Because if I do nothing, the bugger'll think he has me bet.

HARRY You sit there, Hugh.

O'DONNELL Damn it, maybe I could poison him! The very job! Send him a peace offering — a cask of Bordeaux Special!

LOMBARD Has everybody got a copy?

O'DONNELL Or better still you (O'NEILL) send him the Bordeaux. He'd never suspect you. I got a jar of this deadly stuff from Genoa last week — just one drop in your glass and — plunk!

HARRY Go ahead, Peter.

LOMBARD Thank you. Three months —

O'DONNELL All the same that jacket takes years off him.

LOMBARD If I may, Hugh (O'DONNELL) —

O'DONNELL You would never think he was forty-one, would you? Almost forty-two. (*Offering* LOMBARD *the floor*) Peter.

LOMBARD Three months ago you (O'NEILL) wrote again to Philip asking for Spanish arms and money. You have a copy — dated May 14th last.

O'DONNELL I have no copy.

HARRY *points to a paper in front of* O'DONNELL.

Ah. Sorry.

LOMBARD The final sentence reads: 'With such aid we hope to restore the faith of the Church and to secure you a kingdom.'

O'DONNELL I never agreed with that stuff about offering him a kingdom.

LOMBARD I have brought his reply back — the document dated August 3rd. 'I have been informed you are defending the Catholic cause against the English. That this is acceptable to God is proved by the signal victories you have gained — '

O'DONNELL Not against the shit O'Doherty.

LOMBARD 'I hope you will continue to prosper and you need not doubt but I will render you any assistance you may require.' Now after all these years I think I have a very good idea how the Spanish court thinks. They have a natural sympathy and understanding of us because we share the one true faith. And they genuinely abhor England's attempt to impose the new heretical religion on us. But don't assume that that sympathy is unqualified — because it is not. Their interest in us is practical and political. I have had a series of meetings with the Duke of Lerma —

O'DONNELL Whoever he is.

LOMBARD He determines their foreign policy. And every time he says the same thing to me. Spain will help you only if you are useful to us. And when I look at you what do I see? A small island located strategically to the west of our enemy, England. A tiny portion of that island, the area around Dublin, under English rule. A few New English families living in isolation round the country. But by far the greater portion of your island is a Gaelic domain, ruled by Gaelic chieftains. And how do they behave? Constantly at war — occasionally with the English — but always, always among themselves. And how can fragmented and warring tribes be any use to us?

O'DONNELL   Constantly at war? Jesus, I haven't an enemy in the world!

LOMBARD   But what Lerma is really saying is that if we can forge ourselves into a cohesive unit, then, then we can go back to him and say: we are not fragmented; we are not warring; we are a united people; now help us. Now to return to my *Commentarius* — it's the document with the blue cover. The full title is *De Regno Hiberniae Sanctorum Insula Commentarius* —

O'DONNELL   I have no —

HARRY points to the document in front of him.

Ah, sorry.

LOMBARD   My thesis is this. If we are to understand the Irish situation fully we must go back more than four hundred years — to that famous October 17th when Henry II of England landed here. He had in his hand a copy of Pope Adrian IV's Bull, *Laudabiliter*, making him *Dominus Hiberniae* —

O'DONNELL   Whatever that means.

LOMBARD   King of Ireland. And that Bull had two consequences —

O'NEILL   I got married last night.

There is a long, shocked silence.

O'DONNELL   What?

O'NEILL   I got married last night.

O'DONNELL   You're a liar! (*To* HARRY) He's a liar! (*To* O'NEILL) You bugger, you never did!

O'NEILL   Yes.

O'DONNELL   God Almighty! (*To* HARRY) You said he was in Dublin at a meeting of the Council.

HARRY   He was in Dublin.

O'DONNELL   Jesus God Almighty! The bloody jacket — didn't I tell you the tail was high!

LOMBARD   You kept that very quiet, Hugh.

O'DONNELL   Who to, you bugger, you? I have it! — the big red-

	head you had here all last month — that Scotch woman — Annie McDonald!
O'NEILL	No.
LOMBARD	Congratulations.
O'NEILL	Thank you.
O'DONNELL	I've got it! — Brian McSwiney's daughter — the Fanad Whippet — what's her real name? — Cecelia! Jesus, not Cecelia!

O'NEILL *shakes his head.*

	Who then? Come on, man! Tell us!
LOMBARD	Did you say last night?
O'NEILL	In fact at two o'clock this morning. We eloped . . .
O'DONNELL	'We el- '! Sweet Jesus God Almighty! We eloped! (*He drums the table in his excitement*) Lay me down and bury me decent! The hoor eloped! Yipeeeeee!

He embraces O'NEILL.

	Terrific, man! Congratulations!
LOMBARD	Who's the new Countess, Hugh?
O'DONNELL	Jesus, I hope I have the same appetite for it when I'm your age!
O'NEILL	Neither of you knows her. She's from Newry.
O'DONNELL	Magennis! Siobhan Magennis!
O'NEILL	No. She's —
O'DONNELL	The other sister then — the one with the teeth — Maeve!
O'NEILL	I met her first only a few months ago. On her twentieth birthday.
O'DONNELL	She's only — ?!
O'NEILL	Her name is Mabel.
O'DONNELL	(*Very grand*) Mabel.
O'NEILL	She's one of the New English. Her grandfather came over here from Newcastle-under-Lyme in Staffordshire. He was given the Cistercian monastery and lands around Newry and Carlingford — that's what brought them over.

Pause.

O'DONNELL Come on, Hugh. Quit the aul' fooling. Tell us her real —

O'NEILL She is Mabel Bagenal. She is the daughter of the retired Queen's Marshal. She is the sister of Sir Henry Bagenal, the present Queen's Marshal.

Silence.

HARRY Anybody for more wine?

Silence.

LOMBARD Where did you get married?

O'NEILL The Bishop of Meath married us in Drumcondra — on the outskirts of Dublin.

LOMBARD Which Bishop of Meath?

O'NEILL Tom Jones, the Protestant Bishop. Mabel is a Protestant.

O'DONNELL Hold on, Hugh — wait now — wait — wait. You can't marry into the Upstarts! And a sister of the Butcher Bagenal! Jesus, man —

O'NEILL I'm going to ask her to come and meet you.

O'DONNELL Keep her for a month, Hugh — like that McDonald woman — that's the very job — keep her for a month and then kick her out. Amn't I right, Harry? (*To* O'NEILL) She won't mind, Hugh, honest to God. That's what she'll expect. Those New English are all half tramps. Give her some clothes and a few shillings and kick her back home to Staffordshire.

O'NEILL Her home is Newry.

O'DONNELL Wherever she's from. (*To* HARRY) That's all she'll expect. I'm telling you.

O'NEILL I'm going to ask her to join us.

O'DONNELL Amn't I right, Peter?

LOMBARD We have all got to assess the religious and political implications of this association, Hugh.

O'NEILL Marriage, Archbishop.

LOMBARD   Will Spain think so? Will Rome?

O'NEILL   (*Very angry, in Tyrone accent*) I think so. And this
is *my* country. (*Quietly, in his usual accent*) I have
married a very talented, a very spirited, a very
beautiful young woman. She has left her people to
join me here. They will never forgive her for that.
She is under this roof now, among a people she has
been reared to believe are wild and barbarous. I am
having a celebration tonight when I will introduce
her to my people. I particularly ask you two to welcome her here. But if that is beyond you I demand
at least civility.

> *He leaves. Silence.* LOMBARD *begins gathering up
> his papers.* HARRY *helps him. After a very long
> pause:*

O'DONNELL   The bugger's off his aul' head! — that's all there is
to it! She's turned the bugger's aul' head.

HARRY   (*To* LOMBARD) Stay overnight. We can meet again
tomorrow morning.

O'DONNELL   And he let me blather on about the English building new forts — and him jouking about the Newry
fort all the time! That's a class of treachery, Harry
— that's what that is!

HARRY   You're talking rubbish, Hugh.

O'DONNELL   Do you know where the Butcher Bagenal was last
week? In the Finn valley. Raiding and plundering
with a new troop of soldiers over from Chester
— the way you'd blood young greyhounds!
Slaughtered and beheaded fifteen families that were
out saving hay along the river bank, men, women
and children. With the result that at this moment
there are over a hundred refugees in my mother's
place in Donegal Town.

HARRY   (*To* LOMBARD) I'll have copies made of these.

O'DONNELL   I'll tell you something, Harry Hoveden: as long as
he has that Upstart bitch with him there'll be no
welcome for him in Tyrconnell!

LOMBARD *is about to leave with his papers.*

HARRY At least wait and meet her, Peter. For his sake.

> O'NEILL *enters, leading* MABEL *by the elbow.*
> MABEL *is twenty, forthright, determined. Now*
> *she is very nervous. Her accent has traces of*
> *Staffordshire.*

O'NEILL Here we are. I want you to meet two of my friends,
Mabel. Hugh O'Donnell — Sir Hugh O'Donnell —
Earl of Tyrconnell. My wife, Mabel.

MABEL I'm pleased to meet you.

> *She holds out her hand.* O'DONNELL *has to take it.*
> *He does not speak. Pause.*

O'NEILL And Dr Peter Lombard, Titular Bishop of Armagh
and Primate of All Ireland.

MABEL I'm pleased to meet you.

> *Again she holds out her hand. After a pause*
> LOMBARD *takes it. He does not speak. Pause.*

O'NEILL We've got to keep on the right side of Peter: he's
writing our history.

LOMBARD That seems to make you uneasy for some reason.

O'NEILL Not as long as you tell the truth.

LOMBARD You keep insisting on this 'truth', Hugh.

O'NEILL Don't you believe in the truth, Archbishop?

LOMBARD I don't believe that a period of history — a given
space of time — my life — your life — that it contains within it one 'true' interpretation just waiting
to be mined. But I do believe that it may contain
within it several possible narratives: the life of Hugh
O'Neill can be told in many different ways. And
those ways are determined by the needs and the
demands and the expectations of different people
and different eras. What do they want to hear?

How do they want it told? So that in a sense I'm not altogether my own man, Hugh. To an extent I simply fulfil the needs, satisfy the expectations — don't I? (*He turns away*)

HARRY You're looking rested now.

O'NEILL And Harry Hoveden you know.

MABEL Oh yes. I know Harry.

HARRY Do you like the flowers?

MABEL Yes, they're lovely.

O'NEILL Broom.

MABEL Yes.

O'NEILL Spanish broom.

MABEL Yes.

O'NEILL Member of the *genista* family.

MABEL Ah. I wouldn't know that.

O'NEILL Actually that's Spanish broom . . . comes from Spain. They need plenty of water.

MABEL Broom? No, they don't. They need hardly any water at all.

O'NEILL looks accusingly at HARRY.

O'DONNELL I'll have another slug of that wine — if that's all right with you, Hugh.

O'NEILL Of course. Anybody else?

Silence.

HARRY Did you have a rest?

MABEL I lay down but I didn't sleep any — I was too excited. Everything's so . . . And the noise of those cows! I mean, I looked out the window and all I could see was millions of them stretching away to the hills. I mean, I never saw so many cows in one place in all my life. There must be millions of them. Cows and horses.

HARRY We're moving you into the bedroom just above us. It's quieter there.

LOMBARD If you'll pardon me. I've some letters to write.

O'NEILL The celebration begins at nine, Peter.

LOMBARD *exits.*

HARRY (*Taking* O'DONNELL'*s elbow*) And Hugh hasn't eaten since this morning.

O'DONNELL What are you talking about? I ate only —

HARRY We'll join you later.

He steers O'DONNELL *out in front of him. The moment they are alone* O'NEILL *grabs* MABEL *from behind and buries his face in her neck and hair.*

MABEL Oh, my God.

O'NEILL Put your arms around me.

MABEL I'm trembling all over.

O'NEILL I want you now.

MABEL 'Come and meet two friends,' you said.

O'NEILL Now! — now! — now!

MABEL You should have warned me, Hugh.

O'NEILL Let's go upstairs.

MABEL I'm in pieces, I am! Hugh O'Donnell and a popish priest all in a couple of minutes! Did you not see my hand? — it was shaking!

O'NEILL I want to devour you.

MABEL Our Henry calls him the Butcher O'Donnell. He says he strangles young lambs with his bare hands.

O'NEILL That's true.

MABEL Oh God! Are you serious?

O'NEILL And eats them raw.

MABEL Oh God! — you're not serious?

O'NEILL We all do that here.

MABEL Stop it, Hugh. And he speaks so funny! Why doesn't he speak like you?

O'NEILL How do I speak?

MABEL 'How do I speak?' — like those Old English nobs in Dublin.

O'NEILL (*Tyrone accent*) That's why you're fair dying about me.

MABEL   And I met a popish priest, Hugh! That's the first
         time in my life I ever even *saw* one of them! And I
         said, 'I'm pleased to meet you'! Oh, my God, wait
         till my sister Mary hears this!
O'NEILL   And your brother Henry.
MABEL   Our Henry would shoot me, Hugh!
O'NEILL   Would he?
MABEL   You know he would! I shook the hand of a popish
         priest!
O'NEILL   An archbishop.
MABEL   Is that worse?
O'NEILL   Much worse. And look at it.
MABEL   At what?
O'NEILL   Your hand.

She looks at her hand.

It's turning black.

MABEL   It's — ?!

*She suddenly realizes she has been fooled. She
gives a great whoop of laughter and punches him.*

Oh, my God, I actually looked! You're a bastard,
Hugh O'Neill — that's what you are — a real bastard! (*She laughs again, this time on the point of tears*)
Oh, my God, it's a bit too much, Hugh . . . I think
maybe — I think maybe I'm going to cry — and the
stupid thing is that I never ever cry . . . All that
secrecy — running away — the wedding ceremony
— all the excitement — being here — meeting those
people . . . (*now crying*) They weren't very welcoming, Hugh — were they? I mean they couldn't even
speak to me — could they?

O'NEILL   Give them time.

MABEL   Just when I was riding away from home I turned
         round and there was my father looking out the
         landing window. And he smiled and waved — he
         had no idea I was running away. And he'll never

understand why I did. He's a good man and a fair-minded man and he'll try; but it will never make sense to him. And he's going to be puzzled and hurt for the rest of his life.

O'NEILL Shhhhh.

MABEL I'm all right. Just a little bit confused, Hugh. Just a little bit nervous. Everything's so different here. I knew it would be strange — I knew that. But I didn't think it would be so . . . foreign. I'm only fifty miles from home but I feel very far away from everything I know.

O'NEILL Give me your hand.

MABEL It's not black. I'll be all right, Hugh. Just give me time. We're a tough breed, the Upstarts.

O'NEILL I have a present for you.

MABEL Yes?

O'NEILL It's a new invention — a time-piece you carry around with you. It's called a watch.

MABEL A what?

O'NEILL A watch. You wear it on your finger just like a ring.

MABEL Where did you get that thing?

O'NEILL I had it made for you in London; specially.

MABEL Oh, Hugh —

O'NEILL The only other person I know who has one is Queen Elizabeth.

MABEL It's a beautiful thing, Hugh, really beautiful.

O'NEILL Elizabeth wears it on this finger.

MABEL The Queen has one! And I have the only other one! Queen Elizabeth and Countess Mabel — why not?

O'NEILL Why not indeed?

MABEL It really is beautiful. Thank you. Thank you very much. (*She kisses him*) I'm sorry, Hugh. I'll never cry like that again. That's a promise. Never again. Ever. We're a tough breed, the O'Neills.

Quick black.

ACT ONE

Scene Two

Almost a year has passed. The same rooms as in Scene One, but MABEL *has added to the furnishings and the room is now more comfortable and more colourful.*

MABEL *is sitting alone doing delicate and complicated lacework. She works in silence for some time. Then from offstage the sudden and terrifying sound of a young girl shrieking. This is followed immediately by boisterous laughter, shouting, horseplay and a rapid exchange in Irish between a young girl and a young man.*

MABEL *is terrified by the shriek. She drops her lacework. Her eyes are shut tight. She sits frozen in terror for a few seconds — even when it is obvious that the screaming is horseplay. Then in sudden fury she jumps to her feet and goes to the exit left. As she goes — and unseen by her — her sister* MARY *enters right.* MARY BAGENAL *is slightly older than* MABEL. *Like* MABEL *there is a hint of Staffordshire in her accent. And like* MABEL *she is a determined young woman.*

MABEL (*At exit*) Shut up out there! D'you hear me? Just shut up! If you want to behave like savages, go on back to the bogs! (*She is suddenly aware — and embarrassed — that* MARY *has overheard her outburst*) Just horseplay. You would think they were killing each other, wouldn't you? And I'm wasting my breath because they don't understand a word of English.

> *There is an awkward silence.* MABEL *picks up her lacework.*

MARY They're getting my carriage ready. It's a long way back to Newry.

MABEL It's only fifty miles.

MARY I suppose that's all.

MABEL (*Impulsively*) Stay the night, Mary.

MARY I can't.

MABEL Please. For my sake. Please.

MARY I'd like to, Mabel; you know I would but —

MABEL Just one night.

MARY If I'm not home before dark — you know our Henry — he'd be worried sick.

MABEL Let him worry about you for a change.

MARY I really can't, Mabel. Not this time. Anyhow, you and I always fight after a few hours.

MABEL Do we?

MARY Well . . . sometimes.

MABEL In that case.

MARY Next time . . . maybe.

MABEL Next time.

MARY That's a promise.

> *Another brief burst of shrieking and horseplay off.*
> *The sisters smile uneasily at each other. Pause.*

I left a box of nectarine and quince in your pantry. And a few jars of honey. Last year's, I'm afraid. If it crystallizes just dip it in warm water.

MABEL Thank you.

> *Pause.*

MARY They have no bees here, have they?

MABEL No, we haven't.

MARY I've finally persuaded our Henry to move his hives away from the house, thank heavens. Do you remember — just beyond the vegetable garden? — where Father built the fishpond? — that's where they are now. In a semicircle round the pond.

MABEL Yes.

MARY He has over a hundred hives now.

MABEL Has he?

MARY   Maybe more.

MABEL   Really?

MARY   We sold about four thousand pounds of honey last year. To the army mostly. They would buy all he can produce but they don't always pay him. (*Pause*) And do you remember that bog land away to the left of the pond? Well, you wouldn't recognize that area now. We drained it and ploughed it and fenced it; and then planted a thousand trees there in four separate areas: apple and plum and damson and pear. Henry had them sent over from Kent. They're doing beautifully.

MABEL   Good.

MARY   They have no orchards here, have they?

MABEL   No, we haven't.

MARY   Mostly vegetable growing, is it?

MABEL   We go in for pastoral farming — not husbandry; cattle, sheep, horses. We have two hundred thousand head of cattle here at the moment — as you have heard. Did you say something about a herb garden?

MARY   Oh, that's a great success. That little square where we used to have the see-saw — do you remember that patch outside the kitchen window?

MABEL   I'm not gone a year, Mary.

MARY   Sorry. I've brought you some seeds. (*She produces envelopes from her bag*) I've labelled them for you. (*She reads:*) Fennel. Lovage. Tarragon. Dill. Coriander. Borage. I had tansy, too, but I'm afraid it died on me. Do you remember every Easter we used to make tansy pudding and leave it — sorry. Don't plant the fennel near the dill or the two will cross-fertilize.

MABEL   Is that bad?

MARY   You'll end up with a seed that's neither one thing or the other. Borage likes the sun but it will survive wherever you plant it — it's very tough. I should have some valerian seeds later in the year. I'll send you some. Are you still a bad sleeper?

MABEL Was Father conscious at the end?

MARY Father? Conscious? You should have heard him! Leaving personal messages for everybody —

MABEL Messages?

MARY And detailed instructions about everything. The west door of the fort needs new hinges. The last consignment of muskets has defective hammers. Never depend totally on London because they don't really understand the difficult job we're doing over here.

MABEL Personal messages?

MARY He forgot nobody. I'm to take up bookbinding if you don't mind! Henry spends too much time at paperwork and not enough at soldiering. Old Tom, the gardener, should rub beeswax into his arthritic joints. Give a new Bible to the two maids from Tandragee. Half-an-hour before he died he asked what price we were getting for our eggs! Wonderful, wasn't it?

MABEL Yes.

MARY I miss him terribly, Mabel. I know he had a hard life but it was a very full life. You forget that almost single-handed he tamed the whole of County Down and County Armagh and brought order and prosperity to them. And God blessed his great endeavours; and Dad knew that, too. And that was a great consolation to him at the end. (*Pause*) To all of us. (*Pause*) So. (*Pause*) I miss you so much, Mabel.

MABEL I miss you, too.

MARY I locked your bedroom door the day you left and it hasn't been opened since. But the house seems to be getting even bigger and emptier.

MABEL You enjoy the garden, don't you?

MARY Henry says I should get out more — meet more people. Where am I supposed to go out to? We're surrounded by the Irish. And every day more and more of their hovels spring up all along the perimeter of our lands.

MABEL You visit the Freathys, don't you?

MARY   They left. Months ago. Back to Cornwall.

MABEL   Why?

MARY   Couldn't take any more, I suppose. The nearest neighbour we have now is Patrick Barnewall of Rathfriland and that's fifteen miles away.

MABEL   But think of the welcome you always get from Young Patrick! Remember the day he said to you: (*lisping*) 'Mith Mary, come down to the old mill-house with me.' God, we laughed at that for weeks. Do you remember?

MARY   Yes.

MABEL   It became a kind of catchphrase with us — 'Mith Mary' — do you remember?

MARY *cries quietly.*

Here. Come on. We'll have none of that.

MARY   He was sixty-five last week, Young Patrick Barnewall.

MABEL   Are you all right, Mary?

MARY   He wants to marry me, Mabel. I told him I'd think about it.

MABEL   Oh, Mary, you — !

MARY   And I *am* thinking seriously about it.

MABEL   Mary, he's an old — !

MARY   I promised him I'd give him my answer next month. Our Henry thinks very highly of him.

MABEL   Mary, you can't marry Patrick Barnewall.

MARY   We'll see. I'm not sure yet. I think I will.

MABEL   The man's an old fool, Mary! He was always a fool! He has been a joke to us all our years!

MARY   He's still one of us, Mabel. And whatever about his age he's a man of great honour. (*Now formal and distant*) Once more — it's time I was going. I've left nothing behind me, have I? Did you see my new horses? Of course you did. Aren't they handsome? Henry got them from Wales for my birthday. They're very sure-footed and they have tremendous stamina. You'll give my regards to Hugh?

MABEL I don't know where he's got to. He'll be sorry to have missed you.

MARY No, he won't. The twice we met we fought bitterly. I'll try to come again, Mabel — if I get a chance. But you know how angry Henry is.

MABEL Is he still?

MARY He still talks about taking you home by force.

MABEL This is my home, Mary.

The sudden shrieking as before. MARY *moves beside her and speaks with concern and passion.*

MARY No, it's not. This can never be your home. Come away with me now, Mabel.

MABEL Please, Mary —

MARY Yes, I know they have their colourful rituals and their interesting customs and their own kind of law. But they are not civilized, Mabel. And you can never trust them — you must know that now — how treacherous and treasonable they are — and steeped in religious superstition.

MABEL That's enough, Mary.

MARY You talk about 'pastoral farming' — what you really mean is no farming — what you really mean is neglect of the land. And a savage people who refuse to cultivate the land God gave us have no right to that land.

MABEL Stop that at once, Mary!

MARY I'm sure some of them are kind and decent and trustworthy. Of course they are. And yes — I know — Hugh is different — Hugh was educated in England. But his people are doomed in spite of their foreign friends and their popish plotting because their way of life is doomed. And they are doomed because civility is God's way, Mabel, and because superstition must yield before reason. You know in your heart what I'm saying is true.

MABEL I became a Roman Catholic six months ago.

MARY Oh God, Mabel, how could — ?!

MABEL Out of loyalty to Hugh and to his people. As for civility I believe that there is a mode of life here that is at least as honourable and as cultivated as the life I've left behind. And I imagine the Cistercian monks in Newry didn't think our grandfather an agent of civilization when he routed them out of their monastery and took it over as our home.

MARY Hugh has two mistresses! — here! — now! Under this roof! Is that part of his religion?

MABEL That is part of his culture.

MARY For God's sake! Is it part of his culture that he bows and scrapes before the Lord Deputy in Dublin and promises obedience and loyalty for life — and the very next day he's plotting treason with Spain?

MABEL That is politics.

MARY 'Politics'! Listen to yourself. You're becoming slippery like them! You're beginning to talk like them, to think like them! Hugh is a traitor, Mabel — to the Queen, to her Deputy, to everything you and I were brought up to believe in. Do you know what our people call him? The Northern Lucifer — the Great Devil — Beelzebub! Hugh O'Neill is evil incarnate, Mabel! You tell me he has twenty gold and velvet suits — but I have seen him eating with his bare hands! You tell me that he speaks three or four languages and that every leader in Europe respects him — but I can tell you that —

She breaks off because O'NEILL *enters with* HARRY.

HARRY The consignment of lead has arrived from England.

O'NEILL Have you got the import licence?

HARRY Here.

O'NEILL Check the order forms against the customs papers and see that — Mary!

MARY Hello, Hugh.

O'NEILL When did you arrive?

MARY A few hours ago.

O'NEILL Well, this is a surprise.

366

MARY   I'm just about to leave.

They shake hands.

O'NEILL   What's the hurry?
MABEL   She wants to get home before dark.
MARY   Hello, Harry.
HARRY   You're a stranger, Mary. How are you?

They shake hands.

MARY   I'm well, Harry. How are you?
HARRY   Fine, thank you, fine.
O'NEILL   Well, this is unexpected.
MABEL   Isn't she looking well?
O'NEILL   Indeed. And have the sisters had a good long gossip?
MABEL   We're about talked out — aren't we?
O'NEILL   And how's the Queen's Marshal?
MARY   Henry's well, thank you.
O'NEILL   Henry's well.
MARY   Yes.
O'NEILL   Good.
MARY   Yes. (*Pause*) He's very well.
O'NEILL   Splendid. But disquieted, I imagine, by that little difficulty with Maguire down in Fermanagh?
MARY   I don't know anything about that, Hugh.
O'NEILL   Of course not; naturally; affairs of state. But he does have a problem there — or at least so we've heard, Harry, haven't we?
MARY   Henry doesn't discuss those things with me.
O'NEILL   The difficulty — as we understand it — is that London has asked Maguire to make a public profession of his loyalty and obedience — to 'come in' as they coyly phrase it, as in to come in out of the wilderness, the Gaelic wilderness, of course. Nothing more than a token gesture is asked for — the English, unlike us, never drive principles to embarrassing conclusions. For heaven's sake, I've made the

gesture myself, haven't I, Harry? And I've brought young Hugh O'Donnell 'in'. And I assure you, Mary, it means nothing, nothing. And in return for that symbolic . . . courtesy London offers you formal acknowledgement and recognition of what you already are — leader of your own people! Politically quaint, isn't it?

MARY So taking a solemn oath of loyalty to Her Majesty is neither solemn nor binding to you, Hugh?

O'NEILL Good heavens, no! I'm loyal today — disloyal to-morrow — you know how capricious we Gaels are. Anyhow, where was I? Yes, our friend Maguire. Maguire is having difficulty making that little courtesy. And so London gets peevish. And heated messages are exchanged. And terrible threats are made. And who gets hauled in to clean up the mess? Of course — poor old Henry! It's always the Henrys, the menials in the middle, who get the kicks, isn't it?

MARY Our Henry's well able to handle rebels like Maguire.

O'NEILL 'Our Henry'? Nobody better. London couldn't have a more dutiful servant than Our Henry. As you and I know well — but as London keeps forgetting — it's the plodding Henrys of this world who are the real empire-makers. But the point I'm getting to — (*to* HARRY) I'm not being indiscreet, Harry, am I? — the reason I mention the problem at all is that Maguire has thrown the head up and proclaims he'll fight to the death before a syllable of loyalty to a foreign queen will ever issue from his pure lips! I know. I know. Trapped in the old Gaelic paradigms of thought. It's so familiar — and so tedious. But then what does he do? Comes to me who has already made the token gesture, me, the 'compromised' O'Neill in his eyes, comes to me and begs me to fight beside him! Now! Look at the dilemma that places me in, Mary. You do appreciate my dilemma, don't you?

MARY   I don't want to hear anything about this, Hugh.

O'NEILL   I try to live at peace with my fellow chieftains, with your people, with the Old English, with Dublin, with London, because I believe — I know — that the slow, sure tide of history is with me, Mary. All I have to do is . . . just sit — and — wait. And then a situation like this arises and how am I to conduct myself?

MABEL   It's time Mary set off.

O'NEILL   Do I keep faith with my oldest friend and ally, Maguire, and indeed with the Gaelic civilization that he personifies? Or do I march alongside the forces of Her Majesty? And I've marched with them before, Mary. You didn't know that? Oh yes, I've trotted behind the Tudors on several expeditions against the native rebels. I've even fought alongside Our Henry in one little skirmish — oh, years and years ago, when you and Mabel were still playing with your dolls. Oh, yes, that's a detail our annalists in their wisdom choose to overlook, perhaps because they believe, like Peter Lombard, that art has precedence over accuracy. I'm beginning to wonder should we trust historians at all! Anyhow, back to Maguire — and my dilemma. It really is a nicely balanced equation. The old dispensation — the new dispensation. My reckless, charming, laughing friend, Maguire — or Our Henry. Impulse, instinct, capricious genius, brilliant improvisation — or calculation, good order, common sense, the cold pragmatism of the Renaissance mind. Or to use a homely image that might engage you: pasture — husbandry. But of course I'm now writing a cliché history myself, amn't I? Because we both know that the conflict isn't between caricatured national types but between two deeply opposed civilizations, isn't it? We're really talking about a life-and-death conflict, aren't we? Only one will survive. You wouldn't disagree with that, would you?

MABEL   Mary wants to leave, Hugh.

O'NEILL No, no, it's a nice point and I would welcome
Mary's wholesome wisdom. I'll be very direct. Do
I grasp the Queen's Marshal's hand? — using Our
Henry as a symbol of the new order which every
aristocratic instinct in my body disdains but which
my intelligence comprehends and indeed grudg-
ingly respects — because as a boy I spent nine
years in England where I was nursed at the very
wellspring of that new order — think of all those
formative years in the splendid homes of Leicester
and Sidney and indeed at the Court itself — hence
the grand accent, Mary —

MABEL   Hugh, I think —

O'NEILL No — allow me — or — or do I grip the hand of
the Fermanagh rebel and thereby bear public and
imprudent witness to a way of life that my blood
comprehends and indeed loves and that is as old
as the Book of Ruth? My dilemma. Help me, Mary.
Which hand do I grasp? Because either way I make
an enemy. Either way I interfere with that slow
sure tide of history. No, that's unfair. I mustn't
embarrass you. Let's put it another way. Which
choice would history approve? Or to use the Archbishop's language: if the future historian had a
choice of my two alternatives, which would he
prefer for his acceptable narrative? Tell me.

MARY   I don't know anything about history, Hugh.

O'NEILL All right; then which hand do I grasp?

MARY   Queen Elizabeth made you an Earl. And you
accepted that title. And you know that that title
carries with it certain duties and responsibilities.

O'NEILL Those duties I have honoured faithfully.

MARY   Then as long as you continue to do that, Hugh, and
if you are at peace with your conscience you have
no dilemma.

O'NEILL (*To* HARRY) She's right, you know. (*To* MARY) A wise
answer that, Mary. You have an admirably tidy
little mind. That's what I'll do. And hope that his-

tory's approval and the guidance of my conscience
are in accord.

> MARY *gathers her belongings together and*
> *embraces* MABEL.

MARY I'm glad to see you looking so well.
MABEL Write to me.

> *They kiss.*

Thank you for all you brought.
MARY I'll not forget the valerian. Goodbye, Harry.
HARRY Safe journey, Mary.

> *They shake hands.*

MARY Goodbye, Hugh.

> *Hugh is examining the seed packets with excessive*
> *interest.*

O'NEILL Sorry?
MARY Goodbye.
O'NEILL Oh — goodbye — goodbye — remember me to
Our Henry.

> *Both women exit. Long pause.*

HARRY All that will go straight back to the Marshal.
O'NEILL What's that, Harry?
HARRY Everything you said will be reported to Bagenal —
and to London.
O'NEILL That's why I told her.
HARRY You want it known that you've promised Maguire
you'd help him?
O'NEILL I don't think I told her that, did I? (*He reads:*) 'The
coriander seed. Watch this seed carefully as it ripens
suddenly and will fall without warning.' Sounds

like Maguire, doesn't it? — Coriander Maguire.

HARRY Because if you renege on that promise he certainly will fall.

O'NEILL What herb are you, Harry? What about dill? 'Has a comforting and soothing effect.' Close enough. And who is borage? 'Inclined to induce excessive courage, even recklessness.' That's O'Donnell, isn't it? Borage O'Donnell.

HARRY Or are you saying that you're going to take the English side against Maguire, Hugh?

O'NEILL *gathers the envelopes of seeds together.*

In fact are you going to betray your old friend, Maguire?

O'NEILL (*Roaring*) 'Betray my old — '! For Christ's sake, don't you start using language like that to me, Harry! (*Softly*) Maguire is a fool. He's determined to rise up and nobody can stop him and he'll be hacked to pieces and his people routed and his country planted with Upstarts and safe men. It happened to Fitzmaurice. And McDermott. And Nugent. And O'Reilly. And O'Connor. And O'Kelly. Their noble souls couldn't breathe another second under 'tyranny'. And where are they now? Wiped out. And what did they accomplish? Nothing. But because of their nobility, survival — basic, crude, day-to-day survival — is made infinitely more difficult for the rest of us.

HARRY You are unfair to Maguire, Hugh. He's impetuous but he's no fool.

O'NEILL I know — I know — of course I know Maguire's no fool. Maguire has no choice. Maguire has to rise. History, instinct, his decent passion, the composition of his blood — he has no alternative. So he will fulfil his fate. It's not a tragic fate and it's not a heroic fate. But his open embrace of it has elements of both, I suppose. Of course I know all that, for Christ's sake . . .

o'donnell *bursts in. He is breathless with excitement.*

o'donnell News, boys! News! News! News! Wait till you hear the news, Hugh! Big news — huge news — enormous news! Sorry for bursting in on you like this, Harry. Peter Lombard's with me. We've been riding since dawn. God, I'm wild dry — give us a swig of that wine, Harry. This is it, Hugh boy! I'm telling you — this is it!

o'neill This is what?

o'donnell Don't ask me. I can't tell you. Wait for Peter — I can't spoil it on him. But I'll say this much, Hugh O'Neill: I never thought I'd live to see the day! (*He accepts a glass*) Decent man, Harry. (*He toasts*) To the future — to a great, great future — to the three of us —

Enter lombard.

— to the four of us! (*To* lombard) I haven't opened my mouth — have I?

lombard *is equally excited but controlled. He shakes hands with* o'neill *and then* harry.

lombard Hugh. Good to see you.

o'neill Welcome, Peter.

lombard Harry. (*To* o'neill) I was going to send a messenger but I thought it was much too important.

o'donnell Spout it out, Peter!

lombard It really is astonishing news, Hugh.

o'neill It's Spain, isn't it?

o'donnell The aul' wizard. I never said a word.

lombard It's Spain, Hugh. After all these years. God be praised a thousand times. It is indeed Spain.

o'donnell Can you believe it?

lombard Years of begging, cajoling, arguing — years of hoping — years of despairing.

O'DONNELL Years of praying, Peter.

LOMBARD Years of praying indeed. But he has kept his promises, Hugh. Don Francisco Gómez de Sandoval y
Rojas, fifth Marquis of Denia, Duke of Lerma, my
friend, Ireland's friend, he has kept his promise.

O'DONNELL Lerma determines their foreign policy.

O'NEILL *moves away and stands alone downstage.*

HARRY This isn't the first time Lerma has made promises.

LOMBARD Passed by the Council of State last Thursday week.
Signed by King Philip himself the following morning. This isn't a promise. This is guaranteed. And
solid. And substantial.

O'DONNELL Yipeeeeee!

LOMBARD At this moment they are mustering an army and
assembling a fleet.

O'DONNELL Do you see those wee Spanish soldiers in the field,
Harry? Bloody ferrets! Jesus, they'd go down a rabbit hole to get you!

HARRY How solid? How substantial?

LOMBARD At least thirty-five ships — galleons, men-of-war
and some hundred-ton vessels.

HARRY Where are they going to land?

LOMBARD I don't know. That's a military matter.

HARRY But it's crucial. It has got to be somewhere along
the north coast.

LOMBARD I think I heard some mention of Kinsale.

O'DONNELL Wherever that is. Never heard of it.

HARRY Kinsale's out of the question. We'd have to march
an army through the full length of the country to
join forces with them. (*To* O'NEILL) It can't be Kinsale,
Hugh.

LOMBARD Then tell them it can't be Kinsale.

HARRY Who's the commander-in-chief?

LOMBARD Don Juan del Aguila.

O'DONNELL Whoever he is. Don Hugho del Ballyshannon's for
more wine, boys!

HARRY Tell me about Aguila.

LOMBARD He's from the Barraco in the province of Avila. Not
brilliant but very competent, very experienced.

HARRY How many men?

LOMBARD At least six thousand.

HARRY Not enough.

LOMBARD They'll be fully trained and equipped; and it's up
to us to match that number. (*To* O'NEILL) You and
Hugh here have got to tour the whole country and
whip every Gaelic chieftain into shape.

HARRY Where are they mustering their men?

LOMBARD Most of them are Spanish but they hope to levy a
few companies of Italians.

O'DONNELL Do you see those Italians? Bloody savages! The
only time they ever smile is when they're sinking a
sword in you! Jesus, Hugh, we'll go through the
English quicker than a physic!

MABEL *enters.* O'DONNELL *embraces her warmly.*

We're up, Mabel darling! We're up and the Spanish
are beside us!

She looks at O'NEILL.

LOMBARD Forgive us, Mabel. We're a bit elated.

MABEL The Spanish are coming?

O'DONNELL Lift up your heart, Dark Rosie!

LOMBARD The Spanish are coming. At long last. And there's
more, Hugh (O'NEILL). There's still more.

O'DONNELL Belt it out, Archbishop Lombard.

LOMBARD A Bull of Indulgence from His Holiness Pope
Clement VIII.

O'DONNELL Quiet! Quiet! Let the dog see the rabbit!

LOMBARD (*Reading*) 'To the archbishops, bishops, prelates,
chiefs, earls, barons and people of Ireland. En-
couraged by the exhortations of our predecessors
and ourself you have long struggled to recover and
preserve your liberty and to throw off the yoke of
slavery imposed on you by the English, deserters

from the Holy Roman Church. Now, to all of you who follow and assist our beloved son, Hugh O'Neill, and the Catholic army, if you truly repent and confess and if possible receive the Holy Communion, we grant plenary pardon and remission of all sins, as usually granted to those setting out to the war against the Turks for the recovery of the Holy Land. Rome. The Ninth Year of Our Pontificate.'

O'DONNELL Jesus, great word that — 'pontificate'.

LOMBARD Which means, Hugh, that now you aren't fighting a mere war — you are fighting a holy crusade.

O'DONNELL Goddamn bloody right, Peter!

LOMBARD Which means, too, that we are no longer a casual grouping of tribes but a nation state united under the Papal colours.

O'DONNELL Is that big enough news for you, man — eh?

Everybody looks at O'NEILL. *Silence. He walks slowly across the room.*

Hi! Hugh!

Silence.

(*To* OTHERS) What's wrong with the bugger? (*To* O'NEILL) O'Neill! Sir Hugh! Tyrone! Did you hear what the man's just said?

O'NEILL Yes; yes, I heard.

O'DONNELL 'Yes, I heard'! What the hell's wrong with the bugger?

Silence. Then, when O'NEILL *finally speaks, he speaks very softly, almost as if he were talking to himself.*

O'NEILL I'm remembering Sir Henry Sidney and Lady Mary, may they rest in peace. We spent the winters in the great castle at Ludlow in Shropshire. I've few memories of the winters. It's the summers I remem-

ber and the autumns, in Kent, in the family seat
at Penshurst. And the orchards; and the deerpark;
and those enormous fields of wheat and barley. A
golden and beneficent land. Days without blemish.
Every young man's memories. And every evening
after dinner Sir Henry would propose a topic for discussion: Travel — Seditions and Troubles — Gardens
— Friendship and Loyalty — Good Manners — The
Planting of Foreign Countries. And everyone round
the table had to contribute — the family, guests,
even myself, even his son Philip who was younger
than I. And Sir Henry would tease out the ideas
and guide the conversation almost imperceptibly
but very skilfully so that by the time we rose from
the table he had moulded the discourse into a well-
rounded and formal essay on whatever the theme
was. I was only a raw boy at the time but I was conscious not only that new ideas and concepts were
being explored and fashioned but that I was being
explored and fashioned at the same time. And that
knowledge wasn't unflattering. Drake was there
once, I remember. And Frobisher and his officers on
the eve of their first South American voyage. Gross
men; vain men. But Sir Henry's grace and tact
seemed to transform all that naked brutality and
imperial greed into boyish excitement and manly
adventure. He was the only father I ever knew. I
was closer to him and to Lady Mary than I was to
O'Hagan who fostered me. I loved them both very
much.

Anyhow, time came to come home. I was almost
seventeen then. And the night before I left Lady
Mary had an enormous farewell dinner for me —
there must have been a hundred guests. And at
the end of the meal Sir Henry got to his feet — I
knew he was slightly drunk, maybe he was more
drunk than I knew — and he said: 'Our disquisi-
tion tonight will explore a matter of some interest to
England and of particular interest to Master O'Neill

who goes home tomorrow to become a leader of his people. And the matter is this, and I quote from a letter I have just received from my friend, Andrew Trollope. "Those Irishmen who live like subjects play but as the fox which when you have him on a chain will seem tame; but if he ever gets loose, he will be wild again." So. Speak to that, Fox O'Neill.' And then he laughed. And everybody joined in. And then a hundred people were laughing at me . . .

I left the next morning before the household was awake. And ever since — up until this minute — ever since, that trivial little hurt, that single failure in years of courtesy has pulsed relentlessly in a corner of my heart. Until now. And now for no reason that pulse is quiet and all my affection for Sir Henry returns without qualification. (*Pause*) But all that is of no interest to anybody but myself.

O'DONNELL   Damned right it isn't. Bloody pulse — what's he blathering about?

> O'NEILL *claps his hands, dismissing the entire episode. He is now suddenly very brisk and very efficient.*

O'NEILL   The present. (*To* LOMBARD) You're right. Hugh and I will tour the country to gather support. We'll set out next Monday. (*To* O'DONNELL) No cap-in-hand. We go with authority and assurance.

O'DONNELL   Damned right we do!

O'NEILL   (*To* HARRY) Get a letter off to Lerma today. Kinsale is out of the question. If they insist on landing in the south — anywhere in the south — tell them to cancel the expedition. (*To* LOMBARD) What equipment are they bringing?

LOMBARD   Six battery pieces and six hundred hundredweight of powder.

O'NEILL   (*To* HARRY) We'll need at least five hundred small guns. Tell Lerma we're expert in guerrilla warfare but inexperienced in open battle.

LOMBARD And see that Archbishop Oviedo gets a copy —
he's very influential.

HARRY Right.

LOMBARD (*To* O'NEILL) The Pope has ordered him to sail in the
San Andrea — that's the flagship.

O'DONNELL Flagship! (*He salutes*) Jesus, that word flagship's
like music to me!

O'NEILL They're bringing their own saddles?

LOMBARD Yes; but they expect you to supply the horses.

O'NEILL (*To* HARRY) A levy of five horses on every family.
And oatmeal. And butter. (*To* LOMBARD) A Bull of
Indulgence isn't enough. Everybody who opposes
us must be publicly identified. I need a Bull of
Excommunication.

LOMBARD You won't get that, Hugh.

O'NEILL We got one before.

LOMBARD Twenty years ago.

O'NEILL I want a Bull of Excommunication, Peter.

LOMBARD I've tried. I'll try again. Oviedo's our only hope.

O'NEILL (*To* HARRY) Messages to all the Ulster leaders: a meeting here the day after tomorrow — at noon.

HARRY Noon.

O'NEILL Send Brian O'Hagan across to the Earl of Argyle
for mercenaries.

HARRY How many?

O'NEILL As many as he can get. And pay in advance.

HARRY How much money will he need?

O'NEILL Whatever Argyle asks. (*To* O'DONNELL) You're the
expert on horses.

O'DONNELL Bloody right.

O'NEILL (*To* HARRY) Take him up to the upper meadows and
show him the new stock. (*To* O'DONNELL) Pick only
the horses that are strong enough for a long cam-
paign.

O'DONNELL How many are up there?

O'NEILL Something over three thousand.

O'DONNELL I'll have a look.

HARRY *and* O'DONNELL *go to the door.* O'DONNELL *stops there.*

With all the excitement I forgot to tell you the rumour that's going round Dublin: the Lord Deputy's about to proclaim you a traitor.

O'NEILL That'll do no harm at all. Good. Excellent.

O'DONNELL And do you know what they're offering as a reward for you? Go on — guess — guess.

O'NEILL All right. Tell me.

O'DONNELL £2000 alive, £1000 dead. The same as they were offering five years ago — for the shit O'Doherty!

He gives a great whoop and exits.

O'NEILL (*To* LOMBARD) Your network of priests could be useful. How many are you in touch with?

LOMBARD Twenty, twenty-five.

O'NEILL Every week? Every month?

LOMBARD It varies. They have a price on their head, too.

O'NEILL Get in touch with them as soon as possible. Tell them I'll need them as messengers all over Europe.

LOMBARD I'll do what I can.

He goes to the door.

O'NEILL And put Oviedo to work on that Excommunication Bull.

LOMBARD Oviedo can't demand it, Hugh. The decision is the Pope's. Excommunication is a spiritual matter.

O'NEILL Don't play those games with me, Peter. The situation is as 'spiritual' now as it was twenty years ago. I need Excommunication for solidarity here, for solidarity with Europe. I expect you to deliver it.

LOMBARD As I said, I've tried. I'll try again.

He leaves. O'NEILL *goes to the desk and busies himself with papers. Silence.* MABEL *watches him for a while and then goes to him.*

MABEL Stop it, Hugh.

O'NEILL Stop what?

MABEL This Spanish business. Don't let it happen.

O'NEILL Why should I do that?

MABEL Because you know this isn't what you really want to happen.

O'NEILL I've spent twenty years trying to bring it about, haven't I?

MABEL This isn't your way.

O'NEILL But you know what my way is.

MABEL Calculation — deliberation — caution. You inch forward — you withdraw. You challenge — you retreat. You defy — you submit. Every important move you have ever made has been pondered for months.

O'NEILL I have —

MABEL That's why you're the most powerful man in Ireland: you're the only Irish chieftain who understands the political method. O'Donnell doesn't. Maguire doesn't. McMahon doesn't. That's why the Queen is never *quite* sure how to deal with you — you're the antithesis of what she expects a Gaelic chieftain to be. That's your strength. And that's why your instinct now is not to gamble everything on one big throw that is more than risky.

O'NEILL This time Spain is with us.

MABEL Spain is using you.

O'NEILL We're using each other. We've courted each other for years.

MABEL And that has given you some small negotiating power with England. But the manoeuvrings are over now. And I promise you, Hugh, England will throw everything she has into this war.

O'NEILL So will Spain.

MABEL No, she won't. It's not Spain's war. It's your war. And you're taking on a nation state that is united and determined and powerful and led by a very resolute woman.

O'NEILL Is there an echo of pride in that?

MABEL Please, Hugh.

O'NEILL Are we so inconsiderable? We aren't without determination. We aren't disunited.

MABEL Just look calmly at what you are.

O'NEILL I know exactly what we are.

MABEL You are not united. You have no single leader. You
have no common determination. At best you are an
impromptu alliance of squabbling tribesmen —

O'NEILL Careful!

MABEL — grabbing at religion as a coagulant only because
they have no other idea to inform them or give
them cohesion.

Pause.

O'NEILL Is that a considered abstract of the whole Gaelic
history and civilization, Mabel? Or is it nothing
more than an honest-to-goodness, instant wisdom
of the Upstart?

*He is instantly sorry and grabs her and holds her
in his arms.*

I'm sorry, Mabel. Forgive me. I'm very sorry. I'm a
bit on edge. (*He kisses the top of her head*) Of course
you're right. We have no real cohesion. And of
course I'm worried. Even O'Donnell's enthusiasm
worries me: for him it's all a huge adventure —
cattle-raiding on an international scale.

MABEL *moves away.*

And I never quite know what the Archbishop is
thinking.

MABEL He talks about a Catholic Confederation, a Catholic
Army, about you leading Europe in a glorious
Catholic Counter-Reformation. But I always have
the feeling that when he's talking about you and
about Ireland he's really talking in code about Rome
and Roman power. Is that unfair to him?

382

O'NEILL I don't know.

MABEL Just as Spain's only interest is in Spain and in Spanish power. But my only real concern is you, Hugh. This is not going to be just another skirmish at the edge of a forest. This is a war that England must win because her very survival is at stake. And all I know for sure is that when the war is over, whatever the outcome, the Lombards and the Oviedos won't be here — they'll have moved on to more promising territories. (*Pause*) I shouldn't have spoken. (*Pause*) I didn't mean to intrude. (*Pause*) I'm sure I don't really understand the overall thing.

O'NEILL The overall thing.

MABEL That's what matters in the end, isn't it?

O'NEILL The overall thing — we don't even begin to know what it means.

Silence. She gathers her pieces of lace and goes to the door.

MABEL Something Mary told me: a new Lord Deputy is about to be appointed, somebody called Lord Mountjoy. Henry says he's meticulous, and a ruthless fighter. Blount — that's his real name; Charles Blount. That's all she knows. Oh yes — he smokes a lot. It's all very secret. She made me swear not to tell you.

She is about to leave when she is arrested by the controlled passion of o'NEILL's voice.

O'NEILL I have spent my life attempting to do two things. I have attempted to hold together a harassed and a confused people by trying to keep them in touch with the life they knew before they were overrun. It wasn't a life of material ease but it had its assurances and it had its dignity. And I have done that by acknowledging and indeed honouring the rituals and ceremonies and beliefs these people have practised

since before history, long before the God of
Christianity was ever heard of. And at the same time
I have tried to open these people to the strange new
ways of Europe, to ease them into the new assessment of things, to nudge them towards changing
evaluations and beliefs. Two pursuits that can
scarcely be followed simultaneously. Two tasks that
are almost self-cancelling. But they have got to be
attempted because the formation of nations and
civilizations is a willed act, not a product of fate or
accident. And for you to suggest that religion is the
only coagulant that holds us together is to grossly
and ignorantly overlook an age-old civilization. In
one detail you are right: it is not my nature to
gamble everything on one big throw —

MABEL So have your war.

O'NEILL But if I don't move now that civilization is certainly
doomed.

MABEL So go and fight. That's what you've spent your life
doing. That's what you're best at. Fighting to preserve a fighting society. I don't care anymore.

O'NEILL Because you're not quite sure which side you're
on?

MABEL Why do you keep rejecting me, Hugh?

O'NEILL I can see it wouldn't break your heart to see the
Gaelic order wiped out. But let's look at what the
alternative is: the buccaneering, vulgar, material code
of the new colonials —

MABEL (*Leaving*) Excuse me.

O'NEILL The new 'civility' approved, we're told, by God Himself. Isn't that your coagulant — God? No, better
still, God and trade. Now there's a combination.

*She swings back and glares at him in hatred. He
ignores her and pretends to busy himself at the
desk.*

MABEL I want your mistresses out of this house immediately.

O'NEILL　(*Tyrone accent*) Aw, now, sorry, ma'am.

MABEL　What does sorry mean?

O'NEILL　That my mistresses stay.

MABEL　I will not live in the same house as those — those harlots! Get those tramps out of here!

O'NEILL　No.

MABEL　Then I go.

O'NEILL　That's your choice.

Pause. She tries not to cry.

MABEL　I'm pregnant, Hugh.

O'NEILL *goes to the exit.*

O'NEILL　(*Calling*) Harry! Have you a moment?

MABEL　Did you hear what I said?

He returns to the desk.

O'NEILL　That you're pregnant? Yes, I heard. So if all goes well — isn't that the expression? — if all goes well that will be ten legitimate children I'll have sired and about — what? — maybe thirty bastards.

MABEL　Oh, Hugh —

O'NEILL　Or so my people boast. An affectionate attribute every nation bestows on its heroes.

Again he has instant remorse. As she runs to the door he runs after her.

Mabel! Mabel, I'm —

O'DONNELL *dashes on.*

O'DONNELL　A messenger from Spain outside, Hugh! (*To* MABEL) It gets better by the minute! (*To* O'NEILL) The Spanish fleet sails on September 3rd! (*To* MABEL) Maybe you speak Spanish? You should hear your man out

there: 'Beeg fleet — beeg ships'!
O'NEILL Where do they sail from?
O'DONNELL Lisbon. On the first tide.
O'NEILL And where do they land?

HARRY *enters.*

HARRY Did you call me?
O'NEILL Where do they land?
O'DONNELL 'Keen-sall'.
O'NEILL Where — where?
O'DONNELL 'Keen-sall' — Kinsale, I suppose.
O'NEILL Oh, God, no.
O'DONNELL Wherever Kinsale is. This is it, Mabel darling! This is it! Yipeeeeee!

Quick black.

ACT TWO

Scene One

About eight months later. The edge of a thicket somewhere near the Sperrin mountains.

O'NEILL is on his knees. He is using a wooden box as a table and he is writing — scoring out — writing rapidly, with total concentration, almost frantically. Various loose pages on the ground beside him. He looks tired and anxious and harassed. He is so concentrated on his writing that he is unaware of O'DONNELL's entrance. Then, when he is aware, he reaches perfunctorily for the dagger at his side. O'DONNELL, too, looks tired and anxious. He is also spattered with mud and his boots are sodden.

O'DONNELL   It's only me. I suppose you thought something had happened to me.

O'NEILL   You were longer than you thought.

O'DONNELL   I had to make detours going and coming back — the countryside's crawling with troops. And then there were a lot of things to see to at home — disputes — documents — the usual. Look at my feet. These Sperrins aren't mountains — they're bloody bogs! I suppose you wouldn't have a spare pair of boots?

O'NEILL   What you see is all I have.

O'DONNELL   I was afraid you might have had to move on to some new place.

O'NEILL   It's been very quiet here.

O'DONNELL   God, I'm exhausted.

> *He throws himself on the ground and spreads out in exhaustion. His eyes closed. O'NEILL continues writing. Silence.*

O'NEILL Have you any food?

O'DONNELL *opens his leather bag and produces a scone of bread.* O'NEILL *goes to him, takes the bread and eats it hungrily.*

O'DONNELL My mother made me half-a-dozen of them but I met a family begging on the roadside near Raphoe. Everywhere you go there are people scavenging in the fields, hoking up bits of roots, eating fistfuls of watercress. They look like skeletons. Where's Mabel?

O'NEILL Harry took her to relatives of Ruadhaire Dall Ó Cathain's near Dungiven. She wasn't able to keep moving about anymore.

O'DONNELL Proper order, too. When is she due?

O'NEILL Next week probably.

O'DONNELL She's been terrific, Hugh. Not a whimper out of her all these months — and us skulking about like tramps.

O'NEILL I know.

O'DONNELL Next week. Great. At least that'll be something to celebrate. I'm wild dry. Have you any water?

O'NEILL *hands him a bottle.*

O'NEILL Well?

O'DONNELL I hate this aul' brown Tyrone water — with all respects. How do you drink it?

O'NEILL What did you learn?

O'DONNELL I never made Ballyshannon. Dowcra's troops were waiting for me there. I got no further than Donegal Town. My mother says to tell you she was asking for you.

O'NEILL Well?

O'DONNELL Well, it's a complete collapse, she says. The countryside's in chaos, she says: slaughter, famine, disease. There must be eight thousand people crowded into Donegal Town looking for food.

O'NEILL Where's Mountjoy?

O'DONNELL Mountjoy's riding up and down the country and beheading everything that stirs. And every week somebody new caves in; and those that are holding out are being picked off one after the other. But do you know what I heard? Jesus, wait till you hear this, Hugh. We were betrayed at Kinsale! They knew we were going to attack that morning. They were sitting waiting for us. And do you know how they knew? Brian Óg McMahon slipped them the word! Time, place, number of men, everything. And do you know how they bought him? With a bottle of whiskey! Jesus, wouldn't it break your heart? That's what they're all saying at home. There could have been ten million Spanish soldiers and we still wouldn't have won. Because one of our own captains bloody-well betrayed us.

O'NEILL Rubbish.

O'DONNELL What d'you mean — rubbish?

O'NEILL All lies.

O'DONNELL You don't believe me?

O'NEILL You don't believe it yourself.

O'DONNELL It's what everybody at home's saying . . . I don't know . . . maybe . . . but you'll agree those McMahons were always shifty buggers.

O'NEILL How big is the collapse?

O'DONNELL It's all over. It's all finished, Hugh.

O'NEILL Who has submitted? Names.

O'DONNELL My mother says they're crawling in on their hands and knees and offering hostages and money and whatnot. It would be easier to count the handful that are still holding out.

O'NEILL Names.

O'DONNELL Names . . . where do you begin? . . . all right, names . . . Jesus, I just hate saying them . . . Turlough McHenry of the Fews. The two Antrim O'Neills. O'Malley of Mayo. O'Flaherty of Annaly. Maguire of Fermanagh —

O'NEILL Cúchonnacht?

O'DONNELL God, no! The wee get, Connor Roe. Christ, man, aul'

Cúchonnacht's still dodging about the Lisnaskea area with fifteen picked men and hammering away every chance he gets! The McDevitts of Ballybeg, all of them, every branch of the family. The McSwineys of Fanad. Wouldn't it sicken you? — the bloody McSwineys that our family has kept and protected for generations and then when you're down in your luck. (*Suddenly brightening*) But do you know who's holding out? You'd never guess! Still the same wee maggot he always was but at least he hasn't caved in yet. The sheep-stealer! — the shit O'Doherty from Inishowen! Jesus, isn't it well we didn't slip him the Bordeaux Special that time?

O'NEILL   Go on.

O'DONNELL   O'Kelly of Kilconnell. Brave enough; he held out until last Sunday and then do you know what he did? The aul' eejit, Jesus, pompous as ever; he had this blond wig that an aul' aunt had brought home from Paris. Anyhow, he sticks the blond wig on his head, puts on a scarlet jacket, marches into Galway town and offers his surrender — in French! Poor aul' bugger — trying to make a bit of a gesture out of it . . . Anyhow, one swing of an axe and the aul' blond head was rolling about the street . . .

O'NEILL   Go on.

O'DONNELL   Who else? . . . O'Reilly of East Breffni. McWilliam Burke of Connaught. O'Kane —

O'NEILL   Which O'Kane?

O'DONNELL   Your daughter Rose's husband. Sure you always knew he was a bloody weed. Fitzmaurice of Kerry. Donnell McCarthy of Bandon. I can go on forever. O'Dowd. O'Dwyer of Kilnamanagh. God, Hugh, I'm telling you — it's endless.

O'NEILL *picks up his papers and puts them in order. Silence.*

O'NEILL   Where's Chichester?

O'DONNELL   He's taken over your place at Dungannon.

O'NEILL   Hah!

O'DONNELL   He controls the whole of East Ulster. Dowcra controls the whole of West Ulster. Carew controls the whole of Munster. And Mountjoy controls the whole country. (*Pause*) He did a kind of a dirty thing last week, Mountjoy.

O'NEILL *stops and looks at him.*

He smashed the O'Neill crowning stone at Tullyhogue. There was no call for that, was there? (*Pause*) What else is there? The King of France has written to Elizabeth to come to terms with us. Wasting his bloody time. All your Derry lands have been given to Bishop Montgomery and your Armagh lands to the new Protestant bishop there . . . I don't think I heard anything else . . . they've taken over your fishing rights on the Bann and the Foyle . . . And I've resigned, Hugh.

O'NEILL   What do you mean?

O'DONNELL   Handed over to the brother, Rory.

O'NEILL   Oh, Hugh.

O'DONNELL   And I'm leaving at the end of the week.

O'NEILL   Where for?

O'DONNELL   I don't know. Wherever the ship takes me. Maybe Spain. (*Pause. He smiles resolutely and uncertainly*) No, it's not a sudden decision. I've been thinking about it for months, ever since Kinsale. And Rory'll be a fine chieftain — he's a solid man, very calm, very balanced. He hasn't my style or flair, of course; but then I have a fault or two, as you know. The blood gets up too easy and I was always useless at dealing with civil servants and Lord Deputies and people like that. Not like you. Even with my own people, for God's sake: the bloody McSwineys of Fanad couldn't wait to get a thump at me. Anyhow, the chieftain isn't all that important — isn't that what our bards tell us? The land is the goddess that every ruler in turn is married to. We come and we go but she stays the same. And the Tyrconnell goddess is getting a new man. Trouble is, no matter who she's married to, I'll always be in love with her . . . (*He takes a drink of water*) Jesus, that stuff would physic an elephant!

O'NEILL   When are you leaving?

O'DONNELL   Next Friday.

O'NEILL   Where from?

O'DONNELL   I'm getting a ship at a place called Castlehaven — wherever that is.

O'NEILL   Near Skibbereen.

O'DONNELL   Wherever Skibbereen is.

O'NEILL   You'll be back, Hugh.

O'DONNELL   Aye. In a blond wig and a scarlet jacket and leading a hundred thousand Spaniards! And next time we'll land in Derry — better still Rathmullan and my mother'll get landing fees from the buggers — right? (*He laughs*) No, it's all over, Hugh. Finished for all time. Poor aul' Peter Lombard, terrible bleak ending for his history, isn't it? I mean, Jesus, how can the poor man make an interesting story out of a defeat like this — eh? If he'd any sense he'd scrap the whole thing. Yes, there is one thing that might bring me home sometime — to get my sheep back from the shit O'Doherty. Oh, man . . .

> *Impulsively, about to break down, he flings his arms around* O'NEILL. *They embrace for several seconds. Then* O'DONNELL *goes to his bag for a handkerchief.*

What about you? What are you going to do?

O'NEILL   I don't have many choices. And I'm not as young as you.

O'DONNELL   Damned right — twenty years older at least.

O'NEILL   My instinct is to leave like you.

O'DONNELL   What does Mabel think?

O'NEILL   She's urging me to hang on, pick up the pieces, start all over again. They're very tenacious, the New

English.

O'DONNELL Maybe she's right. She's a very loyal wee girl.

O'NEILL Her reasoning is that since the country is in such anarchy Mountjoy has neither the energy nor the resources to impose order; but if I were to make a public declaration of loyalty to the Queen and if she were to reinstate me —

O'DONNELL Are you out of your — ?!

O'NEILL With only nominal authority, without political or military power whatever, then Mabel says I should accept almost any conditions, no matter how humiliating, as long as I'd be restored to my base again and to my own people.

O'DONNELL And why in God's name would Elizabeth restore you?

O'NEILL Because she knows that the only way she can rule Ireland at this point is by *using* someone like me. She hates me — but she can rule through me provided she has control over me. At least that's Mabel's argument. I think I could get enough of my people behind me and she thinks some of the New English would back it — those that are sick of England.

O'DONNELL So you're writing your submission?

O'NEILL What's the alternative? The life of a soured émigré whingeing and scheming round the capitals of Europe.

O'DONNELL Like me.

O'NEILL I didn't mean that, Hugh.

O'DONNELL Show me that. You know, you're a tenacious bugger, too. You and Mabel are well met.

At first O'DONNELL *reads his portions of the submission in mocking and exaggerated tones. He is unaware that* O'NEILL *is deadly serious. But as they proceed through the document —* O'DONNELL *reading his sections,* O'NEILL *speaking his by heart —* O'DONNELL'*s good humour drains away and he ends up as formal and as grave as* O'NEILL.

393

(*Reading*) I, Hugh O'Neill, by the Queen of England, France and Ireland her most gracious favour created Earl of Tyrone, do with all true and humble penitency prostrate myself at her royal feet — (*he drops on his knees*) — absolutely submit myself to her mercy. (*Not reading*) Mercy, Queen, Mercy!

O'NEILL Most sorrowfully imploring her gracious commiseration and appealing only to her princely clemency, without presuming to justify my unloyal proceedings against Her sacred Majesty.

O'DONNELL (*Reading*) May it please Her Majesty to mitigate her just indignation against me for my unnatural rebellion which deserves no forgiveness and for which I can make no satisfaction, even with my life. (*Not reading*) Jesus, you are one great fraud, O'Neill!

O'NEILL I do most humbly beg Her Majesty to restore me to my former living and dignity where as an obedient subject I vow to continue hereafter loyal to her royal person, to her crown, to her prerogatives, and to her English laws.

O'DONNELL Her English — ?! Hey, steady on, man, steady — !

O'NEILL I do renounce and abjure all foreign power whatever and all kind of dependency upon any other potentate but Her Majesty, the Queen of England, France and Ireland —

O'DONNELL (*Reading*) And do vow to serve her faithfully against any foreign power invading her kingdom; and especially do I abjure and renounce all manner of dependency upon the King of Spain and shall be ready with the uttermost of my ability to serve Her Majesty against him or any of his forces or confederates.

O'NEILL I do resign all claim and title to any lands but such as shall now be granted to me; and lastly I offer to the Queen and to her magistrates here my full assistance in anything that may tend to the advancement of her service and the peaceable government of this kingdom.

O'DONNELL (*Reading*) Particularly will I help in the abolishing of all barbarous Gaelic customs which are the seeds of all incivility.

O'NEILL   And for the clearing of all difficult passages and places —

O'DONNELL   (*Reading*) Which are the nurseries —

O'NEILL   Which are the nurseries of rebellion. And I will endeavour to erect habitations —

O'DONNELL   (*Reading*) Civil habitations.

O'NEILL   Civil habitations for myself and for the people of my country to preserve us against any force but the power of the state —

O'DONNELL   (*Reading*) By which power —

O'NEILL   By which power we must rest assured to be preserved as long as we continue in our loyal and faithful duties to Her Majesty —

O'DONNELL   (*Reading*) To her most clement —

O'NEILL   To her most clement, most gracious, most noble and most forgiving majesty.

O'DONNELL   (*Reading*) To whom I now most abjectly and most obediently offer my service and indeed . . . my life . . .

Silence. Then O'NEILL *moves away as if to distance himself from what he has just said.* O'DONNELL *is still on his knees.*

This is the end of it all, Hugh, isn't it? (*Pause*) Jesus.

He gets to his feet, brightening.

All the same, they say she's a peculiar woman, the Queen. Damn it, wouldn't it be a good one if she believed you — eh?

O'NEILL   She won't believe me.

O'DONNELL   But if she did! Damn it, I'd make a submission to her myself!

O'NEILL   Belief has nothing to do with it. As Mabel says, she'll use me if it suits her.

O'DONNELL   And your people?

O'NEILL They're much more pure, 'my people'. Oh, no, they won't believe me either. But they'll pretend they believe me and then with ruthless Gaelic logic they'll crucify me for betraying them.

HARRY enters. He looks quickly first at O'NEILL and then at O'DONNELL — they have not noticed his arrival. He then greets them with deliberate heartiness.

HARRY It wouldn't be hard to surprise you two.

O'DONNELL Harry! How are you, man?

HARRY When did you get back?

O'DONNELL Just arrived.

HARRY We thought we had lost you — (*To* O'NEILL) didn't we?

O'DONNELL I tried to surrender to Dowcra but he wouldn't take me.

O'NEILL How was the journey?

HARRY The journey was fine. We had a fine journey.

O'NEILL And the Ó Cathains were expecting her?

HARRY A big welcoming party. Everything quiet here?

O'NEILL She was in good form when you left her?

HARRY That's a great place they have there. (*To* O'DONNELL) Ethna Ó Cathain and your mother are cousins, aren't they?

O'DONNELL Second cousins.

HARRY Yes, she mentioned that. (*Rummaging in his bag*) And she sent you both some food: some oatmeal bread and milk and what's this — biscuits — strange-looking biscuits —

O'NEILL They know exactly where I am?

HARRY Of course they know; raisins, flour —

O'NEILL And they'll send me word immediately?

HARRY Yes. And she sent this specially to you, Hugh. (*He hands over a bottle to* O'DONNELL)

O'DONNELL Is it whiskey?

HARRY Ten year old.

O'DONNELL Decent woman, Ethna. And thank God I don't put

water in it.

HARRY   Anybody else hungry?

O'NEILL   No, thanks.

O'DONNELL   (*Drinking*) Good luck. Hugh?

O'NEILL   Not for me.

O'DONNELL   What's the news about Dungiven, Harry?

HARRY   (*Eating*) Let me see. Nothing very much. Archbishop Lombard's gone to Rome.

O'DONNELL   For good?

HARRY   They've invented some sort of job for him there.

O'DONNELL   You may be sure aul' Peter'll always land on his feet.

HARRY   And Archbishop Oviedo's gone to England. The morning after Kinsale he headed straight for London to sweeten the authorities there — in case there'd be a backlash against the Catholics in England.

O'DONNELL   They don't miss a beat, those boys, do they? Beautiful stuff this. Sure you don't want some, Hugh?

HARRY   Leave some for the rest of us.

O'NEILL   They have their own physicians, the Ó Cathains, haven't they?

HARRY   Sean Ó Coinne. I met him there. Seemed very competent. What else is new? Oh, yes, Sir Garret Moore wants to get in touch with you — I imagine at Mountjoy's prompting. He wants to explore what areas of common interest might still exist between you and the Crown. The pretext for getting you down to the Boyne is the first run of sea trout. If you were to go I'm sure he'd have some civil servants there.

O'DONNELL   So they do want to talk to you, Hugh. Mabel was right.

HARRY   What else . . . ? There's a rumour that Mountjoy himself may be in trouble because of some woman in England — Lady Penelope Rich? — is that the name? Anyhow, if the scandal becomes public they say Mountjoy may be recalled. What else was there . . . ? Sean na bPunta is still going calmly round the country with his brown leather bag, collecting your

	rents as if the place weren't in chaos! . . . Tadhg Ó
	Cianain is writing a book on the past ten years —
O'DONNELL	Another history! Jesus, if we had as many scones of
	bread as we have historians!
HARRY	It will be a very exact piece of work that Tadhg will
	produce . . . And portions of another book are being
	circulated and it seems the English government is
	paying a lot of attention to it. Written by an English-
	man called Spenser who used to have a place down
	near the Ballyhouras mountains — wherever they
	are — I'm getting like you, Hugh — they're in
	County Cork, aren't they? — anyhow, this Spenser
	was burned out in the troubles after the battle of
	the Yellow Ford . . . (*He suddenly breaks down but*
	continues speaking without stopping) Oh, my God,
	Hugh, I don't know how to say it to you — I don't
	know how to tell you — we had only just arrived
	at Ó Cathain's place —
O'DONNELL	Harry — ?
HARRY	And the journey *had* been fine — she was in won-
	derful form — we sang songs most of the way —
	I taught her 'Tabhair Dom Do Lamh', Ruadhaire
	Dall's song, because the Ó Cathains are relatives of
	his and she could show off before them and we
	laughed until we were sore at the way she pro-
	nounced the Irish words — and she taught me a
	Staffordshire ballad called 'Lord Brand, He was a
	Gentleman' and I tried to sing it in a Staffordshire
	accent — and she couldn't have been better looked
	after — they were all waiting for her — Ethna, the
	doctor Ó Coinne, two midwives, half-a-dozen ser-
	vants. And everything seemed perfectly normal —
	everything *was* fine. She said if the baby was a boy
	she was going to call it Nicholas after her father
	and if it was a girl she was going to call it Joan after
	your mother — and when Ethna asked her were
	you thinking of going into exile she got very agitated
	and she said, 'Hugh?'. She said, 'Hugh would never
	betray his people' — and just then, quite normally,

quite naturally, she went into labour — and whatever happened — I still don't really know — whatever happened, something just wasn't right, Hugh. The baby lived for about an hour — it was a boy — but she never knew it had died — and shortly afterwards Ethna was sitting on a stool right beside her bed, closer than I am to you — and she was sleeping very peacefully — and then she gave a long sigh as if she were very tired and when Ethna put her hand on her cheek . . . It wasn't possible to get word to you — it all happened so quickly — herself and the baby within two hours — the doctor said something about poisoning of the blood — Oh, God, I'm so sorry for you — I'm so sorry for all of us. I loved her, too — you know that — from the very first day we met her — remember that day in May? — her twentieth birthday? — she was wearing a blue dress with a white lace collar and white lace cuffs . . . If you had seen her laid out — she looked like a girl of fourteen, she was just so beautiful . . . God have mercy on her. God have mercy on all of us.

Long silence.

O'NEILL (*Almost in a whisper*) Yes, I think I'll take some of that whiskey now, Hugh. Just a thimbleful, if you please. And no water. Oh, dear God . . .

Quick black.

399

ACT TWO

Scene Two

O'Neill's apartment in Rome many years later.

*When the scene opens the only light on the stage is a candle on a
large desk. This is Lombard's desk; littered with papers; and in the
centre is a large book — the history. The room is scantily furnished
— a small table, some chairs, a stool, a couch.*

*o'NEILL is now in his early sixties. His eyesight is beginning to
trouble him — he carries a walking stick. And he drinks too much.
We first hear his raucous shouting off. When he enters we see that he
is slightly drunk. His temper is volatile and bitter and dangerous. He
is carrying a lighted taper.*

o'NEILL   (*Off*) Anybody at home? Harry? Why are there no
damned lights out here? (*Now on*) Catríona? Your
slightly inebriated husband is back! I really
shouldn't have had that last bottle of — (*He bumps
into a stool and knocks it over. As he straightens it:*)
Forgive me, I do beg your pardon. Perhaps you
could assist me, signor. Am I in the right building?
You see, I'm a foreigner in your city, an émigré
from Ireland in fact — yes, yes, *Irlanda*. Ah! You've
been there? *Bella*, indeed: indeed *bellissima*; you are
very kind. What's that? Oh, yes, that is perfectly true
— everybody does love us. And I'll tell you why,
my friend: because we are a most attractive and
a most loyal people. Now, if you'd be so kind,
I'm trying to make my way to the Palazzo dei
Penitenzieri which is between the Via della
Conciliazione and the Borgo Santo Spirito where I
live with — (*He breaks off suddenly because, holding
his taper up high, he finds himself standing at the desk*

*and looking down at the book. He stares at it for a few
seconds. Very softly)* The right building, indeed. Home.
Everything is in order . . . *(He takes a few steps away
from the desk and calls:)* Archbishop? Harry? *(No
answer. He returns to the book and turns it round so
that he can read it. He leans over the page, his face close
to it and reads:)* 'In the name of God. Herewith I set
my hand to chronicle the life of Hugh O'Neill, Earl
of Tyrone, son of Feardorcha, son of Conn Bacach,
son of Conn Mór, noblest son of noble lineage who
was fostered and brought up by the high-born
nobles of his tribe, the O'Hagans and the O'Quinns,
and who continued to grow and increase in comeliness and urbanity, tact and eloquence, wisdom
and knowledge, goodly size and noble deeds, so
that his name and fame spread throughout the five
provinces of Ireland and beyond — ' *(Suddenly,
violently, angrily he swings away from the desk. He
bellows:)* Where the hell is everybody? Catríona?
Your devoted Earl is home! *(He listens. There is no
sound)* At vespers, no doubt. Or in the arms of
some sweaty Roman with a thick neck and bushy
stomach. *(He goes to the small table and lights the
candles there. Then he empties the dregs from two empty
bottles into a wine glass. As he does these things:)*
Enormously popular in this city, my Countess. Of
course she is still attractive — indeed all the more
attractive since she has gone ever so slightly, almost
judiciously, to seed; no doubt an intuitive response
to the Roman preference for over-ripeness.

Curious people, these Romans: they even find
her vulgar Scottish accent charming. Happily for
them they don't understand a word she . . . *(With
the glass in his hand he has drifted back to — cannot
resist the pull of — the open book. Again myopically he
leans over it and reads:)* 'And people reflected in
their minds that when he would reach manhood
there would not be one like him of the Irish to
avenge their wrongs and punish the plunderings

of his race. For it was foretold by prophets and by predictors of futurity that there would come one like him —

    'A man, glorious, pure, faithful above all
    Who will cause mournful weeping in every
       territory.
    He will be a God-like prince
    And he will be king for the span of — '

(*He shuts the book in fury*) Damn you, Archbishop! But this is one battle I am not going to lose! (*Wheeling away from the table, he bellows:*) Where the hell is everybody?! Catríona, you bitch, where are you? Haaaa-reeee! (*He turns round.* HARRY *is at his elbow. He is embarrassed.*) Ah, there you are. Why do you keep hiding on me? Where the hell is everybody?

HARRY   Catríona has gone out. She says —

O'NEILL   (*Furious again*) Out! Out! Tell me when the hell my accommodating wife is ever in! (*Softly*) Sorry.

HARRY   And the Archbishop is upstairs. You were to have spent the afternoon with him.

O'NEILL   Why would I have done that?

HARRY   He wanted confirmation of some details.

O'NEILL   What are you talking about?

HARRY   For his history.

O'NEILL   'His history'! Damn his history. I haven't eaten all day, Harry. I suppose I ought to be hungry.

HARRY   Let me get you —

O'NEILL   No, I don't want food. What's happened here since morning?

HARRY   A reply from the King of Spain.

O'NEILL   Wonderful!

HARRY   Eventually. Thanking you for your last three letters —

O'NEILL   But —

HARRY   But reminding you again that England and Spain have signed a peace treaty. It's fragile but it's holding.

O'NEILL   The King of Spain has betrayed us, Harry.

HARRY He believes that the interests of Ireland and Spain
are best served by *'inacción'*.

O'NEILL *Inacción.*

HARRY And he urges you to remain in Rome for the time
being.

O'NEILL I have remained in Rome for the time being at his
insistence for the past eight years!

HARRY He says he values your Christian patience.

O'NEILL (*Shouting*) He values my Christian — ! (*Softly*) I'm
going to die in this damned town, Harry. You do
know that, don't you? And be buried here, beside
my son, in the church of San Pietro. (*He laughs*) The
drink makes God-like princes maudlin.

HARRY Not a good day?

O'NEILL Oh, wonderful! Animating! The usual feverish
political activity and intellectual excitement. First
I walked to the top of the Janiculum hill. Then I
walked down again. Then I stood in line at the office
of the Papal Secretary and picked up my paltry
papal pension and bowed and said, *'Grazie. Grazie
molto'*. Then I stood in line at the office of the
Spanish Embassy and picked up my paltry Spanish
pension and bowed and said, *'Gracias. Muchas gracias'*. And then I — (*He breaks off, points to the ceiling*) The Archbishop?

HARRY *nods: Yes.*

(*Whispering*) Then I spent a most agreeable hour
with Maria the Neapolitan.

HARRY That's a new name.

O'NEILL Yes. Wonderful girl, Maria. Steeped in Greek
mythology and speaks half-a-dozen languages.
Anyhow, I left some of my money with her; Spanish
money, of course. And when I was leaving, d'you
know what she said to me, Harry? *'Grazie, signor.
Grazie molto.'*

HARRY *laughs.*

She did. And I believe she meant it. I'm an old man
— I was flattered momentarily.

HARRY And then you met Neachtain Ó Domhnaill and
Christopher Plunkett.

O'NEILL Have you been spying on me?

HARRY They were here this morning looking for you.

O'NEILL And we spent the afternoon together — as you can
see.

HARRY Ó Domhnaill was drunk when he was here.

O'NEILL And once more we went over the master plan to
raise an army and retake Ireland. Spain will provide the men, France will supply the artillery and
the Pope will pay for the transportation. Naturally
O'Neill of Tyrone will lead the liberating host. But
because my eyesight is less than perfect Plunkett
will ride a few paces ahead of me. And because
Plunkett's hearing is less than perfect Ó Domhnaill
will ride a few paces ahead of him. Ó Domhnaill's
delirium tremens has got to be overlooked because he
refuses to acknowledge it himself. Our estimate is
that it may take the best part of a day to rout the
English — perhaps two if they put up a fight. The
date of embarkation — May 19th: you see, the 18th
is pension day.

HARRY What drinking house were you in?

O'NEILL Pedro Blanco's. Full, as usual. Plunkett insisted
the customers were all Englishmen, disguised as
Romans, spying on us. And so for security reasons
our master plan has been code-named — this was
Ó Domhnaill's only inspiration — Operation Turf
Mould . . . I can't stand it much longer, Harry. I
think my mind is beginning to . . . Maybe I should
eat something.

HARRY Good. I'll get you —

O'NEILL Not now. Later. If you would be so kind —

He holds out his glass for HARRY *to fill.*

HARRY Sorry, Hugh. We're out of wine. There's no wine in

404

the house.

O'NEILL Why?

HARRY (*Reluctantly*) The supplier turned me away this afternoon. I'm afraid we've run out of credit.

O'NEILL Who is this supplier?

HARRY His name is Carlo something. We've always dealt with him. His place is at the back of —

O'NEILL And he refused you?

HARRY We already owe him eight hundred ducats.

O'NEILL He refused you?

HARRY He's a decent man but he has six young children.

O'NEILL (*Shouting*) Don't be so damned elusive, Harry. (*Softly*) Did this fellow refuse you?

HARRY He refused me.

O'NEILL And he knew who the wine was for?

HARRY I'm sure he did.

O'NEILL Did you tell him the wine was for Hugh O'Neill?

HARRY I've been going to him ever since we —

O'NEILL Did you specifically tell him the wine was for Hugh O'Neill?

HARRY Yes, of course he knew the wine was for Hugh O'Neill and what he said was that Hugh O'Neill's credit was finished — no payment, no wine. And you might as well know, too, that we owe money to Catríona's tailor and to the baker and that the rent in this place is six months overdue.

O'NEILL (*Icily*) You're shouting at me, Harry.

HARRY Sorry. I can't stand it much longer either, Hugh.

O'NEILL And perhaps this is as good a time as any to take a look at how you're squandering the money I entrust to you to manage my affairs, or perhaps more importantly *why* you're squandering that money. Because my suspicion is that this isn't just your customary ineptitude in money matters —

HARRY *goes to the door.*

HARRY We'll talk tomorrow, Hugh.

O'NEILL What I suspect is that the pride you once professed

in being a servant of the O'Neills is long gone —
and I suppose that's understandable: I can't be of
much use to you anymore, can I?

HARRY You suspect everybody and —

O'NEILL And, because that pride is gone, what I suspect is
that some perverse element in your nature isn't at
all displeased to see Hugh O'Neill humiliated by
this anonymous backstreet wine vendor.

HARRY Hugh —

O'NEILL But it does distress me to see you so soured that it
actually pleases you to have the bailiffs fling O'Neill
out on the street. What's gnawing at you, Harry?
Some bitterness? Some deep disappointment? Some
corroding sense of betrayal?

HARRY Soured? You talk to me about being soured, about
betrayal? (*He controls himself*) Leave the door open
for the Countess.

O'NEILL What was it I called you once, Harry? Was it borage?
No, that was O'Donnell, may he rest in peace; loyal,
faithful Hugh. No, you were . . . dill! The man with
the comforting and soothing effect! And the interesting thing is that I chose Harry Hoveden to be my
private secretary precisely because he wasn't a
Gael. You see, I thought a Gael might be vulnerable
to small, tribal pressures — to little domestic loyalties — an almost attractive human weakness when
you come to think of it. So instead I chose one of
the Old English because he would be above that
kind of petty venality. So I chose Harry Hoveden
because he claimed to admire Hugh O'Neill and
everything Hugh O'Neill was attempting to do
for his people and because when he left the Old
English and joined us he protested such fealty and
faithfulness not only to Hugh O'Neill but to the
whole Gaelic nation.

HARRY If you weren't so drunk, Hugh —

He breaks off because LOMBARD *enters.*

O'NEILL The fault, of course, is mine. I suppose that easy rejection of his old loyalties and the almost excessive display of loyalty to us ought to have alerted me. Certainly Mabel was never taken in by it.

HARRY I'm sorry for you, Hugh. You have become a pitiable, bitter bastard.

O'NEILL Don't you believe in loyalty anymore, Harry? In keeping faith? In fealty?

> LOMBARD *assesses the situation instantly and accurately and in response he assumes a breezy, energetic manner which he sustains right through the scene. As he enters he holds up a bottle.* O'NEILL *immediately regrets his outburst but is unable to apologize and slumps sulkily in a chair.*

LOMBARD I've come at a bad moment, have I? No? Good. And look what I have here. You'd never guess what this is, Harry.

HARRY A bottle.

LOMBARD Brilliant. D'you see, Hugh?

O'NEILL Yes.

LOMBARD Arrived this very day. From home. But it's a very special bottle, Harry. *Poitín.* Waterford *poitín.* I was never much help to their spiritual welfare but they certainly don't neglect the state of my spirit! (*He laughs*) Have you some glasses there? (*To* O'NEILL) Catríona says she'll be late, not to wait up for her. Something about a tailor and a dress fitting. (*To* HARRY) Good man. This, I assure you, is ambrosia.

HARRY Not for me, Peter. But he needs some very badly.

> *As* HARRY *leaves* LOMBARD *calls after him.*

LOMBARD I'll leave this aside for you and if you feel like joining us later . . . And for the Earl himself, just a drop. It's pure nectar, Hugh. (*He takes a sip and relishes it*) Tell me this: are the very special delights of this world foretastes of eternity or just lures to perdition? It's

407

from my own parish; a very remote place called Affane, about ten miles from Dungarvan. And it has been made there for decades by an old man who claims he's one of Ormond's bastards. If he is, God bless bastards — God forgive me. (*He takes another sip*) Exquisite, isn't it? Affane must be an annex of heaven — or Hades.

o'neill *puts his untouched drink to the side.*

o'neill I'll try it later, Peter.

LOMBARD Of course. Now. (*Going to his desk*) You're not too tired to help me check a few details, are you? Splendid. (*He sees the book has been closed*) You know, Hugh, you were very naughty today.

o'neill Was I?

LOMBARD You and I were to have spent the afternoon on this.

o'neill What's that?

LOMBARD My history. (*He laughs*) 'My history'! You would think I was Thucydides, wouldn't you? And, if the truth were told, I'm so disorganized I'm barely able to get all this stuff into chronological order, not to talk of making sense of it. But if I'm to write about the life and times of Hugh O'Neill the co-operation of the man himself would be a help, wouldn't it?

o'neill Sorry, Peter.

LOMBARD No harm done. Here we are — let me tell you the broad outline.

o'neill I had a bad day.

LOMBARD I know. Pension day. That's understandable.

o'neill A stupid, drunken day with Plunkett and Ó Domhnaill.

LOMBARD I saw them this morning. A sorry sight. They were two great men once.

o'neill And I was cruel to Harry just now.

LOMBARD I sensed something was amiss.

o'neill I told him Mabel didn't trust him. That was a damned lie. Mabel loved Harry.

LOMBARD I know she did. And Harry understands. We all
understand. It's been a difficult time for you, Hugh.
That's why this history is important — is vitally
important. These last years have been especially
frustrating. But what we must remember — what I
must record and celebrate — is the *whole* life, from
the very beginning right through those glorious
years when aspiration and achievement came together and O'Neill was a household name right
across Europe. Because they were glorious, Hugh.
And they are a cause for celebration not only by us
but by the generations that follow us. Now. (*He
finds his outline*) I think this is it — is it? Yes, it is.

O'NEILL Mabel will be in the history, Peter?

LOMBARD Mabel? What sort of a question is that? Of course
Mabel will be in the history.

O'NEILL Central to it, Peter.

LOMBARD And so will your first wife, Brian MacFelim's
daughter. And so will your second, the wonderful
Siobhan. And so will Mabel. And so will our beautiful Catríona — she says not to wait up for her. They'll
all be mentioned. What a strange question! (*Confidentially*) But I've got to confess a secret unease,
Hugh. The fact that the great Hugh O'Neill had
four wives — and there were rumours of a fifth
years and years ago, weren't there? — long before
you and I first met — but the fact that O'Neill had
four, shall we say, acknowledged, wives, do you
think that may strike future readers as perhaps . . .
a surfeit? I'm sure not. I'm sure I'm being too sensitive. Anyhow, we can't deliberately suppress what
we know did happen, can we? So. Back to my overall framework.

O'NEILL This is my last battle, Peter.

LOMBARD Battle? What battle?

O'NEILL That (*book*).

LOMBARD What are you talking about?

O'NEILL That thing there.

LOMBARD Your history?

O'NEILL   *Your* history. I'm an old man. I have no position, no power, no money. No, I'm not whingeing — I'm not pleading. But I'm telling you that I'm going to fight you on that and I'm going to win.

LOMBARD   Fight — ? What in the name of God is the man talking about?

O'NEILL   I don't trust you. I don't trust you to tell the truth.

LOMBARD   To tell the truth in — ? Do you really think I would — ?

O'NEILL   I think you are not trustworthy. And that (*book*) is all that is left to me.

LOMBARD   You *are* serious! Hugh, for heaven's sake — ! (*He bursts out laughing*)

O'NEILL   Go ahead. Laugh. But I'm going to win this battle, Peter.

LOMBARD   Hold on now — wait — wait — wait — wait. Just tell me one thing. Is this book some sort of a malign scheme? Am I doing something reprehensible?

O'NEILL   You are going to embalm me in — in — in a florid lie.

LOMBARD   Will I lie, Hugh?

O'NEILL   I need the truth, Peter. That's all that's left. The schemer, the leader, the liar, the statesman, the lecher, the patriot, the drunk, the soured, bitter émigré — put it *all* in, Peter. Record the *whole* life — that's what you said yourself.

LOMBARD   Listen to me, Hugh —

O'NEILL   I'm asking you, man. Yes, damn it, I am pleading. Don't embalm me in pieties.

LOMBARD   Let me tell you what I'm doing.

O'NEILL   You said Mabel will have her place. That place is central to me.

LOMBARD   Will you listen to me?

O'NEILL   Can I trust you to make Mabel central?

LOMBARD   Let me explain what my outline is. May I? Please? And if you object to it — or to any detail in it — I'll rewrite the whole thing in any way you want. That is a solemn promise. Can I be fairer than that? Now. I start with your birth and your noble genealogy and I look briefly at those formative years when you were fostered with the O'Quinns and the O'Hagans and received your early education from the bards and the poets. I then move —

O'NEILL England.

LOMBARD What's that?

O'NEILL I spent nine years in England with Leicester and Sidney.

LOMBARD You did indeed. I have all that material here. We then look at the years when you consolidated your position as the pre-eminent Gaelic ruler in the country, and that leads on to these early intimations you must have had of an emerging nation state. And now we come to the first of the key events: that September when all the people of Ulster came together at the crowning stone at Tullyhogue outside Dungannon, and the golden slipper is thrown over your head and fastened to your foot, and the white staff is placed in your right hand, and the True Bell of St Patrick peals out across the land, and you are proclaimed . . . The O'Neill.

O'NEILL That was a political ploy.

LOMBARD It may have been that, too.

O'NEILL The very next month I begged Elizabeth for pardon.

LOMBARD But an occasion of enormous symbolic importance for your people — six-hundred-and-thirty continuous years of O'Neill hegemony. Right, I then move on to that special relationship between yourself and Hugh O'Donnell; the patient forging of the links with Spain and Rome; the uniting of the whole of Ulster into one great dynasty that finally inspired all the Gaelic chieftains to come together under your leadership. And suddenly the nation state was becoming a reality. And talking of Hugh O'Donnell — (*He searches through a pile of papers*) This will interest you. Yes, maybe this will put your mind at ease. Ludhaidh O'Cleary has written a life of Hugh and this is how he describes him.

	Listen to this. 'He was a dove in meekness and gentleness and a lion in strength and force. He was a sweet-sounding trumpet — '
O'NEILL	'Sweet-sounding'!
LOMBARD	Listen! '— with power of speech and eloquence, sense and counsel, with a look of amiability in his face which struck everyone at first sight.'

      O'NEILL *laughs.*

O'NEILL	'A dove in meekness'!
LOMBARD	But you'll have to admit it has a ring about it. Maybe you and I remember a different Hugh. But maybe that's not the point.
O'NEILL	What is the point? That's certainly a bloody lie.
LOMBARD	Not a lie, Hugh. Merely a convention. And I'll come to the point later. Now, the second key event: the Nine Years War between yourself and England, culminating in the legendary battle of Kinsale and the crushing of the most magnificent Gaelic army ever assembled.
O'NEILL	They routed us in less than an hour, Peter. Isn't that the point of Kinsale?
LOMBARD	You lost a battle — that has to be said. But the telling of it can still be a triumph.
O'NEILL	Kinsale was a disgrace. Mountjoy routed us. We ran away like rats.
LOMBARD	And again that's not the point.
O'NEILL	You're not listening to *me* now. We disgraced ourselves at Kinsale.
LOMBARD	And then I come to my third and final key point; and I'm calling this section — I'm rather proud of the title — I've named it 'The Flight of the Earls'. That has a ring to it, too, hasn't it? That tragic but magnificent exodus of the Gaelic aristocracy —
O'NEILL	Peter —
LOMBARD	When the leaders of the ancient civilization took boat from Rathmullan that September evening and set sail for Europe.

O'NEILL   As we pulled out from Rathmullan the McSwineys stoned us from the shore!

LOMBARD   Then their journey across Europe when every crowned head welcomed and fêted them. And then the final coming to rest. Here. In Rome.

O'NEILL   And the six years after Kinsale — before the Flight of the Earls — aren't they going to be recorded? When I lived like a criminal, skulking round the countryside — my countryside! — hiding from the English, from the Upstarts, from the Old English, but most assiduously hiding from my brother Gaels who couldn't wait to strip me of every blade of grass I ever owned. And then when I could endure that humiliation no longer I ran away! If these were 'my people' then to hell with my people! The Flight of the Earls — you make it sound like a lap of honour. We ran away just as we ran away at Kinsale. We were going to look after our own skins! That's why we 'took boat' from Rathmullan! That's why the great O'Neill is here — at rest — here — in Rome. Because we ran away.

LOMBARD   That is my outline. I'll rewrite it in any way you want.

O'NEILL   That is the truth. That is what happened.

LOMBARD   How should it be rewritten?

O'NEILL   Those are the facts. There is no way you can make unpalatable facts palatable. And your point — just what is your point, Peter?

LOMBARD   I'm no historian but —

O'NEILL   Then don't write my history. Or maybe you could trust me to write it myself: one of the advantages of fading eyesight is that it gives the imagination the edge over reality.

LOMBARD   May I try to explain something to you, Hugh? May I tell you what my point is?

O'NEILL   I'm weary of all this.

LOMBARD   People want to know about the past. They have a genuine curiosity about it.

O'NEILL   Then tell them the whole truth.

413

LOMBARD That's exactly what my point is. People think they
just want to know the 'facts'; they think they believe in some sort of empirical truth, but what they
really want is a story. And that's what this will be:
the events of your life categorized and classified
and then structured as you would structure any
story. No, no, I'm not talking about falsifying, about
lying, for heaven's sake. I'm simply talking about
making a pattern. That's what I'm doing with all this
stuff — offering a cohesion to that random catalogue of deliberate achievement and sheer accident
that constitutes your life. And that cohesion will be
a narrative that people will read and be satisfied
by. And that narrative will be as true and as objec-
tive as I can make it — with the help of the Holy
Spirit. Would it be profane to suggest that that was
the method the Four Evangelists used? — took the
haphazard events in Christ's life and shaped them
into a story, into four complementary stories. And
those stories are true stories. And we believe them.
We call them gospel, Hugh, don't we? (*He laughs
suddenly and heartily*) Would you look at that man?
What are you so miserable about? Think of this
(*book*) as an act of *pietas*. Ireland is reduced as it has
never been reduced before — we are talking about
a colonized people on the brink of extinction. This
isn't the time for a critical assessment of your 'ploys'
and your 'disgraces' and your 'betrayal' — that's
the stuff of another history for another time. Now
is the time for a hero. Now is the time for a heroic
literature. So I am offering Gaelic Ireland two things.
I'm offering them this narrative that has the elements
of myth. And I'm offering them Hugh O'Neill as a
national hero. A hero and the story of a hero.
(*Pause*) It's a very worldly nostrum for a clergyman
to propose — isn't it? I suppose, if I were a holy
man, not some kind of a half priest, half schemer,
I suppose I would offer them God and prayer and
suffering. But there are times when a hero can be as

important to a people as a God. And isn't God —
or so I excuse my perfidy — isn't God the perfect
hero?

A very long silence. LOMBARD *gathers up his papers
and closes the book.* O'NEILL *assimilates what he has
heard.*

O'NEILL How do you write about Harry?

LOMBARD What is the 'truth' about Harry? Well, we know, for
example, that his Old English family threw him out,
that he was destitute and that when you offered
him a job, any job, he grabbed at it. We know, for
example, that he was once passionately loyal to the
Queen but that, when he joined you, he seemed
to have no problem in betraying that loyalty. Or
simply — very simply — we know for example
that Harry Hoveden was a man who admired and
loved you without reservation and who has dedicated his whole life to you. For all I know there
may be other 'truths' about Harry.

O'NEILL Which are you recording?

LOMBARD I know which one history prefers. As I keep telling
you, histories are stories, Hugh, and stories prefer
faithful friends, don't they? And isn't that the
absolute truth about Harry? — is Harry Hoveden
not a most faithful friend?

Another long silence.

O'NEILL And Mabel?

LOMBARD Yes?

O'NEILL (*Shouting*) Don't play bloody games with me, Archbishop! You know damned well what I'm asking
you!

LOMBARD You're asking me how Mabel will be portrayed.

O'NEILL (*Softly*) Yes, I'm asking you how Mabel will be portrayed.

LOMBARD I've tried to explain that at this time the country

needs a —

O'NEILL   How-will-Mabel-be-portrayed?

Pause.

LOMBARD   The story of your life has a broad but very specific
sweep, Hugh —

O'NEILL   Peter, just — !

LOMBARD   And all those ladies you chose as your wives —
splendid and beautiful and loyal though they un-
doubtedly were — well, they didn't contribute sig-
nificantly to — what was it Mabel herself used to
call it? — to the overall thing — wasn't that it?
I mean they didn't re-route the course of history,
did they? So I have got to be as fair as I can to *all*
those ladies without diminishing them, without
inflating them into something they were not, without lying about them. I mean our Catríona, our
beautiful Catríona, would be the last to claim some
historical eminence, wouldn't she? But they all did
have their own scales; and they recognized what
those dimensions were; and in fairness to them we
should acknowledge those dimensions accurately.

O'NEILL   So Mabel . . . ?

LOMBARD   (*Pretending irritation*) You're incorrigible, Hugh
O'Neill! You know that, don't you? You never give
up. All I've got down on paper is a general outline
and a couple of opening pages and the man keeps
badgering me about minor details!

O'NEILL   So Mabel . . . ?

LOMBARD   Let me ask you a question. In the big canvas of
national events — in your exchanges with popes
and kings and queens — is that where Mabel herself thought her value and her importance resided?
Is that how she saw herself? But she had her own
value, her own importance. And at some future
time and in a mode we can't imagine now I have
no doubt that story will be told fully and sym-
pathetically. It will be a domestic story, Hugh; a

love story; and a very beautiful love story it will be. But in the overall thing, Hugh . . . How many heroes can one history accommodate? And how will I emerge myself, for heaven's sake? At best a character in a sub-plot. And isn't that adequate for minor people like us? Now, Hugh, tell me, how do you want to rewrite my outline?

O'NEILL The overall thing — yes, that was her expression.

LOMBARD I made you a solemn promise. I'll rewrite it in any way you want. What changes do you want me to make? (*Pause*) Not necessarily anything major. (*Pause*) Even small adjustments. (*Pause*) Just say the word. (*Pause*) Now I'm badgering you — amn't I? Forgive me. And if any idea or suggestion does occur to you over the next weeks or months, sure I'll be here, won't I? Neither of us is going anywhere — unless Plunkett and Ó Domhnaill recruit us for their next expedition. Now. It's time for a drink. We've earned it. My poor mouth's dry from blathering. Affane — where are you?

O'NEILL A lure to perdition — is that what you called it?

LOMBARD A foretaste of immortality. It really is wonderful. Easy — easy — don't gulp it down. Sip it slowly. Savour it.

HARRY *enters, carrying a bottle.*

Ah, Harry! We're just about to kill this bottle of *poitín*. But, as the man says, it's not going to die without the priest. Will somebody please hit me every time I make one of those hoary clerical jokes? What's that you have?

HARRY A bottle of wine.

LOMBARD Where did that come from?

HARRY I got it ten minutes ago.

O'NEILL I thought we had no money?

HARRY It's only cheap chianti.

O'NEILL Where did the money come from?

HARRY I had an old pair of shoes I didn't want. The porter

had some bottles to spare. Who wants a glass?

LOMBARD Do you know what you are, Harry? A loyal and faithful man. Now that is a truth!

He pauses beside HUGH *as he goes to the desk. Privately.*

Trust it, Hugh. Trust it. (*Aloud*) To all of us. May we live for ever — in one form or another. And now I'm going to give the first public recital of *The History of Hugh O'Neill*. In the name of God — I know the opening by heart! In the name of God. Herewith I set my hand to chronicle the life of Hugh O'Neill —

When O'NEILL *speaks he speaks almost in a whisper in counterpoint to* LOMBARD's *public recitation. His English accent gradually fades until at the end his accent is pure Tyrone.*

O'NEILL By the Queen of England, France and Ireland her most gracious favour created Earl of Tyrone —

LOMBARD Son of Feardorcha, son of Conn Bacach, son of Conn Mór, noblest son of noble lineage, who was fostered and brought up by the high-born nobles of his tribe —

O'NEILL I do with all true and humble penitency prostrate myself at your feet and absolutely submit myself to your mercy, most sorrowfully imploring your commiseration and appealing only to your clemency —

LOMBARD He continued to grow and increase in comeliness and urbanity, tact and eloquence, wisdom and knowledge, goodly size and noble deeds so that his name and fame spread throughout the five provinces of Ireland and beyond —

O'NEILL May it please you to mitigate your just indignation against me for my betrayal of you which deserves no forgiveness and for which I can make no satisfaction, even with my life —

LOMBARD   And people reflected in their minds that when he would reach manhood there would not be one like him of the Irish to avenge their wrongs and punish the plunderings of his race —

O'NEILL   Mabel, I am sorry . . . please forgive me, Mabel . . .

LOMBARD   For it was foretold by prophets and by predictors of futurity that there would come one like him —
　　'A man, glorious, pure, faithful above all
　　Who will cause mournful weeping in every
　　　　territory.
　　He will be a God-like prince
　　And he will be king for the span of his life.'

O'NEILL *is now crying. Bring down the lights slowly.*

DANCING
AT LUGHNASA

Characters

MICHAEL, young man, narrator
KATE, forty, schoolteacher
MAGGIE, thirty-eight, housekeeper
AGNES, thirty-five, knitter
ROSE, thirty-two, knitter
CHRIS, twenty-six, Michael's mother
GERRY, thirty-three, Michael's father
JACK, fifty-three, missionary priest

MICHAEL, who narrates the story, also speaks the lines of the Boy, i.e. himself when he was seven.

ROSE is 'simple'. All her sisters are kind to her and protective of her. But Agnes has taken on the role of special protector.

Time and Place

Act One: A warm day in early August 1936.
Act Two: Three weeks later.

The home of the Mundy family, two miles outside the village of Ballybeg, County Donegal, Ireland.

Set

Slightly more than half the area of the stage is taken up by the kitchen on the right (left and right from the point of view of the audience). The rest of the stage — the remaining area stage left — is the garden adjoining the house. The garden is neat but not cultivated. Upstage centre is a garden seat.

The (unseen) Boy has been making two kites in the garden and pieces of wood, paper, cord, etc. are lying on the ground close to the garden seat. One kite is almost complete.

There are two doors leading out of the kitchen. The front door leads to the garden and the front of the house. The second in the top right-hand corner leads to the bedrooms and to the area behind the house.

One kitchen window looks out front. A second window looks on to the garden.

There is a sycamore tree off right. One of its branches reaches over part of the house.

The room has the furnishings of the usual country kitchen of the thirties: a large iron range, large turf box beside it, table and chairs, dresser, oil lamp, buckets with water at the back door, etc., etc. But because this is the home of five women the austerity of the furnishings is relieved by some gracious touches — flowers, pretty curtains, an attractive dresser arrangement, etc.

Dress

Kate, the teacher, is the only wage-earner. Agnes and Rose make a little money knitting gloves at home. Chris and Maggie have no income. So the clothes of all the sisters reflect their lean circumstances. Rose wears wellingtons even though the day is warm. Maggie wears large boots with long, untied laces. Rose, Maggie and Agnes all wear the drab, wrap-around overalls/ aprons of the time.

In the opening tableau Father Jack is wearing the uniform of a British Army officer chaplain — a magnificent and immaculate uniform of dazzling white; gold epaulettes and gold buttons, tropical hat, clerical collar, military cane. He stands stiffly to attention. As the text says, he is 'resplendent', 'magnificent'. So resplendent that he looks almost comic opera.

In this tableau, too, Gerry is wearing a spotless white tricorn hat with splendid white plumage. (Soiled and shabby versions of Jack's uniform and Gerry's ceremonial hat are worn at the end of the play, i.e. in the final tableau.)

Dancing at Lughnasa was first performed at the Abbey Theatre, Dublin, on 24 April 1990, with the following cast:

KATE	Frances Tomelty
MAGGIE	Anita Reeves
ROSE	Bríd Ní Neachtain
AGNES	Bríd Brennan
CHRIS	Catherine Byrne
MICHAEL	Gerard McSorley
GERRY	Paul Herzberg
JACK	Barry McGovern

Directed by	Patrick Mason
Designed by	Joe Vanek
Lighting by	Trevor Dawson

This production transferred to the National Theatre, London, in October 1990, with the following changes of cast:

KATE	Rosaleen Linehan
GERRY	Stephen Dillane
JACK	Alec McCowen

In memory of
those five brave Glenties women

ACT ONE

When the play opens MICHAEL *is standing downstage left in a pool of light. The rest of the stage is in darkness. Immediately* MICHAEL *begins speaking, slowly bring up the lights on the rest of the stage.*

Around the stage and at a distance from MICHAEL *the other characters stand motionless in formal tableau.* MAGGIE *is at the kitchen window (right).* CHRIS *is at the front door.* KATE *is at extreme stage right.* ROSE *and* GERRY *sit on the garden seat.* JACK *stands beside* ROSE. AGNES *is upstage left. They hold these positions while* MICHAEL *talks to the audience.*

MICHAEL   When I cast my mind back to that summer of 1936 different kinds of memories offer themselves to me. We got our first wireless set that summer — well, a sort of a set; and it obsessed us. And, because it arrived as August was about to begin, my Aunt Maggie — she was the joker of the family — she suggested we give it a name. She wanted to call it Lugh* after the old Celtic God of the Harvest. Because in the old days August the First was *Lá Lughnasa*, the feast day of the pagan god, Lugh; and the days and weeks of harvesting that followed were called the Festival of Lughnasa. But Aunt Kate — she was a national schoolteacher and a very proper woman — she said it would be sinful to christen an inanimate object with any kind of name, not to talk of a pagan god. So we just called it Marconi because that was the name emblazoned on the set.

    And about three weeks before we got that wireless my mother's brother, my Uncle Jack, came home from Africa for the first time ever. For twenty-five years he had worked in a leper colony there, in a

*Lugh – pronounced 'Loo'. *Lughnasa* — pronounced 'Loo-na-sa'.

remote village called Ryanga in Uganda. The only time he ever left that village was for about six months during World War I when he was chaplain to the British Army in East Africa. Then back to that grim hospice where he worked without a break for a further eighteen years. And now in his early fifties and in bad health he had come home to Ballybeg — as it turned out — to die.

And when I cast my mind back to that summer of 1936 these two memories — of our first wireless and of Father Jack's return — are always linked. So that when I recall my first shock at Jack's appearance, shrunken and jaundiced with malaria, at the same time I remember my first delight, indeed my awe, at the sheer magic of that radio. And when I remember the kitchen throbbing with the beat of Irish dance music beamed to us all the way from Athlone, and my mother and her sisters suddenly catching hands and dancing a spontaneous stepdance and laughing — screaming! — like excited schoolgirls, at the same time I see that forlorn figure of Father Jack shuffling from room to room as if he were searching for something but couldn't remember what. And even though I was only a child of seven at the time I know I had a sense of unease, some awareness of a widening breach between what seemed to be and what was, of things changing too quickly before my eyes, of becoming what they ought not to be. That may have been because Uncle Jack hadn't turned out at all like the resplendent figure in my head. Or maybe because I had witnessed Marconi's voodoo derange those kind, sensible women and transform them into shrieking strangers. Or maybe it was because during those Lughnasa weeks of 1936 we were visited on two occasions by my father, Gerry Evans, and for the first time in my life I had a chance to observe him.

The lighting changes. The kitchen and garden are now

> *lit as for a warm summer afternoon.*
>
> MICHAEL, KATE, GERRY *and* FATHER JACK *go off. The others busy themselves with their tasks.* MAGGIE *makes a mash for hens.* AGNES *knits gloves.* ROSE *carries a basket of turf into the kitchen and empties it into the large box beside the range.* CHRIS *irons at the kitchen table. They all work in silence. Then* CHRIS *stops ironing, goes to the tiny mirror on the wall and scrutinizes her face.*

CHRIS   When are we going to get a decent mirror to see ourselves in?

MAGGIE   You can see enough to do you.

CHRIS   I'm going to throw this aul' cracked thing out.

MAGGIE   Indeed you're not, Chrissie. I'm the one that broke it and the only way to avoid seven years' bad luck is to keep on using it.

CHRIS   You can see nothing in it.

AGNES   Except more and more wrinkles.

CHRIS   D'you know what I think I might do? I think I just might start wearing lipstick.

AGNES   Do you hear this, Maggie?

MAGGIE   Steady on, girl. Today it's lipstick; tomorrow it's the gin bottle.

CHRIS   I think I just might.

AGNES   As long as Kate's not around. 'Do you want to make a pagan of yourself?'

> CHRIS *puts her face up close to the mirror and feels it.*

CHRIS   Far too pale. And the aul' mousy hair. Needs a bit of colour.

AGNES   What for?

CHRIS   What indeed.

> *She shrugs and goes back to her ironing. She holds up a surplice.*

Make a nice dress that, wouldn't it? . . . God forgive
me . . .

*Work continues. Nobody speaks. Then suddenly and
unexpectedly* ROSE *bursts into raucous song:*

ROSE 'Will you come to Abyssinia, will you come?
Bring your own cup and saucer and a bun . . . '

*As she sings the next two lines she dances — a
gauche, graceless shuffle that defies the rhythm of the
song.*

'Mussolini will be there with his airplanes in the air,
Will you come to Abyssinia, will you come?'
Not bad, Maggie — eh?

MAGGIE *is trying to light a very short cigarette butt.*

MAGGIE You should be on the stage, Rose.

ROSE *continues to shuffle and now holds up her apron
skirt.*

ROSE And not a bad bit of leg, Maggie — eh?
MAGGIE Rose Mundy! Where's your modesty!

MAGGIE *now hitches her own skirt even higher than*
ROSE*'s and does a similar shuffle.*

Is that not more like it?
ROSE Good, Maggie — good — good! Look, Agnes, look!
AGNES A right pair of pagans, the two of you.
ROSE Turn on Marconi, Chrissie.
CHRIS I've told you a dozen times: the battery's dead.
ROSE It is not. It went for me a while ago.

*She goes to the set and switches it on. There is a sudden,
loud three-second blast of 'The British Grenadiers'.*

You see! Takes aul' Rosie!

> *She is about to launch into a dance — and the music suddenly dies.*

CHRIS Told you.

ROSE That aul' set's useless.

AGNES Kate'll have a new battery back with her.

CHRIS If it's the battery that's wrong.

ROSE Is Abyssinia in Africa, Aggie?

AGNES Yes.

ROSE Is there a war there?

AGNES Yes. I've told you that.

ROSE But that's not where Father Jack was, is it?

AGNES (*Patiently*) Jack was in Uganda, Rosie. That's a different part of Africa. You know that.

ROSE (*Unhappily*) Yes, I do . . . I do . . . I know that . . .

> MAGGIE *catches her hand and sings softly into her ear to the same melody as the 'Abyssinia' song:*

MAGGIE 'Will you vote for De Valera, will you vote?
If you don't we'll be like Gandhi with his goat.'

> ROSE *and* MAGGIE *now sing the next two lines together:*

'Uncle Bill from Baltinglass has a wireless up his —

> *They dance as they sing the final line of the song:*

'Will you vote for De Valera, will you vote?'

MAGGIE I'll tell you something, Rosie: the pair of us should be on the stage.

ROSE The pair of us should be on the stage, Aggie!

> *They return to their tasks.* AGNES *goes to the cupboard for wool. On her way back to her seat she looks out the window that looks on to the garden.*

AGNES   What's that son of yours at out there?

CHRIS   God knows. As long as he's quiet.

AGNES   He's making something. Looks like a kite.

She taps on the window, calls 'Michael!' and blows a kiss to the imaginary child.

Oh, that was the wrong thing to do! He's going to have your hair, Chris.

CHRIS   Mine's like a whin-bush. Will you wash it for me tonight, Maggie?

MAGGIE   Are we all for a big dance somewhere?

CHRIS   After I've put Michael to bed. What about then?

MAGGIE   I'm your man.

AGNES   (*At window*) Pity there aren't some boys about to play with.

MAGGIE   Now you're talking. Couldn't we all do with that?

AGNES   (*Leaving window*) Maggie!

MAGGIE   Wouldn't it be just great if we had a — (*Breaks off*) Shhh.

CHRIS   What is it?

MAGGIE   Thought I heard Father Jack at the back door. I hope Kate remembers his quinine.

AGNES   She'll remember. Kate forgets nothing.

Pause.

ROSE   There's going to be pictures in the hall next Saturday, Aggie. I think maybe I'll go.

AGNES   (*Guarded*) Yes?

ROSE   I might be meeting somebody there.

AGNES   Who's that?

ROSE   I'm not saying.

CHRIS   Do we know him?

ROSE   I'm not saying.

AGNES   You'll enjoy that, Rosie. You loved the last picture we saw.

ROSE   And he wants to bring me up to the back hills next Sunday — up to Lough Anna. His father has a boat there. And I'm thinking maybe I'll bring a bottle of milk with me. And I've enough money saved to buy a packet of chocolate biscuits.

CHRIS Danny Bradley is a scut, Rose.

ROSE I never said it was Danny Bradley!

CHRIS He's a married man with three young children.

ROSE And that's just where you're wrong, missy — so there! (*To* AGNES) She left him six months ago, Aggie, and went to England.

MAGGIE Rose, love, we just want —

ROSE (*To* CHRIS) And who are you to talk, Christina Mundy! Don't you dare lecture me!

MAGGIE Everybody in the town knows that Danny Bradley is —

ROSE (*To* MAGGIE) And you're jealous, too! That's what's wrong with the whole of you — you're jealous of me! (*To* AGNES) He calls me his Rosebud. He waited for me outside the chapel gate last Christmas morning and he gave me this. (*She opens the front of her apron. A charm and a medal are pinned to her jumper*) 'That's for my Rosebud,' he said.

AGNES Is it a fish, Rosie?

ROSE Isn't it lovely? It's made of pure silver. And it brings you good luck.

AGNES It is lovely.

ROSE I wear it all the time — beside my miraculous medal. (*Pause*) I love him, Aggie.

AGNES I know.

CHRIS (*Softly*) Bastard.

> ROSE *closes the front of her apron. She is on the point of tears. Silence. Now* MAGGIE *lifts her hen-bucket and, using it as a dancing partner, she does a very fast and very exaggerated tango across the kitchen floor as she sings in her parodic style the words from 'The Isle of Capri':*

MAGGIE 'Summer time was nearly over;
Blue Italian skies above.

I said, "Mister, I'm a rover.
Can't you spare a sweet word of love?"'

*And without pausing for breath she begins calling
her hens as she exits by the back door:*

Tchook-tchook-tchook-tchook-tchook-tchook-
tchook-tchookeeeee . . .

> MICHAEL *enters and stands stage left.* ROSE *takes the
> lid off the range and throws turf into the fire.*

CHRIS For God's sake, I have an iron in there!

ROSE How was I to know that?

CHRIS Don't you see me ironing? (*Fishing with tongs*) Now
you've lost it. Get out of my road, will you!

AGNES Rosie, love, would you give me a hand with this
(*wool*)? If we don't work a bit faster we'll never get
two dozen pairs finished this week.

> *The convention must now be established that the
> (imaginary) Boy* MICHAEL *is working at the kite
> materials lying on the ground. No dialogue with the
> Boy* MICHAEL *must ever be addressed directly to adult*
> MICHAEL, *the narrator. Here, for example,* MAGGIE *has
> her back to the narrator.* MICHAEL *responds to* MAGGIE
> *in his ordinary narrator's voice.* MAGGIE *enters the
> garden from the back of the house.*

MAGGIE What are these supposed to be?

BOY Kites.

MAGGIE Kites! God help your wit!

BOY Watch where you're walking, Aunt Maggie — you're
standing on a tail.

MAGGIE Did it squeal? — haaaa! I'll make a deal with you,
cub: I'll give you a penny if those things ever leave
the ground. Right?

BOY You're on.

434

She now squats down beside him.

MAGGIE I've new riddles for you.

BOY Give up.

MAGGIE What goes round the house and round the house and sits in the corner? (*Pause*) A broom! Why is a river like a watch?

BOY You're pathetic.

MAGGIE Because it never goes far without winding! Hairy out and hairy in, lift your foot and stab it in — what is it?

Pause.

BOY Give up.

MAGGIE Think!

BOY Give up.

MAGGIE Have you even one brain in your head?

BOY Give up.

MAGGIE A sock!

BOY A what?

MAGGIE A sock — a sock! You know — lift your foot and stab it — (*She demonstrates. No response*) D'you know what your trouble is, cub? You-are-buck-stupid!

BOY Look out — there's a rat!

She screams and leaps to her feet in terror.

MAGGIE Where? — where? — where? Jesus, Mary and Joseph, where is it?

BOY Caught you again, Aunt Maggie.

MAGGIE You evil wee brat — God forgive you! I'll get you for that, Michael! Don't you worry — I won't forget that!

She picks up her bucket and moves off towards the back of the house. Stops.

And I had a barley sugar sweet for you.

BOY Are there bits of cigarette tobacco stuck to it?

435

MAGGIE   Jesus Christ! Some day you're going to fill some
         woman's life full of happiness. (*Moving off*) Tchook-
         tchook-tchook-tchook . . .

         Again she stops and throws him a sweet.

         There. I hope it chokes you.

              MAGGIE *exits.*

         Tchook-tchook-tchook-tchook-tchookeeeee . . .
MICHAEL When I saw Uncle Jack for the first time the reason I
         was so shocked by his appearance was that I expected
         — well, I suppose, the hero from a schoolboy's book.
         Once I had seen a photograph of him radiant and
         splendid in his officer's uniform. It had fallen out of
         Aunt Kate's prayer book and she snatched it from
         me before I could study it in detail. It was a picture
         taken in 1917 when he was a chaplain to the British
         forces in East Africa and he looked — magnificent.
         But Aunt Kate had been involved locally in the War
         of Independence; so Father Jack's brief career in the
         British Army was never referred to in that house. All
         the same the wonderful Father Jack of that photo was
         the image of him that lodged in my mind.
            But if he was a hero to me he was a hero and a
         saint to my mother and to my aunts. They pored
         over his occasional letters. They prayed every night
         for him and for his lepers and for the success of his
         mission. They scraped and saved for him — sixpence
         here, a shilling there — sacrifices they made willingly,
         joyously, so that they would have a little money to
         send to him at Christmas and for his birthday. And
         every so often when a story would appear in the
         Donegal Enquirer about 'our own leper priest', as they
         called him — because Ballybeg was proud of him,
         the whole of Donegal was proud of him — it was
         only natural that our family would enjoy a small
         share of that fame — it gave us that little bit of status

in the eyes of the parish. And it must have helped my aunts to bear the shame Mother brought on the household by having me — as it was called then — out of wedlock.

> KATE *enters left, laden with shopping bags. When she sees the Boy working at his kites her face lights up with pleasure. She watches him for a few seconds. Then she goes to him.*

KATE Well, that's what I call a busy man. Come here and give your Aunt Kate a big kiss.

> *She catches his head between her hands and kisses the crown of his head.*

And what's all this? It's a kite, is it?

BOY It's two kites.

KATE (*Inspecting them*) It certainly is two kites. And they're the most wonderful kites I've ever seen. And what are these designs?

> *She studies the kite faces which the audience cannot see.*

BOY They're faces. I painted them.

KATE (*Pretending horror*) Oh, good Lord, they put the heart across me! You did those? Oh, God bless us, those are scarifying? What are they? Devils? Ghosts? I wouldn't like to see those lads up in the sky looking down at me! Hold on now . . .

> *She searches in her bags and produces a small, wooden spinning top and whip.*

Do you know what this is? Of course you do — a spinning top. Good boy. And this — this is the whip. You know how to use it? Indeed you do. What do you say?

BOY   Thanks.

KATE   Thank you, Aunt Kate. And do you know what I
       have in here? A new library book! With coloured pic-
       tures! We'll begin reading it at bedtime.

       *Again she kisses the top of his head. She gets to her
       feet.*

       Call me the moment you're ready to fly them. I
       wouldn't miss that for all the world.

       She goes into the kitchen.

       D'you know what he's at out there? Did you see,
       Christina? Making two kites!

CHRIS Some kites he'll make.

KATE   All by himself. No help from anybody.

AGNES You always said he was talented, Kate.

KATE   No question about that. And very mature for his years.

CHRIS Very cheeky for his years.

ROSE   I think he's beautiful, Chris. I wish he was mine.

CHRIS Is that a spinning top he has?

KATE   It's nothing.

       MICHAEL *exits left.*

CHRIS Oh, Kate, you have him spoiled. Where did you get
       it?

KATE   Morgan's Arcade.

CHRIS And I'm sure he didn't even thank you.

ROSE   I know why you went into Morgan's!

KATE   He did indeed. He's very mannerly.

ROSE   You wanted to see Austin Morgan!

KATE   Every field along the road — they're all out at the hay
       and the corn.

ROSE   Because you have a notion of that aul' Austin Morgan!

KATE   Going to be a good harvest by the look of it.

ROSE   I know you have! She's blushing! Look! Isn't she
       blushing?

438

CHRIS *holds up a skirt she is ironing.*

CHRIS You'd need to put a stitch in that hem, Rosie.

ROSE (*To* KATE) But what you don't know is that he's going with a wee young thing from Carrickfad.

KATE Rose, what Austin Morgan does or doesn't do with —

ROSE Why are you blushing then? She's blushing, isn't she? Why-why-why, Kate?

KATE (*Sudden anger*) For God's sake, Rose, shut up, would you!

ROSE Anyhow, we all know you always had a —

AGNES Rosie, pass me those steel needles — would you, please?

Pause.

CHRIS (*To* KATE) Are you tired?

KATE *flops into a seat.*

KATE That road from the town gets longer every day. You can laugh if you want but I *am* going to get that old bike fixed up and I *am* going to learn to ride this winter.

AGNES Many about Ballybeg?

KATE Ballybeg's off its head. I'm telling you. Everywhere you go — everyone you meet — it's the one topic: Are you going to the harvest dance? Who are you going with? What are you wearing? This year's going to be the biggest ever and the best ever.

AGNES All the same I remember some great harvest dances.

CHRIS Don't we all.

KATE (*Unpacking*) Another of those riveting Annie M P Smithson novels for you, Agnes.

AGNES Ah. Thanks.

KATE *The Marriage of Nurse Harding* — oh, dear! For you, Christina. One teaspoonful every morning before breakfast.

CHRIS What's this?

KATE Cod liver oil. You're far too pale.

CHRIS Thank you, Kate.

KATE Because you take no exercise. Anyhow, I'm in the chemist's shop and this young girl — a wee slip of a thing, can't even remember her name — her mother's the knitting agent that buys your gloves, Agnes —

AGNES Vera McLaughlin.

KATE Her daughter whatever-you-call-her.

ROSE Sophia.

KATE Miss Sophia, who must be all of fifteen; she comes up to me and she says, 'I hope you're not going to miss the harvest dance, Miss Mundy. It's going to be just *supreme* this year.' And honest to God, if you'd seen the delight in her eyes you'd think it was heaven she was talking about. I'm telling you — off its head — like a fever in the place. That's the quinine. The doctor says it won't cure the malaria but it might help to contain it. Is he in his room?

CHRIS He's wandering about out the back somewhere.

KATE I told the doctor you thought him very quiet, Agnes.

AGNES *has stopped knitting and is looking abstract-edly into the middle distance.*

AGNES Yes?

KATE Well, didn't you? And the doctor says we must remember how strange everything here must be to him after so long. And on top of that Swahili has been his language for twenty-five years; so that it's not that his mind is confused — it's just that he has difficulty finding the English words for what he wants to say.

CHRIS No matter what the doctor says, Kate, his mind is a bit confused. Sometimes he doesn't know the difference between us. I've heard him calling you Rose and he keeps calling me some strange name like —

KATE Okawa.

CHRIS That's it! Aggie, you've heard him, haven't you?

KATE Okawa was his houseboy. He was very attached to him. (*Taking off her shoe*) I think I'm getting corns in this foot. I hope to God I don't end up crippled like poor Mother, may she rest in peace.

AGNES Wouldn't it be a good one if we all went?

CHRIS Went where?

AGNES To the harvest dance.

CHRIS Aggie!

AGNES Just like we used to. All dressed up. I think I'd go.

ROSE I'd go, too, Aggie! I'd go with you!

KATE For heaven's sake, you're not serious, Agnes — are you?

AGNES I think I am.

KATE Hah! There's more than Ballybeg off its head.

AGNES I think we should all go.

KATE Have you any idea what it'll be like? — crawling with cheeky young brats that I taught years ago.

AGNES I'm game.

CHRIS We couldn't, Aggie — could we?

KATE And all the riff-raff of the countryside.

AGNES I'm game.

CHRIS Oh God, you know how I loved dancing, Aggie.

AGNES (*To* KATE) What do you say?

KATE (*To* CHRIS) You have a seven-year-old child — have you forgotten that?

AGNES (*To* CHRIS) You could wear that blue dress of mine — you have the figure for it and it brings out the colour of your eyes.

CHRIS Can I have it? God, Aggie, I could dance non-stop all night — all week — all month!

KATE And who'd look after Father Jack?

AGNES (*To* KATE) And you look great in that cotton dress you got for Confirmation last year. You're beautiful in it, Kate.

KATE What sort of silly talk is —

AGNES (*To* KATE) And you can wear my brown shoes with the crossover straps.

KATE This is silly talk. We can't, Agnes. How can we?

ROSE Will Maggie go with us?

CHRIS Will Maggie what! Try to stop her!

KATE Oh God, Agnes, what do you think?

AGNES We're going.

KATE Are we?

ROSE We're off! We're away!

KATE Maybe we're mad — are we mad?

CHRIS It costs four-and-six to get in.

AGNES I've five pounds saved. I'll take you. I'll take us all.

KATE Hold on now —

AGNES How many years has it been since we were at the harvest dance? — at any dance? And I don't care how young they are, how drunk and dirty and sweaty they are. I want to dance, Kate. It's the Festival of Lughnasa. I'm only thirty-five. I want to dance.

KATE (*Wretched*) I know, I know, Agnes, I know. All the same — oh my God — I don't know if it's —

AGNES It's settled. We're going — the Mundy girls — all five of us together.

CHRIS Like we used to.

AGNES Like we used to.

ROSE I love you, Aggie! I love you more than chocolate biscuits!

> ROSE *kisses* AGNES *impetuously, flings her arms above her head, begins singing 'Abyssinia' and does the first steps of a bizarre and abandoned dance. At this* KATE *panics.*

KATE No, no, no! We're going nowhere!

CHRIS If we all want to go —

KATE Look at yourselves, will you! Just look at yourselves! Dancing at our time of day? That's for young people with no duties and no responsibilities and nothing in their heads but pleasure.

AGNES Kate, I think we —

KATE Do you want the whole countryside to be laughing at us? — women of our years? — mature women, *dancing*? What's come over you all? And this is Father Jack's home — we must never forget that — ever. No, no, we're going to no harvest dance.

ROSE But you just said —

KATE And there'll be no more discussion about it. The
      matter's over. I don't want it mentioned again.

> *Silence.* MAGGIE *returns to the garden from the back
> of the house. She has the hen-bucket on her arm and
> her hands are cupped as if she were holding some-
> thing fragile between them. She goes to the kite
> materials.*

MAGGIE The fox is back.

BOY Did you see him?

MAGGIE He has a hole chewed in the henhouse door.

BOY Did you get a look at him, Aunt Maggie?

MAGGIE Wasn't I talking to him. He was asking for you.

BOY Ha-ha. What's that you have in your hands?

MAGGIE Something I found.

BOY What?

MAGGIE Sitting very still at the foot of the holly tree.

BOY Show me.

MAGGIE Say please three times.

BOY Please-please-please.

MAGGIE In Swahili.

BOY Are you going to show it to me or are you not?

MAGGIE (*Crouching down beside him*) Now, cub, put your ear
        over here. Listen. Shhh. D'you hear it?

BOY I think so . . . yes.

MAGGIE What do you hear?

BOY Something.

MAGGIE Are you sure?

BOY Yes, I'm sure. Show me, Aunt Maggie.

MAGGIE All right. Ready? Get back a bit. Bit further. Right?

BOY Yes.

> *Suddenly she opens her hands and her eyes follow
> the rapid and imaginary flight of something up to
> the sky and out of sight. She continues staring after
> it. Pause.*

What was it?

MAGGIE Did you see it?

BOY I think so . . . yes.

MAGGIE Wasn't it wonderful?

BOY Was it a bird?

MAGGIE The colours are so beautiful. (*She gets to her feet*) Trouble is — just one quick glimpse — that's all you ever get. And if you miss that —

She moves off towards the back door of the kitchen.

BOY What was it, Aunt Maggie?

MAGGIE Don't you know what it was? It was all in your mind. Now we're quits.

KATE (*Unpacking*) Tea . . . soap . . . Indian meal . . . jelly . . .

MAGGIE I'm sick of that white rooster of yours, Rosie. Some pet that. Look at the lump he took out of my arm.

ROSE You don't speak to him right.

MAGGIE I know the speaking he'll get from me — the weight of my boot. Would you put some turf on that fire, Chrissie; I'm going to make some soda bread.

She washes her hands and begins baking.

ROSE (*Privately*) Watch out. She's in one of her cranky moods.

KATE Your ten Wild Woodbine, Maggie.

MAGGIE Great. The tongue's out a mile.

ROSE (*Privately*) You missed it all, Maggie.

MAGGIE What did I miss this time?

ROSE We were all going to go to the harvest dance — like the old days. And then Kate —

KATE Your shoes, Rose. The shoemaker says, whatever kind of feet you have, only the insides of the soles wear down.

ROSE Is that a bad thing?

KATE That is neither a bad thing nor a good thing, Rose. It's just — distinctive, as might be expected.

ROSE *grimaces behind* KATE's *back.*

Cornflour . . . salt . . . tapioca — it's gone up a penny for some reason . . . sugar for the bilberry jam — if we ever get the bilberries . . .

AGNES and ROSE exchange looks.

MAGGIE (*Privately to* ROSE) Look at the packet of Wild Woodbine she got me.

ROSE What's wrong with it?

MAGGIE Only nine cigarettes in it. They're so wild one of them must have escaped on her.

They laugh secretly.

CHRIS Doesn't Jack sometimes call you Okawa, too, Maggie?

MAGGIE Yes. What does it mean?

CHRIS Okawa was his houseboy, Kate says.

MAGGIE Dammit. I thought it was Swahili for gorgeous.

AGNES Maggie!

MAGGIE That's the very thing we could do with here — a houseboy.

KATE And the battery. The man in the shop says we go through these things quicker than anyone in Ballybeg.

CHRIS Good for us.

She takes the battery and leaves it beside Marconi.

KATE I met the parish priest. I don't know what has happened to that man. But ever since Father Jack came home he can hardly look me in the eye.

MAGGIE That's because you keep winking at him, Kate.

CHRIS He was always moody, that man.

KATE Maybe that's it . . . The paper . . . candles . . . matches . . . The word's not good on that young Sweeney boy from the back hills. He was anointed last night.

MAGGIE I didn't know he was dying!

KATE Not an inch of his body that isn't burned.

AGNES Does anybody know what happened?

KATE Some silly prank up in the hills. He knows he's dying, the poor boy. Just lies there, moaning.

CHRIS What sort of prank?

KATE How would I know?

CHRIS What are they saying in the town?

KATE I know no more than I've told you, Christina.

Pause.

ROSE (*Quietly, resolutely*) It was last Sunday week, the first night of the Festival of Lughnasa; and they were doing what they do every year up there in the back hills.

KATE Festival of Lughnasa! What sort of —

ROSE First they light a bonfire beside a spring well. Then they dance round it. Then they drive their cattle through the flames to banish the devil out of them.

KATE Banish the — ! You don't know the first thing about what —

ROSE And this year there was an extra big crowd of boys and girls. And they were off their heads with drink. And young Sweeney's trousers caught fire and he went up like a torch. That's what happened.

KATE Who filled your head with that nonsense?

ROSE They do it every Lughnasa. I'm telling you. That's what happened.

KATE (*Very angry, almost shouting*) And they're savages! I know those people from the back hills! I've taught them! Savages — that's what they are! And what pagan practices they have are no concern of ours — none whatever! It's a sorry day to hear talk like that in a Christian home, a Catholic home! All I can say is that I'm shocked and disappointed to hear you repeating rubbish like that, Rose!

ROSE (*Quietly, resolutely*) That's what happened. I'm telling you.

Pause.

MAGGIE All the same it would be very handy in the winter

446

time to have a wee houseboy to feed the hens:
'Tchook-tchook-tchook-tchook-tchook-tchook-
tchook-tchookeeeee . . . '

> FATHER JACK *enters by the back door. He looks frail
> and older than his fifty-three years. Broad-brimmed
> black hat. Heavy grey top coat. Woollen trousers that
> stop well short of his ankles. Heavy black boots. Thick
> woollen socks. No clerical collar. He walks — shuffles
> quickly — with his hands behind his back. He seems
> uneasy, confused. Scarcely any trace of an Irish accent.*

JACK I beg your pardon . . . the wrong apartment . . . forgive me . . .

KATE Come in and join us, Jack.

JACK May I?

MAGGIE You're looking well, Jack.

JACK Yes? I expected to enter my bedroom through that . . .
what I am missing — what I require . . . I had a handkerchief in my pocket and I think perhaps I —

CHRIS (*Taking one from the ironing pile*) Here's a handkerchief.

JACK I thank you. I am grateful. It is so strange: I don't
remember the — the architecture? — the planning? —
what's the word? — the layout! — I don't recollect
the layout of this home . . . scarcely. That is strange,
isn't it? I thought the front door was there. (*To* KATE)
You walked to the village to buy stores, Agnes?

KATE It's Kate. And dozens of people were asking for you.

JACK They remember me?

KATE Of course they remember you! And when you're feeling stronger they're going to have a great public
welcome for you — flags, bands, speeches, everything!

JACK Why would they do this?

KATE Because they're delighted you're back.

JACK Yes?

KATE Because they're delighted you're home.

JACK I'm afraid I don't remember them. I couldn't name

ten people in Ballybeg now.

CHRIS It will all come back to you. Don't worry.

JACK You think so?

AGNES Yes, it will.

JACK Perhaps . . . I feel the climate so cold . . . if you'll forgive me . . .

AGNES Why don't you lie down for a while?

JACK I may do that . . . thank you . . . you are most kind . . .

He shuffles off. Pause. A sense of unease, almost embarrassment.

KATE (*Briskly*) It will be a slow process but he'll be fine. Apples . . . butter . . . margarine . . . flour . . . And wait till you hear! Who did I meet in the post office! Maggie, are you listening to me?

MAGGIE Yes?

KATE You'll never believe it — your old pal, Bernie O'Donnell! Home from London! First time back in twenty years!

MAGGIE Bernie . . .

KATE Absolutely gorgeous. The figure of a girl of eighteen. Dressed to kill from head to foot. And the hair! — as black and as curly as the day she left. I can't tell you — a film star!

MAGGIE Bernie O'Donnell . . .

KATE And beside her two of the most beautiful children you ever laid eyes on. Twins. They'll be fourteen next month. And to see the three of them together — like sisters, I'm telling you.

MAGGIE Twin girls.

KATE Identical.

MAGGIE Identical.

KATE Nora and Nina.

ROSE Mother used to say twins are a double blessing.

MAGGIE Bernie O'Donnell . . . oh my goodness . . .

KATE And wait till you hear — they are pure blonde! 'Where in the name of God did the blonde hair come from?' I asked her. 'The father, Eric,' she says. 'He's from

Stockholm.'

AGNES Stockholm!

ROSE Where's Stockholm, Aggie?

KATE So there you are. Bernie O'Donnell married to a Swede. I couldn't believe my eyes. But the same bubbly, laughing, happy Bernie. Asking about everybody by name.

> MAGGIE *goes to the window and looks out so that the others cannot see her face. She holds her hands, covered with flour, out from her body.*

CHRIS She remembered us all?

KATE Knew all about Michael; had his age to the very month. Was Agnes still the quickest knitter in Ballybeg? Were none of us thinking of getting married? — and weren't we wise!

ROSE Did she remember me?

KATE 'Rose had the sweetest smile I ever saw.'

ROSE There!

KATE But asking specially for you, Maggie: how you were doing — what you were doing — how were you looking — were you as light-hearted as ever? Every time she thinks of you, she says, she has the memory of the two of you hiding behind the turf stack, passing a cigarette between you and falling about laughing about some boy called — what was it? — Curley somebody?

MAGGIE Curley McDaid. An eejit of a fella. Bald as an egg at seventeen. Bernie O'Donnell . . . oh my goodness . . .

> *Pause.*

AGNES Will she be around for a while?

KATE Leaving tomorrow.

AGNES We won't see her so. That's a pity.

CHRIS Nice names, aren't they? — Nina and Nora.

KATE I like Nora. Nice name. Strong name.

AGNES Not so sure about Nina. (*To* CHRIS) Do you like Nina for a name?

449

CHRIS   Nina? No, not a lot.

KATE   Well, if there's a Saint Nina I'm afraid she's not in my prayer book.

AGNES   Maybe she's a Swedish saint.

KATE   Saints in Sweden! What'll it be next!

ROSE   Mother used to say twins are a double blessing.

KATE   (*Sharply*) You've offered us that cheap wisdom already, Rose.

Pause.

CHRIS   You've got some flour on your nose, Maggie.

MAGGIE When I was sixteen I remember slipping out one Sunday night — it was this time of year, the beginning of August — and Bernie and I met at the gate of the workhouse and the pair of us off to a dance in Ardstraw. I was being pestered by a fellow called Tim Carlin at the time but it was really Brian McGuinness that I was — that I was keen on. Remember Brian with the white hands and the longest eyelashes you ever saw? But of course he was crazy about Bernie. Anyhow, the two boys took us on the bar of their bikes and off the four of us headed to Ardstraw, fifteen miles each way. If Daddy had known, may he rest in peace . . .

    And at the end of the night there was a competition for the Best Military Two-step. And it was down to three couples: the local pair from Ardstraw; wee Timmy and myself — he was up to there on me; and Brian and Bernie . . .

    And they were just so beautiful together, so stylish; you couldn't take your eyes off them. People just stopped dancing and gazed at them . . .

    And when the judges announced the winners — they were probably blind drunk — naturally the local couple came first; and Timmy and myself came second; and Brian and Bernie came third.

    Poor Bernie was stunned. She couldn't believe it. Couldn't talk. Wouldn't speak to any of us for the rest of the night. Wouldn't even cycle home with us.

She was right, too: they should have won; they were just so beautiful together . . .

And that's the last time I saw Brian McGuinness — remember Brian with the . . . ? And the next thing I heard he had left for Australia . . .

She was right to be angry, Bernie. I know it wasn't fair — it wasn't fair at all. I mean they must have been blind drunk, those judges, whoever they were . . .

> MAGGIE *stands motionless, staring out of the window, seeing nothing. The others drift back to their tasks:* ROSE *and* AGNES *knit;* KATE *puts the groceries away;* CHRIS *connects the battery. Pause.*

KATE Is it working now, Christina?
CHRIS What's that?
KATE Marconi.
CHRIS Marconi? Yes, yes . . . should be . . .

> *She switches the set on and returns to her ironing. The music, at first scarcely audible, is Irish dance music — 'The Mason's Apron' — played by a céilí band. Very fast; very heavy beat; a raucous sound. At first we are aware of the beat only. Then, as the volume increases slowly, we hear the melody. For about ten seconds — until the sound has established itself — the women continue with their tasks. Then* MAGGIE *turns round. Her head is cocked to the beat, to the music. She is breathing deeply, rapidly. Now her features become animated by a look of defiance, of aggression; a crude mask of happiness. For a few seconds she stands still, listening, absorbing the rhythm, surveying her sisters with her defiant grimace. Now she spreads her fingers (which are covered with flour), pushes her hair back from her face, pulls her hands down her cheeks and patterns her face with an instant mask. At the same time she opens her mouth and emits a wild, raucous 'Yaaaah!' — and immediately begins to dance, arms, legs, hair, long bootlaces*

flying. And as she dances she lilts — sings — shouts and calls, 'Come on and join me! Come on! Come on!' For about ten seconds she dances alone — a white-faced, frantic dervish. Her sisters watch her.

Then ROSE's *face lights up. Suddenly she flings away her knitting, leaps to her feet, shouts, grabs* MAGGIE's *hand. They dance and sing — shout together;* ROSE's *wellingtons pounding out their own erratic rhythm.*

Now after another five seconds AGNES *looks around, leaps up, joins* MAGGIE *and* ROSE. *Of all the sisters she moves most gracefully, most sensuously. Then after the same interval* CHRIS, *who has been folding Jack's surplice, tosses it quickly over her head and joins in the dance. The moment she tosses the vestment over her head* KATE *cries out in remonstration, 'Oh, Christina — !' But her protest is drowned.* AGNES *and* ROSE, CHRIS *and* MAGGIE, *are now all doing a dance that is almost recognizable. They meet — they retreat. They form a circle and wheel round and round. But the movements seem caricatured; and the sound is too loud; and the beat is too fast; and the almost recognizable dance is made grotesque because — for example — instead of holding hands, they have their arms tightly around one another's neck, one another's waist. Finally* KATE, *who has been watching the scene with unease, with alarm, suddenly leaps to her feet, flings her head back, and emits a loud 'Yaaaah!'*

KATE *dances alone, totally concentrated, totally private; a movement that is simultaneously controlled and frantic; a weave of complex steps that takes her quickly round the kitchen, past her sisters, out to the garden, round the summer seat, back to the kitchen; a pattern of action that is out of character and at the same time ominous of some deep and true emotion.*

Throughout the dance ROSE, AGNES, MAGGIE *and* CHRIS *shout — call — sing to each other.* KATE *makes no sound.*

With this too loud music, this pounding beat, this shouting — calling — singing, this parodic reel, there is a sense of order being consciously subverted, of the women consciously and crudely caricaturing themselves, indeed of near-hysteria being induced. The music stops abruptly in mid-phrase. But because of the noise they are making the sisters do not notice and continue dancing for a few seconds. Then KATE *notices — and stops. Then* AGNES. *Then* CHRIS *and* MAGGIE. *Now only* ROSE *is dancing her graceless dance by herself.*

Then finally she, too, notices and stops. Silence. For some time they stand where they have stopped. There is no sound but their gasping for breath and short bursts of static from the radio. They look at each other obliquely; avoid looking at each other; half smile in embarrassment; feel and look slightly ashamed and slightly defiant. CHRIS *moves first. She goes to the radio.*

CHRIS It's away again, the aul' thing. Sometimes you're good with it, Aggie.

AGNES Feel the top. Is it warm?

CHRIS Roasting.

AGNES Turn it off till it cools down.

CHRIS *turns it off — and slaps it.*

CHRIS Bloody useless set, that.

KATE No need for corner-boy language, Christina.

AGNES There must be some reason why it overheats.

CHRIS Because it's a goddamn, bloody useless set — that's why.

ROSE Goddamn bloody useless.

KATE Are wellingtons absolutely necessary on a day like this, Rose?

ROSE I've only my wellingtons and my Sunday shoes, Kate. And it's not Sunday, is it?

KATE Oh, dear, we're suddenly very logical, aren't we?

MAGGIE (*Lighting a cigarette*) I'll tell you something, girls: this Ginger Rogers has seen better days.

KATE It's those cigarettes are killing you.

MAGGIE (*Exhaling*) Wonderful Wild Woodbine. Next best thing to a wonderful, wild man. Want a drag, Kitty?

KATE Go and wash your face, Maggie. And for goodness' sake tie those laces.

MAGGIE Yes, miss. (*At window*) Where's Michael, Chrissie?

CHRIS Working at those kites, isn't he?

MAGGIE He's not there. He's gone.

CHRIS He won't go far.

MAGGIE He was there ten minutes ago.

CHRIS He'll be all right.

MAGGIE But if he goes down to the old well —

CHRIS Just leave him alone for once, will you, please?

MAGGIE *shrugs and goes out the back door. Pause.*

KATE Who's making the tea this evening?

AGNES Who makes the tea every evening?

CHRIS (*At radio*) The connections seem to be all right.

KATE Please take that surplice off, Christina.

CHRIS Maybe a valve has gone — if I knew what a valve looked like.

KATE Have you no sense of propriety?

CHRIS If you ask me we should throw it out.

AGNES I'd be all for that. It's junk, that set.

ROSE Goddamn bloody useless.

KATE (*To* AGNES) And you'll buy a new one, will you?

AGNES It was never any good.

KATE You'll buy it out of your glove money, will you? I thought what you and Rose earned knitting gloves was barely sufficient to clothe the pair of you.

AGNES This isn't your classroom, Kate.

KATE Because I certainly don't see any of it being offered for the upkeep of the house.

AGNES Please, Kate —

KATE But now it stretches to buying a new wireless. Wonderful!

AGNES I make every meal you sit down to every day of the week —

KATE Maybe I should start knitting gloves?

AGNES I wash every stitch of clothes you wear. I polish your shoes. I make your bed. We both do — Rose and I. Paint the house. Sweep the chimney. Cut the grass. Save the turf. What you have here, Kate, are two unpaid servants.

ROSE And d'you know what your nickname at school is? The Gander! Everybody calls you the Gander!

MAGGIE runs on and goes straight to the window.

MAGGIE Come here till you see! Look who's coming up the lane!

AGNES Who's coming?

MAGGIE I only got a glimpse of him — but I'm almost certain it's —

AGNES Who? Who is it?

MAGGIE (*To* CHRIS) It's Gerry Evans, Chrissie.

CHRIS Christ Almighty.

MAGGIE He's at the bend in the lane.

CHRIS Oh, Jesus Christ Almighty.

The news throws the sisters into chaos. Only CHRIS *stands absolutely still, too shocked to move.* AGNES *picks up her knitting and works with excessive concentration.* ROSE *and* MAGGIE *change their footwear. Everybody dashes about in confusion — peering into the tiny mirror, bumping into one another, peeping out the window, combing hair. During all this hectic activity they talk over each other and weave around the immobile* CHRIS. *The lines overlap:*

KATE How dare Mr Evans show his face here.

MAGGIE He wants to see his son, doesn't he?

KATE There's no welcome for that creature here.

ROSE Who hid my Sunday shoes?

MAGGIE We'll have to give him his tea.

KATE I don't see why we should.

MAGGIE And there's nothing in the house.

KATE No business at all coming here and upsetting everybody.

ROSE You're right, Kate. I hate him!

MAGGIE Has anybody got spare shoelaces?

KATE Look at the state of that floor.

MAGGIE Maybe he just wants to meet Father Jack.

KATE Father Jack may have something to say to Mr Evans. (*Of the ironing*) Agnes, put those clothes away.

> AGNES *does not hear her, so apparently engrossed is she in her knitting.*

MAGGIE My Woodbine! Where's my Woodbine?

ROSE He won't stay the night, Kate, will he?

KATE He most certainly won't stay the night in this house!

MAGGIE Have you a piece of cord, Aggie? Anybody got a bit of twine?

KATE Behave quite normally. Be very calm and very dignified. Stop peeping out, Rose!

ROSE (*At window*) There's nobody coming at all.

> *Silence. Then* AGNES *puts down her knitting, rushes to the window, pushes* ROSE *aside and looks out.*

AGNES Let me see.

ROSE You imagined it, Maggie.

CHRIS Oh God.

ROSE He's not there at all.

AGNES (*Softly*) Yes, he is. Maggie's right. There he is.

ROSE Show me.

KATE Has he a walking stick?

ROSE Yes.

KATE And a straw hat?

ROSE Yes.

KATE It's Mr Evans all right.

AGNES Yes. There he is.

CHRIS Oh sweet God — look at the state of me — what'll I

say to him? — how close is he?

ROSE I couldn't look that man in the face. I just hate him — hate him!

KATE That's a very unchristian thing to say, Rose. (*As* ROSE *rushes off*) There's no luck in talk like that!

CHRIS Look at my hands, Kate — I'm shaking.

> KATE *catches her shoulders.*

KATE You are not shaking. You are perfectly calm and you are looking beautiful and what you are going to do is this. You'll meet him outside. You'll tell him his son is healthy and happy. And then you'll send him packing — yourself and Michael are managing quite well without him — as you always have.

> CHRIS *does not move. She is about to cry.* KATE *now takes her in her arms.*

Of course ask him in. And give the creature his tea. And stay the night if he wants to. (*Firm again*) But in the outside loft. And alone. Now. I brought a newspaper home with me. Did anybody see where I left it?

> CHRIS *now rushes to the mirror and adroitly adjusts her hair and her clothes.*

AGNES Where is he, Maggie?

MAGGIE In the garden.

KATE Agnes, did you see where I left the paper?

MAGGIE It's on the turf box, Kate.

> KATE *reads the paper — or pretends to.* AGNES *sits beside the radio and knits with total concentration.* MAGGIE *stands at the side of the garden window.* GERRY EVANS *enters left, his step jaunty, swinging his cane, his straw hat well back on his head. He knows he is being watched. Although he is very ill-at-ease the smile never leaves his face.* CHRIS *goes out*

to the garden where they meet. GERRY *has an English accent.*

GERRY   How are you, Chrissie? Great to see you.

CHRIS   Hello, Gerry.

GERRY   And how have you been for the past six months?

CHRIS   Thirteen months.

GERRY   Thirteen? Never!

CHRIS   July last year; July the seventh.

GERRY   Wow-wow-wow-wow. Where does the time go? Thirteen months? Phew! A dozen times — two dozen times I planned a visit and then something turned up and I couldn't get away.

CHRIS   Well, you're here now.

GERRY   Certainly am. And that was a bit of good fortune. Last night in a bar in Sligo. Bump into this chappie with a brand new Morris Cowley who lets slip that he's heading for Ballybeg in the morning. Ballybeg? Something familiar about that name! So. Here I am. In the flesh. As a matter of interest. Bit of good luck that, wasn't it?

CHRIS   Yes.

GERRY   He just let it slip. And here I am. Oh, yes, wonderful luck.

CHRIS   Yes.

Pause.

MAGGIE   Looks terrified, the poor fella.

KATE   Terrified, my foot.

MAGGIE   Come here till you see him, Aggie.

AGNES   Not just now.

MAGGIE   I'm sure he could do with a good meal.

KATE   I'll give him three minutes. Then if she doesn't hunt him, I will.

GERRY   You're looking wonderful, Chrissie. Really great. Terrific.

CHRIS   My hair's like a whin-bush.

GERRY   Looks lovely to me.

CHRIS Maggie's going to wash it tonight.

GERRY And how's Maggie?

CHRIS Fine.

GERRY And Rose and Kate?

CHRIS Grand.

GERRY And Agnes?

CHRIS Everybody's well, thanks.

GERRY Tell her I was asking for her — Agnes.

CHRIS I would ask you in but the place is —

GERRY No, no, some other time; thanks all the same. The old schedule's a bit tight today. And the chappie who gave me the lift tells me Father Jack's home.

CHRIS Just a few weeks ago.

GERRY All the way from Africa.

CHRIS Yes.

GERRY Safe and sound.

CHRIS Yes.

GERRY Terrific.

CHRIS Yes.

GERRY Lucky man.

CHRIS Yes.

GERRY *uses the cane as a golf club and swings.*

GERRY Must take up some exercise. Putting on too much weight.

KATE He's not still there, is he?

MAGGIE Yes.

KATE Doing what, in God's name?

MAGGIE Talking.

KATE Would someone please tell me what they have to say to each other?

MAGGIE He's Michael's father, Kate.

KATE That's a responsibility never burdened Mr Evans.

CHRIS A commercial traveller called into Kate's school last Easter. He had met you somewhere in Dublin. He had some stupid story about you giving dancing lessons up there.

GERRY He was right.

CHRIS He was not, Gerry!

GERRY Cross the old ticker.

CHRIS Real lessons?

GERRY All last winter.

CHRIS What sort of dancing?

Gerry Strictly ballroom. You're the one should have been giving them — you were always far better than me. Don't you remember?

He does a quick step and a pirouette.

Oh, that was fun while it lasted. I enjoyed that.

CHRIS And people came to you to be taught?

GERRY Don't look so surprised! Everybody wants to dance. I had thousands of pupils — millions!

CHRIS Gerry —

GERRY Fifty-three. I'm a liar. Fifty-one. And when the good weather came they all drifted away. Shame, really. Yes, I enjoyed that. But I've just started a completely new career, as a matter of interest. Never been busier. Gramophone salesman. Agent for the whole country, if you don't mind. 'Minerva Gramophones — The Wise Buy.'

CHRIS Sounds good, Gerry.

GERRY Fabulous. All I have to do is get the orders and pass them on to Dublin. A big enterprise, Chrissie; oh, one very big enterprise.

CHRIS And it's going all right for you?

GERRY Unbelievable. The wholesaler can't keep up with me. Do you see this country? This country is gramophone crazy. Give you an example. Day before yesterday; just west of Oughterard; spots this small house up on the side of a hill. Something seemed just right about it — you know? Off the bike; up the lane; knocks. Out comes this enormous chappie with red hair — what are you laughing at?

CHRIS Gerry —

GERRY I promise you. I show him the brochures; we talk about them for ten minutes; and just like that he takes four

— one for himself and three for the married daughters.

CHRIS He took four gramophones?

GERRY Four brochures!

They both laugh.

But he'll buy. I promise you he'll buy. Tell you this, Chrissie: people thought gramophones would be a thing of the past when radios came in. But they were wrong. In my experience . . . Don't turn round; but he's watching us from behind that bush.

CHRIS Michael?

GERRY Pretend you don't notice. Just carry on. This all his stuff?

CHRIS He's making kites, if you don't mind.

GERRY Unbelievable. Got a glimpse of him down at the foot of the lane. He is just enormous.

CHRIS He's at school, you know.

GERRY Never! Wow-wow-wow-wow. Since when?

CHRIS Since Christmas. Kate got him in early.

GERRY Fabulous. And he likes it?

CHRIS He doesn't say much.

GERRY He loves it. He adores it. They all love school nowadays. And he'll be brilliant at school. Actually I intended bringing him something small —

CHRIS No, no; his aunts have him —

GERRY Just a token, really. As a matter of interest I was looking at a bicycle in Kilkenny last Monday. But they only had it in blue and I thought black might be more — you know — manly. They took my name and all. Call next time I'm down there. Are you busy yourself?

CHRIS Oh, the usual — housework — looking after his lordship.

GERRY Wonderful.

CHRIS Give Agnes and Rose a hand at their knitting. The odd bit of sewing. Pity you don't sell sewing-machines.

GERRY That's an idea! Do the two jobs together! Make an absolute fortune. You have the most unbelievable business head, Chrissie. Never met anything like it.

She laughs.

What are you laughing at?

MAGGIE You should see the way she's looking at him — you'd think he was the biggest toff in the world.

KATE Tinker, more likely! Loafer! Wastrel!

MAGGIE She knows all that, too.

KATE Too? That's all there is.

MAGGIE Come over till you see them, Agnes.

AGNES Not just now.

GERRY You'd never guess what I met on the road out from the town. Talk about good luck! A cow with a single horn coming straight out of the middle of its forehead.

CHRIS You never did!

GERRY As God is my judge. Walking along by itself. Nobody near it.

CHRIS Gerry —

GERRY And just as I was passing it, it stopped and looked me straight in the eye.

CHRIS That was no cow you met — that was a unicorn.

GERRY Go ahead and mock. A unicorn has the body of a horse. This was a cow — a perfectly ordinary brown cow except that it had a single horn just here. Would I tell you a lie?

CHRIS *laughs.*

Go ahead. Laugh. But that's what I saw. Wasn't that a spot of good luck?

CHRIS Was it?

GERRY A cow with a single horn? Oh, yes, that must be a good omen. How many cows like that have you ever met?

CHRIS Thousands. Millions.

GERRY Stop that! I'm sure it's the only one in Ireland; maybe the only one in the world. And I met it on the road to Ballybeg. And it winked at me.

CHRIS You never mentioned that.

GERRY What?

CHRIS That it winked at you.

GERRY Unbelievable. That's what made it all so mysterious. Oh, yes, that must be a fabulous omen. Maybe this week I'm going to sell a gramophone or two after all.

CHRIS But I thought you — ?

GERRY Look! A single magpie! That's definitely a bad omen — one for sorrow. (*Using his stick as a gun*) Bang! Missed. (*Mock serious*) Where's my lucky cow? Come back, brown cow, come back!

They both laugh.

KATE They're not *still* talking, are they?

MAGGIE Laughing. She laughs all the time with him. D'you hear them, Aggie?

AGNES Yes.

KATE Laughing? Absolutely beyond my comprehension.

AGNES Like so many things, Kate.

KATE Two more minutes and Mr Evans is going to talk to me. Laughing? Hah!

GERRY Thinking of going away for a while, Chrissie.

CHRIS Where to?

GERRY But I'll come back to say goodbye first.

CHRIS Are you going home to Wales?

GERRY Wales isn't my home any more. My home is here — well, Ireland. To Spain — as a matter of interest. Just for a short while.

CHRIS To sell gramophones?

GERRY Good God, no! (*Laughs*) You'll never believe this — to do a spot of fighting. With the International Brigade. A company leaves in a few weeks. Bit ridiculous, isn't it? But you know old Gerry when the blood's up — bang-bang-bang! — missing everybody.

CHRIS Are you serious?

GERRY Bit surprised myself — as a matter of interest.

CHRIS What do you know about Spain?

GERRY Not a lot. A little. Enough, maybe. Yes, I know enough. And I thought I should try my hand at something worthy for a change. Give Evans a Big Cause and he won't let you down. It's only everyday stuff he's not successful at. Anyhow, I've still to enlist . . . He's still watching us. He thinks we don't see him. I wouldn't mind talking to him.

CHRIS He's a bit shy.

GERRY Naturally. And I'm a stranger to him practically . . . does he know my name?

CHRIS Of course he knows your name.

GERRY Good. Thanks. Well, maybe not so good. He's a very handsome child. With your eyes. Lucky boy.

'Dancing in the Dark' softly from the radio.

MAGGIE Good for you, Aggie. What did you do to it?

AGNES I didn't touch it.

KATE Turn that thing off, Aggie, would you?

AGNES does not.

GERRY You have a gramophone! I could have got it for you wholesale.

CHRIS It's a wireless set.

GERRY Oh, very posh.

CHRIS It doesn't go half the time. Aggie says it's a heap of junk.

GERRY I know nothing about radios but I'll take a look at it if you —

CHRIS Some other time. When you come back.

Pause.

GERRY And Agnes is well?

CHRIS Fine — fine.

GERRY Of all your sisters Agnes was the one that seemed to

464

object least to me. Tell her I was asking for her.
CHRIS I'll tell her.

They listen to the music.

GERRY Good tune.

Suddenly he takes her in his arms and dances.

CHRIS Gerry —
GERRY Don't talk.
CHRIS What are you at?
GERRY Not a word.
CHRIS Oh God, Gerry —
GERRY Shhh.
CHRIS They're watching us.
GERRY Who is?
CHRIS Maggie and Aggie. From the kitchen window.
GERRY Hope so. And Kate.
CHRIS And Father Jack.
GERRY Better still! Terrific!

> *He suddenly swings her round and round and dances
> her lightly, elegantly across the garden. As he does
> he sings the song to her.*

MAGGIE (*Quietly*) They're dancing.
KATE What!
MAGGIE They're dancing together.
KATE God forgive you!
MAGGIE He has her in his arms.
KATE He has not! The animal!

> *She flings the paper aside and joins* MAGGIE *at the
> window.*

MAGGIE They're dancing round the garden, Aggie.
KATE Oh God, what sort of fool is she?
MAGGIE He's a beautiful dancer, isn't he?

KATE He's leading her astray again, Maggie.

MAGGIE Look at her face — she's easy led. Come here till you see, Aggie.

AGNES I'm busy! For God's sake, can't you see I'm busy!

MAGGIE *turns and looks at her in amazement.*

KATE That's the only thing that Evans creature could ever do well — was dance. (*Pause*) And look at her, the fool. For God's sake, would you look at that fool of a woman? (*Pause*) Her whole face alters when she's happy, doesn't it? (*Pause*) They dance so well together. They're such a beautiful couple. (*Pause*) She's as beautiful as Bernie O'Donnell any day, isn't she?

MAGGIE *moves slowly away from the window and sits motionless.*

GERRY Do you know the words?

CHRIS I never know any words.

GERRY Neither do I. Doesn't matter. This is more important. (*Pause*) Marry me, Chrissie. (*Pause*) Are you listening to me?

CHRIS I hear you.

GERRY Will you marry me when I come back in two weeks?

CHRIS I don't think so, Gerry.

GERRY I'm mad about you. You know I am. I've always been mad about you.

CHRIS When you're with me.

GERRY Leave this house and come away with —

CHRIS But you'd walk out on me again. You wouldn't intend to but that's what would happen because that's your nature and you can't help yourself.

GERRY Not this time, Chrissie. This time it will be —

CHRIS Don't talk any more; no more words. Just dance me down the lane and then you'll leave.

GERRY Believe me, Chrissie; this time the omens are terrific! The omens are unbelievable this time!

*They dance off. After they have exited the music con-
tinues for a few seconds and then stops suddenly in
mid-phrase.* MAGGIE *goes to the set, slaps it, turns it
off.* KATE *moves away from the window.*

KATE   They're away. Dancing.

MAGGIE Whatever's wrong with it, that's all it seems to last
        — a few minutes at a time. Something to do with the
        way it heats up.

KATE   We probably won't see Mr Evans for another year —
        until the humour suddenly takes him again.

AGNES   He has a Christian name.

KATE   And in the meantime it's Christina's heart that gets
        crushed again. That's what I mind. But what really
        infuriates me is that the creature has no sense of ordi-
        nary duty. Does he ever wonder how she clothes and
        feeds Michael? Does he ask her? Does he care?

AGNES *rises and goes to the back door.*

AGNES   Going out to get my head cleared. Bit of a headache
        all day.

KATE   Seems to me the beasts of the field have more con-
        cern for their young than that creature has.

AGNES   Do you ever listen to yourself, Kate? You are such a
        damned righteous bitch! And his name is Gerry! —
        Gerry! — Gerry!

Now on the point of tears AGNES *runs off.*

KATE   And what was that all about?

MAGGIE Who's to say?

KATE   Don't I know his name is Gerry? What am I calling
        him? — St Patrick?

MAGGIE She's worried about Chris, too.

KATE   You see, that's what a creature like Mr Evans does:
        appears out of nowhere and suddenly poisons the
        atmosphere in the whole house — God forgive him, the
        bastard! There! That's what I mean! God forgive me!

MAGGIE *begins putting on her long-laced boots again.*
As she does she sings listlessly, almost inaudibly:

MAGGIE ''Twas on the Isle of Capri that he found her
Beneath the shade of an old walnut tree.
Oh, I can still see the flowers blooming round her,
Where they met on the Isle of Capri.'

KATE If you knew your prayers as well as you know the
words of those aul' pagan songs! . . . She's right: I am
a righteous bitch, amn't I?

MAGGIE 'She was as sweet as a rose at the dawning
But somehow fate hadn't meant it to be,
And though he sailed with the tide in the morning,
Still his heart's in the Isle of Capri.'

She now stands up and looks at her feet.

Now. Who's for a foxtrot?

KATE You work hard at your job. You try to keep the home
together. You perform your duties as best you can —
because you believe in responsibilities and obliga-
tions and good order. And then suddenly, suddenly
you realize that hair cracks are appearing everywhere; that control is slipping away; that the whole
thing is so fragile it can't be held together much
longer. It's all about to collapse, Maggie.

MAGGIE (*Wearily*) Nothing's about to collapse, Kate.

KATE That young Sweeney boy from the back hills — the
boy who was anointed — his trousers didn't catch
fire, as Rose said. They were doing some devilish
thing with a goat — some sort of sacrifice for the
Lughnasa Festival; and Sweeney was so drunk he
toppled over into the middle of the bonfire. Don't
know why that came into my head . . .

MAGGIE Kate . . .

MAGGIE *goes to her and sits beside her.*

KATE And Mr Evans is off again for another twelve months

and next week or the week after Christina'll collapse
into one of her depressions. Remember last winter?
— all that sobbing and lamenting in the middle of
the night. I don't think I could go through that again.
And the doctor says he doesn't think Father Jack's
mind is confused but that his superiors probably had
no choice but send him home. Whatever he means
by that, Maggie. And the parish priest did talk to me
today. He said the numbers in the school are falling
and that there may not be a job for me after the
summer. But the numbers aren't falling, Maggie.
Why is he telling me lies? Why does he want rid of
me? And why has he never come out to visit Father
Jack? (*She tries to laugh*) If he gives me the push all
five of us will be at home together all day long — we
can spend the day dancing to Marconi.

> *Now she cries.* MAGGIE *puts her arm around her.*
> MICHAEL *enters left.*

But what worries me most of all is Rose. If I died —
if I lost my job — if this house were broken up —
what would become of our Rosie?

MAGGIE Shhh.

KATE I must put my trust in God, Maggie, mustn't I? He'll
look after her, won't he? You believe that, Maggie,
don't you?

MAGGIE Kate . . . Kate . . . Kate, love . . .

KATE I believe that, too . . . I believe that . . . I do believe
that . . .

> MAGGIE *holds her and rocks her.* CHRIS *enters quickly
> left, hugging herself. She sees the Boy at his kites,
> goes to him and gets down beside him. She speaks
> eagerly, excitedly, confidentially.*

CHRIS Well. Now you've had a good look at him. What do
you think of him? Do you remember him?

BOY (*Bored*) I never saw him before.

CHRIS Shhh. Yes, you did; five or six times. You've forgotten. And he saw you at the foot of the lane. He thinks you've got very big. And he thinks you're handsome!

BOY Aunt Kate got me a spinning top that won't spin.

CHRIS He's handsome. Isn't he handsome?

BOY Give up.

CHRIS I'll tell you a secret. The others aren't to know. He has got a great new job! And he's wonderful at it!

BOY What does he do?

CHRIS Shhh. And he has bought a bicycle for you — a black bike — a man's bike and he's going to bring it with him the next time he comes.

She suddenly embraces him and hugs him.

BOY Is he coming back soon?

CHRIS (*Eyes closed*) Maybe — maybe. Yes! Yes, he is!

BOY How soon?

CHRIS Next week — the week after — soon — soon — soon! Oh, yes, you have a handsome father. You are a lucky boy and I'm a very, very lucky woman.

She gets to her feet, then bends down again and kisses him lightly.

And another bit of good news for you, lucky boy: you have your mother's eyes!

She laughs, pirouettes flirtatiously before him and dances into the kitchen.

And what's the good news here?

MAGGIE The good news here is . . . that's the most exciting turf we've ever burned!

KATE Gerry's not gone, is he?

CHRIS Just this minute.

AGNES enters through the back door. She is carrying some roses.

He says to thank you very much for the offer of the bed.

KATE Next time he's back.

CHRIS That'll be in a week or two — depending on his commitments.

KATE Well, if the outside loft happens to be empty.

CHRIS And he sends his love to you all. His special love to you, Aggie; and a big kiss.

AGNES For me?

CHRIS Yes! For you!

MAGGIE (*Quickly*) Those are beautiful, Aggie. Would Jack like some in his room? Put them on his windowsill with a wee card — 'ROSES' — so that the poor man's head won't be demented looking for the word. And now, girls, the daily dilemma: what's for tea?

CHRIS Let me make the tea, Maggie.

MAGGIE We'll both make the tea. Perhaps something thrilling with tomatoes? We've got two, I think. Or if you're prepared to wait I'll get that soda bread made.

AGNES I'm making the tea, Maggie.

CHRIS Let me, please. Just today.

AGNES (*Almost aggressively*) I make the tea every evening, don't I? Why shouldn't I make it this evening as usual?

MAGGIE No reason at all. Aggie's the chef. (*Sings raucously:*)
'Everybody's doing it, doing it, doing it.
Picking their noses and chewing it, chewing it,
chewing it . . . '

KATE Maggie, please!

MAGGIE If she knew her prayers half as well as she knows the words of those aul' pagan songs . . . (*Now at the radio*) Marconi, my friend, you're not still asleep, are you?

> FATHER JACK *enters. He shuffles quickly across the kitchen floor, hands behind his back, eyes on the ground, as if he were intent on some engagement elsewhere. Now he becomes aware of the others.*

JACK If anybody is looking for me I'll be down at the bank

of the river for the rest of the ... (*He tails off and looks around. Now he knows where he is. He smiles*) I beg your pardon. My mind was ... It's Kate.

KATE It's Kate.

JACK And Agnes. And Margaret.

MAGGIE How are you, Jack?

JACK And this is — ?

CHRIS Chris — Christina.

JACK Forgive me, Chris. You were only a baby when I went away. I remember Mother lifting you up as the train was pulling out of the station and catching your hand and waving it at me. You were so young you had scarcely any hair but she had managed to attach a tiny pink — a tiny pink — what's the word? — a bow! — a bow! — just about here; and as she waved your hand the bow fell off. It's like a — a picture? — a camera-picture? — a photograph! — it's like a photograph in my mind.

CHRIS The hair isn't much better even now, Jack.

JACK And I remember you crying, Margaret.

MAGGIE Was I?

JACK Yes; your face was all blotchy with tears.

MAGGIE You may be sure — beautiful as ever.

JACK (*To* AGNES) And you and Kate were on Mother's right and Rose was between you; you each had a hand. And Mother's face, I remember, showed nothing. I often wondered about that afterwards.

CHRIS She knew she would never see you again in her lifetime.

JACK I know that. But in the other life. Do you think perhaps Mother didn't believe in the ancestral spirits?

KATE Ancestral — ! What are you blathering about, Jack? Mother was a saintly woman who knew she was going straight to heaven. And don't you forget to take your medicine again this evening. You're supposed to take it three times a day.

JACK One of our priests took so much quinine that he became an addict and almost died. A German priest; Father Sharpeggi. He was rushed to hospital in

Kampala but they could do nothing for him. So
Okawa and I brought him to our local medicine man
and Karl Sharpeggi lived until he was eighty-eight!
There was a strange white bird on my windowsill
when I woke up this morning.

AGNES That's Rosie's pet rooster. Keep away from that thing.

MAGGIE Look what it did to my arm, Jack. One of these days
I'm going to wring its neck.

JACK That's what we do in Ryanga when we want to
please the spirits — or to appease them: we kill a
rooster or a young goat. It's a very exciting exhibi-
tion — that's not the word, is it? — demonstration?
— no — show? No, no; what's the word I'm looking
for? Spectacle? That's not it. The word to describe a
sacred and mysterious . . . ? (*Slowly, deliberately*) You
have a ritual killing. You offer up sacrifice. You have
dancing and incantations. What is the name for that
whole — for that — ? Gone. Lost it. My vocabulary
has deserted me. Never mind. Doesn't matter . . . I
think perhaps I should put on more clothes . . .

Pause.

MAGGIE Did you speak Swahili all the time out there, Jack?

JACK All the time. Yes. To the people. Swahili. When Euro-
peans call, we speak English. Or if we have a — a
visitor? — a visitation! — from the District Commissioner. The present Commissioner knows Swahili but
he won't speak it. He's a stubborn man. He and I
fight a lot but I like him. The Irish Outcast, he calls
me. He is always inviting me to spend a weekend
with him in Kampala — to keep me from 'going
native', as he calls it. Perhaps when I go back. If you
co-operate with the English they give you lots of
money for churches and schools and hospitals. And
he gets so angry with me because I won't take his
money. Reported me to my superiors in Head House
last year; and they were very cross — oh, very cross.
But I like him. When I was saying goodbye to him —

473

he thought this was very funny! — he gave me a present of the last governor's ceremonial hat to take home with — Ceremony! That's the word! How could I have forgotten that? The offering, the ritual, the dancing — a ceremony! Such a simple word. What was I telling you?

AGNES The District Commissioner gave you this present.

JACK Yes; a wonderful triangular hat with three enormous white ostrich plumes rising up out of the crown. I have it in one of my trunks. I'll show it to you later. Ceremony! I'm so glad I got that. Do you know what I found very strange? Coming back in the boat there were days when I couldn't remember even the simplest words. Not that anybody seemed to notice. And you can always point, Margaret, can't you?

MAGGIE Or make signs.

JACK Or make signs.

MAGGIE Or dance.

KATE What you must do is read a lot — books, papers, magazines, anything. I read every night with young Michael. It's great for his vocabulary.

JACK I'm sure you're right, Kate. I'll do that. (*To* CHRIS) I haven't seen young Michael today, Agnes.

KATE Christina, Jack.

JACK Sorry, I —

CHRIS He's around there somewhere. Making kites, if you don't mind.

JACK And I have still to meet your husband.

CHRIS I'm not married.

JACK Ah.

KATE Michael's father was here a while ago . . . Gerry Evans . . . Mr Evans is a Welshman . . . not that that's relevant to . . .

JACK You were never married?

CHRIS Never.

MAGGIE We're all in the same boat, Jack. We're hoping that you'll hunt about and get men for all of us.

JACK (*To* CHRIS) So Michael is a love child?

CHRIS I — yes — I suppose so . . .

JACK He's a fine boy.

CHRIS He's not a bad boy.

JACK You're lucky to have him.

AGNES We're all lucky to have him.

JACK In Ryanga women are eager to have love children. The more love children you have the more fortunate your household is thought to be. Have you other love children?

KATE She certainly has not, Jack; and strange as it may seem to you, neither has Agnes nor Rose nor Maggie nor myself. No harm to Ryanga but you're home in Donegal now and much as we cherish love children here they are not exactly the norm. And the doctor says if you don't take exercise your legs will seize up on you; so I'm going to walk you down to the main road and up again three times and then you'll get your tea and then you'll read the paper from front to back and then you'll take your medicine and then you'll go to bed. And we'll do the same thing tomorrow and the day after and the day after that until we have you back to what you were. You start off and I'll be with you in a second. Where's my cardigan?

JACK *goes out to the garden.* KATE *gets her cardigan.*

MICHAEL Some of Aunt Kate's forebodings weren't all that inaccurate. Indeed some of them were fulfilled before the Festival of Lughnasa was over.

She was right about Uncle Jack. He had been sent home by his superiors, not because his mind was confused, but for reasons that became clearer as the summer drew to a close.

And she was right about losing her job in the local school. The parish priest didn't take her back when the new term began; although that had more to do with Father Jack than with falling numbers.

And she had good reason for being uneasy about Rose — and, had she known, about Agnes, too. But what she couldn't have foreseen was that the home

475

would break up quite so quickly and that when she would wake up one morning in early September both Rose and Agnes would have left for ever.

At this point in MICHAEL's *speech* JACK *picks up two pieces of wood, portions of the kites, and strikes them together. The sound they make pleases him. He does it again — and again — and again. Now he begins to beat out a structured beat whose rhythm gives him pleasure. And as* MICHAEL *continues his speech* JACK *begins to shuffle-dance in time to his tattoo — his body slightly bent over, his eyes on the ground, his feet moving rhythmically. And as he dances — shuffles, he mutters — sings — makes occasional sounds that are incomprehensible and almost inaudible.* KATE *comes out to the garden and stands still, watching him.* ROSE *enters. Now* ROSE *and* MAGGIE *and* AGNES *are all watching him — some at the front door, some through the window. Only* CHRIS *has her eyes closed, her face raised, her mouth slightly open; remembering.* MICHAEL *continues without stopping:*

But she was wrong about my father. I suppose their natures were so out of tune that she would always be wrong about my father. Because he did come back in a couple of weeks as he said he would. And although my mother and he didn't go through a conventional form of marriage, once more they danced together, witnessed by the unseen sisters. And this time it was a dance without music; just there, in ritual circles round and round that square and then down the lane and back up again; slowly, formally, with easy deliberation. My mother with her head thrown back, her eyes closed, her mouth slightly open. My father holding her just that little distance away from him so that he could regard her upturned face. No singing, no melody, no words. Only the swish and whisper of their feet across the grass.

I watched the ceremony from behind that bush.

But this time they were conscious only of themselves and of their dancing. And when he went off to fight with the International Brigade my mother grieved as any bride would grieve. But this time there was no sobbing, no lamenting, no collapse into a depression.

KATE *now goes to* JACK *and gently takes the sticks from him. She places them on the ground.*

KATE We'll leave these back where we found them, Jack. They aren't ours. They belong to the child.

She takes his arm and leads him off.

Now we'll go for our walk.

The others watch with expressionless faces.

ACT TWO

Early September; three weeks later. Ink bottle and some paper on the kitchen table. Two finished kites — their artwork still unseen — lean against the garden seat.

MICHAEL *stands downstage left, listening to* MAGGIE *as she approaches, singing. Now she enters left carrying two zinc buckets of water. She is dressed as she was in Act One. She sings in her usual parodic style:*

MAGGIE   'Oh play to me, Gypsy;
        The moon's high above,
        Oh, play me your serenade,
        The song I love . . . '

> *She goes into the kitchen and from her zinc buckets she fills the kettle and the saucepan on the range. She looks over at the writing materials.*

        Are you getting your books ready for school again?

BOY   School doesn't start for another ten days.

MAGGIE   God, I always hated school. (*She hums the next line of the song. Then she remembers*) You and I have a little financial matter to discuss. (*Pause*) D'you hear me, cub?

BOY   I'm not listening.

MAGGIE   You owe me money.

BOY   I do not.

MAGGIE   Oh, yes, you do. Three weeks ago I bet you a penny those aul' kites would never get off the ground. And they never did.

BOY   Because there was never enough wind; that's why.

MAGGIE   Enough wind! Would you listen to him. A hurricane wouldn't shift those things. Anyhow, a debt is a debt.

One penny please at your convenience. Or the equiv-
alent in kind: one Wild Woodbine. (*Sings:*)
  'Beside your caravan
  The campfire's bright . . .'

*She dances her exaggerated dance across to the table
and tousles the Boy's hair.*

BOY Leave me alone, Aunt Maggie.

MAGGIE 'I'll be your vagabond
  Just for tonight . . .'

BOY Now look at what you made me do! The page is all
blotted!

MAGGIE Your frank opinion, cub: am I vagabond material?

BOY Get out of my road, will you? I'm trying to write a
letter.

MAGGIE Who to? 'That's for me to know and you to find out.'
Whoever it is, he'd need to be smart to read that
scrawl. (*She returns to her buckets*)

BOY It's to Santa Claus.

MAGGIE In September? Nothing like getting in before the rush.
What are you asking for?

BOY A bell.

MAGGIE A bell.

BOY For my bicycle.

MAGGIE For your bicycle.

BOY The bike my Daddy has bought me — stupid!

MAGGIE Your Daddy has bought you a bicycle?

BOY He told me today. He bought it in Kilkenny. So there!

MAGGIE*'s manner changes. She returns to the table.*

MAGGIE (*Softly*) Your Daddy told you that?

BOY Ask him yourself. It's coming next week. It's a black
bike — a man's bike.

MAGGIE Aren't you the lucky boy?

BOY It's going to be delivered here to the house. He
promised me.

MAGGIE Well, if he promised you . . . (*very brisk*) Now! Who can we get to teach you to ride?

BOY I know how to ride!

MAGGIE You don't.

BOY I learned at school last Easter. So there! But you can't ride.

MAGGIE I can so.

BOY I know you can't.

MAGGIE Maybe not by myself. But put me on the bar, cub — magnificent!

BOY You never sat on the bar of a bike in your life, Aunt Maggie!

MAGGIE Oh yes, I did, Michael. Oh yes, indeed I did. (*She gathers up the papers*) Now away and write to Santa some other time. On a day like this you should be out running about the fields like a young calf. Hold on — a new riddle for you.

BOY Give up.

MAGGIE A man goes to an apple tree with two apples on it. He doesn't take apples off it. He doesn't leave apples on it. How does he do that?

BOY Give up.

MAGGIE Think, will you!

BOY Give up.

MAGGIE Well, since you don't know, I will tell you. He takes *one* apple off! Get it? He doesn't take *apples* off! He doesn't leave *apples* on!

BOY God!

MAGGIE You might as well be talking to a turf stack.

> JACK *enters. He looks much stronger and is very sprightly and alert. He is not wearing the top coat or the hat but instead a garish-coloured — probably a sister's — sweater. His dress now looks even more bizarre.*

JACK Did I hear the church bell ringing?

MAGGIE A big posh wedding today.

JACK Not one of my sisters?

MAGGIE No such luck. A man called Austin Morgan and a girl

from Carrickfad.

JACK   Austin Morgan — should I know that name?

MAGGIE   I don't think so. They own the Arcade in the town. And how are you today?

JACK   Cold as usual, Maggie. And complaining about it as usual.

MICHAEL *exits.*

MAGGIE   Complain away — why wouldn't you? And it is getting colder. But you're looking stronger every day, Jack.

JACK   I feel stronger, too. Now! Off for my last walk of the day.

MAGGIE   Number three?

JACK   Number four! Down past the clothes line; across the stream; round the old well; and up through the meadow. And when that's done Kate won't have to nag at me — nag? — nag? — sounds funny — something wrong with that — nag? — that's not a word, is it?

MAGGIE   Nag — yes; to keep on at somebody.

JACK   Yes? Nag. Good. So my English vocabulary is coming back, too. Great. Nag. Still sounds a bit strange.

KATE *enters with an armful of clothes from the clothes line.*

KATE   Time for another walk, Jack.

JACK   Just about to set out on number four, Kate. And thank you for keeping at me.

KATE   No sign of Rose and Agnes yet?

MAGGIE   They said they'd be back for tea. (*To* JACK) They're away picking bilberries.

KATE   (*To* JACK) You used to pick bilberries. Do you remember?

JACK   Down beside the old quarry?

MAGGIE   The very place.

JACK   Mother and myself; every Lughnasa; the annual ritual.

Of course I remember. And then she'd make the most wonderful jam. And that's what you took to school with you every day all through the winter: a piece of soda bread and bilberry jam.

MAGGIE But no butter.

JACK Except on special occasions when you got scones and for some reason they were always buttered. I must walk down to that old quarry one of these days.

'O ruddier than the cherry,
　O sweeter than the berry,
　O nymph more bright,
　Than moonshine night,
　Like kidlings blithe and merry.'

(*Laughs*) Where on earth did that come from? You see, Kate, it's all coming back to me.

KATE So you'll soon begin saying Mass again?

JACK Yes, indeed.

MAGGIE Here in the house?

JACK Why not? Perhaps I'll start next Monday. The neighbours would join us, wouldn't they?

KATE They surely would. A lot of them have been asking me already.

JACK How will we let them know?

MAGGIE I wouldn't worry about that. Word gets about very quickly.

JACK What Okawa does — you know Okawa, don't you?

MAGGIE Your houseboy?

JACK My friend — my mentor — my counsellor — and yes, my houseboy as well; anyhow Okawa summons our people by striking a huge iron gong. Did you hear that wedding bell this morning, Kate?

KATE Yes.

JACK Well, Okawa's gong would carry four times as far as that. But if it's one of the bigger ceremonies he'll spend a whole day going round all the neighbouring villages, blowing on this enormous flute he made himself.

MAGGIE And they all meet in your church?

JACK When I had a church. Now we gather on the common in the middle of the village. If it's an important
ceremony you would have up to three or four hundred people.

KATE All gathered together for Mass?

JACK Maybe. Or maybe to offer sacrifice to Obi, our Great
Goddess of the Earth, so that the crops will flourish.
Or maybe to get in touch with our departed fathers
for their advice and wisdom. Or maybe to thank the
spirits of our tribe if they have been good to us; or to
appease them if they're angry. I complain to Okawa
that our calendar of ceremonies gets fuller every
year. Now at this time of year over there — at the
Ugandan harvest time — we have two very wonderful ceremonies: the Festival of the New Yam and the
Festival of the Sweet Cassava; and they're both dedicated to our Great Goddess, Obi —

KATE But these aren't Christian ceremonies, Jack, are they?

JACK Oh, no. The Ryangans have always been faithful to
their own beliefs — like these two Festivals I'm telling
you about; and they are very special, really magnificent ceremonies. I haven't described those two
Festivals to you before, have I?

KATE Not to me.

JACK Well, they begin very formally, very solemnly with
the ritual sacrifice of a fowl or a goat or a calf down
at the bank of the river. Then the ceremonial cutting
and anointing of the first yams and the first cassava;
and we pass these round in huge wooden bowls.
Then the incantation — chant, really — that expresses
our gratitude and that also acts as a rhythm or per-
cussion for the ritual dance. And then, when the
thanksgiving is over, the dance continues. And the
interesting thing is that it grows naturally into a
secular celebration; so that almost imperceptibly the
religious ceremony ends and the community celebration takes over. And that part of the ceremony is
a real spectacle. We light fires round the periphery
of the circle; and we paint our faces with coloured

powders; and we sing local songs; and we drink palm wine. And then we dance — and dance — and dance — children, men, women, most of them lepers, many of them with misshapen limbs, with missing limbs — dancing, believe it or not, for days on end! It is the most wonderful sight you have ever seen! (*Laughs*) That palm wine! They dole it out in horns! You lose all sense of time!

Oh, yes, the Ryangans are a remarkable people: there is no distinction between the religious and the secular in their culture. And of course their capacity for fun, for laughing, for practical jokes — they've such open hearts! In some respects they're not unlike us. You'd love them, Maggie. You should come back with me!

How did I get into all that? You must stop me telling these long stories. Exercise time! I'll be back in ten minutes; and only last week it took me half-an-hour to do number four. You've done a great job with me, Kate. So please do keep nagging at me.

He moves off — then stops.

It's not Gilbert and Sullivan, is it?

KATE Sorry?

JACK That quotation.

KATE What's that, Jack?

JACK 'O ruddier than the cherry / O sweeter than the berry' — no, it's not Gilbert and Sullivan. But it'll come back to me, I promise you. It's all coming back.

Again he moves off.

KATE Jack.

JACK Yes?

KATE You are going to start saying Mass again?

JACK We've agreed on next Monday, haven't we? Haven't we, Maggie?

MAGGIE Yes.

484

JACK At first light. The moment Rose's white cock crows. A harvest ceremony. You'll have to find a big gong somewhere, Kate.

> *He leaves. Pause.* KATE *and* MAGGIE *stare at each other in concern, in alarm. They speak in hushed voices.*

KATE I told you — you wouldn't believe me — I told you.

MAGGIE Shhh.

KATE What do you think?

MAGGIE He's not back a month yet.

KATE Yesterday I heard about their medicine man who brought a woman back from death —

MAGGIE He needs more time.

KATE And this morning it was 'the spirits of the tribe'! And when I mentioned Mass to him you saw how he dodged about.

MAGGIE He said he'd say Mass next Monday, Kate.

KATE No, he won't. You know he won't. He's changed, Maggie.

MAGGIE In another month, he'll be —

KATE Completely changed. He's not our Jack at all. And it's what he's changed into that frightens me.

MAGGIE Doesn't frighten me.

KATE If you saw your face ... of course it does ... Oh, dear God —

> MAGGIE *now drifts back to the range.* KATE *goes to the table and with excessive vigour wipes it with a damp cloth. Then she stops suddenly, slumps into a seat and covers her face with her hands.* MAGGIE *watches her, then goes to her. She stands behind her and holds her shoulders with her hands.* KATE *grasps* MAGGIE*'s hand in hers.*

MAGGIE All the same, Kitty, I don't think it's a sight I'd like to see.

KATE What sight?

MAGGIE A clatter of lepers trying to do the Military Two-step.

485

KATE God forgive you, Maggie Mundy! The poor creatures are as entitled to —

She breaks off because CHRIS's *laughter is heard off.* KATE *jumps to her feet.*

This must be kept in the family, Maggie! Not a word of this must go outside these walls — d'you hear? — not a syllable!

CHRIS and GERRY enter left. He enters backways, pulling CHRIS who holds the end of his walking stick. Throughout the scene he keeps trying to embrace her. She keeps avoiding him.

GERRY No false modesty. You know you're a great dancer, Chrissie.

CHRIS No, I'm not.

GERRY You should be a professional dancer.

CHRIS You're talking rubbish.

GERRY Let's dance round the garden again.

CHRIS We've done that; and down the lane and up again — without music. And that's enough for one day. Tell me about signing up. Was it really in a church?

GERRY I'm telling you — it was unbelievable.

CHRIS It was a real church?

GERRY A Catholic church as a matter of interest.

CHRIS I don't believe a word of it.

GERRY Would I tell you a lie? And up at the end — in the sanctuary? — there were three men, two of them with trench coats; and between them, behind this lectern and wearing a sort of military cap, this little chappie who spoke in an accent I could hardly understand. Naturally I thought he was Spanish. From Armagh, as it turned out.

CHRIS I'm sure he couldn't understand you either.

GERRY He described himself as the recruiting officer. 'Take it from me, comrade, nobody joins the Brigade without my unanimity.'

She laughs — and avoids his embrace.

CHRIS   It's a wonder he accepted you.

GERRY   'Do you offer your allegiance and your loyalty and your full endeavours to the Popular Front?'

CHRIS   What's the Popular Front?

GERRY   The Spanish government that I'm going to keep in power. 'I take it you are a Syndicalist?' 'No.' 'An Anarchist?' 'No.' 'A Marxist?' 'No.' 'A Republican, a Socialist, a Communist?' 'No.' 'Do you speak Spanish?' 'No.' 'Can you make explosives?' 'No.' 'Can you ride a motorbike?' 'Yes.' 'You're in. Sign here.'

CHRIS   So you'll be a dispatch rider?

GERRY *imitates riding a motorbike.*

And you leave on Saturday?

GERRY   First tide.

CHRIS   How long will you be away?

GERRY   As long as it takes to sort the place out.

CHRIS   Seriously, Gerry.

GERRY   Maybe a couple of months. Everybody says it will be over by Christmas.

CHRIS   They always say it will be over by Christmas. I still don't know why you're going.

GERRY   Not so sure I know either. Who wants salesmen that can't sell? And there's bound to be *something* right about the cause, isn't there? And it's somewhere to go — isn't it? Maybe that's the important thing for a man: a *named* destination — democracy, Ballybeg, heaven. Women's illusions aren't so easily satisfied — they make better drifters. (*Laughs*) Anyhow he held out a pen to sign on the dotted line and it was only when I was writing my name that I glanced over the lectern and saw the box.

CHRIS   What box?

GERRY   He was standing on a box. The chappie was a midget!

CHRIS   Gerry!

GERRY   No bigger than three feet.

CHRIS Gerry, I —

GERRY Promise you! And when we were having a drink afterwards he told me he was invaluable to the Brigade — because he was a master at disguising himself!

CHRIS Gerry Evans, you are —

GERRY Let's go down to the old well.

CHRIS We're going nowhere. Come inside and take a look at this wireless. It stops and starts whenever it feels like it.

GERRY I told you: I know nothing about radios.

CHRIS I've said you're a genius at them.

GERRY Chrissie, I don't even know how to —

CHRIS You can try, can't you? Come on. Michael misses it badly.

She runs into the kitchen. He follows.

You should see Jack striding through the meadow. He looks like a new man.

KATE (*To* GERRY) Were you talking to him?

GERRY He wants to do a swap with me: I'm to give him this hat and he's to give me some sort of a three-cornered hat with feathers that the District Commissioner gave him. Sounds a fair exchange.

MAGGIE Chrissie says you're great with radios, Gerry.

GERRY I'll take a look at it — why not?

MAGGIE All I can tell you is that it's not the battery. I got a new one yesterday.

GERRY Let me check the aerial first. Very often that's where the trouble lies. Then I'll have a look at the ignition and sparking plugs. Leave it to Gerry.

He winks at CHRIS *as he goes out the front door and off right.*

MAGGIE He sounds very knowledgeable.

CHRIS It may be something he can't fix.

KATE I know you're not responsible for Gerry's decisions, Christina. But it would be on my conscience if I didn't tell you how strongly I disapprove of this International Brigade caper. It's a sorry day for Ireland when we send young men off to Spain to fight for godless Communism.

CHRIS For democracy, Kate.

KATE I'm not going to argue. I just want to clear my conscience.

CHRIS That's the important thing, of course. And now you've cleared it.

GERRY *runs on and calls through the window:*

GERRY Turn the radio on, Chrissie, would you?

MAGGIE It's on.

GERRY Right.

He runs off again.

CHRIS Just as we were coming out of the town we met Vera McLaughlin, the knitting agent. (*Softly*) Agnes and Rose aren't back yet?

MAGGIE They'll be here soon.

CHRIS She says she'll call in tomorrow and tell them herself. The poor woman was very distressed.

KATE Tell them what?

CHRIS She's not buying any more handmade gloves.

MAGGIE Why not?

CHRIS Too dear, she says.

KATE Too dear! She pays them a pittance!

CHRIS There's a new factory started up in Donegal Town. They make machine gloves more quickly there and far more cheaply. The people Vera used to supply buy their gloves direct from the factory now.

MAGGIE That's awful news, Chrissie.

CHRIS She says they're organizing buses to bring the workers to the factory and back every day. Most of the people who used to work at home have signed on. She tried to get a job there herself. They told her she was too old. She's forty-one. The poor woman could hardly speak.

MAGGIE Oh God ... poor Aggie ... poor Rose ... what'll they do?

AGNES enters the garden. KATE sees her.

KATE Shhh. They're back. Let them have their tea in peace. Tell them later.

They busy themselves with their tasks. AGNES is carrying two small pails of blackberries which she leaves outside the door of the house. Just as she is about to enter the kitchen a voice off calls her:

GERRY (*Off*) Who is that beautiful woman!

She looks around, puzzled.

AGNES Gerry?
GERRY Up here, Aggie!
AGNES Where?
GERRY On top of the sycamore.

Now she sees him. The audience does not see him.

AGNES Mother of God!
GERRY Come up and join me!
AGNES What are you doing up there?
GERRY You can see into the future from here, Aggie!
AGNES The tree isn't safe, Gerry. Please come down.
GERRY Come up and see what's going to happen to you!
AGNES That branch is dead, Gerry. I'm telling you.

The branch begins to sway.

GERRY Do you think I could get a job in a circus? Wow-wow-wow-wow!
AGNES Gerry —!
GERRY (*Sings*) 'He flies through the air with the greatest of ease — ' Wheeeeeee!

She covers her eyes in terror.

AGNES Stop it, Gerry, stop it, stop it!

GERRY 'That daring young man on the flying trapeze . . . '

AGNES You're going to fall! I'm not looking! I'm not watching! (*She dashes into the house*) That clown of a man is up on top of the sycamore. Go out and tell him to come down, Chrissie.

MAGGIE He's fixing the aerial.

AGNES He's going to break his neck — I'm telling you!

MAGGIE As long as he fixes the wireless first.

KATE How are the bilberries, Agnes?

AGNES Just that bit too ripe. We should have picked them a week ago.

CHRIS Is that a purple stain on your gansey?

AGNES   I know. I'd only begun when I fell into a bush. And look at my hands — all scrabbed with briars. For all the sympathy I got from Rosie. Nearly died laughing at me. How is she now? (*Pause*) Is she still in bed?

CHRIS Bed?

AGNES She wasn't feeling well. She left me and went home to lie down. (*Pause*) She's here, isn't she?

MAGGIE *rushes off to the bedroom.*

KATE I haven't seen her. (*To* CHRIS) Have you?

CHRIS No.

KATE When did she leave you?

AGNES Hours ago — I don't know — almost immediately after we got to the old quarry. She said she felt out of sorts.

CHRIS And she went off by herself?

AGNES Yes.

KATE To come home?

AGNES That's what she said.

MAGGIE *enters.*

MAGGIE She's not in her bed.

AGNES   Oh God! Where could she —

KATE   Start at the beginning, Agnes. What exactly happened?

AGNES   Nothing 'happened' — nothing at all. We left here together — when was it? — just after one o'clock —

CHRIS   That means she's missing for over three hours.

AGNES   We walked together to the quarry. She was chatting away as usual. I had my two buckets and she had —

KATE   Go on — go on!

AGNES   And just after we got there she said she wasn't feeling well. I told her not to bother about the bilberries — just to sit in the sun. And that's what she did.

KATE   For how long?

AGNES   I don't know — five — ten minutes. And then I fell into the bush. And that was when she laughed. And then she said — she said — I've forgotten what she said — something about a headache and her stomach being sick and she'd go home and sleep for a while. (*To* MAGGIE) You're sure she's not in her bed?

MAGGIE *shakes her head.*

KATE   Then what?

AGNES *begins to cry.*

AGNES   Where is she? What's happened to our Rosie?

KATE   What direction did she go when she left you?

AGNES   Direction?

KATE   Stop snivelling, Agnes! Did she go towards home?

AGNES   I think so ... yes ... I don't know ... Maggie —

MAGGIE   She may have gone into the town.

CHRIS   She wouldn't have gone into town in her wellingtons.

AGNES   She was wearing her good shoes.

KATE   Are you sure?

AGNES   Yes; and her blue cardigan and her good skirt. I said to her — I said, 'You're some lady to go picking bilberries with.' And she just laughed and said, 'I'm some toff, Aggie, amn't I some toff?'

MAGGIE Had she a bottle of milk with her?

AGNES I think so — yes — in one of her cans.

MAGGIE Had she any money with her?

AGNES She had half-a-crown. That's all she has.

MAGGIE (*Softly*) Danny Bradley.

KATE What? — who?

MAGGIE Danny Bradley . . . Lough Anna . . . up in the back hills.

CHRIS Oh God, no.

KATE What? — what's this? — what about the back hills?

CHRIS She has some silly notion about that scamp, Bradley. She believes he's in love with her. He gave her a present last Christmas — she says.

KATE (*To* AGNES) What do you know about this Bradley business?

AGNES I know no more than Chris has —

KATE I've often seen you and Rose whispering together. What plot has been hatched between Rose and Mr Bradley?

AGNES No plot . . . please, Kate —

KATE You're lying to me, Agnes! You're withholding! I want the truth!

AGNES Honest to God, all I know is what Chris has just —

KATE I want to know everything you know! Now! I want to —

MAGGIE That'll do, Kate! Stop that at once! (*Calmly*) She may be in the town. She may be on her way home now. She may have taken a weak turn on her way back from the quarry. We're going to find her. (*To* CHRIS) You search the fields on the upper side of the lane. (*To* AGNES) You take the lower side, down as far as the main road. (*To* KATE) You go to the old well and search all around there. I'm going into the town to tell the police.

KATE You're going to no police, Maggie. If she's mixed up with that Bradley creature I'm not going to have it broadcast all over —

MAGGIE I'm going to the police and you'll do what I told you to do.

CHRIS There she is! Look — look! There she is!

She has seen ROSE *through the window and is about to rush out to greet her.* MAGGIE *catches her arm and restrains her. The four sisters watch* ROSE *as she crosses the garden —* CHRIS *and* KATE *from the window,* MAGGIE *and* AGNES *from the door.* ROSE *is unaware of their anxious scrutiny. She is dressed in the 'good' clothes described by* AGNES *and they have changed her appearance. Indeed, had we not seen the* ROSE *of Act One, we might not now be immediately aware of her disability. At first look this might be any youngish country woman, carefully dressed, not unattractive, returning from a long walk on a summer day. She walks slowly, lethargically, towards the house. From her right hand hangs a red poppy that she plucked casually along the road. The face reveals nothing — but nothing is being deliberately concealed. She sees Agnes's cans of fruit. She stops beside them and looks at them. Then she puts her hand into one of the cans, takes a fistful of berries and thrusts the fistful into her mouth. Then she wipes her mouth with her sleeve and the back of her hand. As she chews she looks at her stained fingers. She wipes them on her skirt. All of these movements — stopping, eating, wiping — are done not dreamily, abstractedly, but calmly, naturally. Now she moves towards the house. As she approaches the door* AGNES *rushes to meet her. Instead of hugging her, as she wants to, she catches her arm.*

AGNES Rosie, love, we were beginning to get worried about you.

ROSE They're nice, Aggie. They're sweet. And you got two canfuls. Good for you.

AGNES *leads her into the house.*

AGNES Is your stomach settled?

ROSE My stomach?

AGNES You weren't feeling well — remember? — when we

were at the quarry?

ROSE Oh, yes. Oh, I'm fine now, thanks.

AGNES You left me there and you said you were coming home to lie down. D'you remember that?

ROSE Yes.

CHRIS But you didn't come home, Rosie.

ROSE That's right.

AGNES And we were very worried about you.

ROSE Well . . . here I am.

CHRIS Were you in the town?

AGNES That's why you're all dressed up, isn't it?

CHRIS You went into Ballybeg, didn't you?

Pause. ROSE *looks from one to the other.*

MAGGIE (*Briskly*) She's home safe and sound and that's all that matters. Now I don't know about you girls but I can tell you this chicken is weak with hunger. Let me tell you what's on the menu this evening. Our beverage is the usual hot, sweet tea. There is a choice between caraway-seed bread and soda bread, both fresh from the chef's oven. But now we come to the difficulty: there's only three eggs between the seven of us — I wish to God you'd persuade that white rooster of yours to lay eggs, Rosie.

CHRIS There are eight of us, Maggie.

MAGGIE How are there — ? Of course — the soldier up the sycamore! Not a great larder but a nice challenge to someone like myself. Right. My suggestion is . . . Eggs Ballybeg; in other words scrambled and served on lightly toasted caraway-seed bread. Followed — for those so inclined — by one magnificent Wild Woodbine. Everybody happy?

CHRIS Excellent, Margaret!

MAGGIE Settled.

ROSE *has taken off her shoe and is examining it carefully.*

AGNES   We'll go and pick some more bilberries next Sunday,
        Rosie.

ROSE   All right.

AGNES   Remember the cans you had? You had your own two
        cans — remember? Did you take them with you?

ROSE   Where to, Aggie?

AGNES   Into the town . . . wherever you went . . .

ROSE   I hid them at the quarry behind a stone wall. They're
        safe there. I'll go back and pick them up later this
        evening. Does anybody know where my overall is?

MAGGIE It's lying across your bed. And you'd need to bring
        some turf in, Rosie.

ROSE   I'll change first, Maggie.

MAGGIE Be quick about it.

CHRIS   How many pieces of toast do you want?

MAGGIE All that loaf. And go easy on the butter — that's all
        we have. Now. Parsley. And just a whiff of basil. I
        don't want you to be too optimistic, girls, but you
        should know I feel very creative this evening.

        ROSE *moves towards the bedroom door. Just as she is
        about to exit:*

KATE   I want to know where you have been, Rose.

        ROSE *stops. Pause.*

        You have been gone for the entire afternoon. I want
        you to tell me where you've been.

AGNES   Later, Kate; after —

KATE   Where have you been for the past three hours?

ROSE   (*Inaudible*) Lough Anna.

KATE   I didn't hear what you said, Rose.

ROSE   Lough Anna.

CHRIS   Kate, just leave —

KATE   You walked from the quarry to Lough Anna?

ROSE   Yes.

KATE   Did you meet somebody there?

ROSE   Yes.

KATE Had you arranged to meet somebody there?

ROSE I had arranged to meet Danny Bradley there, Kate. He brought me out in his father's blue boat. (*To* MAGGIE) I don't want anything to eat, Maggie. I brought a bottle of milk and a packet of chocolate biscuits with me and we had a picnic on the lake. (*To* AGNES) Then the two of us went up through the back hills. He showed me what was left of the Lughnasa fires. A few of them are still burning away up there. (*To* KATE) We passed young Sweeney's house — you know, the boy who got burned, the boy you said was dying. Well, he's on the mend, Danny says. His legs will be scarred but he'll be all right. (*To* ALL) It's a very peaceful place up there. There was nobody there but Danny and me. (*To* AGNES) He calls me his Rosebud, Aggie. I told you that before, didn't I? (*To* ALL) Then he walked me down as far as the workhouse gate and I came on home by myself. (*To* KATE) And that's all I'm going to tell you. (*To* ALL) That's all any of you are going to hear.

    She exits, her shoes in one hand, the poppy in the other. MICHAEL *enters.*

KATE What has happened to this house? Mother of God, will we ever be able to lift our heads ever again . . . ?

    Pause.

MICHAEL The following night Vera McLaughlin arrived and explained to Agnes and Rose why she couldn't buy their hand-knitted gloves any more. Most of her home knitters were already working in the new factory and she advised Agnes and Rose to apply immediately. The Industrial Revolution had finally caught up with Ballybeg.

    They didn't apply, even though they had no other means of making a living, and they never discussed their situation with their sisters. Perhaps Agnes made the decision for both of them because she knew Rose wouldn't have got work there anyway. Or perhaps, as Kate believed, because Agnes was too notionate to work in a factory. Or perhaps the two of them just wanted . . . away.

Anyhow, on my first day back at school, when we came into the kitchen for breakfast, there was a note propped up against the milk jug: 'We are gone for good. This is best for all. Do not try to find us.' It was written in Agnes's resolute hand.

Of course they did try to find them. So did the police. So did our neighbours who had a huge network of relatives all over England and America. But they had vanished without trace. And by the time I tracked them down — twenty-five years later, in London — Agnes was dead and Rose was dying in a hospice for the destitute in Southwark.

The scraps of information I gathered about their lives during those missing years were too sparse to be coherent. They had moved about a lot. They had worked as cleaning women in public toilets, in factories, in the Underground. Then, when Rose could no longer get work, Agnes tried to support them both — but couldn't. From then on, I gathered, they gave up. They took to drink; slept in parks, in doorways, on the Thames Embankment. Then Agnes died of exposure. And two days after I found Rose in that grim hospice — she didn't recognize me, of course — she died in her sleep.

Father Jack's health improved quickly and he soon recovered his full vocabulary and all his old bounce and vigour. But he didn't say Mass that following Monday. In fact he never said Mass again. And the neighbours stopped enquiring about him. And his name never again appeared in the *Donegal Enquirer*. And of course there was never a civic reception with bands and flags and speeches.

But he never lost his determination to return to Uganda and he still talked passionately about his life

with the lepers there. And each new anecdote con-
tained more revelations. And each new revelation
startled — shocked — stunned poor Aunt Kate. Until
finally she hit on a phrase that appeased her: 'his
own distinctive spiritual search'. 'Leaping around a
fire and offering a little hen to Uka or Ito or whoever
is not religion as I was taught it and indeed know it,'
she would say with a defiant toss of her head. 'But
then Jack must make his own distinctive search.'
And when he died suddenly of a heart attack —
within a year of his homecoming, on the very eve
of the following *Lá Lughnasa* — my mother and
Maggie mourned him sorely. But for months Kate
was inconsolable.

My father sailed for Spain that Saturday. The last I
saw of him was dancing down the lane in imitation
of Fred Astaire, swinging his walking stick, Uncle
Jack's ceremonial tricorn at a jaunty angle over his
left eye. When he got to the main road he stopped
and turned and with both hands blew a dozen
theatrical kisses back to Mother and me.

He was wounded in Barcelona — he fell off his
motorbike — so that for the rest of his life he walked
with a limp. The limp wasn't disabling but it put an
end to his dancing days; and that really distressed
him. Even the role of maimed veteran, which he
loved, could never compensate for that. He still visited us occasionally, perhaps once a year. Each time
he was on the brink of a new career. And each time
he proposed to Mother and promised me a new bike.
Then the war came in 1939; his visits became more
infrequent; and finally he stopped coming altogether.

Sometime in the mid-fifties I got a letter from a
tiny village in the south of Wales; a curt note from a
young man of my own age and also called Michael
Evans. He had found my name and address among
the belongings of his father, Gerry Evans. He intro-
duced himself as my half-brother and he wanted me
to know that Gerry Evans, the father we shared, had

died peacefully in the family home the previous week. Throughout his final illness he was nursed by his wife and his three grown children who all lived and worked in the village.

My mother never knew of that letter. I decided to tell her — decided not to — vacillated for years as my father would have done; and eventually, rightly or wrongly, kept the information to myself.

MAGGIE, CHRIS, KATE and AGNES now resume their tasks.

CHRIS Well, at least that's good news.
MAGGIE What's that?
CHRIS That the young Sweeney boy from the back hills is going to live.
MAGGIE Good news indeed.

CHRIS goes to the door and calls:

CHRIS Michael! Where are you? We need some turf brought in!

She now goes outside and calls up to Gerry. MICHAEL *exits.*

Are you still up there?
GERRY (*Off*) Don't stand there. I might fall on top of you.
CHRIS Have you any idea what you're doing?
GERRY (*Off*) Come on up here to me.
CHRIS I'm sure I will.
GERRY (*Off*) We never made love on top of a sycamore tree.

She looks quickly around: did her sisters hear that?

CHRIS If you fall and break your neck it'll be too good for you. (*She goes inside*) Nobody can vanish quicker than that Michael fellow when you need him.
MAGGIE (*To* AGNES) I had a brilliant idea when I woke up this

morning, Aggie. I thought to myself: what is it that Ballybeg badly needs and that Ballybeg hasn't got?

AGNES A riddle. Give up.

MAGGIE A dressmaker! So why doesn't Agnes Mundy who has such clever hands, why doesn't she dressmake?

AGNES Clever hands!

MAGGIE *looks around for her cigarettes.*

MAGGIE She'd get a pile of work. They'd come to her from far and wide. She'd make a fortune.

AGNES Some fortune in Ballybeg.

MAGGIE And not only would the work be interesting but she wouldn't be ruining her eyes staring at grey wool eight hours a day. Did you notice how Rosie squints at things now? It's the job for you, Aggie; I'm telling you. Ah, holy God, girls, don't tell me I'm out of fags! How could that have happened?

CHRIS *goes to the mantelpiece and produces a single cigarette.*

Chrissie, you are one genius. Look, Kate. (*Scowls*) Misery. (*Lights cigarette*) Happiness! Want a drag?

KATE What's keeping those wonderful Eggs Ballybeg?

MAGGIE If I had to choose between one Wild Woodbine and a man of — say — fifty-two — widower — plump, what would I do, Kate? I'd take fatso, wouldn't I? God, I really am getting desperate.

JACK *enters through the garden.*

Maybe I should go to Ryanga with you, Jack.

JACK I know you won't but I know you'd love it.

MAGGIE Could you guarantee a man for each of us?

JACK I couldn't promise four men but I should be able to get one husband for all of you.

MAGGIE Would we settle for that?

CHRIS One between the four of us?

JACK That's our system and it works very well. One of you would be his principal wife and live with him in his largest hut —

MAGGIE That'd be you, Kate.

KATE Stop that, Maggie!

JACK And the other three of you he'd keep in his enclosure. It would be like living on the same small farm.

MAGGIE Snug enough, girls, isn't it? (*To* JACK) And what would be — what sort of duties would we have?

JACK Cooking, sewing, helping with the crops, washing — the usual housekeeping tasks.

MAGGIE Sure that's what we do anyway.

JACK And looking after his children.

MAGGIE That he'd have by Kate.

KATE Maggie!

JACK By all four of you! And what's so efficient about that system is that the husband and his wives and his children make up a small commune where everybody helps everybody else and cares for them. I'm completely in favour of it.

KATE It may be efficient and you may be in favour of it, Jack, but I don't think it's what Pope Pius XI considers to be the holy sacrament of matrimony. And it might be better for you if you paid just a bit more attention to our Holy Father and a bit less to the Great Goddess . . . Iggie.

Music of 'Anything Goes' very softly on the radio.

CHRIS Listen.

MAGGIE And they have hens there, too, Jack?

JACK We're overrun with hens.

MAGGIE Don't dismiss it, girls. It has its points. Would you be game, Kate?

KATE Would you give my head peace, Maggie.

CHRIS Gerry has it going!

MAGGIE Tell me this, Jack: what's the Swahili for 'tchook-tchook-tchook-tchook-tchook'?

JACK You'd love the climate, too, Kate.

KATE I'm not listening to a word you're saying.

GERRY runs on.

GERRY Well? Any good?

CHRIS Listen.

GERRY Aha. Leave it to the expert.

JACK I have something for you, Gerry.

GERRY What's that?

JACK The plumed hat — the ceremonial hat — remember?
We agreed to swap. With you in a second.

He goes to his bedroom.

MAGGIE Good work, Gerry.

GERRY Thought it might be the aerial. That's the end of your
troubles.

Listens. Sings a line of the song.

Dance with me, Agnes.

AGNES Have a bit of sense, Gerry Evans.

GERRY Dance with me. Please. Come on.

MAGGIE Dance with him, Aggie.

GERRY (*Sings*) 'In olden times a glimpse of stocking
Was looked on as something shocking — '
Give me your hand.

MAGGIE Go on, Aggie.

AGNES Who wants to dance at this time of —

GERRY pulls her to her feet and takes her in his arms.

GERRY (*Sings*) '. . . anything goes.
Good authors, too, who once knew better words
Now only use four-letter words
Writing prose,
Anything goes . . .'

Bring up the sound. With style and with easy elegance

they dance once around the kitchen and then out to the garden — GERRY *singing the words directly to her face:*

'If driving fast cars you like,
    If low bars you like,
    If old hymns you like,
    If bare limbs you like,
    If Mae West you like,
    Or me undressed you like,
    Why, nobody will oppose.
    When ev'ry night,
    The set that's smart is in-
    truding in nudist parties in
    Studios,
    Anything goes . . . '

They are now in the far corner of the garden.

You're a great dancer, Aggie.
AGNES No, I'm not.
GERRY You're a superb dancer.
AGNES No, I'm not.
GERRY You should be a professional dancer.
AGNES Too late for that.
GERRY You could teach dancing in Ballybeg.
AGNES That's all they need.
GERRY Maybe it is!

He bends down and kisses her on the forehead. All this is seen — but not heard — by CHRIS *at the kitchen window. Immediately after this kiss* GERRY *bursts into song again, turns* AGNES *four or five times very rapidly and dances her back to the kitchen.*

There you are. Safe and sound.
MAGGIE I wish to God I could dance like you, Aggie.
AGNES I haven't a breath.
GERRY Doesn't she dance elegantly?
MAGGIE Always did, our Aggie.

GERRY Unbelievable. Now, Chrissie — you and I.
CHRIS (*Sharply*) Not now. I wonder where Michael's got to?
GERRY Come on, Chrissie. Once round the floor.
CHRIS Not now, I said. Are you thick?
MAGGIE I'll dance with you, Gerry!

She kicks her wellingtons off.

Do you want to see real class?
GERRY Certainly do, Maggie.
MAGGIE Stand back there, girls. Shirley Temple needs a lot of space.
GERRY Wow-wow-wow-wow!
MAGGIE Hold me close, Gerry. The old legs aren't too reliable.

She and GERRY sing and dance:

'In olden times a glimpse of stocking
   Was looked on as something shocking
   But now — '

CHRIS *suddenly turns the radio off.*

CHRIS Sick of that damned thing.
GERRY What happened?
MAGGIE What are you at there, Chrissie?
CHRIS We're only wasting the battery and we won't get a new one until the weekend.
MAGGIE It wasn't to be, Gerry. But there'll be another day.
GERRY That's a promise, Maggie.

He goes to CHRIS at the radio.

Not a bad little set, that.
KATE Peace, thanks be to God! D'you know what that thing has done? Killed all Christian conversation in this country.
CHRIS (*To AGNES, icily*) Vera McLaughlin's calling here tomorrow. She wants to talk to you and Rose.

AGNES What about?

KATE (*Quickly*) I didn't tell you, did I? — her daughter's got engaged!

MAGGIE Which of them?

KATE 'The harvest dance is going to be just supreme this year, Miss Mundy' — that wee brat!

MAGGIE Sophia. Is she not still at school?

KATE Left last year. She's fifteen. And the lucky man is sixteen.

MAGGIE Holy God. We may pack it in, girls.

KATE It's indecent, I'm telling you. Fifteen and sixteen! Don't tell me that's not totally improper. It's the poor mother I feel sorry for.

AGNES What does she want to talk to us about?

CHRIS (*Relenting*) Something about wool. Didn't sound important. She probably won't call at all. (*She turns the radio on again. No sound. To* MAGGIE) Go ahead and dance, you two.

MAGGIE Artistes like Margaret Mundy can't perform on demand, Chrissie. We need to be in touch with other forces first, don't we, Gerry?

GERRY Absolutely. Why is there no sound?

KATE Maggie, are we never going to eat?

MAGGIE Indeed we are — outside in the garden! Eggs Ballybeg *al fresco*. Lughnasa's almost over, girls. There aren't going to be many warm evenings left.

KATE Good idea, Maggie.

AGNES I'll get the cups and plates.

GERRY (*With* CHRIS *at radio*) Are you all right?

CHRIS It's not gone again, is it?

GERRY Have I done something wrong?

CHRIS I switched it on again — that's all I did.

MAGGIE Take out those chairs, Gerry.

GERRY What about the table?

MAGGIE We'll just spread a cloth on the ground.

> MAGGIE *exits with the cloth which she spreads in the middle of the garden.* GERRY *kisses* CHRIS *lightly on the back of the neck.*

GERRY At least we know it's not the aerial.

CHRIS According to you.

GERRY And if it's not the aerial the next thing to check is the ignition.

CHRIS Ignition! Listen to that bluffer!

GERRY Bluffer? (*To* AGNES *as she passes*) Did you hear what she called me? That's unfair, Agnes, isn't it?

> AGNES *smiles and shrugs.*

Let's take the back off and see what's what.

> ROSE *enters the garden from the back of the house. At first nobody notices her. She is dressed as in Act One. In her right hand she holds the dead rooster by the feet. Its feathers are ruffled and it is stained with blood.* ROSE *is calm, almost matter-of-fact.* AGNES *sees her first and goes to her.* CHRIS *and* GERRY *join the others in the garden.*

AGNES Rosie, what is it, Rosie?

ROSE My rooster's dead.

AGNES Oh, Rosie . . .

ROSE (*Holding the dead bird up*) Look at him. He's dead.

AGNES What happened to him?

ROSE The fox must have got him.

AGNES Oh, poor Rosie . . .

ROSE Maggie warned me the fox was about again. (*To* ALL) That's the end of my pet rooster. The fox must have got him. You were right, Maggie.

> *She places it carefully on the tablecloth in the middle of the garden.*

MAGGIE Did he get at the hens?

ROSE I don't think so.

MAGGIE Was the door left open?

ROSE They're all right. They're safe.

MAGGIE That itself.

AGNES We'll get another white rooster for you, Rosie.

ROSE Doesn't matter.

MAGGIE And I'll put manners on him early on.

ROSE I don't want another.

MAGGIE (*Quick hug*) Poor old Rosie. (*As she moves away*) We can hardly expect him to lay for us now . . .

CHRIS Where's that Michael fellow got to? Michael! He hears me rightly, you know. I'm sure he's jouking about out there somewhere, watching us. Michael!

ROSE *sits on the garden seat.*

MAGGIE All right, girls, what's missing? Knives, forks, plates . . . (*She sees* JACK *coming through the kitchen*) Jesus, Mary and Joseph!

> JACK *is wearing a very soiled, very crumpled white uniform — a version of the uniform we saw him in at the very beginning of the play. One of the epaulettes is hanging by a thread and the gold buttons are tarnished. The uniform is so large that it looks as if it were made for a much larger man: his hands are lost in the sleeves and the trousers trail on the ground. On his head he wears a tricorn, ceremonial hat; once white like the uniform but now grubby, the plumage broken and tatty. He carries himself in military style, his army cane under his arm.*

JACK Gerry, my friend, where are you?

GERRY Out here, Jack.

JACK There you are. (*To* ALL) I put on my ceremonial clothes for the formal exchange. There was a time when it fitted me — believe it or not. Wonderful uniform, isn't it?

GERRY Unbelievable. I could do with that for Spain.

JACK It was my uniform when I was chaplain to the British Army during the Great War.

KATE We know only too well what it is, Jack.

JACK Isn't it splendid? Well, it was splendid. Needs a bit of a clean up. Okawa's always dressing up in it. I really must give it to him to keep.

KATE It's not at all suitable for this climate, Jack.

JACK You're right, Kate. Just for the ceremony — then I'll change back. Now, if I were at home, what we do when we swap or barter is this. I place my possession on the ground —

He and GERRY *enact this ritual.*

Go ahead. (*Of hat*) Put it on the grass — anywhere — just at your feet. Now take three steps away from it — yes? — a symbolic distancing of yourself from what you once possessed. Good. Now turn round once — like this — yes, a complete circle — and that's the formal rejection of what you once had — you no longer lay claim to it. Now I cross over to where you stand — right? And you come over to the position I have left. So. Excellent. The exchange is now formally and irrevocably complete. This is my straw hat. And that is your tricorn hat. Put it on. Splendid! And it suits you! Doesn't it suit him?

CHRIS His head's too big.

GERRY (*Adjusting hat*) What about that? (*To* AGNES) Is that better, Agnes?

AGNES You're lovely.

GERRY *does a Charlie Chaplin walk across the garden, his feet spread, his cane twirling. As he does he sings:*

GERRY 'In olden times a glimpse of stocking
Was looked on as something shocking . . .'

JACK (*Adjusting his hat*) And what about this? Or like this? Or further back on my head?

MAGGIE Would you look at them! Strutting about like a pair of peacocks! Now — teatime!

AGNES I'll make the tea.

MAGGIE You can start again tomorrow. Let me finish off

Lughnasa. Chrissie, put on Marconi.

CHRIS I think it's broken again.

AGNES Gerry fixed it. Didn't you?

GERRY Then Chrissie got at it again.

CHRIS Possessed that thing, if you ask me.

KATE I wish you wouldn't use words like that, Christina. There's still great heat in that sun.

MAGGIE Great harvest weather.

KATE I love September.

MAGGIE (*Not moving*) Cooking time, girls.

KATE Wait a while, Maggie. Enjoy the bit of heat that's left.

AGNES *moves beside* ROSE.

AGNES Next Sunday, then. Is that all right?

ROSE What's next Sunday?

AGNES We'll get some more bilberries.

ROSE Yes. Yes. Whatever you say, Aggie.

GERRY *examines the kites.*

GERRY Not bad for a kid of seven. Very neatly made.

KATE Look at the artwork.

GERRY Wow-wow-wow-wow! That is unbelievable!

KATE I keep telling his mother — she has a very talented son.

CHRIS So there, Mr Evans.

GERRY Have you all seen these?

MAGGIE I hate them.

GERRY I think they're just wonderful. Look, Jack.

For the first time we all see the images. On each kite is painted a crude, cruel, grinning face, primitively drawn, garishly painted.

I'll tell you something: this boy isn't going to end up selling gramophones.

CHRIS Michael! He always vanishes when there's work to be done.

MAGGIE I've a riddle for you. Why is a gramophone like a parrot?

KATE Maggie!

MAGGIE Because it . . . because it always . . . because a parrot . . . God, I've forgotten!

> MAGGIE *moves into the kitchen.* MICHAEL *enters. The characters are now in positions similar to their positions at the beginning of the play — with some changes.* AGNES *and* GERRY *are on the garden seat.* JACK *stands stiffly to attention at* AGNES's *elbow. One kite, facing boldly out front, stands between* GERRY *and* AGNES; *the other between* AGNES *and* JACK. ROSE *is upstage left.* MAGGIE *is at the kitchen window.* KATE *is downstage right.* CHRIS *is at the front door. During* MICHAEL's *speech* KATE *cries quietly. As* MICHAEL *begins to speak the stage is lit in a very soft, golden light so that the tableau we see is almost, but not quite, in a haze.*

MICHAEL As I said, Father Jack was dead within twelve months. And with him and Agnes and Rose all gone the heart seemed to go out of the house.

Maggie took on the tasks Rose and Agnes had done and pretended to believe that nothing had changed. My mother spent the rest of her life in the knitting factory — and hated every day of it. And after a few years doing nothing Kate got the job of tutoring the young family of Austin Morgan of the Arcade. But much of the spirit and fun had gone out of their lives; and when my time came to go away, in the selfish way of young men, I was happy to escape.

> *Now fade in very softly, just audible, the music — 'It is Time to Say Goodnight' (not from the radio speaker).*
>
> *And as* MICHAEL *continues, everybody sways very slightly from side to side — even the grinning kites. The movement is so minimal that we cannot be quite*

certain if it is happening or if we imagine it.

And so, when I cast my mind back to that summer of 1936, different kinds of memories offer themselves to me.

But there is one memory of that Lughnasa time that visits me most often; and what fascinates me about that memory is that it owes nothing to fact. In that memory atmosphere is more real than incident and everything is simultaneously actual and illusory. In that memory, too, the air is nostalgic with the music of the thirties. It drifts in from somewhere far away — a mirage of sound — a dream music that is both heard and imagined; that seems to be both itself and its own echo; a sound so alluring and so mesmeric that the afternoon is bewitched, maybe haunted, by it. And what is so strange about that memory is that everybody seems to be floating on those sweet sounds, moving rhythmically, languorously, in complete isolation; responding more to the mood of the music than to its beat. When I remember it I think of it as dancing. Dancing with eyes half closed because to open them would break the spell. Dancing as if language had surrendered to movement — as if this ritual, this wordless ceremony, was now the way to speak, to whisper private and sacred things, to be in touch with some otherness. Dancing as if the very heart of life and all its hopes might be found in those assuaging notes and those hushed rhythms and in those silent and hypnotic movements. Dancing as if language no longer existed because words were no longer necessary . . .

Slowly bring up the music. Slowly bring down the lights.

Acknowledgements

The editor thanks Jean Fallon and Suella Holland for their invaluable contributions to the preparation of this edition. Acknowledgements are also due to Anne Friel and family, Leah Schmidt and Dinah Wood.

Three Sisters was published first by The Gallery Press in 1981.

The Communication Cord was published first by Faber and Faber Limited in 1983 and published by The Gallery Press in 1984.

Fathers and Sons was published first by Faber and Faber Limited in 1987 and published by The Gallery Press in 2013.

Making History was published first by Faber and Faber Limited in 1989.

Dancing at Lughnasa was published first by Faber and Faber Limited in 1990.

Dancing at Lughnasa: Extracts from 'Anything Goes' by Cole Porter © Harms Inc, reproduced by permission of Warner Chappell Music Ltd.